Collateralized Debt Obligations

Structures and Analysis
Second Edition

THE FRANK J. FABOZZI SERIES

Collateralized Debt Obligations

Structures and Analysis
Second Edition

DOUGLAS J. LUCAS

LAURIE S. GOODMAN

FRANK J. FABOZZI

WILEY
John Wiley & Sons, Inc.

Published by John Wiley & Sons, Inc., Hoboken, New Jersey
Published simultaneously in Canada

For general information on our other products and services or for technical support, please
contact our Customer Care Department within the United States at (800) 762-2974, outside
the United States at (317) 572-3993 or fax (317) 572-4002.

Wiley also publishes its books in a variety of electronic formats. Some content that appears in
print may not be available in electronic books. For more information about Wiley products,
visit our web site at www.wiley.com.

ISBN-13 978-0-471-71887-1
ISBN-10 0-471-71887-4

Printed in the United States of America

10 9 8 7 6 5 4 3

DJL
To my wife Elaine, and my children Eric and Benjamin

LSG
To my husband Mark, and my children Louis, Arthur, Benjamin, and Pamela

FJF
To my daughter Patricia Marie

Contents

Preface

The first edition of this book proclaimed "the market for collateralized debt obligations (CDOs) is the fastest growing sector of the asset-backed securities market." Those words are still true four years later as we offer this second edition. In fact, with $200 billion of cash CDOs issued in 2005, another $200 billion of synthetic CDOs issued, and an incalculable amount of tranches referencing credit default swap (CDS) indices traded, the CDO market is probably the fastest growing financial product not only among asset-backed securities, but among *all* financial products.

As we also said four years ago, "there have been numerous and dramatic changes within the CDO market as it has evolved." Since that statement, credit protections on CDOs have been tightened, high-yield loans have replaced high-yield bond collateral, and structured finance collateral, including high-grade collateral, has come to dominate issuance. Among synthetic CDOs, arbitrage and managed arbitraged CDOs have replaced balance sheet transactions, single-tranche CDOs have been created and have risen to dominance, and tranches referencing CDS indices have been created.

This second edition reflects the growing and evolving nature of the CDO market: It contains an additional one-third of text and three-quarters of the book contains new material.

This book covers many different aspects of CDOs and collateral underlying CDOs. Its 24 chapters are divided into eight parts:

- Part One: Introduction to Cash CDOs
- Part Two: Loans and CLOs
- Part Three: Structured Finance CDOs and Collateral Review
- Part Four: Other Types of Cash CDOs
- Part Five: Synthetic CDOs
- Part Six: Default Correlation
- Part Seven: CDO Equity
- Part Eight: Other CDO Topics

Below we provide an overview of each chapter.

PART ONE: INTRODUCTION TO CASH CDOs

In Chapter 1 ("Cash CDO Basics"), we first make the case that it is worth taking the time to understand CDOs. Then, to properly explain CDOs, we break them down into their four moving parts: assets, liabilities, purposes, and credit structures. We explain each building block in detail and create a framework for understanding CDOs that puts old and new CDO variants in context and cuts through confusing financial jargon. Finally, we define the roles of the different parties to a CDO.

In Chapter 2 ("Cash Flow CDOs"), we detail the cash flow credit protection structure, explaining the distribution of cash flows to CDO tranches, the cash flow waterfall, overcollateralization tests, the restrictions imposed on CDO managers, and key factors considered by the rating agencies in the CDO debt rating process. In doing so, we make use of lots of examples from actual CDOs.

PART TWO: LOANS AND CLOs

This section discusses three types of loans underlying collateralized loan obligations (CLOs): U.S. broadly syndicated loans, European broadly syndicated loans, and U.S. middle market loans.

The focus of Chapter 3 ("High-Yield Loans: Structure and Performance") is on U.S. broadly syndicated loans. We discuss the loan market, loan seniority, and lender's control over borrowers, including loan terms and conditions that cover preservation of collateral, appropriation of excess cash flow, control of business risk, performance requirements, and reporting requirements. We conclude the chapter with a discussion of loan default and recovery rates and CLO credit quality.

We begin Chapter 4 ("European Bank Loans and Middle Market Loans") by comparing the U.S. and European markets for broadly syndicated loans. We look at issuance by country, industry, and loan purpose; and at trends in leverage, spreads, and covenant protections. Given the lack of European loan default and recovery studies, the focus of the chapter is on calibrating European loans to default and recovery rates on U.S. loans. We then move on to middle market loans. In the face of tighter spreads for large broadly syndicated loans, some arbitrage CLO managers have delved into these loans to obtain higher spreads. We address the characteristics of middle market loans with particular focus upon their credit quality.

PART THREE: STRUCTURED FINANCE CDOs AND COLLATERAL REVIEW

In Chapters 5 and 6 we describe the collateral underlying structured finance CDOs (SF CDOs). The focus of Chapter 5 ("Review of Structured Finance Collateral: Mortgage-Related Products") is on real estate-related collateral such as residential mortgage-backed securities, mortgage-related asset-backed securities, commercial mortgage-backed securities, and real estate investment trusts. Nonmortgage collateral is the focus of Chapter 6 ("Review of Structured Finance Collateral: Nonmortgage ABS") and includes a discussion of credit card receivable-backed securities, auto loan-backed securities, student loan-backed securities, SBA loan-backed securities, aircraft lease-backed securities, franchise loan-backed securities, and rate reduction bonds

Some of the difficulties in calculating structured finance defaults and recoveries are described in Chapter 7 ("Structured Finance Default and Recovery Rates"). We then detail S&P's and Moody's default and recovery methodologies and results, as well as our methodology for combining their results. We conclude the chapter by considering the best way to use this default and recovery information for *high-grade* SF CDOs.

The similarities of and differences between SF CDOs structures and high-yield corporate CDO structures are explained in Chapter 8 ("Structured Finance Cash Flow CDOs"). A review of the relative credit quality of structured finance debt versus corporate debt as CDO collateral is presented. We conclude the chapter by demonstrating that by using the same criteria to rate all types of CDOs, the rating agencies impose an extra burden on those backed by structured finance collateral. As a result, we argue that ratings on SF CDOs are conservative.

PART FOUR: OTHER TYPES OF CASH CDOs

In Chapter 9 ("Emerging Market CDOs"), we look at CDOs backed by sovereign emerging market bonds, focusing on the differences (that matter) between emerging markets and high-yield corporate deals. We conclude that the rating agencies are far more conservative in their assumptions when rating emerging market deals than in rating high-yield corporate deals.

Market value CDOs are the subject of Chapter 10 ("Market Value CDOs"). While the number of market value deals is small relative to cash flow deals, they are the structure of choice for collateral where the cash flows are difficult to predict. We open the chapter with an overview of the differences between cash flow and market value structures and then examine the mechanics of market value CDOs, focusing on advance rates. An advance rate is the percentage of a particular asset that may be issued as rated debt and is the key to protecting CDO debt holders. Our investigation of market price volatility suggests that the advance rates used by the rating agencies are conservative.

PART FIVE: SYNTHETIC CDOs

In Chapter 11 ("Introduction to Credit Default Swaps and Synthetic CDOs"), we build upon a description of credit default swaps to explain the workings of synthetic CDOs. Synthetic CDOs have evolved from vehicles used by commercial banks to offload commercial loan risk to customized tranches where investors can select the names they are exposed to, the level of subordination that protects them from losses, or the premium they are paid. In the chapter we also explain how the rise of standardized trenches on CDS indices has increased trading liquidity, thereby allowing long-short strategies based on tranche seniority or protection tenor.

In Chapters 12 and 13, we look at two types of synthetic CDO structures. The basic structure and structural nuances of synthetic balance sheet CDOs, the unique challenges confronting the rating agencies in rating them, and the key differences between synthetic and cash transactions are described in Chapter 12 ("Synthetic Balance Sheet CDOs") In Chapter 13 ("Synthetic Arbitrage CDOs"), we describe the advantages of this structure over its cash counterpart. These advantages explain why synthetic arbitrage CDO issuance has grown dramatically and is expected to do so in the future. The advantages are (1) the super-senior piece in a synthetic CDO is generally not funded, (2) there is only a short ramp-up period, and (3) credit default swaps often trade cheaper than the cash bond of the same maturity. We also demonstrate in Chapter 13 how these advantages impact the economics of CDO transactions.

We explain an empirically driven methodology that uses historical default and loss-given-default data to determine how a specific trade would have performed if entered into in the past in Chapter 14 ("A Framework for Evaluating Trades in the Credit Derivatives Market"). More specifically, we show how single name, portfolio, and CDO positions would have performed had they been entered into each year from 1970 through 2000.

The coverage in Chapter 15 ("Structured Finance Credit Default Swaps and Synthetic CDOs") falls neatly into two topics. First, the evolution of structured finance CDS documentation, the competing dealer, and end user templates, and the structured finance CDS terms that best replicate the economics of owning a cash structured finance bond. Second, we address the effect of structured finance CDS on SF CDOs, including managers' newfound flexibility in accessing credit risk, the creation of new SF CDO structures, the outlook for more tiering among CDO managers, and the effect on SF CDO credit quality.

PART SIX: DEFAULT CORRELATION

We define default correlation, discuss its drivers, and show why CDO investors care about it in the first of our two chapters on default correlation, Chapter 16 ("Default Correlation: The Basics"). We provide pictorial representations of default probability and default correlation and derive mathematical formulas relating default correlation to default probability. The difficulty of the problem becomes evident when we show that pairwise default correlations are not sufficient to understand the behavior of a credit risky portfolio and introduce "higher orders of default correlation."

In the second of our chapters on default correlation, Chapter 17 ("Empirical Default Correlation: Problems and Solutions"), we survey the meager work done on historic default correlation. We show that default correlations within well-diversified portfolios vary by the ratings of the credits and also by the time period over which defaults are examined. But in that chapter we also devote a good deal of coverage to describe the major problems in measuring and even thinking about default correlation. The thorniest problem is that when looking at historical rates of default, it is impossible to distinguish default correlation from changing default probability. We compare different approaches of incorporating default correlation into portfolio credit analysis and opine that the approached suggested by Credit Suisse First Boston makes the most direct use of historical data and is the easier to understand, but feel that more work needs to be done on default probability.

PART SEVEN: CDO EQUITY

There are four reasons why investors should consider buying CDO equity: nonrecourse term financing, the forgiving nature of the cash flow CDO structure, two optionalities CDO equity holders enjoy, and the use of CDO equity in a defensive investment strategy. We set forth these reasons in Chapter 18 ("Why Buy CDO Equity?").

In Chapter 19 ("CDO Equity Returns and Return Correlation"), we take on the misguided practice of calculating CDO equity Sharpe ratios and the correlation of CDO equity returns with the returns of other assets. The calculation of these variables is so fundamentally flawed that the results are useless. We delve into the usefulness of historical data in predicting future CDO equity returns and present a simple approach to understanding the relationship between CDO equity returns and the returns of CDO underlying asset portfolios.

PART EIGHT: OTHER CDO TOPICS

In Part Eight of the book we include six chapters that cover a smorgasbord of CDO topics.

A discussion of secondary market developments and pitfalls is provided in Chapter 20 ("Analytical Challenges in Secondary-Market CDO Trading"). However, the bulk of the chapter is on how to evaluate a secondary CDO offering. We show what to look for in a trustee report and what to get out of net asset value analysis. Our most important suggestion is a methodology for selecting default scenarios in cash flow modeling.

The factors that structurers consider in creating CDOs are the subject of Chapter 21 ("The CDO Arbitrage"). We show how to look at the CDO arbitrage and present a "quick and dirty" analysis for benchmarking CDO issuance and then focuses on how the arbitrage dictates deal structure. Spread configurations and the exact collateral used are important in determining optimal deal structure. We explain why the practice of simply looking at percent subordination or percent overcollateralization as an arbiter of tranche quality is misleading.

In Chapter 22 ("How to Evaluate a CDO and Manage a CDO Portfolio"), we look at evaluating CDOs individually and as part of a portfolio. One of the most important points to look for in a CDO purchase is the structural protections inherent in a CDO because there is a natural tension between the interest of debt holders and equity holders. Buyers of CDO debt should look at both the incentive structures in a CDO, as well as how the manager has done on outstanding CDOs. In picking managers, track record cannot be taken at face value. In the chapter we also make the case that investors should buy CDOs backed by different types of collateral and that low-diversity CDOs are not to be shunned.

In Chapter 23 ("Quantifying Single-Name Risk Across CDOs") we quantify the extent of collateral overlap among a sample of CLOs and SF CDOs and propose a simple and consistent measure of single-name risk. We explain that there is little reason to be concerned about single-name risk except at the level of equity and the lowest debt tranche.

In the last chapter, the rating history of 1,000 CDOs and 3,000 CDO tranches across 22 types of CDOs in the United States, Europe, and emerging markets is provided. In that chapter (Chapter 24, "CDO Rating Experience"), we compare CDOs by type and vintage and assess both the frequency and severity of downgrades. Particular attention is paid to the severity of downgrades and a proxy CDO default study is offered.

ACKNOWLEDGMENTS

We gratefully acknowledge the expertise and participation of UBS research personnel. Bill Prophet, Greg Reiter, William Smith, and Tom Zimmerman reviewed drafts and made helpful comments. Wilfred Wong and Tommy Leung contributed analysis to several chapters. Vicki Ye was involved in every step, from background research and data gathering to reviewing and critiquing the final product.

We particularly thank the rating agencies, Moody's Investors Service, Standard & Poor's, and Fitch Ratings, for allowing us to draw upon the wealth of data and expertise they provide to CDO investors. Most specifically, we incorporated material on their rating methodologies, default and recovery studies, and rating transition studies into this book. Special thanks also to S&P LCD, for the variety of loan data and analysis they allow us to use.

Douglas J. Lucas
Laurie S. Goodman
Frank J. Fabozzi

About the Authors

Douglas J. Lucas is an Executive Director at UBS and head of CDO Research. He is ranked top three in CDO research in the *Institutional Investors* fixed income analyst survey. His prior positions include head of CDO research at JPMorgan, co-CEO of Salomon Swapco, and analyst at Moody's Investors Service. While at Moody's he authored the rating agency's first default and rating transition studies, quantified the expected loss rating approach, and developed the rating methodologies for collateralized debt obligations and triple-A special purpose derivatives dealers. He is known for doing some of the first quantitative work in default correlation. Currently Chairman of The Bond Market Association's CDO Research Committee, Douglas has a BA magna cum laude in Economics from UCLA and an MBA with Honors from the University of Chicago.

Laurie S. Goodman is cohead of Global Fixed Income Research and manages U.S. Securitized Products (RMBS, ABS, CMBS, CDO) and Treasury/Agency/Swap Research at UBS. As a mortgage analyst, Laurie has long dominated *Institutional Investor's* MBS categories, placing first in four categories 30 times over the last eight years. In 1993, Laurie founded the securitized products research group at Paine Webber, which merged with UBS in 2000. Prior to that, Laurie held senior fixed income research positions at Citicorp, Goldman Sachs, and Merrill Lynch and gained buy-side experience as a mortgage portfolio manager. She began her career as a Senior Economist at the Federal Reserve Bank of New York. Laurie holds a BA in Mathematics from the University of Pennsylvania, and MA and PhD degrees in Economics from Stanford University. She has published more than 160 articles in professional and academic journals.

Frank J. Fabozzi is an Adjunct Professor of Finance and Becton Fellow in the School of Management at Yale University. Prior to joining the Yale faculty, he was a Visiting Professor of Finance in the Sloan School at MIT. Frank is a Fellow of the International Center for Finance at Yale University and on the Advisory Council for the Department of Operations Research and Financial Engineering at Princeton University. He is the editor of *The Journal of Portfolio Management* and an associate editor of *The Journal of Fixed Income*. He earned a doctorate in economics from the City University of New York in 1972. In 2002 Frank was inducted into the Fixed Income Analysts Society's Hall of Fame. He earned the designation of Chartered Financial Analyst and Certified Public Accountant. He has authored and edited numerous books in finance.

Introduction to Cash CDOs

Cash CDO Basics

Collateralized debt obligations (CDOs) have been around since 1987. Yet it was only in 1998 that annual issuance broke $100 billion. As of 2005, $1.1 trillion of CDOs were outstanding, making CDOs the fastest-growing investment vehicle of the last decade. This growth is a testament to their popularity among asset managers and investors.

A CDO issues debt and equity and uses the money it raises to invest in a portfolio of financial assets such as corporate loans or mortgage-backed securities. It distributes the cash flows from its asset portfolio to the holders of its various liabilities in prescribed ways that take into account the relative seniority of those liabilities. This is just a starting definition, we will fill in the details for this definition over the next few pages.

In this chapter, we first make the case that it is worth taking the time to understand CDOs. Then, to properly explain CDOs, we break them down into their four moving parts: assets, liabilities, purposes, and credit structures. We explain each building block in detail and create a framework for understanding CDOs that puts old and new CDO variants in context and cuts through confusing financial jargon. Next, we define the roles of the different parties to a CDO.

WHY STUDY CDOs?

Before we tell you more about CDOs, you should know why it is worth your time to take notice. There are three compelling reasons:

Reason #1: There are a lot of them. As noted earlier, as of 2005 the total amount of CDOs outstanding is $1.1 trillion. Of course, the mere fact that there is a lot of something is not a recommendation. But the most desirable thing in the world is not very useful if you cannot get your hands on it. The fact that the supply of CDOs is large and growing means that there are a wide variety of different structures to choose from.

Reason #2: They have unique and attractive return profiles. Via CDOs, investors can gain exposures that they could not otherwise obtain, such as investment-grade risk to speculative-grade assets or speculative-grade risk to investment-grade assets. Investors can get levered exposure to an asset portfolio, or the exact opposite, loss-protected exposure to an asset portfolio. Equity in a CDO achieves nonrecourse term leverage. The debt a CDO issues provides higher spreads than similarly rated instruments. Certain types of CDOs provide upside potential with a limit on downside risk. Others provide a surety of constant returns.

Reason #3: They can improve the return profile of an existing portfolio. CDOs offer access to certain assets that many investors could or would not acquire on their own, thereby improving portfolio diversity. CDOs come with built-in diversification and most come with built-in asset management. CDO returns have low correlation to returns of other assets.

UNDERSTANDING CDOs

"Collateralized debt obligations," "arbitrage cash flow CDOs," and "collateralized loan obligations" are similar phrases that could refer to the same type of CDO or to very different types of CDOs. "Structured finance CDOs," "ABS CDOs," and "resecuritizations" are three distinct names all referring to the same type of CDO. The phraseology gets worse with idioms such as "CDO squared" and the perfectly logical expression (once you understand it) "the CDO issues CDOs." Like most finance terms, the emphasis of CDO nomenclature is to distinguish new products from existing products. This often happens at the expense of logical categorization.

Any CDO can be well described by focusing on its four important attributes: assets, liabilities, purposes, and credit structures. Like any company, a CDO has assets. With a CDO, these are financial assets such as corporate loans or mortgage-backed securities. And like any company, a CDO has liabilities. With a CDO, these run the gamut of preferred shares to AAA rated senior debt. Beyond the seniority and subordination of CDO liabilities, CDOs have additional structural credit protections, which fall into the category of either *cash flow* or *market value* protections. Finally, every CDO has a purpose that it was created to fulfill, and these fall into the categories of *arbitrage*, *balance sheet*, or *origination*. In this chapter, we are going to look at the different types of assets CDOs hold, the different types of liabilities CDOs issue, the two different credit structures CDOs employ, and at the three purposes for which CDOs are created.

Assets

CDOs own financial assets such as corporate loans or mortgage-backed securities. A CDO is primarily identified by its underlying assets.

The first CDOs created in 1987 owned high-yield bond portfolios. In fact, before the term "CDO" was invented to encompass an ever-broadening array of assets, the term in use was "collateralized bond obligation" or "CBO." In 1989, corporate loans and real estate loans were used in CDOs for the first time, causing the term "collateralized loan obligation" or "CLO" to be coined. Generally, CLOs are comprised of performing high-yield loans, but a few CLOs, even as far back as 1988, targeted distressed and nonperforming loans. Some cash CLOs comprised of investment-grade loans have also been issued.

Loans and bonds issued by emerging market corporations and sovereign governments were first used as CDO collateral in 1994, thus "emerging market CDO" or "EM CDO." In 1995, CDOs comprised of residential mortgage-backed securities (RMBS) were first issued. CDOs comprised of commercial mortgage-backed securities (CMBS) and asset-backed securities (ABS), or combinations of RMBS, CMBS, and ABS followed but they have never found a universally accepted name. In this book, we use "structured finance CDO" or "SF CDO." However, Moody's champions the term "resecuritizations" and many others use "ABS CDO," even to refer to CDOs with CMBS and RMBS in their collateral portfolios.

It is noteworthy that the collateral diversity we have described so far, between 1987 through 1995, occurred while annual CDO issuance averaged $2 billion and never exceeded $4 billion. As shown in Exhibit 1.1, CDO issuance only really took off in 1996. Issuance jumped to $38 billion in 1996, $82 billion in 1997, and $139 billion in 1998.

The decline in CDO issuance in 2001 and 2002 was due to a difficult corporate credit environment. As a result, corporate bond and loan-backed CDO issuance fell 50% from $100 billion in 2000 to $50 billion in 2002. Since 2002, the steady annual increases in CDO issuance has been fueled by high-yield loan-backed CLOs and SF CDOs. As shown in Exhibit 1.2, these collateral types underlie 91% of CDOs issued thus far

EXHIBIT 1.1   Annual Cash CDO Issuance

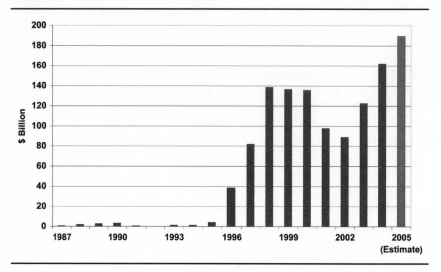

EXHIBIT 1.2   Collateral Backing Cash CDOs in 2005

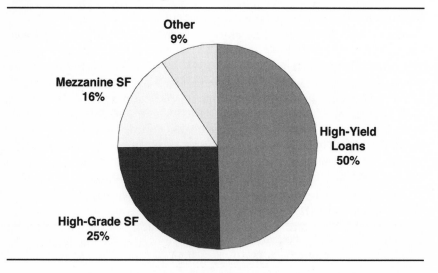

in 2005. Also shown in Exhibit 1.2 is the distinction between mezzanine assets—BBB– and A rated SF—and high-grade AA– and AAA rated SF assets. While mezzanine SF securities have been used in CDOs in quantity as far back as 1998, higher rated SF securities debuted in CDOs in 2003. The majority of the "other" category in the exhibit is comprised of capital notes from banks and insurance companies. CDOs backed by these assets were first issued in 2000. Emerging market debt and high-yield bonds make up most of the remainder of the "other" category in Exhibit 1.2.

The CDO market is opportunistic in the way it drops collateral types that are out of favor with investors and picks up collateral types that are in favor with investors. The best example of this is the switch out of poor-performing high-yield bonds and into well-performing high-yield loans between 2001 and 2003. Also, certain types of ABS present in SF CDOs from 1999 through 2001 disappeared from later vintages: manufactured housing loans, aircraft leases, franchise business loans, and 12b-1 mutual fund fees. All of these assets had horrible performance in older SF CDOs. In their place, SF CDOs have recently focused more on RMBS and CMBS.

Liabilities

Any company that has assets also has liabilities. In the case of a CDO, these liabilities have a detailed and strict ranking of seniority, going up the CDO's capital structure as equity or preferred shares, subordinated debt, mezzanine debt, and senior debt. These *tranches* of notes and equity are commonly labeled Class A, Class B, Class C, and so forth going from top to bottom of the capital structure. They range from the most secured AAA rated tranche with the greatest amount of subordination beneath it, to the most levered, unrated equity tranche. Exhibit 1.3 shows a simplified tranche structure for a CLO.

Special purposes entities like CDOs are said to be "bankrupt remote." One aspect of the term is that they are new entities without

EXHIBIT 1.3 Simple, Typical CLO Tranche Structure

Tranche	Percent of Capital Strucutre	Rating	Coupon
Class A	77.5	AAA	LIBOR + 26
Class B	9	A	LIBOR + 75
Class C	2.75	BBB	LIBOR + 180
Class D	2.75	BB	LIBOR + 475
Preferred shares	8	NR	Residual cash flow

previous business activities. They therefore cannot have any legal liability for sins of the past. Another aspect of their "remoteness from bankruptcy" is that the CDO will not be caught up in the bankruptcy of any other entity, such as the manager of the CDO's assets, or a party that sold assets to the CDO, or the banker that structured the CDO.

Another, very important aspect of a CDO's bankruptcy remoteness, is the absolute seniority and subordination of the CDO's debt tranches to one another. Even if it is a certainty that some holders of the CDO's debt will not receive their full principal and interest, cash flows from the CDO's assets are still distributed according to the original game plan dictated by seniority. The CDO cannot go into bankruptcy, either voluntarily or through the action of an aggrieved creditor. In fact, the need for bankruptcy is obviated because the distribution of the CDO's cash flows, even if the CDO is insolvent, has already been determined in detail at the origination of the CDO.

Within the stipulation of strict seniority, there is great variety in the features of CDO debt tranches. The driving force for CDO structurers is to raise funds at the lowest possible cost. This is done so that the CDO's equity holder, who is at the bottom of the chain of seniority, can get the most residual cash flow.

Most CDO debt is floating rate off LIBOR, but sometimes a fixed rate tranche is structured. Avoiding an asset-liability mismatch is another reason why floating-rate high-yield loans are more popular in CDOs than fixed-rate high-yield bonds. Sometimes a CDO employs short-term debt in its capital structure. When such debt is employed, the CDO must have a standby liquidity provider, ready to purchase the CDO's short-term debt should it fail to be resold or roll in the market. A CDO will only issue short-term debt if its cost, plus that of the liquidity provider's fee, is less than the cost of long-term debt.

Sometimes a financial guaranty insurer will wrap a CDO tranche. Usually this involves a AAA rated insurer and the most senior CDO tranche. Again, a CDO would employ insurance if the cost of the tranche's insured coupon plus the cost of the insurance premium is less than the coupon the tranche would have to pay in the absence of insurance. To meet the needs of particular investors, sometimes the AAA tranche is divided into *senior* AAA and *junior* AAA tranches.

Some CDOs do not have all their assets in place when their liabilities are sold. Rather than receive cash the CDO is not ready to invest, tranches might have a delay draw feature, where the CDO can call for funding within some specified time period. This eliminates the negative carry the CDO would bear if it had to hold uninvested debt proceeds in cash. An extreme form of funding flexibility is a revolving tranche, where the CDO can call for funds and return funds as its needs dictate.

Purposes

CDOs are created for one of three purposes:

> *Balance Sheet.* A holder of CDO-able assets desires to (1) shrink its balance sheet, (2) reduce required regulatory capital, (3) reduce required economic capital, or (4) achieve cheaper funding costs. The holder of these assets sells them to the CDO. The classic example of this is a bank that has originated loans over months or years and now wants to remove them from its balance sheet. Unless the bank is very poorly rated, CDO debt would not be cheaper than the bank's own source of funds. But selling the loans to a CDO removes them from the bank's balance sheet and therefore lowers the bank's regulatory capital requirements. This is true even if market practice requires the bank to buy some of the equity of the newly created CDO.

> *Arbitrage.* An asset manager wishes to gain assets under management and management fees. Investors wish to have the expertise of an asset manager. Assets are purchased in the marketplace from many different sellers and put into the CDO. CDOs are another means, along with mutual funds and hedge funds, for an asset management firm to provide its services to investors. The difference is that instead of all the investors sharing the fund's return in proportion to their investment, investor returns are also determined by the seniority of the CDO tranches they purchase.

> *Origination.* Banks and insurance companies wish to increase equity capital. Here, the example is a large number of smaller-size banks issuing capital notes[1] directly to the CDO simultaneous with the CDO's issuance of its own liabilities. The bank capital notes would not be issued but for the creation of the CDO to purchase them.

Three purposes differentiate CDOs on the basis of how they acquire their assets and focus on the motivations of asset sellers, asset managers, and capital note issuers. From the point of view of CDO investors, however, all CDOs have a number of common purposes, which explain why many investors find CDO debt and equity attractive.

One purpose is the division and distribution of the risk of the CDO's assets to parties that have different risk appetites. Thus, a AAA investor can invest in speculative-grade assets on a loss-protected basis. Or a BB investor can invest in AAA assets on a levered basis.

---

[1] Capital notes are unsecured obligations that are generally ranked lowest in the order of repayment.

EXHIBIT 1.4   CDO Spreads versus Alternative Investments, August 2005

	CLO	SF CDO	Corporates	CMBS	Home Equity	Credit Card	Manf. House
AAA	26	Senior 27 Junior 46	23	26	25	8	67
AA	41	58		45	49		
A	73	145	33	54	65	24	
BBB	178	270	100	110	136	42	
BB	475						

Source: UBS, Salomon Yield Book.

For CDO equity investors, the CDO structure provides a leveraged return without some of the severe adverse consequences of borrowing via repo from a bank. CDO equity holders own stock in a company and are not liable for the losses of that company. Equity's exposure to the CDO asset portfolio is therefore capped at the cost of equity minus previous equity distributions. Instead of short-term bank financing, financing via the CDO is locked in for the long term at fixed spreads to the London interbank offered rate (LIBOR).

For CDO debt investors, CDOs offer spreads that are usually higher than those of alternative investments, particularly for CDOs rated below AA, as shown in Exhibit 1.4. And finally, the CDO structure allows investors to purchase an interest in a diversified portfolio of assets. Often these assets are not available to investors except through a CDO. Exhibit 1.5 summarizes the CDO purposes that we have discussed.

CREDIT STRUCTURES

Beyond the seniority and subordination of CDO liabilities, CDOs have additional structural credit protections, which fall into the category of either *cash flow* or *market value* protections.

The *market value credit structure* is less often used, but easier to explain, since it is analogous to an individual's margin account at a brokerage. Every asset in the CDO's portfolio has an *advance rate* limiting the amount that can be borrowed against that asset. Advance rates are necessarily less than 100% and vary according to the market value volatility of the asset. For example, the advance rate on a fixed rate B rated bond would be far less than the advance rate on a floating rate AAA-rated bond. Both the rating and floating rate nature of the AAA bond

EXHIBIT 1.5 CDO Purposes

	Balance Sheet	Arbitrage	Origination
Provide asset sellers with cheap funding or regulatory capital relief or economic capital relief	X		
Provide asset managers with assets under management and CDO investors with asset management services		X	
Provide banks and insurance companies with cheap equity-like capital			X
Divide and distribute the risk of the CDO assets to parties with differing appetites for risk	X	X	X
Provide equity investors with leveraged exposure to the CDO's assets with non-recourse term financing	X	X	X
Provide debt investors with high ratings-adjusted yields	X	X	X
Provide investors with a diversified investment portfolio, perhaps of hard-to-access assets	X	X	X

indicate that its market value will fluctuate less than the B rated bond. Therefore, the CDO can borrow more against it. The sum of advance rates times the market values of associated assets is the total amount the CDO can borrow.

The credit quality of a market value CDO derives from the ability of the CDO to liquidate its assets and repay debt tranches. Thus, the market value of the CDO's assets are generally measured every day, advance rates applied, and the permissible amount of debt calculated. If this comes out, for example, to $100 million, but the CDO has $110 million of debt, the CDO must do one of two things. It can sell a portion of its assets and repay a portion of its debt until the actual amount of debt is less than the permissible amount of debt. Or the CDO's equity holders can contribute more cash to the CDO. If no effective action is taken, the entire CDO portfolio is liquidated, all debt is repaid, and residual cash given to equity holders. The market value credit structure is analogous to an individual being faced with a collateral call at his (or her) brokerage account. If he does not post additional collateral, his portfolio is at least partially liquidated.

The *cash flow credit structure* does not have market value tests. Instead, subordination is sized so that the *after-default cash flow* of assets is expected to cover debt tranche principal and interest with some degree of certainty. Obviously, the certainty that a AAA CLO tranche, with 23% subordination beneath it, will receive all its principal and interest is greater than the certainty a BB CLO tranche, with only 8% subordination beneath it, will receive all its principal and interest.

All cash flow CDOs have a feature that improves the credit quality of their senior tranches. In the normal course of events, if defaults are not "too high" (a phrase we will shortly explain in detail), cash coupons come in from the CDO's asset portfolio. These dollars are first applied to the CDO's administrative costs, such as those for its trustee and its manager, if it has one. Next, these moneys are applied to interest expense of the CDO's senior-most tranche. Next, moneys are applied to interest expense on the CDO's second most senior tranche and successively moving down the capital structure until all interest on all debt tranches is paid. If the CDO has a manager, an additional fee to that manager might be paid next. Finally, left over, or residual, cash flow is given to the CDO's equity holders.

What if defaults are "too high" (as we promised earlier to explain)? Also, how do we know whether defaults are too high? There are two series of tests, the most important of which is shown below. The key to these tests is that defaulted assets are excluded or severely haircut (counted at a fraction of their par amount) in the definition of "asset par."

Class A par coverage test = Asset par/Class A par

Class B par coverage test = Asset par/(Class A par + Class B par)

Class C par coverage test = Asset par/(Class A par + Class B par + Class C par)

... and so on, for all the debt tranches

To pass these tests, par coverage must be greater than some number, perhaps 120% for the Class A par coverage test, perhaps only 105% for the Class C par coverage test. The more defaulted assets a CDO has, the more likely it will be to fail one or more of these tests. Failure of a par coverage test requires that cash be withheld from paying interest on lower-ranking debt tranches. Instead, cash must be used to pay down principal on the CDO's senior-most debt tranche. If enough cash is available to pay down the senior-most tranche so that the par coverage test is in compliance, remaining cash can be used to make interest payments to lower-ranking tranches and on down the line to the CDO's equity holders. We discuss the cash flow credit structure in much more depth in Chapter 2.

A CDO STRUCTURAL MATRIX

Exhibit 1.6 shows the four CDO building blocks and a variety of options beneath each one. Any CDO can be well described by asking and answering the four questions implied by the exhibit:

- What are its assets?
- What are the attributes of its liabilities?
- What is its purpose?
- What is its credit structure?

This way of looking at CDOs encompasses all the different kinds of CDOs that have existed in the past and all the kinds of CDOs that are currently being produced. For example, the first CDO ever created, back in 1987, had high-yield bond assets, fixed rate debt, a market value credit structure, and was done for balance sheet purposes.[2] We will make further use of this CDO classification system as we turn to the most common types of CDOs offered today.

EXHIBIT 1.6 CDO Structural Matrix

Assets	Liabilities	Purpose	Credit Structure
High-yield loans	Fixed/floating rate	Arbitrage	Cash flow
High-grade structured finance	PIK/non-PIK	Balance sheet	Market value
Mezzanine structured finance	Guaranteed/unen- hanced	Origination	
Capital notes	Short term/long term		
High-yield bonds	Delayed draw/ revolving		
Emerging market debt			

---

[2] Imperial Savings' September 1987 issue, managed by Caywood Christian, underwritten by Drexel Burnham, and rated by S&P.

CDOs BEING OFFERED TODAY

In Exhibit 1.2, we showed that 91% of CDOs issued so far in 2005 are backed by high-yield loans and structured finance (ABS, CMBS, RMBS) assets. Most of these CDOs, as well as the comparatively few CDOs backed by high-yield bonds, investment-grade bonds, and emerging market bonds, use the cash flow credit structure and were done for arbitrage purposes. Exhibit 1.7 shows 2005 CDO issuance by purpose, credit structure, and assets. Note that 81% of CDOs issued in 2005 have been arbitrage cash flow CDOs backed by various types of assets. This is clearly the dominant structure.

PARTIES TO A CDO

A number of parties and institutions contribute to the creation of a CDO. We conclude this introductory chapter with a discussion of the most important roles.

CDO Issuer and Co-Issuer

A CDO is a distinct legal entity, usually incorporated in the Cayman Islands. Its liabilities are called CDOs, so one might hear the seemingly circular phrase "the CDO issues CDOs." Offshore incorporation enables the CDO to more easily sell its obligations to United States and international investors and escape taxation at the corporate entity level. When a CDO is located outside the U.S., it will typically also have a Delaware co-issuer. This entity has a passive role, but its existence in the structure allows CDO obligations to be more easily sold to U.S. insurance companies.

EXHIBIT 1.7   CDO Issuance in 2005

Purpose	Credit Structure	Assets	Share
Arbitrage	Cash flow	HY loans	40%
Arbitrage	Cash flow	HG SF	18%
Arbitrage	Cash flow	Mezz. SF	15%
Arbitrage	Cash flow	Bonds, other	8%
Origination	Cash flow	Capital notes	6%
Balance sheet	Cash flow	Various	8%
Arbitrage	Market value	Various	5%

Asset Manager (Collateral Manager)

Asset managers (or *collateral managers*) select the initial portfolio of an arbitrage CDO and manage it according to prescribed guidelines contained in the CDO's *indenture*. Sometimes an asset manager is used in a balance sheet CDO of distressed assets to handle their workout or sale. A variety of firms offer CDO asset management services including hedge fund managers, mutual fund managers, and firms that specialize exclusively in CDO management.

Asset Sellers

Asset sellers supply the portfolio for a balance sheet CDO and typically retain its equity. In cash CDOs, the assets involved are usually smaller-sized loans extended to smaller-sized borrowers. In the United States, these are called "middle market" loans and in Europe these are called "small and medium enterprise" (SME) loans.

Investment Bankers and Structurers

Investment bankers and *structurers* work with the asset manager or asset seller to bring the CDO to fruition. They set up corporate entities, shepherd the CDO through the debt rating process, place the CDO's debt and equity with investors, and handle other organizational details. A big part of this job involves structuring the CDO's liabilities: their size and ratings, the cash diversion features of the structure, and, of course, debt tranche coupons. To obtain the cheapest funding cost for the CDO, the structurer must know when to use short-term debt or insured debt or senior/junior AAA notes, to name just a few structural options. Another part of the structurer's job is to negotiate an acceptable set of eligible assets for the CDO. These tasks obviously involve working with and balancing the desires of the asset manager or seller, different debt and equity investors, and rating agencies.

Insurers/Guarantors

Monoline bond insurers or *financial guarantors* typically only guarantee the senior-most tranche in a CDO. Often, insurance is used when a CDO invests in newer asset types or is managed by a new CDO manager.

Rating Agencies

Rating agencies approve the legal and credit structure of the CDO, perform due diligence on the asset manager and the trustee, and rate the various seniorities of debt issued by the CDO. Usually two or three of the major rating agencies (Moody's, S&P, and Fitch) rate the CDO's debt. DBRS is a recent entrant in CDO ratings and A. M. Best has rated CDOs backed by insurance company capital notes.

Trustees

Trustees hold the CDO's assets for the benefit of debt and equity holders, enforce the terms of the CDO indenture, monitor and report upon collateral performance, and disburse cash to debt and equity investors according to set rules. As such, their role also encompasses that of collateral custodian and CDO paying agent.

CHAPTER 2

Cash Flow CDOs

As explained in Chapter 1, arbitrage CDOs are categorized as either cash flow transactions or market value transactions. The objective of the asset manager in a cash flow transaction is to generate cash flow for CDO tranches without the active trading of collateral. Because the cash flows from the structure are designed to accomplish the objective for each tranche, restrictions are imposed on the asset manager. The asset manager is very limited in his or her authority to buy and sell bonds. The conditions for disposing of issues held are specified and are usually driven by credit risk management. Also, in assembling the portfolio, the asset manager must meet certain requirements set forth by the rating agency or agencies that rate the deal.

In this chapter we will discuss cash flow transactions. Specifically, we will look at the distribution of the cash flows, restrictions imposed on the asset manager to protect the noteholders, and the key factors considered by rating agencies in rating tranches of a cash flow transaction. In this chapter we focus on establishing a basic understanding of cash flow CDO deals using examples. Only a brief mention will be made of deals backed by other types of collateral. In the following eight chapters, we focus on other collateral types. Chapters 3, 4, and 5 we focus on loan collateral and loan-backed deals (CLOs). In Chapters 6, 7, and 8 we focus on structured finance collateral (MBS/ABS/CMBS/CDO), and the deals backed by this collateral. In Chapter 9 we focus on emerging market collateral.

DISTRIBUTION OF CASH FLOWS

In a cash flow transaction, the cash flows from income and principal are distributed according to rules set forth in the prospectus. The distribution of the cash flows is referred to as the "waterfall." We describe these rules below and will use a representative CDO deal to illustrate them.

The representative CDO deal we will use is a $300 million cash flow CDO with a "typical" cash flow structure. The deal consists of the following:

- $260 million (87% of the deal) Aaa/AAA (Moody's/S&P) floating rate tranche
- $27 million ($17 million fixed rate + $10 million floating rate) Class B notes, rated A3 by Moody's
- $5 million (fixed rate) Class C notes, rated Ba2 by Moody's
- $8 million in equity (called "preference shares" in this deal)

The collateral for this deal consists primarily of investment-grade, commercial mortgage-backed securities (CMBS), asset-backed securities (ABS), real estate investment trusts (REIT), and residential mortgage-backed securities (RMBS); 90% of which must be rated at least "Baa3" by Moody's or BBB– by S&P.[1] The asset manager is a well respected money management firm.

Exhibit 2.1 illustrates the priority of interest distributions among different classes for our sample deal. Interest payments are allocated first to high priority deal expenses such as fees, taxes, and registration, as well as monies owed to the asset manager and hedge counterparties. After these are satisfied, investors are paid in a fairly straightforward manner, with the more senior bonds paid off first, followed by the subordinate bonds, and then the equity classes.

Note the important role in the waterfall played by what is referred to as the *coverage tests*. We will explain these shortly. They are important because before any payments are made on Class B or Class C bonds, coverage tests are run to assure the deal is performing within guidelines. If that is not the case, consequences to the equity holders are severe. Note from Exhibit 2.1 if the Class A coverage tests are violated, then excess interest on the portfolio goes to pay down principal on the Class A notes, and cash flows will be diverted from all other classes to do so. If the portfolio violates the Class B coverage tests, then interest will be diverted from Class C plus the equity tranche to pay down first principal on Class A, or, if Class A is retired, Class B principal.

Exhibit 2.2 shows the simple principal cash flows for this deal. Principal is paid down purely in class order. Any remaining collateral principal from overcollateralization gets passed onto the equity piece.

---

[1] At the time of purchase, the collateral corresponded, on average, to a Baa2 rating.

EXHIBIT 2.1   Interest Cash Flow "Waterfall"

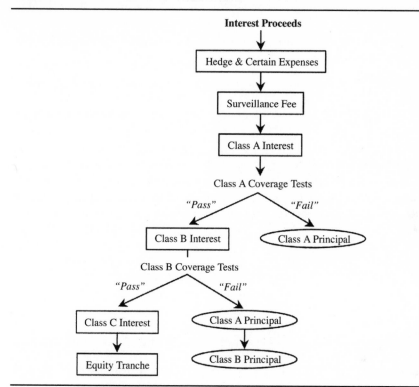

Interest Proceeds

→ Hedge & Certain Expenses

→ Surveillance Fee

→ Class A Interest

→ Class A Coverage Tests

"Pass" → Class B Interest   *"Fail"* → Class A Principal

Class B Coverage Tests

"Pass" → Class C Interest → Equity Tranche

"Fail" → Class A Principal → Class B Principal

EXHIBIT 2.2   Principal Cash Flow "Waterfall"

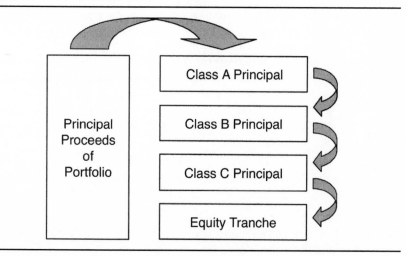

Principal Proceeds of Portfolio

Class A Principal

Class B Principal

Class C Principal

Equity Tranche

RESTRICTIONS ON MANAGEMENT: SAFETY NETS

Noteholders have two major protections provided in the form of tests. They are coverage tests and quality tests. We discuss each type below.

Coverage Tests

Coverage tests are designed to protect noteholders against a deterioration of the existing portfolio. There are actually two categories of tests—*overcollateralization tests* and *interest coverage tests*.

Overcollateralization Tests

The overcollateralization or O/C ratio for a tranche is found by computing the ratio of the *principal* balance of the collateral portfolio over the *principal* balance of that tranche and all tranches senior to it. That is,

$$\text{O/C ratio for a tranche} = \frac{\text{Principal (par) value of collateral portfolio}}{\text{Principal for tranche} + \text{Principal for all tranches senior to it}}$$

The higher the ratio, the greater protection for the note holders. Note that the overcollateralization ratio is based on the principal or par value of the assets.[2] (Hence, an overcollateralization test is also referred to as a *par value test*.) An overcollateralization ratio is computed for specified tranches subject to the overcollateralization test. The overcollateralization test for a tranche involves comparing the tranche's overcollateralization ratio to the tranche's required minimum ratio as specified in the guidelines. The required minimum ratio is referred to as the *overcollateralization trigger*. The overcollateralization test for a tranche is passed if the overcollateralization ratio is greater than or equal to its respective overcollateralization trigger.

Consider our representative CDO. There are two rated tranches subject to the overcollateralization test—Classes A and B. Therefore two overcollateralization ratios are computed for this deal. For each tranche, the overcollateralization test involves first computing the overcollateralization ratio as follows:

$$\text{O/C ratio for Class A} = \frac{\text{Principal (par) value of collateral portfolio}}{\text{Principal for Class A}}$$

---

[2] As explained in Chapter 10, for market value CDOs, overcollateralization tests are based on market values rather than principal or par values.

$$\text{O/C ratio for Class B} = \frac{\text{Principal (par) value of collateral portfolio}}{\text{Principal for Class A} + \text{Principal for Class B}}$$

Once the overcollateralization ratio for a tranche is computed, it is then compared to the overcollateralization trigger for the tranche as specified in the guidelines. If the computed overcollateralization ratio is greater than or equal to the overcollateralization trigger for the tranche, then the test is passed with respect to that tranche.

For our representative deal, the overcollateralization trigger is 113% for Class A and 101% for Class B. Note that the lower the seniority, the lower the overcollateralization trigger. The Class A overcollateralization test is failed if the ratio falls below 113% and the Class B overcollateralization test is failed if the ratio falls below 101%.

Interest Coverage Test

The interest coverage or I/C ratio for a tranche is the ratio of scheduled interest due on the underlying collateral portfolio to scheduled interest to be paid to that tranche and all tranches senior to it. That is,

$$\text{I/C ratio for a tranche} = \frac{\text{Scheduled interest due on underlying collateral portfolio}}{\text{Scheduled interest to that tranche} + \text{Schedule interest to all tranches senior}}$$

The higher the interest coverage ratio, the greater the protection. An interest coverage ratio is computed for specified tranches subject to the interest coverage test. The interest coverage test for a tranche involves comparing the tranche's interest coverage ratio to the tranche's *interest coverage trigger* (i.e., the required minimum ratio as specified in the guidelines). The interest coverage test for a tranche is passed if the computed interest coverage ratio is greater than or equal to its respective interest coverage trigger.

For our representative deal, Classes A and B are subject to the interest coverage test. The following two interest coverage ratios are therefore computed:

$$\text{I/C ratio for Class A} = \frac{\text{Scheduled interest due on underlying collateral portfolio}}{\text{Scheduled interest to Class A}}$$

I/C ratio for Class B

$$= \frac{\text{Scheduled interest due on underlying collateral portfolio}}{\text{Scheduled interest to Class A + Scheduled interest to Class B}}$$

In the case of our representative deal, the Class A interest coverage trigger is 121%, while the Class B interest coverage trigger is 106%.

PIK-ing Occurs When Coverage Tests are Not Met

We showed in Exhibit 2.1 that if the Class A coverage tests are violated, the excess interest on the portfolio goes to pay down principal on the Class A notes, and cash flows will be diverted from the other classes to do so. In this case, what happens to the Class B notes?

They have a *pay-in-kind* or PIK feature. This is a clearly disclosed structural feature in most CDOs where, instead of paying a current coupon, the par value of the bond is increased by the appropriate amount. So if a $5 coupon is missed, the par value increases, say from $100 to $105. The next coupon is calculated based on the larger $105 par amount. The PIK concept originated in the high-yield market, and was employed for companies whose future cash flows were uncertain. The option to pay-in-kind was designed to help these issuers conserve scarce cash or even avoid default. It was imported to the CDO market as a structural feature to enhance the more senior classes.

The PIK-ability of subordinate tranches and the diversion of cash flows to cause early amortization of the Class A tranche naturally strengthens the Class A tranche. The Class A tranche can therefore either achieve a higher rating, or its size can be increased while still maintaining its original rating. CDO equity holders benefit from an overall lower cost of funds: They either have a lower coupon on the Class A tranche; or the Class A tranche, which enjoys the CDO's lowest funding cost, is larger. Either case lowers interest costs to the CDO and thus increases return to equity holders.

The effectiveness of PIK-ing in bolstering the credit quality of the Class A tranche depends upon the amount of collateral cash flow that exists in excess of Class A coupon. The higher the coupon on collateral, and the longer the tenor of collateral, then the more cash flow potentially available for diversion to pay down Class A principal. The effectiveness of PIK-ing (in bolstering the Class A tranche) also depends upon the looseness or tightness of the overcollateralization and interest coverage tests. The tighter the coverage tests are to the CDO's original par and coupon ratios, the sooner a deterioration in those ratios will cause cash flow to be diverted to repay Class A principal.

The effect of cash diversion to the Class A tranche in a high-yield-backed CDO can be dramatic. It is not unusual for subordinate tranches of a CDO to have been downgraded (and to be PIK-ing without any chance of ultimate payment) while the CDO's Aaa tranche maintains its credit quality and rating. That is due to the outlook for Class A receiving full principal and interest because of the diversion of cash to Class A principal.

In determining its optimal capital structure, CDO equity must weigh reduction in the overall cost of CDO debt against the potential for equity to receive less cash flow in severe default scenarios. Distribution of collateral cash flow amongst tranches in a CDO is a zero-sum game. And since equity receives residual cash flow after debt tranches are satisfied, PIK-ing and the diversion of cash flows to Class A principal affects it the most. First, the CDO's average cost of funds increases. Second, the CDO becomes more delevered. Finally, less cash reaches the equity tranche, and that which does is delayed.

Quality Tests

After the tranches of a CDO deal are rated, the rating agencies are concerned that the composition of the collateral portfolio may be adversely altered by the asset manager over time. Tests are imposed to prevent the asset manager from trading assets so as to result in a deterioration of the quality of the portfolio and are referred to as *quality tests*. These tests deal with maturity restrictions, the degree of diversification, and credit ratings of the assets in the collateral portfolio.

CREDIT RATINGS

There are three key inputs to cash flow CDO ratings:

- Collateral diversification
- Likelihood of default
- Recovery rates

While each rating agency uses a slightly different methodology, they reach similar conclusions. For this analysis, we use a variation of Moody's methodology, as it is the most transparent plus allows us to change inputs to show the import and impact of each.

Moody's uses the same objective process for developing liability structures regardless of the type of collateral. Moody's determines losses on each tranche under different default scenarios, and probability-weight those results. The resulting "expected loss" is then compared to the maximum permitted for any given rating. While that whole iterative process makes for a tedious analysis, it does help highlight why, for example, a deal backed by investment-grade corporate bonds will have a very high proportion of triple A tranches and a low proportion of equity compared to a deal backed by high-yield corporate bonds.

Collateral Diversification

Moody's methodology reduces the number of credits in the CDO portfolio to a smaller number of homogenous, uncorrelated credits. For example, for CDOs backed by corporate bonds, a *diversity score* is calculated by dividing the bonds into different industry classifications. These industry classifications are shown in Exhibit 2.3. Each industry group is assumed to have a zero correlation with other industry groups. Two securities from different issuers within the same industry group are assumed to have some correlation to each other. At the extreme, two securities from the same issuer are treated as having 100% correlation, and hence providing zero diversification.

Reducing the portfolio to the number of independent securities allows the use of a binomial probability distribution. This is the distribution that allows one to figure out the probability of obtaining 9 "heads" in 10 flips of the coin. This distribution can also be applied to a weighted coin, where the probability of "heads" is substantially different than the probability of tails. Intuitively, each asset is a separate flip of the coin, and the outcomes ("heads" and "tails") corresponds to "no default" and "default." The use of this probability distribution makes it possible to define the likelihood of a given number of securities in the portfolio defaulting over the life of a deal.

One factor concerning investors in CDOs is the potential for the default on one bond to wipe out the equity. In fact, in addition to the general diversification methodology, there are single-name concentration rules that protect against too large a concentration within securities issued by any single entity. It is customary for issuer exposure to be no more than 2%. To allow asset managers some flexibility, a few exceptions are permitted. In one actual deal, for example, four positions could be as large as 3%, as long as no more than two of these exposures were in the same industry. If two of the exposures greater than 2% were in the same industry, additional restrictions apply.

Historical Defaults

Likelihood of default is provided by the *weighted average rating factor* (WARF). This is a rough guide to the asset quality of a portfolio and is meant to incorporate the probability of default for each of the bonds backing a CDO. To see where this comes from, we need to look at actual default experience on corporate bonds.

EXHIBIT 2.3   Moody's Investors Service—Industry Classifications for Corporate Credits

Listing	Sector
1	Aerospace & Defense
2	Automobile
3	Banking
4	Beverage, Food & Tobacco
5	Buildings and Real Estate
6	Chemicals, Plastics & Rubber
7	Containers, Packaging and Glass
8	Personal and Nondurable Consumer Products
9	Diversified/Conglomerate Manufacturing
10	Diversified/Conglomerate Service
11	Metals & Minerals
12	Ecological
13	Electronics
14	Finance
15	Farming and Agriculture
16	Grocery
17	Health Care, Education, and Childcare
18	Home and Office Furnishings, Housewares and Durable Consumer Products
19	Hotels, Inns and Gaming
20	Insurance
21	Leisure, Amusement, Motion Picture, Entertainment
22	Machinery
23	Mining, Steel, Iron and Nonprecious Metals
24	Oil and Gas
25	Personal, Food and Miscellaneous Services
26	Printing and Publishing
27	Cargo Transport
28	Retail Stores
29	Telecommunications
30	Textiles and Leather
31	Personal Transportation
32	Utilities
33	Broadcasting

Source: Table 6 (Industry Classifications) in Alan Backman and Gerard O'Connor, "Rating Cash Flow Transactions Backed by Corporate Debt 1995 Update," Moody's Investors Service, p. 13. Updated by UBS CDO Desk.

Exhibit 2.4 shows actual average cumulative default rates from 1 to 10 years based on Moody's data from 1983 to 2004. These data show that bonds with an initial rating of Baa3 experienced average default rates of 5.36% after 7 years, and 7.20% after 10 years. Compare that to the B1 default rate of 35.69% after 7 years and 47.43% after 10 years. Generally, as would be expected, bonds with lower ratings exhibit higher default patterns. Moreover, defaults rise exponentially, not linearly, as rating decline.

However, it is difficult to use these data to construct a stylized default pattern, as some anomalies appear. For example, over some time periods, Aaa bonds default more frequently than do Aa1 bonds. And Aa2 bonds default more frequently than either Aa3 or A1 bonds, while A2 bonds default more frequently than A3 bonds. Correspondingly, B2 bonds default less frequently than either Ba3 or B1 bonds.

EXHIBIT 2.4   Average Issuer-Weighted Cumulative Default Rates by Alphanumeric Rating, 1983–2004 Moody's

Cohort Rating	Time Horizon (Years)									
	1	2	3	4	5	6	7	8	9	10
Aaa	0.00	0.00	0.00	0.06	0.18	0.24	0.32	0.40	0.40	0.40
Aa1	0.00	0.00	0.00	0.15	0.15	0.25	0.25	0..25	0.25	0.25
Aa2	0.00	0.00	0.04	0.13	0.28	0.34	0.40	0.48	0.57	0.67
Aa3	0.00	0.00	0.05	0.11	0.18	0.26	0.26	0.26	0.26	0.33
A1	0.00	0.00	0.19	0.30	0.38	0.47	0.50	0.58	0.67	0.84
A2	0.03	0.08	0.22	0.47	0.68	0.89	1.05	1.34	1.59	1.69
A3	0.03	0.21	0.37	0.50	0.65	0.86	1.19	1.38	1.55	1.69
Baa1	0.17	0.50	0.84	1.14	1.46	1.69	1.92	2.05	2.21	2.31
Baa2	0.12	0.40	0.81	1.52	2.11	2.74	3.39	3.98	4.62	5.49
Baa3	0.41	1.07	1.70	2.66	3.60	4.49	5.36	6.15	6.68	7.20
Ba1	0.66	2.07	3.55	5.23	6.76	8.67	9.70	10.85	11.61	12.38
Ba2	0.62	2.22	4.48	6.84	8.82	10.11	11.85	13.13	14.20	14.66
Ba3	2.23	6.10	10.62	15.03	19.14	23.05	26.56	30.00	33.35	36.24
B1	3.03	8.89	14.81	20.09	25.27	30.29	35.69	39.97	43.98	47.43
B2	5.93	13.73	20.58	26.58	31.24	34.54	37.39	39.60	42.19	44.48
B3	10.77	20.43	29.01	36.82	43.55	49.74	54.46	58.40	61.02	62.32
Caa-C	22.24	35.80	46.75	54.60	60.40	65.15	68.30	72.36	75.38	78.81
Investment grade	0.08	0.23	0.43	0.71	0.96	1.21	1.43	1.65	1.84	2.03
Speculative grade	5.26	10.84	16.06	20.63	24.54	28.00	31.04	33.63	35.87	37.66
All rated	1.79	3.66	5.38	6.89	8.13	9.17	10.04	10.75	11.35	11.83

Source: Exhibit 17 in David T. Hamilton, Praveen Vama, Sharon Ou, and Richard Cantor, *Default and Recovery Rates of Corporate Bond Issuers: 1920–2004*, Moody's Investors Service (January 2005), p. 17.

WARF Scores

Moody's smooths these data and constructs a weighted average rating factor (WARF), shown in Exhibit 2.5. Thus, a bond with a Baa1 rating has a Moody's score of 260, while one rated Baa3 would have a WARF score of 610. Note that these scores exhibit the same pattern as did actual default numbers: Scores are nonlinear and increase exponentially as ratings decline. These scores are also dollar-weighted across the portfolio to deliver a WARF for the portfolio.

The weighted average rating factor for the portfolio translates directly into a cumulative probability of default. The cumulative probability of default will be larger the longer the portfolio is outstanding. A WARF score of 610 means that there is a 6.1% probability of default for each of the independent, uncorrelated assets defaulting in a 10-year period. (In general, the WARF score translates directly into the 10-year

EXHIBIT 2.5   Moody's Weighted Average Rating Factor

	WARF
Aaa	1
Aa1	10
Aa2	20
Aa3	40
A1	70
A2	120
A3	180
Baa1	260
Baa2	360
Baa3	610
Ba1	940
Ba2	1,350
Ba3	1,780
B1	2,220
B2	2,720
B3	3,490
Caa1	4,770
Caa2	6,500
Caa3	8,070
Ca/C	10,000

Source: Moody's Investors Service. Reprinted with permission.

"idealized" cumulative default rate.) The same 610 WARF would correspond to a 4.97% probability of default after 8 years, or a 5.57% probability of default after 9 years.

Note that the systematic bias in mapping actual defaults to WARF scores results in the rating methodology being more conservative for investment-grade corporate bonds deals than for high-yield corporate bond deals. This results in WARF scores for investment-grade bonds that are very close to the actual default probabilities, while the actual default rates for high-yield bonds are much higher than the WARF scores would indicate. Thus, for Baa3 rated securities, the WARF score is 610 (which corresponds to a 6.1% probability of default after 10 years), which is also very close to the average cumulative default rate of 7.20% after 10 years. For Baa1 bonds, the WARF is 260, corresponding to a 2.6% probability of default after 10 years. Actual cumulative default rates for Baa1 are a very similar level of 2.31%. By contrast, for bonds rated Ba2 and below (where most of the high-yield universe resides), WARF scores are considerably lower than the actual cumulative default rate. For a B1 bond, for instance, the WARF is 2,220 versus a cumulative default rate of 47.43%.

When the desired rating on the CDO tranche is the same as the rating on the underlying collateral, Moody's will use the probability of default derived from the WARF score. For CDO ratings higher than the ratings on their underlying collateral, Moody's will use a higher default rate. The multiple applied to the idealized cumulative default rate is referred to as a *stress factor*. Thus, for example, in an investment-grade deal (Baa-rated collateral), Moody's uses a factor of 1.0 to rate a Baa tranche. If the rating on the CDO tranche is Aaa, Aa, or A, then Moody's uses a higher factor to stress the default rates.[3]

---

[3] One factor concerning investors is the "credit barbelling" of the portfolio. In a portfolio with investment-grade corporate bonds, for example, that means buying a combination of an A rated security and a Ba rated security that has the same WARF score as the portfolio. Barbelling is used to increase portfolio yield. For example, most investment-grade deals average a Baa3 rating, but also tend to include 10%–25% high-yield issuance. Given that default rates are nonlinear, this is a concern. However, rating agencies are well aware of the incentive to "barbell" a portfolio to increase portfolio yield. So they "correct" for that by treating the high-yield universe as a separate portfolio and examine that piece of the portfolio at a probability of default much higher than would be dictated by probability of default on the overall portfolio. More precisely, their adaptation for "barbelled" portfolios involves running a double binomial probability distribution. In addition, they place strict concentration limitations on the amount of less-than-investment-grade debt that can be held in a portfolio.

Recovery Rates

Moody's recovery rates are dependent on the desired rating of the CDO tranche. To obtain the highest ratings (Aaa and Aa), Moody's generally assumes recovery rates of 30% on unsecured corporate bonds. To obtain an A or Baa rating, recovery assumptions are slightly higher, at 33% and 36%, respectively. It should be understood that actual average recovery rates are higher than these assumptions. A Moody's study covering the period 1981 to 2004 showed that the median, or midpoint, recovery rate for senior unsecured debt was $45.20 ($44.90 average or mean). For subordinated unsecured debt, the median recovery rate was $33.40 ($32.00 average). The bottom line is this: Moody's is again conservative, as it uses a recovery value consistent with subordinated unsecured debt on debt that is in most cases senior—and that builds in "extra" protection for the investors.

Putting It All Together

Moody's has an expected loss permissible for each CDO rating. That expected loss is derived as follows:

Expected loss

$$= \sum_{i=1}^{n} (\text{Loss in default scenario } i) \times (\text{Probability of scenario } i \text{ ocurring})$$

The following example, using an investment-grade corporate CDO, will help clarify this formula. Assume a typical CDO deal with 45 independent assets. Assume further that we are looking at a 10-year deal in which each asset has a probability of default of 5% corresponding to a WARF score of 500, which is well within the category of Baa rated assets. Moreover, we assume a capital structure with 85% of the bonds Aaa rated, 10% Baa rated, and 5% equity. The recovery rate is assumed to be 30%.

To create an example that can be replicated with a simple spreadsheet, we assume all interim cash flows are distributed, and all defaults occur at the end of the life of the deal. Moody's will actually run each scenario through its CDO cash flow model in order to determine the loss to each bond in the CDO structure. Moody's will assume a number of different loss schedules and select the most detrimental.

We have simplified that whole analytical process to make it more transparent. Our methodology overstates losses to the bondholders, since we ignored all overcollateralization and interest coverage tests. As the portfolio deteriorated, those two tests kick in and would cut off cash flow to the equity tranche, redirecting cash flows to pay down the higher-rated tranches. We have also ignored the excess spread on these deals, which provides a very important cushion to the noteholders.

The probability of a scenario in which none of the 45 securities default is (probability of no default)^{45}, or $(0.95)^{45}$. This is equal to 9.94%. If there are zero defaults, there is obviously no loss. The probability of only one loss is found as follows:

$$[(\text{Probability of no default})^{44} \times (\text{Probability of 1 default}) \times 45]$$
$$= (0.95)^{44} \times 0.95 \times 45 = 23.55\%$$

This frequency distribution is shown in the column of Exhibit 2.6, labeled "Probability."

With one default, the defaulted bond comprises $\frac{1}{45}$ of the portfolio, or 2.22%. However, since a 30% recovery rate is assumed, that loss is lowered to 1.56% (2.22 × 0.7). Thus, the "Portfolio Loss" column of Exhibit 2.6 shows that the loss with one default would be 1.56%. But the 5% equity in the deal acts as a buffer, and there would be no loss to the BBB bond. In order to impact the BBB bond, losses must total more than 5%.

Assume four defaults among the 45 assets. This means that 8.89% of the assets ($\frac{4}{45}$) are defaulting, and portfolio loss becomes 6.22% (8.89% × 0.7). The probability of this occurring is 11.37%. If that case does occur, the Baa bond would lose 12.22% of its value. That is, the equity would be eliminated, and the $10 Baa tranche ($10 per $100 par value) would be reduced by ($6.22 − $5.00), or $1.22, for a 12.22% reduction. Thus

$$[(\text{Baa loss}) \times (\text{Probability of loss})] = 1.38\%$$

or

$$[(11.37\% \text{ probability of scenario}) \times (12.22\% \text{ loss if scenario materializes})]$$

Similarly, if there were five defaults (a 4.92% probability), the portfolio loss would be 7.78%. This corresponds to a loss of 27.78% on the Baa bond. The expected loss to the Baa bond in this scenario is (4.91 × 27.78), or 1.3629%. Note that if portfolio losses total more than 15%, the Baa bond is eliminated, and only then does the Aaa bond start incurring losses.

Adding expected losses in each of the scenarios across the binomial probability distribution, we find that the expected loss on this Baa CDO tranche is 3.92%. Realize again that this example is for illustrative purposes and will overstate losses to the bondholders. It ignores overcollateralization and interest coverage ratios and the excess spread in the deal.

EXHIBIT 2.6   Expected Loss on BBB Class, Investment-Grade CDO Deal (Given 45 Assets)

No. of securities: 45
Default probability: 5%
Loss given default: 70%
Portfolio loss for single default: 1.56% ($\frac{1}{45} \times 70\%$)
Expected BBB loss: 3.9205%

No. of Defaults	Portfolio Loss (%)	Probability (%)	BBB Loss (%)	BBB Loss × Probability (%)
0	0.00	9.94	0.00	0.0000
1	1.56	23.55	0.00	0.0000
2	3.11	27.27	0.00	0.0000
3	4.67	20.57	0.00	0.0000
4	6.22	11.37	12.22	1.3895
5	7.78	4.91	27.78	1.3629
6	9.33	1.72	43.33	0.7460
7	10.89	0.50	58.89	0.2973
8	12.44	0.13	74.44	0.0940
9	14.00	0.03	90.00	0.0246
10	15.56	0.01	100.00	0.0052
11	17.11	0.00	100.00	0.0009
12	18.67	0.00	100.00	0.0001
13	20.22	0.00	100.00	0.0000
14	21.78	0.00	100.00	0.0000
15	23.33	0.00	100.00	0.0000
16	24.89	0.00	100.00	0.0000
17	26.44	0.00	100.00	0.0000
18	28.00	0.00	100.00	0.0000
19	29.56	0.00	100.00	0.0000
20	31.11	0.00	100.00	0.0000
21	32.67	0.00	100.00	0.0000
22	34.22	0.00	100.00	0.0000
23	35.78	0.00	100.00	0.0000
24	37.33	0.00	100.00	0.0000
25	38.89	0.00	100.00	0.0000
26	40.44	0.00	100.00	0.0000
27	42.00	0.00	100.00	0.0000
28	43.56	0.00	100.00	0.0000

EXHIBIT 2.6 (Continued)

No. of Defaults	Portfolio Loss (%)	Probability (%)	BBB Loss (%)	BBB Loss × Probability (%)
29	45.11	0.00	100.00	0.0000
30	46.67	0.00	100.00	0.0000
31	48.22	0.00	100.00	0.0000
32	49.78	0.00	100.00	0.0000
33	51.33	0.00	100.00	0.0000
34	52.89	0.00	100.00	0.0000
35	54.44	0.00	100.00	0.0000
36	56.00	0.00	100.00	0.0000
37	57.56	0.00	100.00	0.0000
38	59.11	0.00	100.00	0.0000
39	60.67	0.00	100.00	0.0000
40	62.22	0.00	100.00	0.0000
41	63.78	0.00	100.00	0.0000
42	65.33	0.00	100.00	0.0000
43	66.89	0.00	100.00	0.0000
44	68.44	0.00	100.00	0.0000
45	70.00	0.00	100.00	0.0000

Importance of Diversification

We can now readily show the importance of diversification. No matter how many assets we have, if the probability of default on each is 5% and recovery is 30%, then the expected loss on the portfolio is 3.5%. However, this does not address the distribution of losses, which is certainly important to the bondholders.

In fact, the Baa bondholders are concerned about the likelihood of losses exceeding the amount of equity in the deal, while the Aaa bondholders are concerned about the likelihood of losses exceeding the amount of equity and Baa bonds. The greater the number of assets, the greater the likelihood that losses on those assets will cluster around 3.5% and the lower the likelihood that losses will exceed the 5% equity cushion and impact the Baa piece. On the flipside, the smaller the number of assets, the greater the likelihood that losses will exceed the 5% equity cushion and will hit the Baa bonds.

Exhibit 2.7 shows probability distributions for losses on pools of 15, 30, and 45 securities. Note that the fewer the number of assets, the greater likelihood that losses will exceed a 5% equity cushion.

EXHIBIT 2.7   Benefits of Diversification

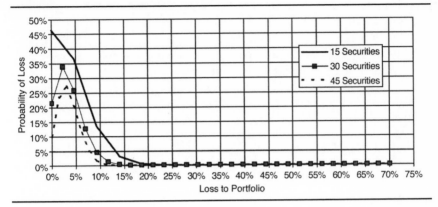

EXHIBIT 2.8   Diversity and Expected Losses (%)

No. of Securities	15	20	25	30	45	60
Aaa losses	0.0273	0.0091	0.0032	0.0012	0.0001	0.0000
Baa losses	9.1520	8.5074	6.8720	5.6216	3.9205	2.9262

Exhibit 2.8 supports the point that with fewer assets, expected losses to the Baa rated tranche are much higher. Thus, for 15 assets, the loss to the Baa tranche is 9.15%; for 30 assets it is 5.62%. For 45 assets, the loss to the Baa tranche is 3.92%; and for 60 assets, it is 2.92%. Note also that the benefits of diversification diminish as more assets are added. The loss to the Baa tranche is 5.5% lower in moving from 15 to 30 assets. It only drops 1.7% in moving from 30 to 45 assets and only 1% from 45 to 60 assets.

What's "Too Much" Diversification?

The above analysis suggests that greater diversification is always better, since it means less variation of collateral returns. However, a higher diversity score also means that it may be likely the asset manager pushed for, and achieved, less equity in the deal. In fact, with a diversity score of 60, the same losses on the Aaa and Baa bonds could have been achieved with less equity (on the order of 4.5% rather than the 5% required on a deal with a diversity score of 45).

Is there any such thing as too much of a diversification "good thing"? That depends on the asset manager. A large, broad-based asset manager may have considerable strength across all sectors and should be able to handle the analysis—and risks—of a highly diverse portfolio. Even here, a very high diversity score can limit flexibility by requiring an asset manager with broad expertise to invest in an industry he does not like. Whether or not flexibility is being limited too much by a very high diversity score is dependent on the range of assets employed and the strengths of a particular asset manager.

Too much diversification is even more a major problem for a smaller asset manager, where the portfolio may have selective strengths in fewer industries. This asset manager may be stretching to take on additional diversity to achieve a lower required equity. Investors should certainly be wary of deals in which very high diversity scores are achieved by managers straying from their fields of expertise.

Loss Distribution Tests

As can be seen from the discussion above, Moody's approach to rating CDOs involves (1) developing a diversity score; (2) calculating a weighted-average rating factor; (3) using the binomial distribution to determine the probability of a specific number of defaults; and (4) calculating the impact of those defaults on bonds within the CDO structure. One element needed to calculate that impact is a distribution of defaults and losses across time. Let us look at this distribution of defaults and losses.

Moody's stresses bonds via six different loss distributions, and a bond must pass each test. The six loss distributions are shown in Exhibit 2.9. Moody's basic approach assumes 50% of the losses will occur at a single point in time, and that remaining losses are evenly distributed over a 5-year period. This single 50% loss is assumed to occur at a different point in each of the six tests. For example, Test 1 assumes that the single 50% loss occurs at the beginning of the deal.

EXHIBIT 2.9   Moody's Loss Distribution Tests

| Year | Percent of Total Losses Occurring at Start of Each Year | | | | | |
	Test 1	Test 2	Test 3	Test 4	Test 5	Test 6
1	50	10	10	10	10	10
2	10	50	10	10	10	10
3	10	10	50	10	10	10
4	10	10	10	50	10	10
5	10	10	10	10	50	10
6	10	10	10	10	10	50

Source: Moody's Investors Service. Reprinted with permission.

Liability Structure

The structure of the liabilities will be primarily determined by the credit quality of the assets, the amount of diversification, and excess spread. That is, the combination of credit quality, diversification of assets, and excess spread dictate expected losses on each tranche. That is then compared to losses allowed to achieve a given rating. Realize that the structures have been optimized. If a structurer sees one of the tranches passing expected loss tests by a large margin, that means there is room to improve the arbitrage. That can be accomplished by leveraging the structure more (i.e., reducing equity, reducing the amount of mezzanine bonds, or both).

The results above clearly indicate that with less diversification, more equity is needed. Indeed, it's ludicrous to think a CDO can achieve a Baa rating with 15 securities, equity of 5%, and an expected loss of 9.15%. As diversification declines, equity must rise. However, the rating agency methodology indicates, for example, that in an investment-grade, corporate-backed CDO deal, in comparison to a high-yield corporate bond-backed deal, a very diversified portfolio of highly rated collateral can be structured with a high percentage of Aaa bonds and a low percent of equity.

Capital Structures versus Collateral

Exhibit 2.10 compares typical capital structures for deals backed by investment-grade corporate bonds, high-yield bonds, mezzanine (primarily BBB rated) SF collateral, and high-yield loans. The comparisons are generic, and assume the CDO transaction contains only bonds rated Aaa and Baa, plus equity.

While most deals of a given genre have Aaa and mezzanine percentages within the bands shown in Exhibit 2.10, differences between deals stem from the fact that there is often further optimization of the deal structure (introduction of an A rated class, for example, lowers the percentages of both Aaas and Baas).

EXHIBIT 2.10   Liability Structure of Cash Flow Deals (% of Deal)

	Investment-Grade Corporate Bond CBO	High-Yield Bond CBO	Mezz. SF CDO	High-Yield Loan CDO
Aaa	82–85	73–75	78–83	75–80
Baa	10–15	10–14	13–17	10–15
Equity	3.5–5	13–15	4–6	8–10

Focus on Exhibit 2.10 more closely. High-yield deals require a much higher percentage of equity and, correspondingly, carry a much lower percentage of triple A tranches than investment-grade corporate bonds or mezzanine SF CDOs. They require more equity than high-yield loan deals.

In a cash flow structure, bondholders are protected not only by the equity, but by the excess spread of the assets over the liabilities. This excess spread cushion is even more important in CDO deals backed by high-yield bonds than in deals backed by higher-rated collateral. The protection provided by that excess spread is actually heightened further by the overcollateralization and interest coverage tests. These two tests can be tripped at higher thresholds on high-yield deals than on invest-ment-grade corporate CDOs or SF CDOs or high-yield loan deals.

As can be seen in Exhibit 2.11, at the Baa level, typical overcollater-alization tests are 105 to 112 on a high-yield CBO versus 103 to 105 on an investment-grade corporate CBO deal. Typical interest coverage tests are 110 to 120 at the Baa level, rather than 100 to 105 on investment-grade corporate deals. So as collateral deteriorates, the overcollateral-ization and interest coverage tests are breached. When the Baa overcol-lateralization or interest coverage tests are breached, then the cash flow spigot is turned away from the equity tranche, and onto paying down the Aaa bonds. When Aaa overcollateralization or interest coverage tests are breached, then interest payments to the Baa tranche are sus-pended and those flows go toward paying off the Aaa class. Again, these triggers provide important protection to the bondholders on all deals, but particularly so on lower-rated collateral deals due to the higher thresholds and greater excess spread.

While the simple, intuitive framework presented in this chapter misses intricacies of an actual deal, it is clear that a higher probability of default on each security must be accompanied by a capital structure with more equity and less Aaa debt. So to achieve the same loss on each tranche, the tranche in the CDO backed by high-yield bonds needs to

EXHIBIT 2.11   Overcollateralization and Interest Coverage Test (%)

	Aaa		Baa	
	O/C	I/C	O/C	I/C
High-yield CBO	115–130	120–130	105–112	110–120
Investment-grade corp. CBO	108–115	115–125	103–105	100–105
Mezz. SF CDO	110–125	115–125	103–105	100–105
High-yield CLO	109–115	110–120	103–105	105–115

have greater subordination. In the simple framework presented, the typical high-yield capital structure (75% Aaas, 15% Baa, and 10% equity) with a diversity score of 45 produces the same losses as does the investment-grade deal with 82% Aaa's, 13% Baa, and 5% equity, as the latter has a lower probability of defaults.

Uses of Interest Rate Swaps and Caps in CDO Transactions

We have mentioned that a wide variety of collateral can be used to back CDO deals. Some of this collateral (high-yield bonds, investment-grade bonds) have fixed rate coupons, some (high-yield loans) have floating-rate coupons. SF collateral may be fixed or floating. The liabilities are usually LIBOR-based floating instruments. To convert a fixed rate asset into a floating rate liability, it is necessary to use either an interest rate swap or a cap.

Exhibit 2.12 shows how this is done. The CDO enters into a swap with an interest rate swap counterpart. The CDO pays a fixed rate coupon to the swap counterparty, and receives a LIBOR-based coupon from the swap counterparty. Exhibit 2.13 shows a bond-backed CDO using an interest rate cap. With an interest rate cap, the CDO makes an upfront payment, and receives a payment only if LIBOR is over a certain prespecified level. This protects the deal against the scenario in which LIBOR spikes, and the fixed rate coupons on the assets are insufficient to cover the cash flow on the liabilities.

EXHIBIT 2.12   Bond-Backed CDO and Interest Rate Swap

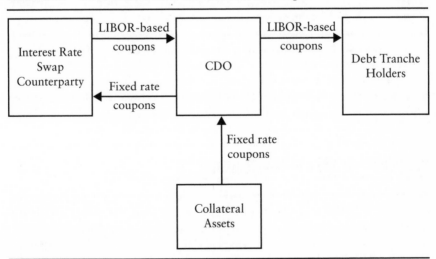

EXHIBIT 2.13   Bond-Backed CDO and Interest Rate Cap

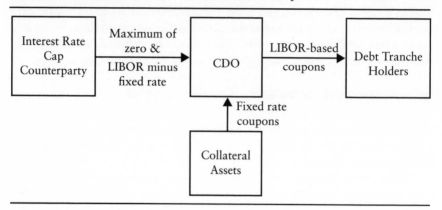

The use of an interest rate swap or cap requires assumptions about the cash flows on the assets. If the assets run off more quickly than anticipated, the CDO can be left with the swaps in place, and no assets. This was a problem for a number of high-yield bond CDOs in the 2001–2002 period, which has used swaps to convert fixed rate assets into floating-rate liabilities. In the 2001–2002 recession, defaults on high-yield bonds were considerably higher than the levels assumed by the structure. Since the collateral was fixed rate and the liabilities were floating, virtually all the deals had interest rate swaps or caps in place. When the assets defaulted, the CDOs which had employed swaps still had the obligation to pay fixed and receive floating on the swaps. With the Fed easing during this period, interest rates had declined, and the result was that the fixed rate paid by the CDOs was well above current market rates. Their choice was to keep paying it, or to buy back the swap by making a one-time payment to the interest rate swap counterparty.

Since that experience CDOs have employed greater use of floating rate assets (high-yield loans, SF collateral) and have been conservative in the number of swaps used in CDO transactions.

CALL PROVISIONS IN CDO TRANSACTIONS

We conclude this chapter with a discussion of commonly used optional redemption features in CDO transactions. The most common is that the deal is callable at par by the equity holders, after a prespecified lockout. The call is generally exercised when the deal is doing very well, and the collateral can be liquidated at a healthy net profit. The deal is more apt to be called when the spreads on the debt tranches have narrowed. That is, the equity holders are looking at the possibility of liquidating the deal, paying off the debt holders, and putting the collateral into a new deal where the debt holders are paid a narrower spread. When evaluating CDOs that have been outstanding for a few years and are being traded in the secondary market, call provisions can be important to the valuation of the securities.

Call Protection for Bond Investors

There are many different variations of the basic CDO structure in which the deal is callable at par after a preset lockout period. Two of the most common variations protecting bondholders are prepayment penalties and coupon step-ups.

Prepayment penalties can take two forms: Either the investor is compensated with a premium call, or there is a "make-whole" provision. The most typical premium call is an amount equal to one-half the annual coupon, which steps down over time. Essentially, the effect of the prepayment penalties is to make the call less attractive to the asset manager.

Coupon step-ups are somewhat rare in deals. If the tranche is not called on a certain date, the coupon "steps-up" to a higher level. A coupon step-up is only used if the asset manager wants to signal to investors that it is unlikely that the deal will extend beyond a certain point. For example, deals backed by collateral with long legal final maturities are more apt to have a coupon step-up to quell investor concerns about extension risk.

Variations of Call Provisions that Benefit Equity Holders

Not all call provisions will be exercised because the deal is going well. Sometimes if the deal is going very poorly, the equity holders may choose to liquidate because the deal is worth more "dead" than alive. This is particularly true towards the end of the deal because the expenses of running a small deal with low leverage are too high and a "clean-up call" is beneficial.

There are also customized call provisions to protect the equity holders from the whims of an asset manager. Some CDO deals have "partial calls," which allows each group of equity holders to exercise authority over their own piece of the deal. This is different from typical structures, in which the deal is only callable in whole by a majority of the equity interests. It is clear that the value of the deal on an ongoing basis will be different for the asset manager (who earns management fees) and an equity holder (who does not). In certain rare cases, a majority of equity holders may replace the asset manager. This is most common in those deals in which the asset manager does not own a piece of the equity. Both of these call provisions are meant to protect the equity holder (who is not the asset manager) at the expense of the asset manager.

Loans and CLOs

High-Yield Loans: Structure and Performance

High-yield corporate loans are an important source of collateral for U.S. collateralized debt obligations (CDOs). In each of the years 2001 through 2005, high-yield loans (also known as leveraged loans) have made up one-fourth to one-third of arbitrage cash flow CDOs. And collateralized loan obligations (CLOs) backed by high-yield loans have outperformed CDOs backed by other forms of corporate debt such as high-yield and investment grade bonds. This is correctly attributed to the superior credit performance of loans and the conservative structure of CLOs. Yet many CDO investors are unfamiliar with high-yield loans.

In this chapter, we attempt to fill that knowledge gap by answering the following questions:

- What exactly is a "loan"?
- How do lenders maintain their senior interest in the borrower's assets?
- How are borrowers prevented from taking actions detrimental to lender's interests?
- What are the trends in loan market size, spreads, and terms?

We also review historical evidence of loan credit quality. Compared to corporate bonds, loans are less likely to default *and* have higher recoveries if they do default. We think this is because, relative to bond ratings, ratings on loans are more timely and accurate. These factors have led to the excellent credit performance of CLOs.

However, quantitative measures of risk and reward for recently issued loans have been mixed. Over the last two-and-a-half years, borrower lever-

---

We thank Jonathan Sprague for his help in this chapter.

age has increased while loan spreads have decreased. But loan default rates are at historic lows, and run much lower than those of high-yield bonds. And the floating rate nature of loans makes them attractive at a time when interest rates are expected to rise and ideal to support the floating rate liabilities of a CLO. Given these contradictory factors, it is a good time for investors to better familiarize themselves with high-yield loans and CLOs.

THE LOAN MARKET

A *syndicated loan* is a single loan with a single set of terms, but multiple lenders, each lender of which provides a portion of the funds. A *high-yield loan*, or *leveraged loan*, is a loan extended to a speculative-grade borrower (i.e., a borrower rated below investment grade, or below BBB–/ Baa3) or an unrated loan priced at LIBOR plus 125 basis points or more. When market participants refer to "loans," especially in the context of a CLO, they generally mean *broadly syndicated* (to 10 or more bank and nonbank investors) high-yield loans. Generally, they also mean *senior secured loans*, which sit at the topmost rank in the borrower's capital structure. And generally, they mean *larger* loans (greater than $100 million) to *larger* companies (greater than $50 million earnings before deductions for interest, taxes, depreciation, and amortization, EBITDA).

Corporate borrowers take loans out to refinance existing debt; for acquisitions and buyouts; to recapitalize their mix of loans, bonds, and equity; and to add on to an existing loan. High-yield loans have been syndicated and sold to nonbank institutional investors since the late 1980s, but institutional investors only became a significant factor in the market in 1995. Exhibit 3.1 shows the history of high-yield loan syndication and the split of loans retained by banks versus those purchased by institutional investors.[1]

Over time, the proportion of syndicated high-yield loans sold to institutional investors has grown to the point where institutions now purchase over 60% of loans, as shown in Exhibit 3.2. The growing role of institutional investors in the loan market is the direct result of the high capital

---

[1] We thank Steven Miller and Standard & Poor's Leveraged Commentary and Data (S&P LCD) for sharing their understanding of and data describing the leveraged loan market. Particularly helpful to this report were "A Syndicated Loan Primer" in *A Guide to the Loan Market*, Standard & Poor's, October 2002; *Leveraged Lending Review 2Q05*, Standard & Poor's LCD, July 2005; *Q4 04 Institutional Loan Default Review*, S&P LCD, January 2005; unpublished data made available to us; and, finally, conversations with members of S&P LCD's staff. S&P LCD's web site is at www.pmdzone.com.

cost to banks of holding loans. End investors are more efficient holders of loan assets, especially B rated loans, and institutional purchases of loans are part of the general trend of commercial bank disintermediation.

EXHIBIT 3.1   Syndicated High-Yield Loan Issuance

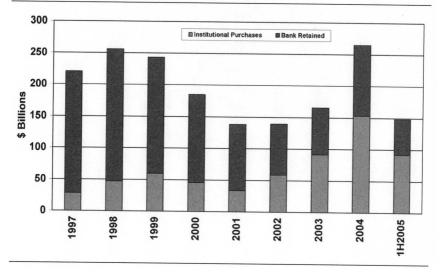

Source: S&P LCD.

EXHIBIT 3.2   Proportion of Syndicated High-Yield Loans Purchased by Institutions

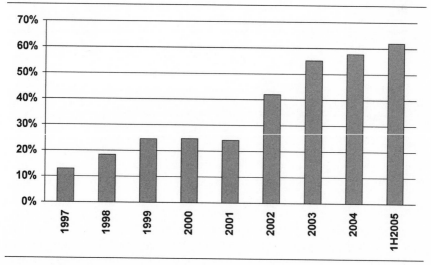

Source: S&P LCD.

EXHIBIT 3.3   Syndicated High-Yield Loan Outstandings by Industry

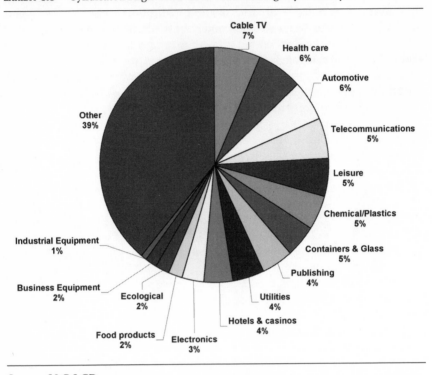

Source: S&P LCD.

These loans are made to a wide variety of borrowers, as illustrated in Exhibit 3.3, which shows outstanding high-yield loans by the borrower's industry.

THE SYNDICATION PROCESS

Syndication allows a borrower to negotiate loan terms once, yet access multiple lenders. Conflicts in priority, which would arise if a borrower serially negotiated loans, are eliminated, as all lenders share equally in rights under the resulting *credit agreement*. The credit agreement is structured, and the process is managed, by an arranger, which is typically a commercial or investment bank.

Syndication first came to prominence in the 1970s, when governments of many less-developed countries, particularly from Latin America and Eastern Europe, took out large loans from Western banks, which were flush with petrodollar deposits. That period came to an end with a string of defaults and reschedulings in the 1980s. Companies and investors involved in M&A and LBO deals then became the most prominent borrowers, but that trend was dampened in the late 1980s by a number of events: the defaults of Federated and Ames, the collapse of the UAL loan syndicate, the stock market crash of 1987, and tighter Federal Reserve guidelines on banks holding highly leveraged transactions. But the syndication market rebounded strongly in the mid-1990s led by general corporate borrowing, along with some revived M&A activity.

The loan market's ups and downs have fostered innovation in the design of syndicated loans. For example, loans may be *underwritten* or done on a *best effort* basis. In the former, the arrangers guarantee that the entire loan will be placed, and must take onto their books (and thus fund) any portion that is not subscribed for by other banks or investors. In a best effort deal, should the loan fail to be fully subscribed, the pricing or the size may be adjusted. A similar technique is the use of *market flex language*, which became more common after the turmoil of the Russian debt crisis of 1998. With market flex, borrowers typically give arrangers the flexibility to adjust loan terms and loan pricing to ensure that the loan is fully subscribed, usually with an upper limit on what the borrower will accept. Typically, that means increasing the loan's spread above its reference rate. A *reverse market flex* tightens the spread in response to oversubscription or other market conditions.

Prospective borrowers interview potential arrangers as to their syndication strategy, loan terms, and their views on loan pricing. Once chosen, the arranger prepares an *information memo* or *bank book* containing information on the borrower, the borrower's industry, loan terms, and the borrower's financial projections. This document is confidential and made available only to qualified banks and accredited investors. It places the reader of the document in the position of having private information about the company, or brings him "over the wall," the metaphorical dividing line between public and private information. In fact, once a bank or institutional investor reads the bank book, it is forbidden from purchasing the borrower's public securities, such as common stock and bonds, until the information is stale or superseded by publicly disseminated information. Sometimes the bank book is stripped of financial projections and other private material for institutional investors that buy public securities and do not want to be restricted in their activities.

When a loan is closed, its final terms are documented in a *credit agreement* and a *security agreement*. Afterward, *liens* that embody lender's rights to the borrower's collateral are *perfected*, with UCC registrations filed in relevant jurisdictions. However, credit agreements are often amended in ways ranging from the waiver of a specific covenant to complex changes in "RATS" (rate, amortization, term, and security).

Minor changes require a simple majority vote to pass while RATS-level issues require 100% concurrence.

LOAN STRUCTURE AND LEADERS

We have spoken so far as if the borrower is taking out a single loan. Usually, the credit agreement includes a *revolving line of credit* (RC) and one or more *term loans* with increasing maturities: term loan A (TLa), term loan B (TLb), etc. Sometimes the revolving line of credit can be drawn upon and converted into a term loan. Another classification of loans under the credit agreement is *pro rata loans* versus *institutional loans*. Pro rata loans are distributed to banks, and usually consist of the revolving line of credit and term loans maturing in three to five years. Institutional loans are distributed to nonbank institutional investors and usually include term loans maturing in five to seven years. Pro rata loans usually have significant amortization before maturity while institutional loans usually have a token 1% per year pay down before otherwise bullet maturities.

Major institutional investors include CLOs, prime funds, and finance companies. CLOs bought 64% of institutional loans over the 12 months ending June 2005, as shown in Exhibit 3.4. Prime funds, origi-

EXHIBIT 3.4   Institutional Loan Purchasers, 12 Months, Ending June 2005

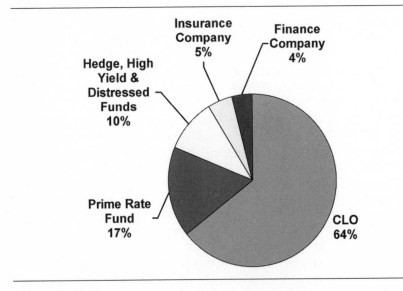

Source: S&P LCD.

nally named when loans were commonly indexed off the prime rate rather than LIBOR, bought 17% of institutional loans over the same period. (LIBOR superseded prime as the reference rate of choice in the 1990s as LIBOR was seen as more transparent and market-sensitive than prime.) Hedge funds, high-yield bond funds, and distressed debt funds bought 10% of new loan issuance and insurance companies bought 5%. Finance companies invested in 4% of institutional loans, particularly smaller loans carrying wide spreads and involving time-intensive monitoring of collateral.

The number of active institutional investors in the syndicated loan market is larger than the number of active banks in the market. Over the 12 months ending June 2005, 140 institutional investors have bought ten or more loans versus 61 banks with that same level of activity. The rise of institutional loans has spawned credit ratings of these instruments. All three major rating agencies now have dedicated staffs opining on the credit quality of loans.

LOAN INTEREST RATES AND UPFRONT FEES

Loan pricing, both interest rate and upfront fees, depends primarily on three factors:

1. The borrower's credit quality
2. New issue supply versus demand
3. The size of the loan

The effect of a loan's credit quality upon loan pricing is obvious. But, as we will discuss later in detail, the intrinsic credit risk of a borrower can at least be partially ameliorated by a loan's terms. New issue supply versus demand relates to the balance or imbalance between the amount of loans coming to market and the credit appetite of banks and institutional lenders. The driving technical in the loan market over the last two-to-three years has been the net cash inflow into single-purpose investment vehicles such as prime funds and CLOs. S&P LCD estimates that in 2003 and 2004 these investment vehicles have taken in $11 billion more than the growth in the dollar amount of outstanding loans. As a result, cash balances at these funds have risen and they have been eager to invest in loans at lower spreads. This has caused a general tightening of loan spreads over that time.

The effect of loan size is not completely obvious or consistent. Supply-demand factors work on an individual name basis just as they do for the market as a whole. In this respect, the larger the loan coming to market, the higher spreads will have to be to clear the name in the market. On the other hand, for purposes of liquidity with respect to future trading of a loan, investors prefer large loan sizes so that more investors and dealers will be familiar with the loan. In balancing these opposing factors, the wisdom in the market is that loans between $200 million and $1 billion price best.

Other factors affecting the attractiveness of a loan, if not actual loan pricing, include the borrower's equity investors, the relationship of the arranger to the borrower, and the expertise and reputation of the arranger. Ownership of a borrower by a leveraged buyout company with a reputation for quality transactions will help the borrower get better loan pricing. Another positive is if the loan arranger is also an equity investor in the borrower. Finally, arrangers who have good records for either avoiding or working out problem loans, and who provide good post-closing service to other lenders, can obtain better pricing for their borrowers.

Loan spreads were in decline from the end of 2002 to mid-2005. Spreads for B rated loans declined 180 basis points and spreads for BB-rated loans declined 202 basis points since the fourth quarter of 2002, as shown in Exhibit 3.5. The major upward blip in the exhibit is due to the credit contraction following 9/11.

EXHIBIT 3.5   Institutional Loan Spreads to LIBOR

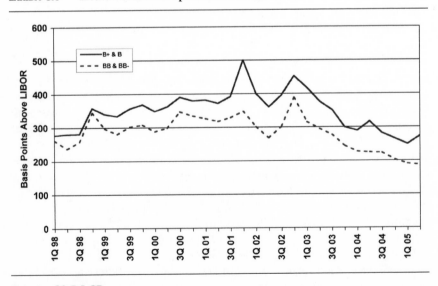

Source: S&P LCD.

Average upfront fees for pro rata loans in the first half of 2005 averaged 42 basis points. These fees are deducted from the amount banks pay for the loan, so the loan is funded at par minus fees. Pro-rata upfront fees have been falling of late, having come down from a high of 76 basis points in 2003. Upfront fees for institutional loans are just about a thing of the past, only averaging seven basis points in the first half of 2005. Upfront fees vary according to loan maturity, with smaller loans commanding higher upfront fees.

An interesting aspect of loan pricing is the borrower's right to switch interest payments from one floating index to another. Possibilities include spreads to prime, LIBOR, and CD rates. Accompanying the change in interest index is the frequency with which interest rates reset. The prime rate resets daily; LIBOR and CD reset every one, three, or 12 months.

Another unique aspect of loan interest payments is the use of pricing grids to adjust required interest payments in reaction to the borrower's evolving credit quality. For investment grade borrowers, changes in spreads usually key off of the borrower's public ratings. For speculative grade borrowers, changes in spreads usually key off the borrower's financial ratios. Pricing grids are most often used for lower-quality speculative-grade borrowers and there is more room in pricing grids for spreads to decrease than increase. As the credit quality of borrowers has been improving, the percentage of institutional loans with pricing grids has been declining. From a peak of 57% in 1998, the presence of pricing grids dropped to only 22% of institutional loans in the second quarter of 2005.

LOAN CREDIT QUALITY

We show two measures of loan credit quality, leverage and interest coverage. Our leverage measure is total debt divided by EBITDA. As shown in Exhibit 3.6, this measure of leverage for large (issuers with EBITDA greater than $50 million) syndicated loan borrowers has improved from 5.9 in 1997 to 5.2 in the first half of 2005. More recently, however, this ratio has increased, from 4.1 in 2001 to 5.2. The proportion of total debt made up of bank debt has increased over the years. From 69% of total debt in 1997 and 60% in 1998, bank debt's share increased to 78% in the first half of 2005. The increasing proportion of bank debt to total debt has stalemated the falling ratio of total debt to EBITDA. Meaning, that bank debt to EBITDA, at 4.0 times, is almost the same as it was in 1997 at 4.1. But bank debt to EBITDA, now at 4.0 is greater than it was in 2002 when it was 2.6. To put it succinctly, leverage is better now than in 1997 and 1998, but worse than 1999 through 2004.

EXHIBIT 3.6   Average Leverage of Large Syndicated Loan Borrowers

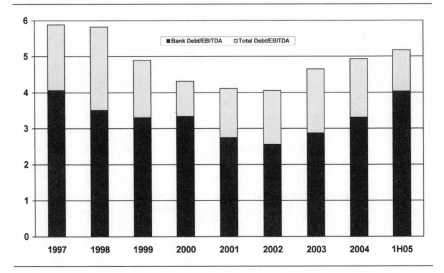

Source: S&P LCD.

Our interest coverage measure is EBITDA, with and without capital expenses (CapEx), divided by total interest expense. As shown in Exhibit 3.7, this measure of borrower's interest coverage in the syndicated loan market has improved from 1.9 in 1997 to 2.9 in the first half of 2005. Overall, the trend is the result of declining LIBOR and declining loan spreads.

LENDER'S LIABILITY

Bank loan participants have a special relationship with borrowers, as indicated by their receipt of private information in the bank book and as we will see later when we discuss loan terms. The downside of a lender's relationship with a borrower is the risk of "lender liability," a set of legal theories and claims under which a borrower may sue a lender. In its most basic form, lender liability arises if a lender violates an implied or contractual duty of good faith and fair dealing towards the borrower. But a higher standard of conduct is demanded of the lender if, through its influence over the borrower, the lender has assumed fiduciary responsibilities. This fiduciary duty might even extend to the borrower's other creditors and subject the lender to claims from them, too.

EXHIBIT 3.7   Average Interest Coverage of Large Syndicated Loan Borrowers

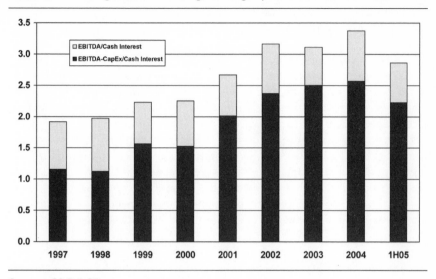

Source: S&P LCD.

In asserting its contractual rights, a lender must be careful to maintain an arm's length relationship with the borrower and avoid becoming the borrower's de facto consultant, advisor, officer, or board of directors. Finally, a lender subjects itself to liability if it fails to sell seized collateral in a commercially reasonable manner. One punishment open to courts against lenders who have misbehaved is to subordinate their claim against the borrower to that of other creditors of the borrower. CLOs mitigate this risk by limiting their investment in revolving loans so that failure to fund a loan cannot be the basis of a lender liability assertion.

OVERVIEW OF LOAN TERMS

Loan terms are embodied in loan credit agreements in three forms: the borrower's representations and warranties, affirmative covenants, and negative covenants. In this chapter, we ignore the specific form of loan terms and organize our discussion with respect to the underlying purpose of those terms. We divide loan terms into the following purposes, which we will discuss in detail:

- Preservation of collateral
- Appropriation of excess cash flow

- Control of business risk
- Performance requirements
- Reporting requirements

In the following discussion of loan terms, we continue to focus on loans to speculative grade credits. For these loans, compliance with terms is tested on an ongoing basis. In contrast, for loans to investment grade borrowers, compliance is often tested only upon the incurrence of some event, such as an acquisition or the issuance of additional debt. Furthermore, loans to speculative credits are almost always senior secured while loans to investment grade credits are usually unsecured. Tight, perpetually tested loan terms and secured interest in collateral keeps speculative grade borrowers on a short leash.

Borrowers commonly breach loan terms, especially performance requirements such as interest coverage ratios. Borrowers also commonly ask permission to breach a loan term, such as for the sale of an asset. Both situations provide lenders with the opportunity to demand further concessions from the borrower. In return for a waiver of a loan term and for not calling the loan immediately due and payable, lenders might, for example, discontinue advances under the revolving line of credit, curtail capital expenditures, increase mandatory amortization schedules, or increase the loan's spread. Banks usually renegotiate loan terms with borrowers long before bankruptcy or even severe impairment. This gives them the opportunity to speed up loan amortization or gain further control over the borrower's assets before bankruptcy occurs.

Preservation of Collateral

The borrower represents that lenders have a legal, valid, and enforceable security interest in the assets the borrower has pledged to secure the loan. Generally, this means *all* the assets of the firm, even assets acquired after the loan is closed, but sometimes a loan is only backed by specific assets. While investment grade companies can get away with springing liens, which create security interests if the borrower is downgraded below investment grade, speculative grade borrowers must pledge collateral as a precondition to receiving a loan.

Obviously, the value and liquidity of collateral are major factors determining the credit quality of a loan. A large amount of readily salable assets is better than a small amount of specialized assets that have little use to any other party than the borrower. Assets that fluctuate greatly in value are obviously less attractive. As a general rule, 50% of inventory and 80% of receivables are readily financeable. The loan value of plant, property, and equipment varies, but generally senior secured loans make up half of a borrower's total liabilities and equity.

To maintain the lender's interest in the collateral, the borrower is forbidden from pledging collateral to other creditors. The borrower must also pay its taxes to prevent government authorities from gaining a superseding claim on pledged collateral. To protect the value of collateral, the borrower pledges to perform proper maintenance. The borrower also pledges to insure collateral.

Appropriation of Excess Cash Flow

Unfettered, a borrower could take out a loan, sell its assets, dividend the proceeds of both the loan and the asset sale to equity holders, and leave lenders with an empty corporate shell. Borrowers, however, are quite fettered: Excess cash flow from the borrower's ordinary and extraordinary business activities must be used to prepay its loans.

"Excess cash flow" is typically defined as cash flow minus cash expenses, required dividends, debt repayments, capital expenditures, and changes in working capital. Typically, 50%–75% of this must be used to prepay loans. Similarly, 50%–100% of proceeds from new equity issuance, 100% of proceeds from new debt issuance, and 100% of asset sales (not already prohibited, as mentioned above) must be used to prepay loans. An acceptable level of annual capital expenditure is usually set out in the credit agreement.

In practice, troubled borrowers often approach lenders for permission to realize *some* proceeds from the sale of assets. Depending upon the borrower's circumstances, lenders generally agree, so long as the majority of proceeds from the asset sale are used to prepay loans.

Control of Business Risk

Lenders are obviously disadvantaged when a borrower's business becomes more risky. Less obvious, perhaps, is that the borrower's equity holders might *gain* an advantage if the borrower's business becomes more risky. An extreme example illustrates the differing incentives.

Suppose a company has declined in value to the point that its market value equals the par value of its bank loan. Lenders would like the borrower to sell itself and pay off the loan. In this case, the borrower's equity holders are assured of receiving zero residual value. Equity holders, on the other hand, would rather the firm sell its assets and buy lottery tickets. Most likely, this will be a losing proposition. There is a chance that winnings will be enough to not only pay off lenders, but also provide some residual value to equity holders.

From a lender's perspective, 100% assurance of payback is better than less than 100% probability of payback. From a shareholder's perspective, a small positive probability of receiving residual value is better than zero probability of receiving any cash.

To control a borrower's business risk, loan documents place restrictions on the borrower's ability to take on more risk via investments, mergers, acquisitions, and the extension of guarantees. Borrowers are also prohibited from issuing more debt, even debt ranking below the loan in priority. At first, this last requirement may seem unnecessary–how can debt below the loan negatively affect loan lenders? But lenders do not want borrowers to increase their probability of default by becoming more levered, so they want to have control over any new borrower financing.

Performance Requirements

Violations of performance requirements, based on accounting measures, give lenders the right to accelerate a loan, making it become due and payable immediately. In practice, this threat gives lenders negotiating power over borrowers when these measures are violated. Banks would rather exercise control over a borrower early on and by doing so, hopefully avoid more serious problems later. Accounting measures of performance usually address coverage, leverage, liquidity, tangible net worth, and capital expenditures. The following are common variants:

- *Coverage*, the ratio of (1) cash flow or earnings to (2) debt service or fixed charges (debt service + amortization + capital expenditures + rent).
- *Leverage*, the ratio of (1) loan debt or total debt to (2) equity or cash flow.
- *Liquidity*, the current ratio of (1) cash + marketable securities + accounts receivable + inventory to (2) accounts payable + short term debt or the quick ratio, which is the current ratio without inventories in the numerator.
- *Tangible net worth*, the dollar amount of net worth – intangible assets.
- *Maximum capital expenditures*, the dollar amount of purchases of plant, property, and equipment.
- Minimum dollar amounts of *cash flow* or *net worth*.

On average, loans have four required performance measures. The frequency that specific performance requirements show up in loan terms, based on 311 recent loans made over the 12 months ending June 2005, is shown in Exhibit 3.8.

EXHIBIT 3.8   Frequency of Performance Requirements

Requirement	Percent of Transactions	Comments
Total debt/EBITDA	84	Leverage ratio
Capex	53	Dollar limit on capital expenditures
Fixed charge coverage	51	Coverage ratio
Interest coverage	45	Coverage ratio
Cash interest coverage	22	Coverage ratio
Sr. debt/EBITDA	20	Leverage ratio
Other	14	Often specialized to borrower
EBITDA	12	Minimum dollar requirement
Net worth	6	Minimum dollar requirement
Debt service coverage	5	Coverage ratio
Operating leases	3	Maximum dollar limit
Debt/EBITDAR	2	Leverage ratio

Source: S&P LCD.

Many speculative grade loans are made under the assumption that financial performance will improve. This is particularly the case in acquisition financing, where economies of scale or asset sales or other factors are expected to improve the financial performance of the combined entity going forward. In these cases, target financial ratios are tightened over time.

The calculation of these variables can vary from being based on generally accepted accounting principals to harsher measures. For example, noncash revenue might be excluded from coverage calculations while noncash expenses are included.

Reporting Requirements

To facilitate the lender's monitoring of the borrower, the borrower is required to supply certain reports and documents, which may include:

- Quarterly and annual financial statements.
- Immediate notice of non-compliance with loan terms and periodic certification of compliance with loan terms.
- Budgets and financial projections, budget versus actual comparisons, and revised budgets.
- Account receivable analysis.
- Property, plant, and equipment appraisals.

■ Proof of insurance.
■ Financial statements, reports, and proxy statements sent to shareholders, the SEC, or other regulators.
■ Any information that lenders reasonably request.

LOAN TERMS VERSUS BOND TERMS

When Fitch compared loan agreements and bond indentures for speculative grade credits, they counted 20 covenants for the former versus six for the later. Fitch also found that debt limitations in bond indentures were usually subject to an incurrence test based on leverage or interest coverage tests. The loose definition of these tests made them ineffectual, in the rating agency's opinion. Restrictions on payments in bond indentures did not always include loans, advances, and investments. Bond debtors were also allowed to merge with few requirements or restrictions.

Fitch's overall conclusion regarding bond indentures was that "the scope of the restrictions and the level of compliance required of the borrower are generally loose and add little value in protecting bondholders."[2]

A TALE OF TWO LOANS

Lessons sometimes have to be relearned in the financial markets, particularly when new participants enter a market. For example, the fact that a loan is senior secured does not in itself guarantee the loan's credit quality. Early in the evolution of the syndicated bank loan market, new participants had to learn the ropes.

Northern[3] was a retail store chain with a terrific market share in its home base. That is the end of its good points. The stores and their equipment were old, and they were in bad locations. A larger well-capitalized store chain had saturated the market in a state next door and was poised to invade Northern's territory.

If anyone knew these facts, they kept quiet about them. Northern's equity buyout firm was simultaneously doing another deal in another part of the country. It did not, let us put it gently, volunteer a lot of negative facts about Northern. The arranger of the loan was looking forward to a very lucrative fee from underwriting a public bond for Northern that

---

[2] Mariarosa Verde, *Loan Preserver: The Value of Covenants*, Fitch, March 4, 1999.
[3] We disguise the names of the two troubled borrowers to cut down on the hate mail we receive.

was structured to be *pari passu* to the loan. It later became public that the arranger retained only a few hundred thousand dollars of the loan.

The *coup de grace* of this disaster was that the loan was made to the holding company without any guarantees from the firm's operating subsidiaries. As the holding company's only asset was common stock in its subsidiaries, lenders at the holding company level were structurally subordinate to the debt holders of those subsidiaries. The only source of funds to pay the holding company level loan was common stock dividends from operating subsidiaries. Those dividends could be paid to the holding company only after the subsidiaries had satisfied their own debt holders.

When Northern's senior secured debt traded down into the mid-teens, a vulture fund swooped in to buy it up. After amassing a large position, they visited the stores. Wrong sequence. The bargain they thought they had found turned out to be no bargain at all. The final distribution to lenders including the vulture fund was a nickel on the dollar.

Several years later, another case showed how market expertise had evolved. Southern was a good retail store chain horribly over-leveraged. On the day their loan closed, it was obvious to some observers that the chain stood a good chance of heading into trouble. The company's business plan depended on selling off divisions of the company to pay off debt and provide a liquidating dividend to equity holders. The problem was that at the time the loan was made, a number of retailers were already engaged in the same strategy. As more retail chains went on the auction block, bids for these businesses became thinner and shorter.

Yet some of the pessimistic observers who felt the company was shaky still participated in the senior secured loan to Southern. Why? They predicted that even if the company spiraled down into bankruptcy, lenders would still receive principal and interest. They were right. As Southern sold divisions for prices far below their projections, the company began to fail on specific loan terms. The friendly happy bankers who took Southern executives on golf outings were replaced by *un*friendly *un*happy bankers who approached the workout specialist in *A Man in Full* in temperament, if not finesse.

Lenders took advantage of every breach Southern made in the terms of its loan agreement to extract cash out of the company's operations to pay down loan balances. When the company eventually filed for bankruptcy, less than 40% of the original loan balance was still outstanding. Senior secured lenders received all principal and accrued interest. Thus, good loan structuring overcame a bad financial plan.

THE SECONDARY MARKET

The sobering tale of Northern touched on a hitherto unexplored point—
the existence of a vigorous secondary market for loans. Banks, of
course, have long sold portions of their loan portfolios, often in
response to regulations regarding concentration or credit risk. But interest in the trading of syndicated loans exploded in the 1990s, with volume rising from $8 billion in 1991 to $145 billion in 2003, a 1,700%
jump. During the same period, the primary market expanded just
450%. As in the primary market, institutions (including CLOs, insurers,
and hedge funds) have come to play an increasingly important role.
While many participants are simply adjusting their loan portfolios,
some investors appear to be looking to take advantage of price movements and discrepancies, just as in other financial markets.

Loans in the secondary market change hands either by *assignment*
or by *participation*. With assignment, the buyer becomes the lender of
record with all related rights and powers. However, the consent of the
borrower is usually required. With participation, the buyer receives the
right to repayment, but the original lender remains the lender of record
and is responsible for collecting amounts from the borrower and for-
warding them on to the participant. In this case, the borrower's consent
is usually not required, but the buyer shoulders a greater credit risk
because participation does not create a contractual link between the
participant and the borrower. So the participant may be left with no
recourse should the original lender become insolvent. As a consequence,
CLOs buy loans via assignment.

One of the factors behind the surge of interest in the secondary market for loans is the increasing amount of available information. Since
loans are private contracts between lenders and borrowers, very little
public information used to be available. That has changed over the last
18 years. In 1987, Loan Pricing Corporation (LPC) launched its flagship
Gold Sheets weekly publication covering the loan market.[4] In 1995,
market participants including banks, brokers, and investors created the
non-profit Loan Syndications and Trading Association (LSTA), which
has created standard documentation for the industry.[5] S&P began rating
syndicated loans that same year. LPC and LSTA also began gathering
mark-to-market pricing data in the mid-1990s, and LSTA joined with
S&P to create a secondary market index. S&P Leverage Commentary
and Data (S&P LCD) was formed in 1996 and began publishing volumi-
nous data on the market. LoanX (now part of Markit Partners) began

---

[4] The data are available at www.loanpricing.com.
[5] The web site is at www.lsta.org.

EXHIBIT 3.9 Cumulative Returns of High-Yield Loans

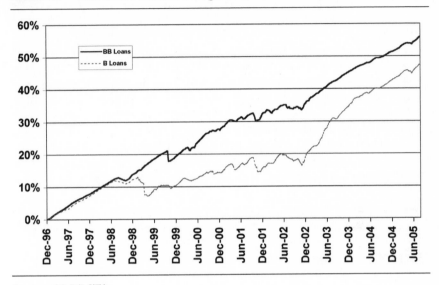

Source: S&P/LSTA.

offering loan pricing in 1999. CUSIPs finally made their loan market debut in 2004, finally simplifying loan identification.

Given that much of secondary market trading is focused on leveraged loans and distressed loans (defined as trading for less than 90 cents on the dollar), it is remarkable that the S&P/LSTA index (see Exhibit 3.9 shows a positive return for every year since its launch. While the index admittedly has only a short nine-year history, it does cover one recessionary period, further underlining the attractive qualities of loans relative to other securities. Of course, high-yield loans have a number of things going for them: their floating rate, low duration nature, and their senior secured status being prominent.

LOAN RECOVERY RATES

Historical recovery studies confirm the advantage of bank loan lenders' senior position in the borrower's assets. Fitch and Moody's have looked at defaulted credits that had both loans and bonds in their capital structure at the time they went into default. As measured shortly after default, Fitch found that defaulted loans priced at an average of 69% in 2002, while defaulted bonds from the same credits priced at an average of 31%.[6] This produces a loan-loss-to-bond-loss ratio of 45% [(1 − 69%)/(1 − 31%)]. Moody's study looked at loan and bond defaults over a longer time period, and calculated loan-loss-to-bond-loss ratios of 55% for senior unsecured bonds and 43% for subordinate bonds.[7]

Exhibits 3.10 and 3.11 show more detail on recoveries of loans and bonds of different seniorities. Exhibit 3.10 focuses on recoveries in 2004 while Exhibit 3.11 shows recoveries over multiple years, depending on the length of time covered in the survey. Recovery in the Moody's data is the bid price for defaulted bonds and loans a few weeks after default. Recovery in the S&P data is after-default cash flows present valued back to the time of default. In all cases, loan recoveries clearly outperform bond recoveries. The recovery rates in these two exhibits are based on the outstanding par of the loans and bonds. But remember, loan amounts decline because of (1) scheduled amortization, (2) sweeps from excess cash flow and the sale of assets, and (3) forced paydown as a condition for the waiver of violations of loan terms. Given loan amor-

EXHIBIT 3.10   Loan and Bond Recovery Rates in 2004

Debt Type	Recovery Rate
Moody's Sr. Secured Loans	96%
Moody's Sr. Unsecured Bonds	50%
Moody's Subordinated Bonds	44%

Source: Moody's, S&P.

EXHIBIT 3.11   Loan and Bond Recovery Rates in Recent Years

Rating Agency/Debt Type	Recovery Rate
S&P Sr. Secured by All Assets, 50% debt cushion 1988–2003	90%
S&P All Seniority Loans 1988–2003	78%
Moody's Sr. Secured Loans 1982–2004	70%
Moody's Sr. Unsecured Bonds 1982–2004	45%
Moody's Subordinated Bonds 1982–2004	33%

Source: S&P LCD, Moody's, S&P.

---

[6] Mariarosa Verde and Paul Mancuso, *High-yield Defaults 2002: The Perfect Storm,* Fitch, February 19, 2003.

[7] Kenneth Emery, Richard Cantor, and Roger Arner, *Recovery Rates On North American Syndicated Bank Loans, 1989–2003,* Moody's Investors Service, March 2004.

tization, losses as a percent of the original loan amount are even smaller than would be indicated by these recovery rates.[8]

S&P notes that ultimate recovery is usually much higher than market prices immediately after default. After tracing payments to defaulted loan holders throughout the bankruptcy process, the rating agency calculates average ultimate recovery on loans in 2002 at 72% versus a 53% average market price shortly after default. Historically, the difference between ultimate recovery and the price immediately after default is greater. From 1980 through 2002, ultimate recovery on bank loans was 82% versus a 60% market price immediately after default, according to S&P.

LOAN DEFAULT RATES

More surprising than differences in loan-bond *recoveries* are differences in loan-bond *default rates,* which are at historic lows. Exhibit 3.12 shows defaults according to year of issuance by broadly syndicated institutional loan borrowers that make public filings to the Security and Exchange Commission. The restriction to public filers is necessary to be able to identify defaulters. As shown in Exhibit 3.12, S&P LCD has followed loan borrower defaults by year of issuance since 1995. Each row of the exhibit shows how many borrowers took out loans in a particular year, and how many of those borrowers subsequently defaulted on those loans. For example, 138 borrowers took out loans in 2000, and of those, 11 defaulted in 2001, 15 in 2002, 2 in 2003, 1 in 2004, and none in the first half of 2005. Note that a data point in the study incorporates all of a borrower's institutional loans, so multiple institution loans (such as B and C term loans) taken out by the same borrower are treated as a single data point in the statistics.

Total defaults in any particular year are shown in the bottom row of Exhibit 3.12. The nine defaults recorded in 2004 are the lowest number of loan defaults in any year since 1999. In fact, the *combined* number of borrower defaults in 2003, 2004, and the first half of 2005 (21) are less than that of any single year since 1999, despite an increasing number of borrowers. Exhibit 3.13 shows the decline of loan defaults another way, by the 12-month rolling average of loan defaults. The solid line in the exhibit is the number of defaulting loans in the past 12 months divided by the total number of loans outstanding. The dotted line in the exhibit is

---

[8] David T. Hamilton et al, *Default & Recovery Rates of Corporate Bond Issuers: 1920 –2004,* Moody's, January 2005. David Keisman and Jane Zennario, *2003 Recovery Highlights,* Standard & Poor's, February 6, 2004.

EXHIBIT 3.12 High-Yield Loan Default Data: Number of Public Filers and Subsequent Defaulters

Year of Origination	Public Filers	1995	1996	1997	1998	1999	2000	2001	2002	2003	2004	1H2005
1995	27	—	—	—	—	—	1	—	—	—	—	—
1996	66		—	—	—	—	1	—	—	—	—	—
1997	107			—	3	2	10	3	1	—	—	—
1998	188				1	7	11	7	6	4	—	—
1999	165					—	7	13	3	2	2	—
2000	138						—	11	15	2	1	—
2001	114							2	3	—	1	—
2002	167								1	3	2	—
2003	289									—	3	—
2004	435										—	1
Totals	1,696	0	0	0	4	9	30	36	29	11	9	1

Source: S&P LCD.

EXHIBIT 3.13   12-Month Trailing Loan Default Rate

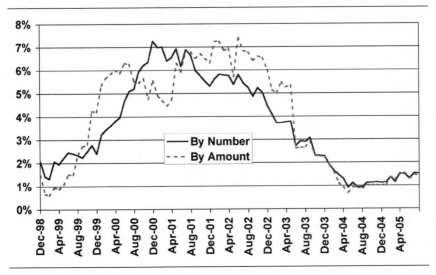

Source: S&P LCD.

the par value of defaulting loans divided by the total par value of loans outstanding. By either measure, loan defaults at 1.5% over the 12 months ending August 2005 are about at their lowest level ever.

Besides the instantaneous picture of loan defaults shown in Exhibit 3.13, we would also like to understand how defaults have occurred over time as loans season. Exhibit 3.14 reassembles the data in Exhibit 3.12 into *cumulative default rates*. It also shows the variability in default rates among *borrowers from different issuance years* (also referred to as *issuance cohorts or vintages*). In Exhibit 3.14, the default experience of each issuance cohort is placed on the same scale of loan seasoning on the horizontal axis. For example, the default history of the 2000 issuance cohort is represented by the line that reaches the 21% default rate mark on the vertical axis at 4.5 years of seasoning on the horizontal axis. The cumulative default rate is calculated as the number of defaulting borrowers (11 + 15 + 2 +1 = 29) divided by the total number of borrowers (138) to create a 21% default rate (29/138). These defaults occurred over five years, as 2000 issuance cohort loans were made, on average, on June 30, 2000, and the loans are tracked through June 30, 2005.

In Exhibit 3.14, the highest two lines at six years of loan seasoning represent the 1997 and 1998 issuance cohorts with 17.8% and 19.1% cumulative default rates, respectively. The lowest two lines at six years of seasoning represent the 1995 and 1996 issuance cohorts, with 3.7%

EXHIBIT 3.14   Cumulative Default Rates of 1995–2004 Issuance Cohorts

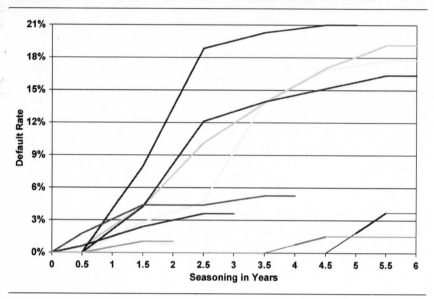

Source: S&P LCD, UBS Calculations.

and 1.5% cumulative default rates, respectively. The 1995 and 1996 cohorts had their first defaults after three years of seasoning, as represented by their cumulative default lines rising above the horizontal axis after 3.5 and 4.5 years.

In Exhibit 3.15, we average individual issuance cohort experience and compare cumulative default rates for loans to those of BB and B senior unsecured bonds.[9] We calculate our averages in two ways, by weighting the experience of each issuance cohort equally and by weighting the experience of each issuance cohort by the number of borrowers in the cohort.[10] For a truer loan-bond comparison, we use the history of corporate bond defaults over the same time period as covered by the data we have on loan defaults.

---

[9] Diane Vazza, Devi Aurora, and Ryan Schneck, *Annual Global Corporate Default Study: Corporate Defaults Poised to Rise in 2005*, Standard & Poor's, January 2005.

[10] We use the rating agency default study method of calculating marginal default rates (the default rate, for example, within the first year, second year, third year, etc., after the cohort is formed) for each cohort and adding average *marginal* default rates together to create *average cumulative* default rates. This uses all available data and avoids the possibility, suffered by other methods, of creating *declining* cumulative default rates.

The results in Exhibit 3.15 show that loan default rates are generally lower than corporate bond default rates. Loan default rates are less than BB bond default rates averaging across all tenors. And loan default rates are 40% that of B bond default rates averaging across all tenors. But one thing missing from Exhibit 3.15 is the default rates for loans of different ratings. The exhibit combines all loans, thus creating a blended loan rating quality we estimate at B+.

But S&P LCD also reports loan default data by borrower rating. In Exhibit 3.16, we perform the same comparison of loan and bond defaults as in Exhibit 3.15, but this time separating out BB/BB– loans and B+/B loans. Again, to make a truer loan-bond comparison, we use the history of corporate bond defaults over the same time period as the data we have on loan defaults. The line items for various loan and bond defaults in Exhibit 3.16 are sorted in ascending order of their six-year default rate. The exhibit shows that BB/BB– loan default rates are most similar to BBB bond default rates, and B+/B loan default rates are most similar to BB bond default rates.

So What's Going on Here?

We think one reason for loan defaults being lower than bond defaults is that loan ratings are generally more up-to-date than bond ratings. Rating agencies have a bias against making rating changes.[11] If a company's fortunes have changed, positively or negatively, its ratings do not necessarily fully reflect that current credit condition. Many companies taking out loans, however, do not have existing ratings, so there is no ratings history to restrain a rating analyst's judgment. Also, many loan packages are accomplished in the context of a complete top-to-bottom restructuring of all the issuer's debt. Thus, a new loan has the effect of starting the ratings process over with a clean slate.

But how have the two collateral types actually performed within high-yield loan and high-yield bond CDOs? Has the general superiority of loans over bonds carried over into CDO portfolios?

HIGH-YIELD LOAN CLO VERSUS HIGH-YIELD BOND CBO PERFORMANCE

We look at two measures of a CDO's collateral performance: par overcollateralization and average collateral rating. We use Moody's mea-

---

[11] Jerome S. Fons, *Understanding Moody's Corporate Bond Ratings and Rating Process*, Moody's Investors Service, May 2002.

EXHIBIT 3.15 Average Cumulative Default Rates for High-Yield Loans and Bonds, 1995–2004 Issuance Cohorts

Years	1	2	3	4	5	6	Annualized
Year-Weighted Cumulative Default Rates							
High-yield loans	1.5%	4.4%	7.2%	9.1%	10.6%	11.4%	1.9%
BB rated bonds	1.2%	3.4%	6.2%	9.0%	11.7%	14.2%	2.4%
B rated bonds	5.4%	12.0%	17.5%	22.3%	26.0%	29.6%	4.9%
Issuer Weighted Cumulative Default Rates							
High-yield loans	1.4%	4.6%	8.0%	10.2%	11.7%	12.4%	2.1%
BB rated bonds	1.2%	3.6%	6.7%	9.5%	12.1%	14.5%	2.4%
B rated bonds	5.6%	12.6%	18.4%	23.3%	27.1%	30.4%	5.1%

Source: S&P LCD, UBS Calculations.

68

EXHIBIT 3.16 Average Cumulative Default Rates for High-Yield Loans and Bonds, 1998–2004 Issuance Cohorts

	1	2	3	4	5	6	Average
Year-Weighted Cumulative Default Rates							
BBB corporate bond	0.4%	1.1%	2.0%	3.1%	4.1%	4.6%	0.8%
BB/BB– loan	0.9%	3.0%	4.2%	5.3%	7.0%	7.8%	1.3%
BB corporate bond	1.4%	4.2%	7.8%	11.0%	13.7%	15.5%	2.6%
B+/B loan	4.5%	9.6%	13.1%	15.3%	17.8%	19.2%	3.2%
B corporate bond	6.3%	14.4%	21.1%	26.9%	30.4%	32.9%	5.5%
Issuer-Weighted Cumulative Default Rates							
BBB corporate bond	0.3%	1.1%	2.0%	3.1%	4.0%	4.4%	0.7%
BB/BB– loan	0.8%	2.6%	3.7%	4.4%	5.7%	6.3%	1.0%
BB corporate bond	1.4%	4.2%	7.8%	10.8%	13.4%	15.0%	2.5%
B+/B loan	3.1%	8.1%	11.7%	13.5%	15.9%	17.3%	2.9%
B corporate bond	6.1%	14.1%	20.8%	26.3%	29.7%	32.2%	5.4%

Source: S&P LCD, UBS Calculations.

surement of annual overcollateralization deterioration, which is based on the trend of overcollateralization for the CDO's junior-most debt tranche.[12] And we use Moody's measure of the collateral's weighted average rating (WARF) to estimate the collateral's annual increase in expected loss.[13] This is done by translating an increase in the collateral's WARF into an increase in 10-year default probability, multiplying that by a default loss assumption, and annualizing.

In Exhibit 3.17, we chart high-yield bond and high-yield loan CDO OC and WARF deterioration for issuance cohorts from 1996 through 2003. Annual OC deterioration increases to the right of the exhibit and annual WARF deterioration increases to the top of the exhibit. Generally, high-yield *bond* CBOs portfolios have much had more OC and WARF deterioration than high-yield *loan* CLO portfolios.[14]

The superior performance of loan over bond CDO portfolios has carried into rating agency CDO downgrades. Exhibit 3.18 shows Moody's cumulative rating downgrades for high-yield bond and high-yield loan CDOs in the following different ways:

---

[12] *Moody's Deal Score Report: CDO Deal Summary Performance May 2005*, Moody's Investors Service, July 29, 2005. Per Moody's, average annual OC Loss is calculated based on a CDO's most junior Moody's-rated tranche OC test as: [Initial (Effective Date) OC – Current OC]/Initial OC/Number of years since deal's closing date. OC levels are calculated by Moody's consistently across all CDOs independent of a CDO Trustee's calculation and may differ from the levels calculated in accordance with a deal's indenture. OC levels for purposes of this calculation are [Performing Collateral Par + (Market Value of Defaulted Collateral/Reinvestment Price)] + Cash in Principal Account]. Moody's assumes the following reinvestment prices: bonds at 90%; loans at 95%; SF tranches at 90%.

[13] Per Moody's, WARF Increase measures the extent of compliance or violation of a CDO's Moody's Weighted Average Rating Factor Test calculated as: [(Adjusted weighted average rating factor – Test level)/Test level]. Adjusted weighted average rating factor is calculated by Moody's, independent of the reported Moody's Rating Factor that is calculated and reported by the CDO Trustee. WARF Increase is based on individual security credit ratings obtained directly from Moody's internal ratings database. To the extent Moody's cannot obtain a rating from their own ratings database, they rely on ratings reported by the Trustees. WARF Increase excludes defaulted securities, whereas some CDOs include defaulted securities in their reported Moody's Rating Factors. Also, this calculation is not adjusted for securities that are on Moody's Watchlist, whereas many CDOs adjust their rating factor calculation by treating such securities as if they had been downgraded (if on Watch for downgrade) or upgraded (if on Watch for upgrade). *Note:* In this study, we have turned Moody's WARF Increase calculation into an *absolute* percentage increase in idealized 10-year expected loss.

[14] The best performing CBO cohort is from 2002 and the worst performing CLO cohort is from 1997.

EXHIBIT 3.17   High-Yield Bond and High-Yield Loan Collateral Portfolio
Deterioration

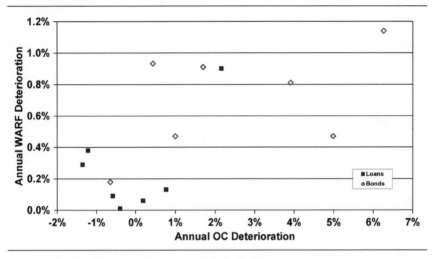

Source: Moody's Investors Service, UBS Calculations.

- The first panel shows the percent of CDOs with one or more tranches downgraded. The statistic is shown by issuance year and then summarized across all issuance years at the right of the exhibit. In every instance, across all issuance years, more high-yield bond CBOs have suffered one or more tranche downgrades than high-yield loan CLOs.
- The second panel shows the percent of CDO tranches downgraded. In every instance, across all issuance years, more high-yield bond CBO tranches have been downgraded than high-yield loan CLO tranches.
- The third panel shows average rating changes by number of rating notches. These are the 1s, 2s, and 3s that Moody's assigns to their letter ratings. Thus, a rating change from A1 to A2 is a one-notch change and a rating change from A1 to Baa1 is a three notch rating change. High-yield loan CLO downgrades have been less severe than high-yield bond CBO downgrades in each issuance year.
- The fourth panel shows the percent of tranches originally rated Aa1, Aa2, or Aa3 that have been downgraded below Baa3. No Aa high-yield loan CLO tranches have ever had that significant a downgrade, but plenty of Aa high-yield bond CBO tranches have.

While Exhibit 3.18 shows the superior performance of CLOs over CBOs, it also shows a distinct difference in the performance of CLOs issued between 1996 to 1998 and those issued later. CLOs issued in the earlier period have performed far less well in comparison to later CLO vintages. One reason for this poor performance is the presence of high-yield bonds within these CLOs. Some of these CLOs had high-yield bond buckets of 20%, which turned out to be unfortunate. In spite of the poorer performance of 1996 to 1998 CLOs, none of their tranches originally rated A3 or higher has been downgraded below Baa3. This is a better performance than that of investment grade bonds from the 1996–1998 era, which experienced more severe downgrades and even some defaults.

EXHIBIT 3.18   Comparison of HY CBO and HY CLO Downgrades, by Vintage

Percent of CDOs with One or More Tranches Downgraded

	Issuance Year								All Vintages
	1996	1997	1998	1999	2000	2001	2002	2003	
HY Bond CBOs	100	100	96	88	74	38	0	0	75
HY Loan CLOs	67	83	82	4	13	4	3	0	16

Cumulative Percent of Tranches Downgraded

	Issuance Year								All Vintages
	1996	1997	1998	1999	2000	2001	2002	2003	
HY Bond CBOs	83	95	87	87	65	29	0	0	68
HY Loan CLOs	67	57	50	3	9	3	1	0	8

Average Cumulative Rating Notch Downgrade

	Issuance Year								Avg Drift/ Year
	1996	1997	1998	1999	2000	2001	2002	2003	
HY Bond CBOs	7.3	9.7	7.9	9.1	4.3	0.8	0.0	0.0	0.8
HY Loan CLOs	3.3	6.0	2.9	0.1	0.3	−0.1	0.0	0.0	0.2

Percent of Aa CDO Tranches Downgraded Below Baa3

	Issuance Year								All Vintages
	1996	1997	1998	1999	2000	2001	2002	2003	
HY Bond CBOs	25	47	46	50	14	0	0	na	35
HY Loan CLOs	0	0	0	0	0	0	0	0	0

Source: Moody's Investors Service, UBS Calculations.

Besides poor collateral performance, CBOs suffered as a result of their interest rate hedging. To manage the interest rate mismatch risk of the CBO's fixed rate collateral and floating rate liabilities, CBOs entered into agreements to pay fixed and receive floating on interest rate swaps. As interest rates fell from 2000 to 2003, CBOs were net payers on these swaps. This would not have been bad if their portfolios and liabilities were still in tack. CBOs would have used fixed rate payments on their collateral portfolios to pay the fixed rate on the swap, and used the floating rate payment coming from the swap to pay the floating rate on their liabilities. But bond defaults had diminished CBO collateral portfolios and the working of overcollateralization triggers had accelerated principal paydown of CBO liabilities. This caused the notional amount of the interest rate swap to be greater than the amount of the assets and liabilities in many CBOs. As a result, many CBOs were overhedged resulting in losses in their hedge positions.

The poor performance of CBOs in comparison to CLOs was not lost on CDO investors. Since 1987, high-yield bond backed CBOs had been the dominant type of CDO. As late as 1999, issuance of arbitrage CBOs outnumbered issuance of arbitrage CLOs by two to one. But in 2000, CLO issuance caught up with CBO issuance and by 2002 the tally was eight to one in favor of CLOs. At the same time, bond buckets in CLOs shrank from up to 20% in 1996 to 1998, to virtually zero a few years later.

Another factor causing the switch from bonds to loans was the belief that interest rates were eventually going to rise and floating rate loans were a better investment than fixed rate bonds.

Aside from the lack of interest rate hedging, CLOs are structured similarly to CBOs. CLOs generally have smaller equity tranches, around 8% to 10% of the capital structure of CBOs and 6% to 9% for CLOs. CLO AAA tranches are about 75% to 80% of the capital structure versus 75% to 78% for CBO AAA tranches. WARFs are generally lower for CLOs than CBOs. Overcollateralization and interest coverage triggers are normally higher for CLOs than CBOs, as shown in Exhibit 3.19.

EXHIBIT 3.19 Typical Overcollateralization and Interest Coverage Triggers

	Overcollateralization		Interest Coverage	
	CBO	CLO	CBO	CLO
Aaa	125	138	113	126
A	116	129	109	119
Baa	111	121	104	110
<Baa	106	111	101	106

CONCLUSION

We provided a guided tour of high-yield loans. About $290 billion of high-yield loans were sold in the 12 months ending June 2005 and 37% of that volume ended up in CLOs.

Bank loan lenders achieve credit quality by their secured position in the borrower's assets and the control they exercise over the borrower. Their control stems from loan terms and conditions that cover preservation of collateral, appropriation of excess cash flow, control of business risk, performance requirements, and reporting requirements.

Over the last eight-and-a-half years, loan credit quality has improved, as measured by the decline in borrower leverage (from 5.9 to 4.9) and increase in interest coverage (from 1.9 to 2.9). However, within this general improvement, leverage has increased since 2002 and interest coverage has decreased since 2002. But the superior credit quality of loans is reflected in their rates of default recovery and, unexpectantly, in their rates of default. Superior loan collateral quality carries over within CLOs in lower levels of overcollateralization and WARF deterioration. Finally, good CLO performance is reflected in the low instance and low severity of rating downgrades.

CHAPTER 4

European Bank Loans and Middle Market Loans

In this chapter we review the features of two types of loans found in collateralized loan obligations (CLOs): European bank loans (specifically, European high-yield syndicated loans) and middle market loans.

EUROPEAN BANK LOANS

European CLO (ECLO) issuance is still small in comparison to U.S. CLOs, yet from many perspectives, there are solid reasons for investors to take a closer look at ECLOs:

- For U.S. CDO investors, ECLOs provide an opportunity to diversify away from the U.S. asset underlyings.
- For U.S. and Asian corporate investors, ECLOs provide access to European corporate credit risk.
- For investors who are not "natural" Euro-investors, an ECLO provides exposure to that currency.
- For a European investor, ECLOs offer cheap EuroLIBOR floaters across the ratings spectrum.
- For all fixed income investors, floating rate instruments such as ECLOs are a good idea if interest rates rise.
- For all CDO investors, in some ways European loans are the ideal collateral for a CDO.

Here we describe the important characteristics of European loans underlying ECLOs. We begin by comparing the U.S. and European loan markets. Next, we focus on senior secured loans, covering their volume of issuance and the distribution of their issuance by country, industry, and purpose of the loan. We look at trends in the leverage and interest coverage of borrowers, loan spreads, and covenant protections. Because European *mezzanine* loans are an increasing proportion of ECLO asset portfolios, we also describe these loans.

We subsequently turn our attention to estimating default and recovery assumptions for ECLO cash flow modeling. Given the lack of European loan default and recovery studies, we focus on calibrating European loans to rating agency bond default studies and U.S. loan recovery studies. Finally, we say a few words about past European loan performance in ECLOs.

U.S. versus European Loan Markets

The first thing an investor should understand about the European (including U.K.) loan market is the relatively low participation of non-bank institutions. Over the 12 months ending 9/30/2005, only 37% of European loan issuance was purchased by nonbanks.[1] By contrast, in the United States, 66% of loans are purchased by nonbank institutions.

We think the markedly different participation of nonbanks lies behind the different credit and pricing practices on the two sides of the Atlantic. In Europe, the lending decision is "yes or no." In the United States, the lending decision is "at what spread?" The European bank perspective is whether or not it wants to have the credit on its books. The U.S. capital markets perspective is that institutional buyers are willing to accept higher risk for higher return. So in the United States, a sufficient spread will typically allow a corporate of lesser credit to execute a loan.

Once a credit is accepted for a loan in Europe, there is little distinction in pricing between stronger and weaker credits. Institutional loans are almost always priced according to their maturity with revolvers and short tenor loans having a spread of +225, intermediate tenor loans having a spread of +275, and the longest maturing loans having a spread of +325. In contrast, with the U.S. market, there is no meaningful difference in pricing between BB and B rated European loans.

Both the strict pass/no pass credit gatekeeping by European banks and the lack of spread variability among European loans work in favor of the ECLO investor, especially an ECLO debt investor. Theses characteristics assure a certain credit quality level in the ECLO portfolio and limit the opportunity for asset managers to buy higher yielding and more risky collateral.

---

[1] All market statistics on European senior secured loans are courtesy of S&P LCD, *LCD European Leveraged Loan Review 3Q05*, S&P LCD, October 2005.

The lack of differentiation in spreads by credit quality also means that there are few opportunistic refinancings by improving European credits to achieve lower-cost financing. This is good for all ECLOs investors, as a corporate that increases its credit standing cannot automatically call their loans and exit the ECLO portfolio. The ECLO does not suffer the "adverse exit" of improving loans as readily as U.S. CLOs do.

European loan spreads are surprisingly constant over time and there are few opportunistic refinancings from a general fluctuation in spreads. In the United States, market technicals associated with the demand for loans by institutional investors make loan spreads volatile. Again, this is good for all ECLO investors, as high-yielding loans are not replaced by low yielding ones.

Approximately 12% of U.S. loans are purchased by funds open to investment by institutional accounts. In Europe, however, very few such investment opportunities exist. So ECLOs are about the only way a nonbank investor can gain exposure to European loans.

The lack of institutional investors does inhibit the transparency of the European loan market. Only 18% of European loans are publicly rated, as opposed to 85% in the U.S. ECLO investors depend upon bank underwriting standards and the nonpublic rating estimates given by rating agencies to loan collateral in ECLOs. But the fact of a European loan default or restructuring does not always escape the wood-panel walls of a European bank's conference room and reach outside ears. Thus, European loan default and recovery data is hard to come by, and tends toward the anecdotal. This is why later on in this chapter we spend so much time calibrating European loan default and recovery experience to that of better-documented U.S. experience.

The Seniority of a Senior Secured Loan

Senior secured loans sit at the top of a firm's capital structure and, ideally, enjoy security of collateral, priority over other creditors, and control of the bankruptcy process. We say "ideally" because the actual degree of security, priority, and control a senior secured lender enjoys varies by legal jurisdiction. In a series of publications,[2] Fitch assessed the protections afforded bank loan lenders in different European legal jurisdictions.

---

[2] See Faith Bartlett, *Regimes, Recoveries and Loan Ratings: The Importance of Insolvency Legislation*, Fitch IBCA, October 1999 and David Staples, et al., *Understanding the Spanish Insolvency Regime*, Fitch IBCA, June 1, 2000. Fitch provides an update on the status of French insolvency reform in Edward Eyerman, Sophie Coutaux, and Janet Fisher, *France's Insolvency Reforms: Chapter 11 Lessons from Mario Monti*, FitchRatings, November 6, 2003.

Fitch finds that among the jurisdictions surveyed, U.K. law offers loan lenders the greatest degree of protection. Under U.K. law, the taking of security is strongly supported, a senior lender's priority is difficult to challenge, and lenders control the insolvency procedure. In contrast, Fitch finds that loan lenders in France have the least protection. Under French law, nonspecialist courts are free to decide the degree to which security and priority are honored and have complete discretion over the insolvency procedure.

The variability of legal protections afforded bank lenders affects the differential Fitch and other rating agencies make between the rating of a corporate's senior secured loan and the rating of its senior unsecured bonds. The difference in ratings indicates the rating agency's view as to the degree of relative protection afforded senior bank loan lenders. In Exhibit 4.1, we greatly simplify Fitch's detailed analysis into a rough estimate of the *average* rating notch difference between a corporation's senior secured loans and its senior unsecured bonds.

Exhibit 4.1 shows Fitch making the least credit rating distinction between senior secured loans and senior unsecured debt in France (about half a ratings notch, on average) and the greatest rating distinction in the United Kingdom (about three rating notches). Spain, the United States, and Germany fall in between these extremes.

It would be wrong, however, to automatically assume that an ECLO comprised of U.K. loans was better or safer than an ECLO comprised of French loans. A CDO's credit quality arises from the balance between the risks of a CDO's asset portfolio and the strengths of the CDO's subordination, cash flow mechanisms, and other protections. All things equal, ratings agencies and investors are going to demand that an ECLO comprised of French corporates have more credit enhancements than one comprised of otherwise identical U.K. corporates. The issue is how to assess the relative risks of French and U.K. loans and apply commensurate credit protections. We will return to this topic with a vengeance later in this chapter.

EXHIBIT 4.1 Rating Notch Difference Between a Corporate's Senior Secured Loan and Senior Unsecured Bond Ratings

France	0.5
Spain	1.5
United States	2
Germany	2.5
United Kingdom	3

Source: UBS calculations from Fitch.

Market Data

Total European syndicated loan issuance (both the pro rata loans that are retained by banks and the institutional loans that are sold to non-banks) was set to reach a new high in 2005 at perhaps €120 billion. Since 2000, European loan issuance has ranged from 26% to 33% of U.S. loan issuance. Institutional loans (the loans purchased by nonbank institutions) have been a growing percentage of the European loan market. In 1999, the €4 billion of institutional loans issued were 11% of the total European loan market. In the nine months ending September 30, 2005, the €43 billion of institutional loans issued were 47% of the total European loan market. Recent loan issuance has been tilted toward telecom and retail firms. Loans to telecom and media have declined drastically, from 1999 and 2000 when they were half of all loan volume.

Within European loan issuance, the dominance of U.K. loans has diminished from 45% in 1998 to 20% over the first nine months of 2005. Combined, French and German loan issuance has varied between 20% to 40% of total loan issuance since 2000. Over the first nine months of 2005, U.K., German, and French issuance has been 20%, 20%, and 19%, respectively.

European loan issuance is dominated by LBOs (initial buyout plus subsequent refinancings and recapitalizations). Ordinary refinancings, made purely to achieve a lower funding cost, play a relatively minor role because of the points we made previously about the European consistency of loan spreads over time and across different degrees of credit quality. This contrasts to the case in the United States, where M&A (LBOs plus corporate acquisitions) and refinancings are about equally important and together dominate loan issuance.

Credit Trends

As shown in the top panel of Exhibit 4.2, leverage of European loan borrowers has never been higher. This, in general, follows the U.S. pattern. Interest coverage, however, is not so diminished due to relatively low EuroLIBOR rates. Compared to the United States (bottom panel of Exhibit 4.2), senior debt leverage ratios and total debt leverage ratios are higher in any European country than the United States. With respect to interest coverage, Germany is the only country with a higher coverage ratio than the U.S. on any measure.

In comparison to French and German loans, U.K. loans,which enjoy the best legal protections, have high leverage and very low interest coverage. We begin to wonder whether the judicial protection enjoyed by U.K. bank loan lenders gives them confidence to extend credit to riskier corporates. France, in contrast, which has the least lender protections,

EXHIBIT 4.2   Senior Secured Loan Issuance Average Pro Forma Credit Statistics

	Observations	Debt/ EBITDA	Senior Debt/ EBITDA	EBITDA/ Cash Interest	EBITDA – Cap X/Cash Interest
1997	18	4.9	3.7	3.1	2.2
1998	42	4.8	3.7	3.0	1.9
1999	43	4.7	3.8	2.9	1.8
2000	63	4.4	3.6	2.9	1.7
2001	72	4.2	3.4	3.4	2.0
2002	87	4.2	3.4	3.4	2.2
2003	101	4.3	3.5	3.6	2.4
2004	130	4.6	3.6	3.5	2.4
3Q2005	121	5.2	4.1	3.2	2.2

	Observations	Debt/ EBITDA	Senior Debt/ EBITDA	EBITDA/ Cash Interest	EBITDA – Cap X/Cash Interest
France	22	5.4	4.4	3.5	2.1
Germany	26	4.7	3.6	3.8	2.5
Italy	6	5.2	4.2	3.1	2.0
Netherlands	9	4.7	3.8	2.9	2.1
Spain	4	7.2	5.5	2.4	1.8
Sweden	6	5.9	4.5	2.7	2.2
United Kingdom	28	5.2	4.3	2.6	1.9
United States		4.2	3.5	3.6	2.8

Source: S&P LCD.

also has the worst leverage among the three countries, as shown in Exhibit 4.2. In this analysis, German loans seem to have "belt and suspenders" when it comes to their credit. Germany has the second best lender protections and about the best credit statistics of European countries in Exhibit 4.2.

Ultimately, these credit trends and distinctions mean little to the ECLO debt investor as long as they are somehow taken into account in the balance we have spoken of before, between the risks of a CDO's asset portfolio and the strengths of a CDO's subordination, cash flow mechanisms, and other protections. If, for example, credit distinctions are taken into account in the rating of European loans (and there is every indication that they are), the issue becomes whether the CDO structure provides credit protections commensurate with the varying risks of its collateral. We renew our promise to return to this topic later in this chapter.

Loan Spreads

As we stated before, European loan spreads are remarkable for showing little volatility and little difference by rating. Only recently have B+/B European loans had an average spread to EuroLIBOR very different than BB/BB– European loans; 289 basis points to 264 basis points, respectively. Exhibit 4.3 shows European BB and B spreads closely inter-twined since the second half of 1999 and only separating in 2005. In a reversal, European spreads have been wider than equivalently rated U.S. loans, also shown in Exhibit 4.3. In fact, BB/BB– European loans are 2 basis points wider over EuroLIBOR than B+/B U.S. loans are over LIBOR. This is because volatile U.S. loan spreads tightened so much over the first nine months of 2005. By rating, European loan spreads have remained pretty constant.

A 50-50 mixture of BB and B European loans yields 55 basis points more than the same ratings mixture of U.S. loans. This is a very interesting fact, especially to potential ECLO equity investors. In terms of *after-default yield*, the European loan portfolio could suffer 55 basis points of

EXHIBIT 4.3   Institutional Loan Spreads

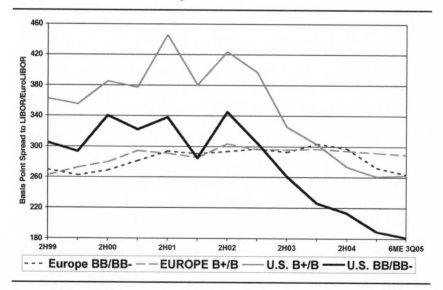

Source: S&P LCD.

credit losses annually before its spread to EuroLIBOR equaled the U.S. loan portfolio's spread to LIBOR. This is a bigger difference than it seems at first. Given a 70% loan recovery rate, 55 basis points of annual credit losses are associated with 1.8% annual defaults, which, as we shall see (we keep promising), is a lot of loan defaults. All other things equal, this excess spread allows ECLO equity to be more highly leveraged (excess spread is a substitute for subordination) and enjoy higher potential returns.

Institutional spreads in the major countries, the United Kingdom, Germany, and France, are very similar. From 1998 through 2005, each country's loan spreads have been the tightest and the widest. At September 30, 2005, 12 basis points separate the tightest (France at +213) and the widest (Germany at +225) country spreads.

Interestingly, the bigger difference in European loan spreads is between their *ranking in amortization.* As in the United States., a "loan" to a European corporate typically consists of a revolving loan and two or more term loans of different maturities. The revolving loans and the fastest amortizing term loan, "Term Loan A" or "Tla," are retained by banks. TLas have seven-year terms, on average. TLb and TLc and sometimes TLd loans are available for nonbank institutional buyers (almost always ECLOs) and have terms of eight years, on average. Roughly 70% of institutional loans are TLb loans.

Exhibit 4.4 shows an almost constant relationship between the spreads of TLb and TLc. Since 1998, the difference in average spreads has varied between 43 and 62 basis points, and usually runs between 43 and 53 basis points. The vast majority of European loans are executed at standard pricing of +225 for revolvers and TLa, +275 for TLb, and +25 for TLc.

Exhibits 4.3 and 4.4 demonstrate a feature of European loans we have previously remarked on: that European loan spreads have been remarkably stable over time. Either by rating or by loan sequence, spreads are surprisingly constant. In our view, this makes European loans significantly more attractive, given how spreads on just about every other fixed income asset have tightened over 2003 to 2005.

Covenants

Financial ratios are an early warning device for loan lenders. Their purpose is to be tripped by a deteriorating borrower before that borrower's financial condition has become unsalvageable. The breakage of a covenant allows bank lenders to assert control over the borrower by threatening to foreclose on the loan. Obviously, this threat is more effective in a jurisdiction where lenders enjoy more rights in bankruptcy. Nevertheless, loan covenants are used in all jurisdictions in great similarity, as shown in Exhibit 4.5. Compared to the U.S. loan market, the frequency of using any of the covenants shown in the exhibit is almost always greater in Europe.

EXHIBIT 4.4   European TLb and TLc Spreads

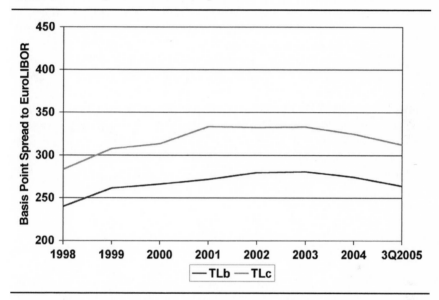

Source: S&P LCD.

EXHIBIT 4.5   Frequency of Loan Covenants

	All Europe	U.K.	Continent
Capital expenditures	82%	85%	81%
Cash interest coverage	29%	33%	27%
Debt service coverage	77%	78%	73%
Debt/EBITDA	96%	89%	97%
Fixed charge coverage	10%	11%	9%
Interest coverage	66%	63%	66%
Senior debt/EBITDA	26%	22%	28%
Senior interest coverage	8%	15%	5%

Source: S&P LCD.

Mezzanine Loans

ECLOs usually include allocations for European mezzanine loans ranging from maximums of 10% to 30%. However, some have been comprised entirely of mezzanine loans. Mezzanine loans are a substitute for high-yield bonds in a European corporate's capital structure, popular with all but the very largest corporates (those issuing more than €500 million of subordinated debt). Mezzanine loans are contractually subordinate to and have longer maturities than senior secured loans, but generally have similar covenants to senior secured loans.[3] In general, mezzanine loans are rated zero to one notch above an entity's senior unsecured rating or implied senior unsecured rating.

Mezzanine loan return is comprised of a cash coupon and par accretion. At September 30, 2005, the average cash coupon was 455 basis points above EuroLIBOR and average par accretion was 5.31%.[4] Prior to 2003, most of a mezzanine loan's return was comprised of its cash coupon. Another trend in mezzanine loans is away from attached warrants. In 2002 and 2003, about half of all mezzanine loans had warrants. In 2005, only 20% of mezzanine loans have warrants. Mezzanine issuance was about €6.1 billion in the first nine months of 2005, up from under €2 billion in the full years 2000 and 2001.

Fitch reports a 3.5% annual default rate on mezzanine debt in the first half of 2005.[5] Fitch also provides some color on the recoveries of defaulted mezzanine loans:

- Some borrowers caught up on missed interest payments.
- One mezzanine loan was equitized with quite a bit of loss.
- One troubled borrower sold itself and mezzanine investors recovered in full.
- One loan was further subordinated and its cash and pay-in-kind interest were reduced.

---

[3] In the U.S., "subordinated" loans are often made at the holding company level. The holding company generally receives cash flow from its operating companies via equity or subordinated debt interests that the holding company has in its operating companies. Thus, a loan at the holding company level is *structurally* subordinate because cash generated by operating companies is first available to the operating company's senior creditors. For a good discussion of the credit characteristics of European mezzanine loans, see Rachel Hardee, Pablo Mazzini, and Tony Stringer, *European Mezzanine Reconsidered,* FitchRatings, October 16, 2003.

[4] All European mezzanine loan statistics are courtesy of Sucheet Gupte, Marina Lukatsky, and Ruth Yang, *LCD European Mezzanine Review 3Q05,* S&P LCD, October 2004.

[5] Rachel Hardee and Pablo Mazzini, *The European Mezzanine Market in 2003: Still Upwardly Mobile?,* Fitch Ratings, March 1, 2004.

So, should an ECLO investor be concerned or pleased that there is a bucket for mezzanine loans in the ECLO it is considering? Let us get to the question of comparing the riskiness of loans of different ratings, from different countries, and of different seniority.

Quantifying European Loan Credit Quality

As we have mentioned, very little hard data exist on historical European loan defaults and recoveries. To make a rough estimate of these statistics, we are going to translate the rating on a European senior secured loan into a prediction of default probability and loss in the event of default. To do this, we will rely on historical default and recovery studies from the rating agencies, which are based mainly on U.S. bonds and loans. The validity of this approach rests on the consistency of ratings across different geographies. We believe this approach will offer insight into the risk of European loans, especially on their relative credit risk across different jurisdictions.

Recall the one, two, or three rating notch distinctions between a credit's senior secured loan rating and that same credit's senior unsecured bond rating that we developed in Exhibit 4.1. Historically, the assumption has been that when a corporate credit goes into bankruptcy, it defaults on *all* of its debts, both bonds and loans. Rating distinctions between senior secured loans and senior unsecured bonds (and for that matter between senior bonds and subordinate bonds) are therefore the result of rating agencies factoring "loss in the event of default" or "loss given default" into their ratings. Under this assumption, one looks to corporate bond default studies to estimate a loan borrower's *probability of default* and to loan recovery studies to estimate a loan's *loss in the event of default.*[6]

The use of bond default studies in this way is only a little tricky. In default studies by Moody's and S&P, corporates are categorized by the rating of their *senior unsecured bonds.* If a corporate has no senior unsecured bonds outstanding, the corporate is categorized by what its senior unsecured bonds *would* be rated *if* it issued senior unsecured bonds. So a BB– default rate in a default study does not address the historic default propensity of BB– bonds or loans. Rather, it addresses the historic default rate of corporates with a BB– senior unsecured rating or an *implied* BB– senior unsecured rating. To estimate the default probability of a loan from a historical study, one must first find or estimate

---

[6] In an ideal rating agency world, a loan and a bond of the same rating have the same *expected loss,* that is, the product of default probability and loss in the event of default. The bond would have a lower default probability and higher loss severity in comparison to the equally rated loan.

the rating the loan borrower has or would have on its senior unsecured debt. As we see from the Fitch reports, the senior unsecured rating is zero to three rating notches below the corporate's senior secured loan rating, depending on the legal jurisdiction of the borrower. The default rates published in the studies under senior unsecured ratings provide the historic default rate of such corporates.

Bond Defaults versus Loan Defaults

But there is a twist. It turns out that there is a lower historic default rate of loans versus bonds, even between loans and bonds issued by the same corporates. The model of a corporate going into bankruptcy and defaulting on *all* of its debt is incomplete, especially so as applied to European bank loans. A recent study by Moody's compares defaults on loans and bonds solely among corporates simultaneously issuing both types of indebtedness.[7]

The Moody's article shows that 23% of the time in the U.S. and 49% of the time in Europe, a corporate default does not involve formal court-refereed insolvency proceedings. In such cases, a corporate will often not default on its loan. In these informal insolvency circumstances, Moody's statistics show loans remaining current and undefaulted 87% of the time in the United States, and 55% of the time in Europe. With respect to U.S. loan defaults, if one multiplies the 23% of cases where there is no formal insolvency proceedings with the 87% of such cases where loans remain current and undefaulted, then in 20% (87% × 23%) of default situations, corporates default on their bonds, but not their loans. We show this clearly in Exhibit 4.6. The exhibit also shows that in Europe, the equivalent percentage of total defaults where corporates default on their bonds, but not their loans, is 27%.[8]

So now we understand that loans default less frequently than would be indicated by rating agency default studies that focus on bond defaults. This is particularly true with respect to European credits. Although the Moody's study does not say so, we assume that a dispro-portionate number of cases where loans remain current while bonds

---

[7] Kenneth Emery, Richard Cantor, and Roger Arner, *Relative Default Rates On Corporate Loans And Bonds*, Moody's Investors Service, September 2003.
[8] It seems that even if a corporate is in bankruptcy, it is not 100% certain it will default on its loans. In fact, we think it is fairly common for a bankruptcy judge to direct a corporate to keep its loan payments current when it is clear bank lenders will not suffer default losses or when continuation of loan payments is necessary to afford the borrower the assets it needs to continue in operation. We have no data on how often this happens. But we think the no-loan default rate in the bottom of Exhibit 4.6 is probably higher than determined by Moody's.

EXHIBIT 4.6   Bond Defaults without Loan Defaults

	U.S.	Europe
Percent of corporate defaults that do not involve formal bankruptcy proceedings	23	49
Times the percent of these defaults where loans remain undefaulted	87	55
Percent of all corporate defaults where loans remain undefaulted	20	27

Source: Moody's Investors Service.

default are in the United Kingdom and Germany rather than in France and Spain. In the more bank lender-friendly countries, we would expect bondholders to be less litigious and more willing to settle claims outside of formal court-refereed bankruptcy proceedings. After all, they have little to gain by seeing the obligor and other creditors in court.

However, Moody's study only looks at issuers of both bonds and loans. This is an atypical capital structure in Europe, where a corporate is more likely to issue senior secured loans and mezzanine loans rather than senior secured loans and subordinated bonds. Our own study of bond and loan default rates shows a greater difference in loan and bond defaults than the Moody's study. As presented in Chapter 3, U.S. loan defaults using S&P LCD data are about half that of bonds. Our explanation, based on our understanding of rating agency practices, is that loan ratings are more up to date and accurate than bond ratings. Rating agencies have a bias against making rating changes, but many corporates taking out a loan do not have existing ratings. In other cases, existing ratings can be ignored because the new capital structure of the corporate is so different from its previous structure.

Given our results and Moody's results, it would seem that a better default discount to apply to loans is in the range of 20% to 50% for U.S. loans. For the *average* across European jurisdictions, the relevant range would seem to be from 27% to 50%. Furthermore, given the differentiation in rights afforded lenders, it seems to us that German and U.K. loans should have a higher "default discount" than would U.S. loans. Conversely, French and Spanish loans should have a lower "default discount" than U.S. loans.

Loan Recoveries

With respect to historic loan recovery, Moody's studies, weighted toward U.S. loans, show an average senior secured loan recovery of

71%, based on market quotations one month after bankruptcy.[9] S&P's loan recovery studies, also weighted toward U.S. loans, show an average recovery of 83%, based on the present value of post-default cash flows.[10] Based on Fitch's analysis of legal regimes, we would assume that German and U.K. loans are likely recover more than U.S. loans, since Fitch makes a greater distinction between the ratings of senior secured loans and senior unsecured bonds from issuers in these jurisdictions than they make for U.S. issuers. By the same token, we would assume that French and Spanish loans would likely recover less than U.S. loans, since Fitch makes either no distinction or a smaller distinction between the ratings of senior secured loans and senior unsecured bonds from these jurisdictions than they do between loans and bonds from U.S. issuers.

A Recipe for Euro Loan Default and Recovery Assumptions

Given all that we've just covered, how can a European loan buyer or a buyer of ECLO obligations develop base case default and recovery rates assumptions for senior secured and mezzanine loans across different European jurisdictions? Here is our recipe:

1. Determine the borrower's senior unsecured rating. If no senior unsecured debt is outstanding (and it will not be, in the typical capital structure of a speculative-grade loan borrower), but the bank loan is rated or has an estimated rating, Exhibit 4.1 can be used to notch down the senior secured bank loan rating to an implied senior unsecured rating. For jurisdictions where the average ends in a "0.5%," we would average the default rates of the bracketing rating categories. For mezzanine loans, which Fitch says are rated zero to one notch above the credit's senior unsecured bond rating, we will notch down one-half a rating and take the average of the bracketing rating categories.
2. Find the historical default rate for the proper senior unsecured rating and tenor in a rating agency default study. We suggest that S&P's seven-year default rate be annualized.
3. Reduce the bond study default rates for the lower default rates of loans. We suggest deducing by 40% for U.K. and German loans, 30% for U.S. loans, and 20% for French, Spanish, and mezzanine loans.

---

[9] Greg M. Gupton, et al., *Bank Loan Loss Given Default*, Moody's, November 2000 and David Hamilton et al., *Default and Recovery Rates of Corporate Bond Issuers: A Statistical Review of Moody's Ratings Performance*, 1920–2003, Moody's Investors Service, January 2004.
[10] David Keisman, *Recovery Trends and Analysis*, PowerPoint presentation, Standard and Poor's, March 24, 2004.

4. Adjust recovery rates according to the difference between the corporate's senior secured rating and its senior unsecured rating. For senior secured bank loan recovery one month after default, we suggest 80% for U.K. loans, 75% for German loans, 70% for U.S. loans, 65% for Spanish loans, and 55% for French loans. For mezzanine loans, since they are rated higher than a senior unsecured bond but lower than a senior secured loan, we suggest Moody's senior secured *bond* recovery of 52%.[11]

5. Stress default and recovery assumptions up from this base case scenario.

Exhibit 4.7 shows how this would play out for BB– loans from different jurisdictions. In the first column, we list the jurisdiction of the senior secured loan or state that we are referring to mezzanine loans generally. In the second column, we translate the loan's BB– rating into the corporate's senior unsecured bond rating as described in step 1 above. In the third column, we take S&P seven-year default rate[12] for the appropriate senior unsecured bond rating and annualized it to create a *constant annual default rate* (CADR). In the fourth column, we show the discount rates that take into account the fact that loans default less frequently than bonds. In the fifth column, we adjust the default study-based CADR in third column by the loan default discounts in the fourth column. In the next-to-the-last column, we show the loan recovery assumptions as described in step 4. Finally, in the last column, we multiply the annual default rate of the fifth column by one minus the recovery rate of in the sixth column to get an annual loss rate.

Exhibit 4.7 shows CADRs, after discounting for the lower default rate of loans versus bonds, ranging from 2.7% to 3.8% for the BB– loans from different jurisdictions, including mezzanine loans. This is a pretty big spread, but when recoveries are factored in and we compute an annual *loss* rate in the exhibit's last column, the range narrows to

---

[11] Moody's addresses this issue explicitly in David Teicher, "Moody's Recovery Rate Assumptions for U.S. Corporate loans and Bonds: Picking Up the Pieces," in *CDO Rating Factors*, Moody's Investors Service, March 17, 2004. For senior secured loans rated two notches above the corporate's senior unsecured rating, the rating agency's assumed recovery for cash flow modeling purposes is 60%. If the loans are one rating notch higher, assumed recovery is 50%, and if the loans are rated equal to the senior unsecured bonds, assumed recovery is 45%. For a mezzanine loan rated one notch higher than the corporate's senior unsecured rating, assumed recovery is 42.5%. Obviously, these recovery rates incorporate a significant stress when compared to historic loan recovery rates.

[12] Brooks Brady and Diane Vazza, *Corporate Defaults in 2003 Recede From Recent Highs,* Standard & Poor's, January 27, 2004.

EXHIBIT 4.7 Calibration of BB– European Loans to U.S. Default and Recovery Studies

Loan Jurisdiction	Implied Senior Unsecured Rating	CADR Based on S&P's 7-Year Bond Default Rate	Loan Default Discount	After Loan Default Discount CADR	Loan Recovery	Annual Loss = CADR × (1 – Loan Recovery)
United Kingdom	B–	6.3%	40%	3.8%	80%	0.8%
German	B/B–	5.7%	40%	3.4%	75%	0.9%
United States	B	5.1%	30%	3.6%	70%	1.1%
Spain	B+/B	4.4%	20%	3.6%	65%	1.2%
France	BB–/B+	3.4%	20%	2.7%	55%	1.2%
Mezzanine Loan	BB–/B+	3.4%	20%	2.7%	52%	1.3%
Average		4.7%		3.3%	66%	1.1%

Source: UBS Calculations from rating agency studies.

0.8% to 1.3%. Theoretically, if all BB-rated loans are somehow "equal," they should be equal on the dimension of annual loss, rather than default rate. Exhibit 4.7 is more consistent with respect to losses than it is with defaults.

We see in the exhibit, for loans of the same rating (BB– in this case), U.K. and German loans are less risky than U.S. loans, while Spanish, French, and mezzanine loans are riskier. Somewhat miraculously, if one created a European loan portfolio consisting of 20% senior secured loans from each of the U.K., Germany, Spain, and France and another 20% of mezzanine loans, all rated BB–, their average annual loss would equal that of U.S. senior secured loans rated BB–. That is, of course, based on following all the steps of our logic and assumptions.

European Loans Within ECLOs

One point that concerns us is the performance of a particular asset class *within* the CDO structure. It does not matter if an asset class' performance is generally exemplary if somehow within CDOs it performs poorly. This would happen if, for example, CDO managers systematically purchased the worst examples of a generally good asset class. This has happened before, as with the concentration in manufactured housing, aircraft leases, mutual fund fees and franchise loans in some structured finance CDOs of 2000 and 2001. We have also seen vastly different collateral performance among high-yield bond CBOs.

But of the more than 35 ECLOs issued, we cannot find any tranche in any ELCO that has experienced a downgrade by any rating agency. In about half those ECLOs we were able to get at least some statistics on overcollateralization, interest coverage, and weighted average collateral rating. While performance is not uniform, and some ECLOs are weakened, on a whole they look very good.

MIDDLE MARKET LOANS

U.S. collateralized loan obligations (CLOs) are increasingly including *middle market commercial loans* in their collateral portfolios. This is the result of the popularity of CLOs and the finite supply of large loans (a.k.a. broadly syndicated high-yield loans of $250 million or more). U.S. CLO issuance was on track to equal $28 billion in 2005, more than double issuance in 2003. Meanwhile, loan amortization in seasoned CLO portfolios requires those CLOs to make replacement purchases.

The need for collateral in new and old CLOs has made CLOs the biggest buyer of large loans. Specifically, in the first nine months of

2005, CLOs purchased 62% of all large loan production not retained banks. And because bank retention of loans was at historically low levels, CLOs purchased 45% of *total* large loan issuance.

In the face of shrinking allocations and tighter spreads brought on by the demand for large loans, some arbitrage CLO managers are delving into middle market loans. We therefore thought it appropriate to address this relatively new CDO collateral asset. We address the characteristics of middle market loans with particular focus upon credit quality. However, the lack of default studies (which we had for U.S. large loans in Chapter 3) or comparative credit analysis (as we had for European loans earlier in this chapter) makes the credit analysis of middle market loans more difficult.

Nevertheless, looking at financial statement data, default recovery studies, rating agency default models, and the conservative treatment of middle market loans by the rating agencies, we conclude that middle market loan credit quality is at least comparable to similarly rated large loan credit quality. Furthermore, the conservative treatment of unrated middle market loans by the rating agencies tends to overstate the risk of these loans and cause CLOs to include extra credit protection in their structures.

Middle Market Loan Definition and Market Data

There is no standard definition of a middle market loan (MML). S&P *Leverage Commentary and Data* (S&P LCD) defines MMLs as "loans to corporates with EBITDA less than $50 million." These loans average $110 to $120 million in size.

Generally, just as with large loans, MMLs are syndicated among several banks, as their size is substantial enough that they are too big for any one bank to hold. Bilateral loan agreements between a single bank and a borrower are not usually considered to be a MML and in any case are not important to the arbitrage CLO market. Like larger loans, MMLs are usually secured by *all* the assets of the borrower, although some MMLs are secured by a subset of the borrower's assets. Only a small percentage of loans are unsecured and these tend to be smaller loans backed by personal guarantees from the business owner.

It bears mentioning that "middle market loan" means different things to different lending institutions. For some banks, it is strictly *cash flow lending* based on the flow of incoming receivables. Spreads may be low for this type of lending, which resembles trade receivable factoring. *Asset-based* middle market loans, done for larger amounts and longer terms, more closely resemble broadly syndicated loans in structure and risk. Also, the type of middle loans being securitized in CLOs has evolved. The first MML CLOs resembled balance sheet transactions. However, the nonbank originators of these loans did not spin them off into a CLO to shrink their balance sheets or reduce their capital requirements. Instead, the motivation was to achieve a lower cost of funds while retaining almost all of the loans' risk. Newer MML CLOs are done for arbitrage purposes where a manager purchases loans from various originators and manages the portfolio for fee revenue. As with arbitrage CLOs comprised of larger loans, equity investors participate in arbitrage MML CLOs to take a levered position in the loan portfolio.

MML volume dropped drastically from 2000 to 2001, from $35 billion to $12 billion. The decline in loan volume was due to consolidation among banks and a pullback from taking on corporate credit risk. Even though MML volume has been increasing, it is still well below 2000 levels. MML volume in 2005 was on track to be $28 billion.

In comparison to MML volume, U.S. large loan issuance is on track to reach $270 billion in 2005, about 10 times the size of expected MML issuance. So, while MMLs can be a significant contributor of collateral to CLOs, they do not have the aggregate volume to become the dominant CLO collateral.

In the first nine months of 2005, MML borrowers came from a variety of industries. In the same period, 30% for acquisitions of one company by another and 30% of loans were taken out to enable cash dividends or stock repurchases. 28% of MMLs loans financed leverage buy outs, either instigated by management or by a financial sponsor (such as KKR/Kohlberg Kravis Roberts or The Carlye Group) and 12% for refinancing existing debt.

Just as with larger more broadly syndicated loans, nonbank institutional investors purchase an increasing amount of MMLs. In fact, 66% of MMLs and larger loans were sold as institutional loans in the first nine months of 2005. In comparison to their holdings of large loans, U.S banks and finance companies hold more MMLs while non-U.S. banks purchase fewer MMLs.

Credit Spreads and Credit Ratings

Credit spreads for MMLs are much more generous than for large loans, as shown in Exhibit 4.8. In the exhibit, we compare institutional MMLs to institutional larger loans. In 1998, spreads on MMLs were 26 basis points higher than on large loans. In the third quarter of 2005, the differential expanded to 124 basis points. This, of course, is the source of attraction of MMLs to CLO managers: wider spread for similar collateral.

EXHIBIT 4.8   Institutional Loan Spreads

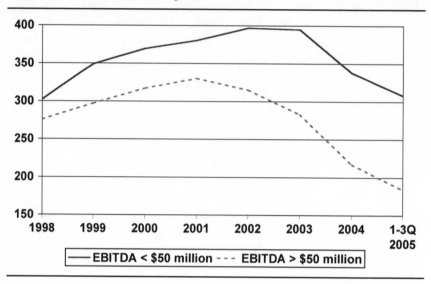

Source: S&P LCD.

Middle Market Loans in CLOs

But the real credit question for CLO equity purchasers is whether MML's increased spread is offset by increased credit risk. Because CDO equity benefits from *after-default spread*, the absolute levels of nominal spread and credit losses do not matter, but the difference between them does. The presence of MMLs in a CLO is beneficial to equity investors, even if the rating agencies underestimate MML credit risk, as long as an MML's higher spread compensates for any increased risk. If an MML's increased spread is not more than offset by increased credit loss, CLO equity investors are better off with MMLs than with large loans in a CLO's collateral portfolio.

The credit question is different for CLO debt investors. Excess spread does not accrue to CDO debt holders, nor does it particularly help them from a credit perspective. Agency CDO rating models allow for the trade-off between asset spread and subordination. Specifically, the higher spread of MMLs allows lower subordination levels, at least in rating agency models. So, in the absence of investor demand for higher subordination, the question for CLO debt investors is how MML and larger loans compare, *rating-for-rating*. If MMLs are safer than large loans, on a *rating-adjusted basis*, CLO debt investors benefit.

Exhibit 4.9 shows that in comparing MMLs and larger loans "rating-for-rating," we are basically talking about the B rating category for

EXHIBIT 4.9 Ratings of Middle Market Loans, 1-3Q 2005

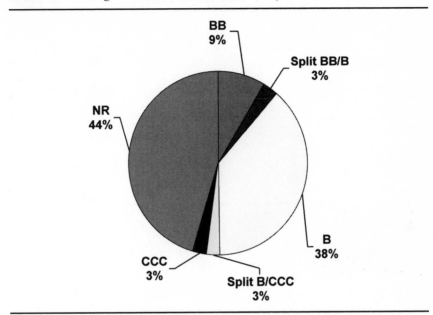

Source: S&P LCD.

MMLs. As can be calculated from the exhibit, most rated MMLs are rated B (68%) or split rated B (79%). This is in contrast to large loans, where the majority of rated loans (50%) are rated BB– or higher. Moreover, almost all of the 44% of MMLs that are unrated would be treated as if they were rated B or lower by the rating agencies in their CDO rating methodologies. This is partly due to inherent rating agency conservatism in dealing with obligors without official published ratings. As we have said, what matters to CLO debt investors is the credit quality of assets on a *ratings-adjusted basis*. Consequently, when we compare MMLs to large loans below, we are seriously disadvantaging MMLs by comparing a B rated asset to a BB/B rated asset.

Borrower Leverage

One thing that MML obligors have going for them over larger loan obligors is lower *total leverage*. Exhibit 4.10 shows MML obligors, those with EBITDA less than $50 million, contrasted to obligors with EBITDA greater than $50 million. We show the average leverage ratio of new loan obligors in the year of origination. The exhibit also shows that while large loan leverage has risen since about 2002, MML leverage has remained stable.

EXHIBIT 4.10   Actual Leverage of Loan Borrowers Total Debt/EBITDA

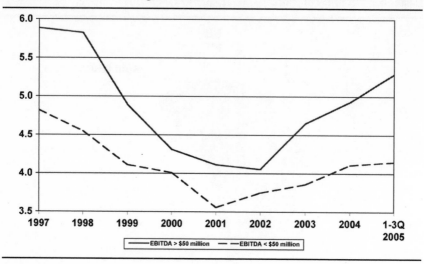

Source: S&P LCD.

EXHIBIT 4.11   Actual Leverage of Loan Borrowers Senior Debt/EBITDA

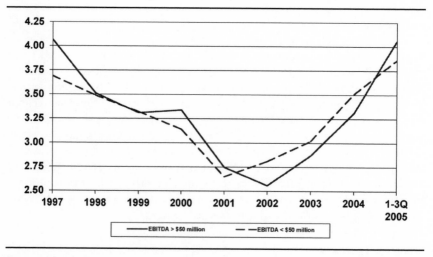

Source: S&P LCD.

But it is also true that *senior debt leverage* for MML obligors is
about the same as for obligors of larger loans. This is simply because
MML obligors tend not to have very much subordinate debt. This is
shown in Exhibit 4.11, which displays average senior debt leverage for
borrowers in the year of loan origination.

EXHIBIT 4.12   Corporate Debt Recoveries, 1987–2004

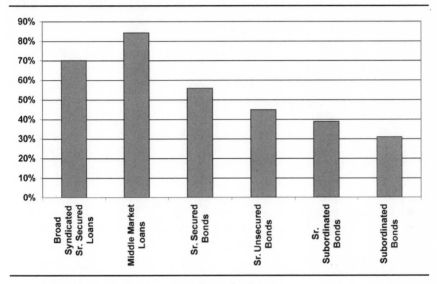

Source: Moody's Investors Service and Standard & Poor's.

Theoretically, lower total leverage and higher senior debt leverage should work in opposite directions upon MML credit quality. All things equal, lower total debt leverage means that MML obligors are less likely to go into default, because debt holders have a greater equity cushion below them. However, all things equal, higher senior debt leverage means that senior debt default severity will be higher because senior debt has less *subordinate* debt below it to absorb losses. In practice, middle market loans have recovered more than other loans, as shown in Exhibit 4.12. The exhibit shows the average present values of after-default cash flows on various forms of corporate debt, including MMLs and all loans. Average recovery of MMLs, defined as loans from obligors with $50 million to $250 million of total debt outstanding, averaged 84% versus 70% for loans from all obligors.

Rating Agency Assessment of Middle Market Loans

MML quality is only half of the credit equation for a MML CLO debt investor. The other half is structural protections, such as subordination and cash diversion mechanisms, embodied in the CLO to protect its debt. In a CDO, there are no bad assets, only assets whose risks are not properly addressed by the CDO structure.

In a CDO, rating agency required credit enhancement is driven by collateral ratings. Since MMLs are typically unrated, required credit enhancement in a MML CLO is driven by the *shadow ratings* on MMLs. Shadow ratings are nonpublic ratings that the rating agencies assign solely for the purpose of sizing credit enhancement in a CDO. We believe these shadow ratings are typically conservative; that is, unrated MMLs are shadow rated *too low* in comparison to publicly rated bonds and large loans. When these too-low shadow ratings are put into the rating agency analysis, the rating agencies demand more credit enhancement than they would if they had fairly assessed the quality of the MML collateral.

We compared the financial ratios of *shadow* rated companies in a recent MML CLO to the financial ratios of *publicly* rated companies. In the MML CLO, the average total leverage ratio (Total Debt/EBITDA) for 40 companies whose loans were shadow rated B was 4.3×. This compares to a higher 5.4× total leverage ratio for publicly rated B companies. By the single measure of total leverage, most of the shadow rated B companies should have been shadow rated BB. Sixteen of the 40 shadow rated B companies had lower total leverage than the average for publicly rated BB companies. Another 14 shadow rated B companies had leverage that was closer to the average of publicly rated BB companies than to the average of publicly rated B companies. All told, 30 of the 40 companies in the MML CDO had leverage ratios suggesting a rating higher than their B shadow rating.

Some credit analysts argue that smaller companies are inherently less creditworthy than larger companies because the access of smaller companies to funding sources is limited. Others argue that tighter covenants on smaller credits make up for the lack of funding sources. Default studies do bear out that all other things equal, smaller companies are more likely to default. Company size is something that Moody's KMV takes into account in their default probability modeling. In other words, Moody's KMV assigns higher default probabilities and lower ratings to smaller companies than larger companies, all other credit factors equal.

As we mention earlier, the advantage of Moody's KMV analysis of financial data is that it assesses the effect of historical financial ratios upon default probability in an objective manner. In other words, the statistical model is incapable of overweighting one financial variable because of a prejudice. So it is interesting that Moody's KMV ratings of MMLs, taking into account the historical relationship between firm size and default probability, leads to much higher ratings then those Moody's assigns to MMLs when rating a MML CLO.

We examined another MML CLO portfolio, which included 30 Moody's shadow rated MMLs. In every case, the shadow rating was lower than the Moody's KMV rating. In fact, shadow ratings were an average of 3.8 rating notches lower than Moody's KMV's ratings and ranged from one numerical rating notch to six numerical rating notches lower. This suggests to us that Moody's loan shadow rating process is very conservative, even taking into account the effect smaller firm size might have upon credit quality. Treating MML collateral three or four notches lower than actual credit quality significantly increases subordination and other credit enhancements to the benefit of CDO debt tranches.

CONCLUSION

Given their favorable spreads and increased use in CLOs, we thought it was worth devoting a chapter focused on European high-yield syndicated loans and U.S. middle market loans.

We have discussed the differences between the European and U.S. loan markets. The relative lack of institutional investors in the European loan market creates positive features for ECLO investors. The on/off nature of bank credit extension in Europe and the lack of credit spread differentiation makes for better credit quality portfolios and limits the opportunity for managers to go after higher yielding and higher risk assets. Stable loan spreads, by credit quality and over time, limit the adverse selection risk of having good loans called out of the ECLO portfolio. European loans spreads have been remarkably constant over the last two years while spreads of almost every other asset have declined.

However, the European loan market is not as transparent as the U.S. loan market, and little hard data is available on loan defaults and recoveries. Also, the protections afforded bank loan lenders vary greatly by jurisdiction within Europe. We offered a methodology to determine base case European loan default and recovery assumptions on a jurisdiction-by-jurisdiction basis. Using rating agency default and recovery studies, we estimated that German and U.K. loans have lower annualized losses than equally rated U.S. loans. Conversely, French, Spanish, and mezzanine loans have higher annualized losses than equally rated U.S. loans.

Finally, the performance of European loans within previous ECLOs has been good.

We defined middle market loans according to S&P LCD's definition as is loans to corporates with less than $50 million of EBITDA. We also noted the changing purpose of MML CLOs from balance sheet motivations to arbitrage motivations.

We made the point that in substituting MMLs for large loans, CLO equity holders care about the after-default spread of one versus the other. MMLs begin with a nominal spread advantage. For CLO debt holders, the issue is the relative credit quality of MMLs versus large loans on a rating-by-rating basis. Comparisons of the MML market with the large loan market are inherently unfair to MMLs, as those loans are typically rated B, versus the B and BB ratings of large loans.

We showed that MML obligors have lower total leverage ratios and higher senior debt ratios than large loan obligors. MMLs have had higher rates of recovery than loans in general. Finally, we showed that the rating agencies are very conservative in assigning shadow ratings to MMLs, which increases the credit protection afforded MML CLO debt holders.

The credit quality of MMLs in a particular CLO depends upon the risk appetite and credit skills of that particular CLO manager. From our survey of MMLs, we believe that plenty of B rated MMLs are equal or better in credit quality to B rated large loans. So the presence of MMLs in a CLO probably improves collateral credit quality.

Structured Finance CDOs and Collateral Review

Review of Structured Finance Collateral: Mortgage-Related Products

Structured finance (SF) collateralized debt obligations are CDOs backed by asset-backed securities (ABS), mortgage-backed securities (MBS), and real estate investment trusts (REITs). To evaluate SF CDOs, the first step is to understand the investment characteristics and features of structured finance products. A review of structured finance products is provided in this chapter and the next. In this chapter, we cover structured finance products backed by mortgage-related products: residential MBS, residential real estate-backed ABS, commercial MBS, and REITs. In the next chapter we cover nonmortgage asset-backed securities In Chapter 7, we discuss default and recovery rates for each type of collateral. SF cash flow CDOs will be discussed in Chapter 8.

RESIDENTIAL MORTGAGE-BACKED SECURITIES

Mortgage-backed securities (MBS) are securities backed by a pool (collection) of mortgage loans. While any type of mortgage loans, residential or commercial, can be used as collateral for a mortgage-backed security, most are backed by residential mortgages. Mortgage-backed securities include: (1) mortgage passthrough securities, (2) collateralized mortgage obligations, and (3) stripped mortgage-backed securities.

We begin our discussion with the raw material for a residential mortgage-backed security (RMBS)—the mortgage loan. A mortgage loan, or simply mortgage, is a loan secured by the collateral of some specified real estate property, which obliges the borrower to make a predetermined series of payments. The mortgage gives the lender the right if the borrower defaults to "foreclose" on the loan and seize the property in order to ensure that the debt is paid off. The interest rate on the mortgage loan is called the *mortgage rate*.

There are many types of mortgage designs available in the United States. A mortgage design is a specification of the interest rate, term of the mortgage, and manner in which the borrowed funds are repaid. The two most popular fixed rate mortgage designs are the fixed rate, level payment, fully amortized mortgage and the adjustable rate mortgage.

The basic idea behind the design of the *fixed rate, level payment, fully amortized mortgage* is that the borrower pays interest and repays principal in equal monthly installments during the term of the mortgage. Each monthly mortgage payment for this mortgage design is due on the first of each month and consists of:

1. Interest of $\frac{1}{12}$ of the annual interest rate times the amount of the outstanding mortgage balance at the beginning of the previous month.
2. A repayment of a portion of the outstanding mortgage balance (principal).

The difference between the monthly mortgage payment and the portion of the payment that represents interest equals the amount that is applied to reduce the outstanding mortgage balance. The monthly mortgage payment is designed so that after the last scheduled monthly payment of the loan is made, the amount of the outstanding mortgage balance is zero (i.e., the mortgage is fully repaid or amortized).

The portion of the monthly mortgage payment applied to interest declines each month, and the portion applied to reducing the mortgage balance increases. The reason for this is that as the mortgage balance is reduced with each monthly mortgage payment, the interest on the mortgage balance declines. Because the monthly mortgage payment is fixed, an increasingly larger portion of the monthly payment is applied to reduce the principal in each subsequent month.

In an *adjustable rate mortgage* (ARM) the rate paid by the borrower adjusts on a given schedule, generally once or twice a year, based on an index (generally LIBOR or Constant Maturity Treasury, CMT) plus a margin. Oftentimes, the initial rate is fixed for a number of years and then reset annually thereafter. This is referred to as a *hybrid ARM*. The most common periods to initial reset are 3, 5, 7, and 10 years. Thus, a loan with a fixed rate for the first 3 years, and resetting annually thereafter, is referred to as a 3/1 hybrid.

With the dramatic rise in home prices between 2000 and 2005, there has been a large increase in interest-only (IO) mortgages. These are mortgages in which the borrower pays the interest-only amount for a number of years. The mortgage begins to amortize when the IO period is over. For example, it is very common to find 5/1 ARMs in which the borrower pays interest only for the first 5 years. There are also 5/1 ARMs in which the borrower pays interest only for a 10-year period; and 30- and 40-year fixed rate mortgages with 10-year IO periods are becoming increasingly common.

Every mortgage loan must be serviced. The servicing fee is a portion of the mortgage rate. The interest rate that the investor receives is said to be the net interest or net coupon.

Prepayments

Homeowners have the right to pay off all or part of their mortgage balance prior to the maturity date. Payments made in excess of the scheduled principal repayments are called *prepayments*. The effect of prepayments is that the amount and timing of the cash flows from a mortgage are not known with certainty. This risk is referred to as *prepayment risk*.

The majority of mortgages outstanding do not penalize the borrower from prepaying any part or all of the outstanding mortgage balance. In recent years, mortgage originators have begun originating *prepayment penalty mortgages* (PPMs). The basic structure of a PPM is as follows. There is a specified time period, the lockout period, where prepayments carry a stiff penalty. Depending on the structure, a certain amount of prepayments may be made during the lockout period without the imposition of a prepayment penalty. The motivation for the PPM is that it reduces prepayment risk for the lender during the lockout period.

Mortgage Passthrough Securities

Investing in mortgages exposes an investor to default risk and prepayment risk. Buying mortgages one by one is extremely cumbersome. A more efficient way is to invest in a *mortgage passthrough security*. This is a security created when one or more holders of mortgages form a pool (collection) of mortgages and sell shares or participation certificates in the pool. A pool may consist of several thousand or only a few mortgages. When a mortgage is included in a pool of mortgages that is used as collateral for a mortgage passthrough security, the mortgage is said to be securitized.

The cash flows of a mortgage passthrough security depend on the cash flows of the underlying pool of mortgages. As explained in the previous section, the cash flows consist of monthly mortgage payments representing interest, the scheduled repayment of principal, and any prepayments.

Payments are made to security holders each month. Neither the amount nor the timing, however, of the cash flows from the pool of mortgages is identical to that of the cash flows passed through to investors. The monthly cash flows for a passthrough are less than the monthly cash flows of the underlying mortgages by an amount equal to servicing and other fees. The other fees are those charged by the issuer or guarantor of the passthrough for guaranteeing the issue. The coupon rate on a passthrough, called the *passthrough coupon rate*, is less than the mortgage rate on the underlying pool of mortgage loans by an amount equal to the servicing fee and guarantee fee. The latter is a fee charged by an agency (discussed later) for providing one of the guarantees discussed later.

Not all of the mortgages that are included in a pool of mortgages that are securitized have the same mortgage rate and the same maturity. Consequently, when describing a passthrough security, a *weighted average coupon rate* and a *weighted average maturity* are determined. A weighted average coupon rate, or WAC, is found by weighting the mortgage rate of each mortgage loan in the pool by the amount of the mortgage balance outstanding. A weighted average maturity, or WAM, is found by weighting the remaining number of months to maturity for each mortgage loan in the pool by the amount of the mortgage balance outstanding.

Issuers of Passthrough Securities

Issuers of passthrough securities include (1) the Government National Mortgage Association (Ginnie Mae); (2) the Federal National Mortgage Association (Fannie Mae); (3) the Federal Home Loan Mortgage Corporation (Freddie Mac); and (4) private issuers. While the first three are only a small part of the collateral in an SF cash flow CDO deal, they are discussed here for completeness. Private issuers will be discussed in the parts of this chapter that cover nonagency MBS and ABS backed by real estate.

Government National Mortgage Association passthroughs are guaranteed by the full faith and credit of the U.S. government. Therefore, Ginnie Mae passthroughs are viewed as risk-free in terms of default risk just like Treasury securities.

Fannie Mae and Freddie Mac are government-sponsored enterprises that issue mortgage passthrough securities. Although a guarantee of Fannie Mae or Freddie Mac is not a guarantee by the U.S. government, most market participants view the passthroughs that they issue as similar, although not identical, in credit worthiness to Ginnie Mae passthroughs. Fannie Mae and Freddie Mac passthroughs are referred to as *conventional passthroughs*. However, some market participants lump them together with Ginnie Mae passthroughs and refer to them as "agency" passthroughs.

Prepayment Conventions and Cash Flows

The difficulty in estimating the cash flows of a mortgage passthrough is due to prepayments. The only way to project cash flows is to make some assumptions about the prepayment rate over the life of the underlying mortgage pool. The prepayment rate is sometimes referred to as the "prepayment speed." Two conventions have been used as a benchmark for prepayment rates: conditional prepayment rate and Public Securities Association prepayment benchmark.

Conditional Prepayment Rate   One convention for projecting prepayments and the cash flows of a passthrough assumes that some fraction of the remaining principal in the pool is prepaid each month for the remaining term of the mortgage. The prepayment rate assumed for a pool, called the *conditional prepayment rate* (also known as *constant prepayment rate* or CPR), is based on the characteristics of the pool (including its historical prepayment experience) and the current and expected future economic environment. The CPR is an annual rate. To estimate monthly prepayments, the CPR must be converted into a monthly prepayment rate, commonly referred to as the *single monthly mortality rate* (SMM).

Adjustable rate mortgages, particularly hybrid ARMs tend to prepay very rapidly at the reset. Thus, the convention for these loans is to use *conditional prepayment rate to balloon* (CPB). That is, if a mortgage is said to prepay at 15% CPB, this mean that prepayments are 15% per annum on the remaining balance until the reset. At the reset, the mortgage is assumed to prepay at par.

PSA Prepayment Benchmark   The Public Securities Association (PSA) prepayment benchmark is expressed as a monthly series of CPRs. The PSA benchmark assumes that prepayment rates are low for newly originated mortgages and then will speed up as the mortgages become seasoned. Specifically, the PSA benchmark assumes the following prepayment rates for 30-year mortgages:

- A CPR of 0.2% for the first month, increased by 0.2% per year per month for the next 30 months when it reaches 6% per year.
- A 6% CPR for the remaining years.

This benchmark is referred to as "100% PSA" or simply "100 PSA." Slower or faster speeds are then referred to as some percentage of

PSA. For example, 50 PSA means one-half the CPR of the PSA benchmark prepayment rate; 150 PSA means 1.5 times the CPR of the PSA benchmark prepayment rate; 300 PSA means three times the CPR of the benchmark prepayment rate. A prepayment rate of 0 PSA means that no prepayments are assumed.

Average Life

The stated maturity of a mortgage passthrough security is an inappropriate measure of its final maturity because of principal repayments over time. Instead, market participants calculate an *average life* for a mortgage-backed security. The average life of a mortgage-backed security is the average time to receipt of principal payments (scheduled principal payments and projected prepayments), weighted by the amount of principal expected. That is,

$$\text{Average life} = \sum_{t=1}^{T} \frac{t \times \text{Projected principal received at time } t}{12 \times \text{Total principal}}$$

where T is the last month that principal is expected to be received.

Contraction Risk and Extension Risk

An investor who owns passthrough securities does not know what the cash flows will be because that depends on prepayments. As noted earlier, this risk is called prepayment risk.

To understand the significance of prepayment risk, suppose an investor buys a 10% coupon at a time when mortgage rates are 10%. Let us consider what will happen to prepayments if mortgage rates decline to, say, 6%. There will be two adverse consequences.

First, a basic property of fixed income securities is that the price of an option-free bond will rise when interest rates decline. But in the case of a passthrough security, the rise in price will not be as large as that of an option-free bond because a fall in interest rates will give the borrower an incentive to prepay the loan and refinance the debt at a lower rate. Thus, the upside price potential of a passthrough security is truncated because of prepayments. The second adverse consequence is that the cash flows must be reinvested at a lower rate. These two adverse consequences when mortgage rates decline are referred to as *contraction risk*. This characteristic of a security is referred to *negative convexity*. Negative convexity means that when interest rates decline, the percentage price gain is not as great as the percentage price decline for a large rise in interest rates.

Now let us look at what happens if mortgage rates rise to say 13%. The price of the passthrough, like the price of any bond, will decline. But again it will decline more because the higher rates will tend to slow down the rate of prepayment, in effect increasing the amount invested at the coupon rate, which is lower than the market rate. Prepayments will slow down because homeowners will not refinance nor partially prepay their mortgages when mortgage rates are higher than the contract rate. Of course, this is just the time when investors want prepayments to speed up so that they can reinvest the prepayments at the higher market interest rate. This adverse consequence of rising mortgage rates is called *extension risk*.

Therefore, prepayment risk encompasses contraction risk and extension risk. Prepayment risk makes passthrough securities unattractive for certain individuals and financial institutions to hold for purposes of accomplishing their investment objectives. Some individuals and institutional investors are concerned with extension risk and others with contraction risk when they purchase a passthrough security. Is it possible to alter the cash flows of a passthrough to reduce the contraction risk and extension risk for institutional investors? This can be done, as explained when we cover collateralized mortgage obligations.

Stripped Mortgage-Backed Securities

A mortgage passthrough security distributes the cash flow from the underlying pool of mortgages on a pro rata basis to the securityholders. A stripped mortgage-backed security is created by altering that distribution of principal and interest from a pro rata distribution to an unequal distribution. The result is that the securities created will have a price/yield relationship that is different from the price/yield relationship of the underlying passthrough security.

In the most common type of stripped mortgage-backed securities, all the interest is allocated to one class (called the *interest-only* or *IO class*) and all the principal to the other class (called the *principal-only* or *PO class*). The IO class receives no principal payments.

The PO security, also called a *principal-only mortgage strip*, is purchased at a substantial discount from par value. The return an investor realizes depends on the speed at which prepayments are made. The faster the prepayments, the higher the investor's return. An IO, also called an *interest-only mortgage strip*, has no par value. In contrast to the PO investor, the IO investor wants prepayments to be slow because the IO investor receives interest only on the amount of the principal outstanding. When prepayments are made, less dollar interest will be received as the outstanding principal declines. If prepayments are too fast, the IO investor may not recover the amount paid for the IO even if the security is held to maturity. An interesting characteristic of an IO is that its price tends to move in the same direction as the change in interest rates.

Both POs and IOs exhibit substantial price volatility when mortgage rates change.

Collateralized Mortgage Obligations

As just explained, an investor in a mortgage passthrough security is exposed to extension risk and contraction risk. Some investors are concerned with extension risk and others with contraction risk when they invest in a passthrough. An investor may be willing to accept one form of prepayment risk but seek to avoid the other. By redirecting how the cash flows of passthrough securities are paid to different bond classes that are created, securities can be created that have different exposure to prepayment risk. When the cash flows of mortgage-related products are redistributed to different bond classes, the resulting securities are called *collateralized mortgage obligations*. The creation of a CMO cannot eliminate prepayment risk; it can only redistribute the two forms of prepayment risk among different classes of bondholders.

The basic principle is that redirecting cash flows (interest and principal) to different bond classes—*tranches*—mitigates different forms of prepayment risk. It is never possible to eliminate prepayment risk. If one tranche in a CMO structure has less prepayment risk than the mortgage passthrough securities that are collateral for the structure, then another tranche in the same structure has greater prepayment risk than the collateral.

Issuers of CMOs are the same three entities that issue agency passthrough securities: Freddie Mac, Fannie Mae, and Ginnie Mae. CMOs issued by any of these entities are referred to as *agency CMOs*.

When an agency CMO is created, it is structured so that even under the worst circumstances regarding prepayments, the interest and principal payments from the collateral will be sufficient to meet the interest obligation of each tranche and pay off the par value of each tranche. Defaults are ignored because the agency that has issued the passthroughs used as collateral is expected to make up any deficiency. Thus, the credit risk of agency CMOs is minimal.

Types of CMO Structures

In all CMO structures there are rules for the priority of distribution of the interest and principal cash flows from the collateral. There is a wide range of CMO structures. In a *sequential-pay CMO structure,* the deal is structured so that each class of bond is retired sequentially. That is, no bond class receives a principal payment until bond classes with higher principal payment priorities are fully paid off. There are some bond classes that receive only interest. These are referred to as *notional IOs* or *structured IOs*.

A *planned amortization class* (PAC) CMO structure bond is one in which a schedule of principal payments is set forth in the prospectus. The PAC bondholders have priority over all other bond classes in the structure with respect to the receipt of the scheduled principal payments. While there is no assurance that the principal payments will be actually realized so as to satisfy the schedule, a PAC bond is structured so that if prepayment speeds are within a certain range, the collateral will throw off sufficient principal to meet the schedule of principal payments.

The greater certainty of the cash flow for the PAC bonds comes at the expense of the non-PAC classes, called the *support* or *companion bonds*. These tranches absorb the prepayment risk. Consequently, support bonds in a CMO structure expose investors to the greatest level of prepayment risk. Because of this, investors must be particularly careful in assessing the cash flow characteristics of support bonds to reduce the likelihood of adverse portfolio consequences due to prepayments.

The support bond typically is divided into different bond classes, including sequential-pay support bond classes. The support bond can even be partitioned to create support bond classes with a schedule of principal payments. That is, support bond classes that are PAC bonds can be created. In a structure with a PAC bond and a support bond with a PAC schedule of principal payments, the former is called a PAC I bond or Level I PAC bond and the latter a PAC II bond or Level II PAC bond. While PAC II bonds have greater prepayment protection than the support bond classes without a schedule of principal repayments, the prepayment protection is less than that provided by PAC I bonds.

Nonagency Mortgage-Backed Securities

Mortgage loans used as collateral for agency and conventional residential mortgage-backed securities are conforming loans. These are loans that meet the underwriting standards of Ginnie Mae, Fannie Mae, or Freddie Mac. The collateral for residential nonagency mortgage-backed securities (referred to as nonagency securities hereafter) consists of nonconforming loans (i.e., loans that do not conform to the underwriting standards of the agency).

Nonagency securities can be either passthroughs or CMOs. In the agency/conventional market, CMOs are created from pools of passthrough securities. In the nonagency market, a CMO can be created from either a pool of passthroughs or unsecuritized mortgage loans. It is uncommon for nonconforming mortgage loans to be securitized as passthroughs and then the passthroughs carved up to create a CMO. Instead, in the nonagency market a CMO is typically carved out of mortgage loans that have not been securitized as passthroughs. Since a mortgage loan is referred to as a "whole loan," nonagency CMOs are also referred to as *whole-loan CMOs*.

Types of Nonconforming Loans

A loan may be nonconforming for one or more of the following reasons:

1. The mortgage balance exceeds the amount permitted by the agency.
2. The borrower characteristics fail to meet the underwriting standards established by the agency.
3. The loan characteristics fail to meet the underwriting standards established by the agency.
4. The applicant fails to provide full documentation as required by the agency.

There are alternative execution channels for originators seeking to sell nonconforming loans for any of the aforementioned reasons.

Prime A Loans   These are loans with excellent credit. A mortgage loan that is nonconforming merely because the mortgage balance exceeds the maximum permitted by the agency guideline is called a *jumbo loan*. Most prime loans are jumbos. A minority of loans in prime pools are conforming in terms of size. Many of the conforming sized Prime A loans in nonagency pools could be sold into agency pools but the originator finds the price execution more favorable in nonagency form (IO loans, for example).

Alternative-A Loans   With respect to the characteristics of the borrower, a loan may fail to qualify because the borrower's credit history does not meet the underwriting standards or the *debt-to-income* (DTI) *ratio* exceeds the maximum permitted. Borrowers who do satisfy the underwriting standards with respect to borrower characteristics are referred to as *A credit borrowers* or *prime borrowers*.

Alternative-A loans (Alt-A loans) are made to borrowers whose qualifying mortgage characteristics do not conform to the underwriting criteria established by the agencies but whose borrower characteristics do. For instance, the borrower may be self-employed and may not be able to provide all the necessary documentation for income verification. In such respects, Alt-A loans allow reduced or alternate forms of documentation to qualify for the loan. Or the borrower may need the loan for an investor property and while the loan-to-value (LTV) ratio is less than 80%, it may lie just outside the maximum deemed acceptable by the agencies. An Alt-A loan borrower, however, should not be confused with borrowers with blemished credits, which is discussed in the next section below.

The typical Alt-A borrower will have an excellent credit rating—referred to as an "A" rating, and hence the loan is referred to as an Alt-A loan—which is especially important to the originator since the credit quality of the borrower must compensate for the lack of other necessary documentation.

What is appealing to borrowers about the Alt-A program is the flexibility that the program offers in terms of documentation, and borrowers are willing to pay a premium for the privilege. Typically, rates on Alt-A loans range between 25 and 75 basis points above the rate on otherwise comparable standard mortgage rates.

Subprime Loans   *B and C borrowers* or *subprime borrowers* are borrowers who fail to satisfy the underwriting standards of the agencies because of borrower characteristics. These characteristics include a compromised credit history and a payment-to-income ratio that is too high. Borrowers who apply for subprime loans include both those who have or had credit problems due to difficulties in repayment of debt brought on by an adverse event, such as job loss or medical emergencies, to those that continue to mismanage their debt and finances.

The distinguishing feature of a subprime mortgage is that the potential universe of subprime mortgagors can be divided into various risk grades, ranging from B through D. The risk gradation is a function of past credit history and the magnitude of credit blemishes existing in the history.[1] Additionally, some of the higher grades in this loan category have also been labeled as "fallen angels" to indicate the fact that the creditworthiness of such borrowers was hampered by a life event, such as job loss or illness. Since such borrowers tend to pose greater credit risk, subprime mortgages command a pricing premium over standard mortgages.

Subprime mortgages are often referred to as home equity loans, even though most of them are first liens, because most of the homeowners who borrow through them do so in order to take equity out of their homes. The term *home equity loan* (HEL) and subprime mortgage are often used interchangeably to designate these loans. Many of these borrowers have been living in their homes for 10 or more years, and need money for a variety of reasons including school expenses, a home addition or a new car. Often, these homeowners already have a mortgage on their home. By refinancing into a larger mortgage, they can draw on and

---

[1] The loans are actually scaled by originators from B to D. Every originator establishes its own profiles for classifying a loan into a risk category.

use their home equity. Thus, subprime mortgage pools contain loans used both for the purpose of refinancing or purchase, with more used for refinancing.

Home equity loans, like prime and Alt A mortgages, may be either fixed or adjustable rate. Adjustable rate loans are most typically 2/28s or 3/27s (interest rate fixed for a 2- or 3-year period, then floating for 28 or 27 years, with the coupon payments adjusted to a market index such as 1-month LIBOR).

High LTV Loans   A characteristic that may result in a loan failing to meet underwriting standards is that the loan-to-value (LTV) ratio exceeds the maximum established by the agency or the loan is not a first-mortgage lien. There are lenders who specialize in loans that exceed the maximum LTV. These lending programs are sometimes referred to as *high LTV* or *125 LTV* programs because the lender may be willing to lend up to 125% of the appraised or market value of the property.

Basically, the lender is making a consumer loan based on the credit of the borrower to the extent that the loan amount exceeds the appraised or market value of the home. For this reason, lenders with high LTV programs have limited these loans to A credit borrowers. Mortgage-related products in which the underlying loans are 125 LTV loans are considered part of the ABS market.

Defining Characteristics

Exhibit 5.1 presents the main characteristics of different sectors of the nonagency market. It covers such loan and borrower characteristics such as lien status, loan size limit and average, minimum and average FICO score (a credit score), LTV (loan-to-value), occupancy (investor versus owner), documentation (full versus nonfull), loan purpose (purchase, cash-out refinancing or rate refinancing), and AAA credit support.

The nonagency sectors of the MBS market are defined by how they differ from agency collateral. In Exhibit 5.1, the highlighted variables identify characteristics that most clearly define each sector. For example, *Prime A* loans have the same credit and documentation as agency loans, but are larger than the conforming limit ($417,000 as of 2006). *Alt-As* have, for the most part, the same credit as agencies, may or may not be within conforming size limits, but have occupancy or documentation issues that land them outside the agency (and Jumbo) underwriting guidelines. Subprime home equity loans (sometimes referred to as B&C) have borrower credits falling below agency standards. *HELOCs* (not shown in the exhibit) differ in that they are open-ended (i.e. revolving) lines of credit as opposed to closed-end, fully amortizing loans.

EXHIBIT 5.1 Loan and Borrower Characteristics, by Product Type

	Agency*	Prime A	Alt-A	Subprime	Hi-LTV 1st	125 Hi-LTV
Lien	1st	1st	1st	80–90% 1st	1st	2nd
Loan limit	≤ Agency	> Agency	none	none	none	none
Avg. loan size	150,000	430,000	375,000	120,000	185,000	35,000
Credit	Agency	A	A/A–	A–/C	A	A
FICO: Min.	660	640	640	500	580	620
Avg.	720	730	700	600	712	700
Avg. LTV	70%	70%	75%	80%	102%	115%
Occupancy	Owner	Owner	20% Investor	10% Investor	5% Investor	Owner
Documentation	Full	10% Nonfull	50% Nonfull	25% Nonfull	20% Nonfull	Full
Loan purpose						
Purchase	NA	45	45	27	85	0
Cash out	NA	15	35	66	10	95
Rate refi.	NA	40	20	7	5	5
AAA Credit Support	Agency	2.50%–3.00%	5.00%–6.00%	20%–35%	20%–30%	40%–50%

*FNMA and FHLMC.

These are the main characteristics separating and defining the major types of loans in the nonagency market. However, as shown in Exhibit 5.1, there are other ways in which these loans differ from agency collateral. It is important to understand those differences in order to project prepayment speeds and credit performance. Also, with the advent of automated underwriting, the agencies and mortgage originators consider a large number of loan and borrower characteristics, relying less on the traditional risk measures of LTV, FICO, and DTI.

We will go into greater detail about some of the highlights of Exhibit 5.1.

Lien Status

Lien status is one of the most simple distinctions between mortgage sectors. All agency, Jumbo, and most Alt-A loans are first-lien mortgages. All traditional HELOCs are second-lien mortgages (although a few small programs feature first-lien HELOC). Subprime collateral is more heterogeneous; most are now first-lien mortgages, although some issuers include from 5% to 10% seconds into their deals. The 125 product, a relatively small part of the home equity market, is all seconds. In contrast, as its name implies, hi-LTV firsts are all first liens, and their LTVs are lower than in the hi-LTV second-lien sector (averaging 102% as opposed to that latter group's 115%).

Loan Limit and Size

Because the benefit of a refinancing is largely determined by the size of a loan, prepayment speeds are closely related to *average loan size*. Hence, size is a very important characteristic of the different mortgage sectors. Thus the considerable research into the impact of size on prepayment speeds is not at all surprising.

All agency loans must be within the conforming limit set in January 2006. (The limit is $417,000 in 2006, up from $359,650 in 2005.) The average agency loan size is around $150,000. However, even within agency pools, size plays an important role. Investors will pay up for pools with small loan balances, because they have been less prepayment-sensitive than pools containing large loan balances.

Loans carrying agency credit and meeting all other agency criteria except size fall into the Jumbo sector. The average size of Jumbos is around $430,000. Investors also pay up in this sector for pools with smaller-than-average loan size.

Alt-A loans can be either conforming or not. Hence, the average loan size, at $280,000, falls roughly midway between Agencies and Prime A. This sector has less well defined parameters than do other areas, and average size within individual issuer programs can vary by a larger degree.

Subprime loans are typically smaller than agency loans. Fixed rate subprime loans average about $90,000, while subprime ARMs are around $140,000 for an overall average of about $130,000. Their relatively small loan size is caused by two factors. Individuals taking out a subprime loan have lower income and, hence smaller homes and lower loan balances than the average homeowner. Also, originators are cautious about making large loans to individuals with less-than-perfect credit.

Because subprime loans, in general, are less refinancable than Jumbo or agency loans, there has been less emphasis on loan size prepayment analysis in subprime than in other sectors. However, in subprime, size is still important from a credit perspective. During 2001, several issuers reduced their origination of very small loans (say, less than $40,000) because those were found to have a disproportionate amount of losses.

Note also that HELOCs, as seconds, have smaller average loan size than do sectors that are all, or mostly, first-lien mortgages.

Credit

For a loan to qualify for inclusion in an agency pool, the borrower must have a "prime", or A, credit rating. A similar credit rating is required for a Prime A loan, as well as, for the most part, Alt-A loans (although recently some Alt-A issuers are including a few A– loans in their securitizations). In general, if a borrower does not meet agency credit standards, the borrower is required to take out a subprime loan and pay a higher loan rate.

Subprime issuers securitize loans from borrowers having credit ratings that range from A– to C or even D. These credit ratings vary among issuers, but they all refer to such credit items as number of late payments on consumer or mortgage loans. In the high LTV sector, originators typically lend only to A credit borrowers because by its very nature a second-lien mortgage is a higher risk loan than would be a first-lien mortgage to that same borrower.

FICO Score

One particular type of credit score, the *FICO* score, has grown to outsized importance in recent years. Initially, FICO scores were used by consumer lenders and not by mortgage lenders because the score was designed to predict borrower credit behavior over a fairly short period of time (about 2 to 3 years). Until several years ago, only a few mortgage issuers used this information to screen borrowers.

But when investors began demanding more credit information, issuers started using FICO scores. So even though FICO was not designed for mortgage credits, it is still a readily available credit score, is widely understood and recognized, and is consistent from issuer to issuer. Additionally, FICO scores are tabulated by an independent credit organization using a model created by Fair, Isaac and Company, and not by the issuers themselves. Today, if a FICO score is unavailable on a nonagency deal, many investors will not consider it.

The agency cutoff for FICO was 620, but recently that limit was moved up to 660. In the Jumbo and Alt-A sectors, the minimum score is between 640 and 660, depending on the issuer. In subprimes, most issuers use 500 or 550 as a cutoff. Average FICOs in the Jumbo, Alt-A, and subprime sectors are around 730, 715, and 620, respectively.

FICO, of course, plays a key role in determining credit performance in various parts of the nonagency market. Delinquency and losses are directly related to the distribution of FICO scores in a loan pool. However, FICO scores also play an important role in prepayment speeds. Lower credit subprime borrowers often refinance when they improve their credit. For example, a C credit borrower who kept current for a year or so on consumer and mortgage loans may be eligible for a B credit loan carrying a much lower interest rate. This "credit curing" refinancing represents a major part of the base case prepayment speed in subprime lending. That is also why average base case speeds in subprime are around 25% CPR, versus 6% to 8% CPR in the agency market.[2]

Additionally, because lower credit borrowers face higher closing costs and points to refinance, subprime loans are much less sensitive to changes in interest rates than are agency loans. Hence, credit (e.g., FICO score) is an important determinant of prepayments, as well as of delinquency and loss rates.

Debt-to-Income Ratio

Whereas FICO score is used as an indicator of an individual's willingness to repay their loan, debt-to-income (DTI) ratio is a measure of their ability to repay it. (DTIs are not provided in Exhibit 5.1.) Two DTI ratios are commonly used in mortgage underwriting, the front-end and back-end. The *front-end ratio* divides a homeowner's housing-related payments (including principal, interest, real estate taxes, and home insurance payments) by gross income. A *back-end ratio* divides total monthly debt payments (including housing related payments plus all

---

[2] See "Credit Refis, Credit Curing, and the Spectrum of Mortgage Rates," *Mortgage Strategy*, UBS, May 21, 2002.

credit card and auto debt, as well as child payments and other long-term obligations) by gross income.

In the agency market, 28% and lower is an acceptable front-end ratio and 38% an acceptable back-end ratio. Some exceptions may be made for compensating factors, such as a high FICO score.

Prime A and Alt-A DTI guidelines are similar to those used by the Agencies. However, in subprimes, DTI ratios are considerably higher. While they vary among issuers, the back-end DTI ratio in subprime deals in 2005 averaged around 60%.

Loan-to-Value

For many years, loan-to-value was the principal factor used by rating agency models in determining expected losses. Today, rating agency models are much more complex, often using FICO scores and other quantitative variables to forecast credit performance. However, LTV is still a primary variable in credit performance and, to a lesser extent, prepayments. A high LTV typically indicates a buyer is stretching to make monthly mortgage payments. Hence, high LTV is often associated with a high DTI ratio as well as other weak credit indicators.

There is also a direct link between LTV and loss severity. Traditionally, the Agencies would not wrap loans that had LTVs over 85%, and any loan above 80% needed mortgage insurance. In recent years, the Agencies instituted programs encouraging homeownership, which now allow LTVs of up to 95%. The additional risk represented by these loans is absorbed by mortgage insurance companies. Higher risk sectors, such as Alt-A and subprime, allow higher LTVs (5% to 10% higher) than do agency or Jumbo.

Occupancy

Investor properties are fairly rare in agency or most Jumbo pools, but are seen frequently in Alt-A and sometimes in subprime deals. Alt-A deals in particular can have as much as 20% investor properties. The *occupancy* variable is primarily a credit issue. Because owners of investment properties are not constrained by the same behavioral and social factors which discourage homeowner defaults and bankruptcies, default rates end up being higher on investor properties. Additionally, since investor properties are typically rental units, loss severities can be much higher than on owner-occupied dwellings.

Documentation

Documentation is the key issue defining Alt-A product. Many home-owners who own their own business lack the traditional *documentation* (such as employment and income verification) that lenders like from borrowers; hence, they become Alt-A material. In recent years, as many as 50% to 85% of loans in an Alt-A deal may be *nonfull documentation*, depending on the issuer. The Agencies require *full documentation* on purchase loans. And while Jumbo lenders permit a nonfull documentation loan, they also require compensating factors, such as low LTV or high FICO. Not surprisingly, nonfull documentation loans have higher default rates than full documentation loans.

Loan Purpose

While *loan purpose* is only a modestly important variable in determining credit performance and prepayments, it helps define several nonagency sectors. In the Jumbo and Alt-A sectors, rate- and cash-out refiinancings rise sharply during a refiancing wave. In subprimes, cash-out refinancings are a major component of prepayment speed, even outside rate-refinancing periods. The typical subprime borrower has been in a home for 10 years and is taking equity out to pay for a new car, send a child to school or expand the home. However, purchase loans are a much smaller part of the subprime market than they are in either the Jumbo or Alt-A sectors. In the 125 hi-LTV sector, virtually all loans are second-lien loans made for credit card debt consolidation, so that the sector lacks purchase money loans. In contrast, in hi-LTV first-lien loans (a product aimed at young, well-paid workers), virtually all loans are purchase money.

Deals with Mixed Collateral

There are deals in which the underlying collateral is mixed with various types of mortgage-related loans. That is, the collateral backing a deal may include collateral that is a combination of mortgages and products that are classified as asset-backed securities—home equity loans and manufactured housing loans—and are discussed later. The Securities Data Corporation (SDC) has established criteria for classifying a mortgage product with mixed collateral as either a nonagency MBS or an asset-backed security (ABS), which we discuss next. The purpose of the classification is not to aid in the analysis of these securities, but rather to construct the so-called league tables for ranking investment banking firms by deal type.

PSA Standard Default Assumption Benchmark

A standardized benchmark for default rates was introduced by the then named Public Securities Association (now called the *Bond Market Association*). The PSA standard default assumption (SDA) benchmark gives the annual default rate for a mortgage pool as a function of the seasoning of the mortgages.

The PSA SDA benchmark, or 100 SDA, specifies the following:

1. The default rate in month 1 is 0.02% and increases by 0.02% up to month 30 so that in month 30 the default rate is 0.60%.
2. From month 30 to month 60, the default rate remains at 0.60%.
3. From month 61 to month 120, the default rate declines by 0.00095% per month from 0.60% to 0.03%.
4. From month 120 on, the default rate remains constant at 0.03%.

As with the PSA prepayment benchmark, multiples of the benchmark are found by multiplying the default rate by the assumed multiple. A "0 SDA" means that no defaults are assumed.

Credit Enhancements

Like agency mortgages, a large number of individual loans are grouped, or pooled into a trust. The cash flows from those loans are used to pay the principal and interest on the trust. The major difference between agency and nonagency securities has to do with guarantees. With a nonagency security there is no explicit or implicit government guarantee of payment of interest and principal as there is with an agency security. The absence of any such guarantee means that the investor in a nonagency security is exposed to credit risk. This is why the rating agencies rate nonagency securities.

To obtain a credit rating, all nonagency securities are credit enhanced. That means that credit support is provided for one or more bondholders in the structure. Typically a double-A or triple-A rating is sought for the most senior tranche in a deal. The amount of credit enhancement necessary depends on rating agency requirements. There are two general types of credit enhancement structures: external and internal.

External Credit Enhancements   External credit enhancements come in the form of third-party guarantees that provide for first loss protection against losses up to a specified level, for example, 10%. The most common forms of external credit enhancement are (1) a corporate guarantee, (2) a letter of credit, (3) pool insurance, and (4) bond insurance.

Pool insurance policies cover losses resulting from defaults and foreclosures. Policies are typically written for a dollar amount of coverage that continues in force throughout the life of the pool. Some policies are written so that the dollar amount of coverage declines as the pool seasons as long as two conditions are met: (1) The credit performance is better than expected; and (2) the rating agencies that rated the issue approve. Because only defaults and foreclosures are covered, additional insurance must be obtained to cover losses resulting from bankruptcy (i.e., court-mandated modification of mortgage debt—"cram down"), fraud arising in the origination process, and special hazards (i.e., losses resulting from events not covered by a standard homeowner's insurance policy).

Bond insurance provides the same function as in municipal bond structures. Typically, bond insurance is not used as the primary protection, but to supplement other forms of credit enhancement.

A nonagency security with external credit support is subject to the credit risk of the third-party guarantor. If the third-party guarantor is downgraded, the issue itself could be subject to downgrade even if the structure is performing as expected.

External credit enhancements do not materially alter the cash flow characteristics of a CMO structure except in the form of prepayment. In case of a default resulting in net losses within the guarantee level, investors will receive the principal amount as if a prepayment has occurred. If the net losses exceed the guarantee level, investors will realize a shortfall in the cash flows.

Internal Credit Enhancements   Internal credit enhancements come in more complicated forms than external credit enhancements and may alter the cash flow characteristics of the loans even in the absence of default. The most common forms of internal credit enhancements are reserve funds, overcollateralization, and senior-subordinated structures.

Reserve funds come in two forms: cash reserve funds and excess servicing spread. *Cash reserve funds* are straight deposits of cash generated from issuance proceeds. In this case, part of the underwriting profits from the deal are deposited into a fund, which typically invests in money market instruments. Cash reserve funds are typically used in conjunction with some form of external credit enhancement.

Excess servicing spread accounts involve the allocation of excess spread or cash into a separate reserve account after paying out the net coupon, servicing fee, and all other expenses on a monthly basis. For example, suppose that the gross weighted average coupon (gross WAC) is 7.75%, the servicing and other fees are 0.25%, and the net weighted average coupon (net WAC) is 7.25%. This means that there is an excess servicing spread of 0.25%. The amount in the reserve account will gradually increase and can be used to pay for possible future losses.

With *overcollateralization*, the value of the collateral exceeds the value of the structure's obligations. For example, if a structure has two tranches with an aggregate par value of $300 million, then that is the amount of the liability. The amount of the collateral backing the structure must be at least equal to the amount of the liability. If the amount of the collateral exceeds the amount of the liability of the structure, the deal is said to be overcollateralized. The amount of overcollateralization represents a form of internal credit enhancement because it can be used to absorb losses. If the liability of the structure is $300 million and the collateral's value is $320 million, then the structure is overcollateralized by $20 million. Thus, the first $20 million of losses will not result in a loss to any of the tranches in the structure.

In a *senior-subordinated structure,* there is a senior tranche and at least one junior or subordinated tranche. The credit enhancement for the senior tranches comes from the junior tranches.

The basic concern in the senior-subordinated structure is that while the subordinated tranches provide a certain level of credit protection for the senior tranche at the closing of the deal, the level of protection changes over time due to prepayments. The objective after the deal closes is to distribute any prepayments such that the credit protection for the senior tranche does not deteriorate over time.

There is a well-developed mechanism used to address this concern called the *shifting interest mechanism.* Here is how it works. The percentage of the principal balance of the subordinated tranche to that of the principal balance for the entire deal is called the *level of subordination* or the *subordinate interest.* The higher the percentage, the greater the level of protection for the senior tranches. The subordinate interest changes after the deal is closed because the subordinate securities do not receive their pro rata share of prepayments. These cash flows are directed to pay down the senior tranches. That is, the subordinate interest shifts (hence the term "shifting interest"). The purpose of a shifting interest mechanism is to allocate prepayments so that the subordinate interest is maintained at an acceptable level to protect the senior tranche. In effect, by paying down the senior tranche more quickly, the amount of subordination is maintained at the desired level. The prospectus will provide the shifting interest percentage schedule.

Prepayments

Dealers involved in the underwriting and market making of nonagency mortgage-backed securities have developed prepayment models for these loans. Several firms have found that the key difference between the prepayment behavior of borrowers of nonconforming mortgages and conforming mortgages is the important role played by the credit characteristics of the borrower.

Borrower characteristics and the seasoning process must be kept in mind when trying to assess prepayments for a particular deal. In the prospectus of an offering, a base-case prepayment assumption is made—the initial speed and the amount of time until the collateral is seasoned. The prepayment benchmark can be expressed as a percent of the PSA curve or may be issuer specific. The prospectus may spell out a *prospectus prepayment curve* or PPC. As with the PSA benchmark described earlier in this chapter, slower or faster prepayment speeds are a multiple of the PPC.

Unlike the PSA prepayment benchmark, the PPC is not generic. By this it is meant that the PPC is issuer specific. In contrast, the PSA prepayment benchmark applies to any type of collateral issued by an agency for any type of loan design. This feature of the PPC is important for an investor to keep in mind when comparing the prepayment characteristics and investment characteristics of the collateral between issuers and issues (new and seasoned).

Deal Structures

Depending on the collateral, the deal coupon may be a fixed rate security, adjustable rate security, or as a security whose rate is fixed for a number of years and then floats. A fixed rate security is generally backed by fixed rate collateral. Hybrid collateral may be used to back deals where the coupon is fixed for a number of years, then floats, or deals where the coupon is floating from the very beginning. For prime and Alt-A ARMs, the former structure is more frequently employed. For home equity (subprime) loans, the latter is more typical. In a floating-rate security, the reference rate is typically one-month LIBOR. Because of the mismatch between (1) the fixed rate paid on the loans for the initial period and 1-month LIBOR, (2) the mismatch between the rate after the reset on the collateral (6-month LIBOR, 1-year CMT, 1-year LIBOR) and the 1-month LIBOR reset on the deal, and (3) the periodic and life caps on the underlying loans, there is a cap on the coupon rate for the floater. Unlike the typical floater, which has a cap that is fixed throughout the security's life, the effective cap of a HEL floater is variable. The effective cap, referred to as the *available funds cap*, will depend on the amount of funds generated by the net coupon on the principal, less any fees.

The AAA tranche is often sequentially tranched, to direct cash flows thrown off in a given timeframe to those investors who value it the most highly. In addition, AAA tranches have been structured to give some senior tranches greater prepayment protection than other senior tranches. The two types of structures that do this are the planned amortization class (PAC) tranche discussed earlier and the *nonaccelerating senior* (NAS) tranche. An NAS tranche receives principal payments according to a schedule. The schedule is not a dollar amount. Rather, it is a principal schedule that shows for a given month the share of pro rata principal that must be distributed to the NAS tranche. The NAS tranche usually receives no principal payments for a preset number of years.

Manufactured Housing-Backed Securities

Manufactured housing-backed securities are backed by loans for manufactured homes. In contrast to site-built homes, manufactured homes are built at a factory and then transported to a manufactured home community or private land. The loan may be either a mortgage loan (for both the land and the home) or a consumer retail installment loan.

Manufactured housing-backed securities are issued by Ginnie Mae and private entities. The former securities are guaranteed by the full faith and credit of the U.S. government. The manufactured housing loans that are collateral for the securities issued and guaranteed by Ginnie Mae are loans guaranteed by the Federal Housing Administration (FHA) or Veterans Administration (VA). Loans not backed by the FHA or VA are called *conventional loans*. Manufactured housing-backed securities that are backed by such loans are called *conventional manufactured housing-backed securities*. These securities are issued by private entities.

The typical term for a manufactured home loan is 15 to 20 years. The loan repayment is structured to fully amortize the amount borrowed. Therefore, as with residential mortgage loans and HELs, the cash flow consists of net interest, regularly scheduled principal, and prepayments. However, prepayments are more stable for manufactured housing-backed securities because they are not sensitive to refinancing. There are several reasons for this. First, the loan balances are typically small so that there is no significant dollar savings from refinancing. Second, the rate of depreciation of mobile homes may be such that in the earlier years depreciation is greater than the amount of the loan paid off. This makes it difficult to refinance the loan. Finally, borrowers are typically of lower credit quality and therefore find it difficult to obtain funds to refinance. The same credit enhancements applicable to mortgage products and described above are also applicable to this product.

COMMERCIAL MORTGAGE-BACKED SECURITIES

Commercial mortgage-backed securities (CMBSs) are backed by a pool of commercial mortgage loans on income-producing property—multifamily properties (i.e., apartment buildings), office buildings, industrial properties (including warehouses), shopping centers, hotels, and health care facilities (i.e., senior housing care facilities). There are three types of CMBS deal structures that have been of interest to bond investors: (1) liquidating trusts; (2) multiproperty single borrower; and (3) multiproperty conduit. The liquidating or nonperforming trusts are a small segment of the CMBS market. This segment, as the name implies, represents CMBS deals backed by nonperforming mortgage loans. The fastest growing segment of the CMBS is conduit-originated transactions. Conduits are commercial-lending entities that are established for the sole purpose of generating collateral to securitize.

Credit Risk

Unlike residential mortgage loans where the lender relies on the ability of the borrower to repay and has recourse to the borrower if the payment terms are not satisfied, commercial mortgage loans are nonrecourse loans. This means that the lender can only look to the income-producing property backing the loan for interest and principal repayment. If there is a default, the lender looks to the proceeds from the sale of the property for repayment and has no recourse to the borrower for any unpaid balance. Basically, this means that the lender must view each property as a standalone business and evaluate each property using measures that have been found useful in assessing credit risk.

While fundamental principles of assessing credit risk apply to all property types, traditional approaches to assessing the credit risk of the collateral differs for CMBS than for nonagency MBS and real estate-backed ABS discussed earlier. For MBS and ABS backed by residential property, typically the loans are lumped into buckets based on certain loan characteristics and then assumptions regarding default rates are made regarding each bucket. In contrast, for commercial mortgage loans, the unique economic characteristics of each income-producing property in a pool backing a CMBS requires that credit analysis be performed on a loan-by-loan basis not only at the time of issuance, but monitored on an ongoing basis.

Regardless of the property type, the two measures that have been found to be key indicators of the potential credit performance is the debt-to-service coverage ratio and the loan-to-value ratio.

The *debt-to-service coverage* (DSC) ratio is the ratio of the property's net operating income (NOI) divided by the debt service. The NOI is defined as the rental income reduced by cash operating expenses (adjusted for a replacement reserve). A ratio greater than 1 means that the cash flow from the property is sufficient to cover debt servicing. The higher the ratio, the more likely that the borrower will be able to meet debt servicing from the property's cash flow.

For all properties backing a CMBS deal, a weighted average DSC ratio is computed. An analysis of the credit quality of an issue will also look at the dispersion of the DSC ratios for the underlying loans. For example, one might look at the percentage of a deal with a DSC ratio below a certain value.

Studies of residential mortgage loans have found that the key determinant of default is the LTV. The figure used for "value" in this ratio is either market value or appraised value. In valuing commercial property, there can be considerable variation in the estimates of the property's market value. Thus, analysts tend to be skeptical about estimates of market value and the resulting LTVs reported for properties. But, the lower the LTV, the greater the protection afforded the lender.

Another characteristic of the underlying loans that is used in gauging the quality of a CMBS deal is the prepayment protection provisions. We discuss these provisions later. Finally, there are characteristics of the property that affect quality. Specifically, analysts and rating agencies look at the concentration of loans by property type and by geographical location.

Basic CMBS Structure

As with any structured finance transaction, sizing will determine the necessary level of credit enhancement to achieve a desired rating level. For example, if certain DSC and LTV ratios are needed, and these ratios cannot be met at the loan level, then subordination is used to achieve these levels.

The rating agencies will require that the CMBS transaction be retired sequentially, with the highest-rated bonds paying off first. Therefore, any return of principal caused by amortization, prepayment, or default will be used to repay the highest-rated tranche.

Interest on principal outstanding will be paid to all tranches. In the event of a delinquency resulting in insufficient cash to make all scheduled payments, the transaction's servicer will advance both principal and interest. Advancing will continue from the servicer for as long as these amounts are deemed recoverable.

Losses arising from loan defaults will be charged against the principal balance of the lowest-rated CMBS tranche outstanding. The total loss charged will include the amount previously advanced as well as the actual loss incurred in the sale of the loan's underlying property.

The investor must be sure to understand the cash flow priority of any prepayment penalties and/or yield maintenance provisions because this can impact a particular bond's average life and overall performance.

Structural Call Protection

The degree of call protection available to a CMBS investor is a function of the following two characteristics: call protection available at the loan level and call protection afforded by the actual CMBS structure. At the commercial loan level, call protection can take the following forms: prepayment lockout, defeasance, prepayment penalty points, and yield maintenance charges.

A *prepayment lockout* is a contractual agreement that prohibits any prepayments during a specified period of time, called the lockout period. The lockout period at issuance can be from two to five years.

After the lockout period, call protection comes in the form of either prepayment penalty points or yield maintenance charges. With *defeasance*, rather than prepaying a loan, the borrower provides sufficient funds for the servicer to invest in a portfolio of Treasury securities that replicates the cash flows that would exist in the absence of prepayments. *Prepayment penalty points* are predetermined penalties that must be paid by the borrower if the borrower wishes to refinance. *Yield maintenance charge*, in its simplest terms, is designed to make the lender indifferent as to the timing of prepayments. The yield maintenance charge, called the "make-whole charge" in the corporate area, makes it uneconomical to refinance solely to get a lower mortgage rate.

The other type of call protection available in CMBS transactions is structural. That is, because the CMBS bond structures are sequential-pay (by rating), the AA-rated tranche cannot pay down until the AAA is completely retired, and the AA-rated bonds must be paid off before the A-rated bonds, and so on. However, principal losses due to defaults are impacted from the bottom of the structure upward.

Call provisions at both the loan and structure level make contraction risk less likely. Therefore unlike some of the mortgage assets described earlier, they are not likely to exhibit negative convexity.

Balloon Maturity Provisions

Many commercial loans backing CMBS transactions are balloon loans that require substantial principal payment at the end of the term of the loan. If the borrower fails to make the balloon payment, the borrower is in default. The lender may extend the loan, and in so doing may modify the original loan terms. During the workout period for the loan, a higher interest rate will be charged, the default interest rate.

The risk that a borrower will not be able to make the balloon payment because either the borrower cannot arrange for refinancing at the balloon payment date or cannot sell the property to generate sufficient funds to pay off the balloon balance is called *balloon risk*. Because the term of the loan will be extended by the lender during the workout period, balloon risk is also referred to as extension risk.

REAL ESTATE INVESTMENT TRUST DEBT

REITs are companies that buy, develop, manage, and sell real estate assets. One special feature of REITs is that they qualify as passthrough entities and are therefore free from taxation at the corporate level. REITs must comply with a number of Internal Revenue Code provisions to qualify for that tax-free status. In particular, REITs must pay dividends equaling at least 90% of their taxable income, and more than 75% of total investment assets must be in real estate assets. Their major business activity is the generation of property income, and no more than 30% of gross income can come from the sale of real estate property held for less than four years. So they are clearly "buy and operate" entities, not flippers or traders.

REIT Taxonomy

REITs fall into three broad categories: equity REITs, mortgage REITs, and hybrid REITs.

Equity REITs are the dominant category, representing about 95% of total market capitalization. Their revenues are derived principally from rents. Equity REITs invest in and own properties (and are thus responsible for the equity or value of their real estate assets). Equity REITs differ by specialization. Some focus on a specific geographic area (a specific region, state or metropolitan area), others focus on a specific property type (such as retail properties, industrial facilities, strip malls, office buildings, apartments or health care facilities). Still other REITs have a broad focus, and invest in a variety of assets across a wide spectrum of locations. The most important asset holdings are retail properties, residential properties, and industrial offices.

Mortgage REITs represent between 3% and 4% of total REIT market capitalization. These REITs provide mortgage money to owners of real estate, and purchase existing mortgages and mortgage-backed securities. Their revenues are generated primarily by interest they earn on the mortgage loans. Mortgage REITs have become a considerably less important part of the market over time. In 1990, they had represented about 29% of total REIT market capitalization.

Hybrid REITS represent less than 2% of the market. They combine the investment strategies of equity REITs and mortgage REITS by investing in both properties and mortgages.

Mortgage REITs are rarely used in CDO deals. CDO managers are interested exclusively in equity REITs. This is because recovery assumptions for mortgage REIT debt are much more stringent than for equity REIT debt. In SF CDO deals, recovery assumptions are dependent on the bond's percentage representation of initial capital. Recovery rates on typical subordinated CMBS/ABS/MBS assets are 30% to 35%. For equity REITs, Moody's assumes a recovery rate of 40%, which reflects the strong covenant packages that we will discuss later. Thus, assumed recovery rates for equity REITs are very similar to those on subordinate CMBS/ABS/MBS assets. By contrast, on health care REITs, which carry special risks due to significant government regulation of their ownership and operation, and mortgage REITs, which tend to be highly leveraged, Moody's assumes only a 10% recovery rate.

REIT Capitalization

The REIT capital structure consists of secured bank loans, unsecured debentures, preferred stock, and equity. Because an equity REIT can buy and sell assets and change financial ratios, debt covenants are one of the most important protections available for holders of unsecured REIT debt.

Here we look more closely at REIT debt covenants, and learn how minimum ratios compare to those on CMBS. We will find BBB rated REIT debt has ratios very similar to single-A rated CMBS debt. We will also learn that, in practice, REITs hold ratios even much higher than those provided by the covenants.

REIT Debt Covenants

Investors in REIT debt will find the covenants quite significant in providing protection. Standard covenants are shown in Exhibit 5.2. A typical REIT covenant package includes the following:

1. Total debt cannot exceed 60% of total assets.
2. Unencumbered assets must represent at least 150% of unsecured debt.
3. Secured debt cannot exceed 40% of total assets.
4. Interest coverage must be greater than 1.5×.

While these look very different from levels that mortgage market junkies are accustomed to, they are easily translated. In fact, they parallel very closely A ratings for CMBS. Let us look of each of these more closely.

The debt/adjusted total assets ratio is very close to an LTV in the CMBS market: It measures the value of the loan versus the value of the property. This ratio must be no more than 60%. In fact, for single-A rated CMBS debt, the implied LTV is generally in the range of 60% to 65%.

EXHIBIT 5.2   Senior Unsecured REIT Debt: Comparison to CMBS

Covenant	Required Ratio	Comparable CMBS Ratio
Debt/Adjusted total assets	No more than 60%	LTV
Total unencumbered assets/Unsecured debt	At least 150%	LTV
Secured debt/Adjusted total assets	No more than 40%	Percent of debt that is senior
Consolidated income available for debt service/Annual debt service	At least 1.5×	DSCR

Generally in a CMBS conduit deal, total LTV is 75%. However, approximately 15% of the deal is subordinated to the single-A tranche, so we can multiply the LTV on the deal by 0.85. This gives 64% LTV (0.75 × 0.85).

The total unencumbered assets/unsecured debt ratio must be at least 150% in a REIT. This leverage ratio is actually a very close relative of LTV measures used in CMBS. It says that unsecured debt cannot be more than 66% of total unencumbered assets. Again, these levels are very similar to the LTVs for single-A rated CMBS debt.

The next ratio is secured debt/adjusted total assets. Since REIT debt is senior, but unsecured, this ratio measures the percent of debt ahead of the bondholder in a REIT capital structure. That ratio must be no greater than 40%. In a CMBS deal, there is approximately 25% subordination under the AAA. The AA and A are generally about 5% each. So the single-A rated CMBS bond has 80% of the deal ahead of it. Thus, the BBB rated REIT has a much lower percent of the deal with a prior claim on the assets, which provides a heavy measure of protection.

The final ratio, consolidated income available for debt service/annual debt service, is very close to a debt service coverage ratio (DSCR). This measures how much income cushion there is to pay bondholders the interest due them. This ratio must be at least 1.5× on a REIT deal. For a single A class on a CMBS deal, it is right around the same level. That is, the deal typically has a 1.25× DSCR at the whole loan level. With 85% of the deal senior, or *pari passu*, to the single A (15% subordination), we obtain a DSCR of 1.47× (1.25/0.85) on the single A CMBS.

Reasons for Tough Ratings

The minimum covenant restrictions for BBB rated REIT debt are very close to the ratios that are required for a single-A rating in the CMBS market. Moody's acknowledges this by saying "REIT ratings tend to run several grades lower than commercial mortgage backed securities (CMBS)

ratings for pools with comparable asset classes and financial ratios."[3] The reasons for the tougher grading scale for REIT debt are fourfold.

- REITS may substantially alter the composition of their portfolio assets unlike a CMBS, which involves fixed pools. So REIT assets can be purchased and sold, while CMBS assets can only leave the pool, and none can be added.[4]
- Financial ratios of a REIT can change over time, but the capital structure of a CMBS is permanent. REIT covenants typically allow significantly greater leverage than the capital structure currently in place. This gives REITs more financial flexibility, but could jeopardize bondholders.
- REIT debt is unsecured, whereas first mortgage positions of CMBS are secured.
- And finally, REIT debt is in the form of bonds, while most CMBS debt is in passthroughs. Thus the REIT debt must be paid in full on a specific day, which is a more stringent hurdle than that for a passthrough completing payment by a stated final maturity.

Investors should realize that not only are covenants in a REIT extremely conservative, but most BBB rated REITs have ratios far more conservative than what covenants actually permit.

Reasons REITs Are Included in CDOs

REITs have become a very important part of structured finance CDOs, comprising 10% to 50% of total assets on a number of deals. REIT debt is included because:

- REITs do not have negative convexity and hence help minimize the negative convexity for the CDO.
- REITs provide valuable diversification for CDO deals.
- REIT yields are somewhat higher than CMBS yields for assets with similar ratings.

Minimizing Negative Convexity

REIT debt generally has 10 to 12 year final maturities and excellent call protection. The call protection occurs because the securities are noncallable bullets or have yield maintenance provisions. The yield maintenance provisions (or "make whole" provisions) are very similar to those

---

[3] See Moody's Investors Service, "Credit Rating Evaluation of REITs" (December 9, 1994).
[4] In a FASIT structure, substitutions are permissible.

found in CMBS deals, with most deals using a discount rate of Treasuries plus 25 basis points. If a deal carrying yield maintenance provisions is called, bondholders will be owed the difference between the value of the cash flows, discounted at Treasuries plus 25 basis points, and par. Calling yield maintenance deals usually represents a windfall to the investor.

To illustrate, assume an investor hypothetically purchased a new par REIT bond, with a 10-year maturity and a coupon of 8.35%, selling exactly at par. (Also assume that the 10-year Treasury note is 5.85%, implying the REIT debt has a spread of 250 bps to the 10-year.) If the bond is called immediately, its value (at a Treasury plus 25 basis points discount rate) is $116.66. Thus, investors receive a $16.66 windfall. If interest rates have fallen, the value of the bond is even larger. In practice, this means that REIT debt is rarely called. It is totally noneconomic to refinance, as bondholders receive more than the savings from any refinancing following lower rates.

This call protection is important because both residential, mortgage-backed securities and mortgage-related ABS have some amount of negative convexity. The convexity problem is minimized in any CDO by limiting the amount of negative convex paper in that deal. Thus the deals must use a heavy component of nonmortgage-related ABS paper, CMBS paper, and REIT paper.

Diversification

REIT paper provides valuable diversification for CDO deals. CDO ratings are derived by reducing the asset pool to a set of nearly homogenous, uncorrelated assets. Structured finance-backed CDOs generally have much lower diversity scores than do high-yield CDOs, since there are substantially fewer categories. On a structured finance deal, a typical diversity score is 15 to 20, compared to the typical 50 to 60 on a high-yield deal. So for convexity purposes, it is important to include nonmortgage-related assets, as well as CMBS and REITs. However, availability of nonmortgage-related subordinated tranches is very limited, and Moody's has only three CMBS categories. By contrast, there are 8 REIT categories, as shown in Exhibit 5.3. Thus, REITs turn out to be a very valuable source of diversification for CDO deals.

Some Yield Pickup to CMBS

Investors are able to obtain this diversification and collateral availability advantage without giving up yield. In fact, REITs actually yield more than do comparably rated CMBS.

EXHIBIT 5.3   Moody's Industry Classifications

Industry Classifications	Category
CMBS	
Conduit	1
Credit tenant leases	2
Large loan	3
REIT	
Hotel and leisure	4
Residential	5
Office	6
Retail	7
Industrial	8
Health care	9
Diversified	10
Self Storage	11

Source: Moody's Investors Service, "The Inclusion of Commercial Real Estate Assets in CDOs," October 8, 1999.

One would think that with such conservative rating methodology on ratios, REITs would tend to trade tighter than CMBS. In fact, the reverse is the case. REITs tend to trade wider at each rating level. Industrial and residential REITs generally tend to trade 5 to 10 basis points wider than equivalently rated CMBS debt at the BBB and BB levels. Retail/storage REITs tend to trade about 30 to 35 basis points wider.

A number of investors have expressed frustration that REIT spreads do not follow the same patterns as those on other corporate bonds. In fact, REIT debt tends to track CMBS debt very closely in the BBB categories.

A Final Advantage

In addition to giving managers a wider choice of available assets, we have argued that REITs add diversification to CDO deals. We also have explained that REIT covenants are approximately as conservative at the BBB level as are CMBS ratios at the single-A level. Moreover, most REITs tend to have actual financial ratios far more conservative than what their covenants allow. The final advantage stems from the fact that REITs are actually wider in yield than comparably rated CMBS debt. In short, REIT exposure should be looked at as a "plus" within the context of a structured finance REIT.

CHAPTER 6

Review of Structured Finance Collateral: Nonmortgage ABS

We continue with our review of structured finance collateral in this chapter. Here we cover credit card receivable-backed securities, auto loan-backed securities, student loan-backed securities, SBA loan-backed securities, aircraft lease-backed securities, franchise loan-backed securities, and rate reduction bonds.

CREDIT CARD RECEIVABLE-BACKED SECURITIES

A major sector of the ABS market is that of securities backed by credit card receivables. Credit cards are issued by banks (e.g., Visa and MasterCard), retailers (e.g., JC Penney and Sears), and travel and entertainment companies (e.g., American Express). Credit card deals are structured as a master trust. With a master trust the issuer can sell several series from the same trust.

Cash Flow

For a pool of credit card receivables, the cash flow consists of finance charges collected, fees, and principal. Finance charges collected represent the periodic interest the credit card borrower is charged based on the unpaid balance after the grace period. Fees include late payment fees and any annual membership fees.

Interest to security holders is paid periodically (e.g., monthly, quarterly, or semiannually). The interest rate may be fixed or floating—roughly half of the securities are floaters. The floating rate is uncapped.

A credit card receivable-backed security is a nonamortizing security. For a specified period of time, referred to as the lockout period or revolving period, the principal payments made by credit card borrowers comprising the pool are retained by the trustee and reinvested in additional receivables to maintain the size of the pool. The lockout period can vary from 18 months to 10 years. So, during the lockout period, the cash flow that is paid out to security holders is based on finance charges collected and fees.

After the lockout period, the principal is no longer reinvested but paid to investors. This period is referred to as the principal-amortization period, and the various types of structures are described later.

Performance of the Portfolio of Receivables

Several concepts must be understood in order to assess the performance of the portfolio of receivables and the ability of the issuer to meet its interest obligation and repay principal as scheduled.

The gross yield includes finance charges collected and fees. Charge-offs represent the accounts charged off as uncollectible. Net portfolio yield is equal to gross portfolio yield minus charge-offs. The net portfolio yield is important because it is from this yield that the bondholders will be paid. So, for example, if the average yield (WAC) that must be paid to the various tranches in the structure is 5% and the net portfolio yield for the month is only 4.5%, there is the risk that the bondholder obligations will not be satisfied.

Delinquencies are the percentages of receivables that are past due for a specified number of months, usually 30, 60, and 90 days. They are considered an indicator of potential future charge-offs.

The monthly payment rate (MPR) expresses the monthly payment (which includes finance charges, fees, and any principal repayment) of a credit card receivable portfolio as a percentage of credit card debt outstanding in the previous month. For example, suppose a $500 million credit card receivable portfolio in January realized $50 million of payments in February. The MPR would then be 10% ($50 million divided by $500 million).

There are two reasons why the MPR is important. First, if the MPR reaches an extremely low level, there is a chance that there will be extension risk with respect to the principal payments on the bonds. Second, if the MPR is very low, then there is a chance that there will not be sufficient cash flows to pay off principal. This is one of the events that could trigger early amortization of the principal (described as follows).

At issuance, portfolio yield, charge-offs, delinquency, and MPR information are provided in the prospectus. Information about portfolio performance is thereafter available from various sources.

Early Amortization Triggers

There are provisions in credit card receivable-backed securities that require early amortization of the principal if certain events occur. Such provisions, which are referred to as either early amortization or rapid amortization, are included to safeguard the credit quality of the issue. The only way that principal cash flows can be altered is by triggering the early amortization provision.

Typically, early amortization allows for the rapid return of principal in the event that the three-month average excess spread earned on the receivables falls to zero or less. When early amortization occurs, the credit card tranches are retired sequentially (i.e., first the AAA bond, then the AA rated bond, and so on). This is accomplished by paying the principal payments made by the credit card borrowers to the investors instead of using them to purchase more receivables. The length of time until the return of principal is largely a function of the monthly payment rate. For example, suppose that a AAA tranche is 82% of the overall deal. If the monthly payment rate is 11%, then the AAA tranche would return principal over a 7.5-month period (82%/11%). An 18% monthly payment rate would return principal over a 4.5-month period (82%/18%).

Monthly information is available on each deal's trigger formula and base rate. The trigger formula is the formula that shows the condition under which the rapid amortization will be triggered. The base rate is the minimum payment rate that a trust must be able to maintain to avoid early amortization.

AUTO LOAN-BACKED SECURITIES

Auto ABS are issued by:

1. The financial subsidiaries of auto manufacturers (domestic and foreign).
2. Commercial banks.
3. Independent finance companies and small financial institutions specializing in auto loans.

In terms of credit, borrowers are classified as either prime, nonprime, or subprime. Each originator employs its own criteria for classifying borrowers into these three broad groups. Typically, prime borrowers are those that have had a strong credit history that is characterized by timely payment of all their debt obligations. The FICO score of prime borrowers is generally greater than 680. Nonprime borrowers have usually had a few delinquent payments. Nonprime borrowers, also called near-prime borrwers, typically have a FICO score ranging from the low 600s to the mid-600s. When a borrower has a credit history of missed or major problems with delinquent loan payments and the borrower may have previously filed for bankruptcy, the borrower is classified as subprime. The FICO score for subprime borrowers typically is less than the low 600s.[1]

Cash Flows and Prepayments

The cash flow for auto loan-backed securities consists of regularly scheduled monthly loan payments (interest and scheduled principal repayments) and any prepayments. For securities backed by auto loans, prepayments result from:

1. Sales and trade-ins requiring full payoff of the loan.
2. Repossession and subsequent resale of the automobile.
3. Loss or destruction of the vehicle.
4. Payoff of the loan with cash to save on the interest cost.
5. Refinancing of the loan at a lower interest cost.

While refinancings may be a major reason for prepayments of mortgage loans, they are of minor importance for automobile loans. Moreover, the interest rates for the automobile loans underlying some deals are substantially below market rates (*subvented rates*) since they are offered by manufacturers as part of a sales promotion.

Prepayments for auto loan-backed securities are measured in terms of the absolute prepayment speed (ABS). The ABS is the monthly prepayment expressed as a percentage of the original collateral amount. As explained earlier, the SMM is a monthly prepayment rate that expresses prepayments based on the prior month's balance.

Structures

When auto ABS were first issued, the typical structure was a grantor trust that issued passthrough certificates. A major drawback with using grantor trusts in creating efficient structures is the inability to time tranche securities. That is, while an issuer can use a grantor trust to create subordinate interests and thereby issue multiple bond classes, each with a *different* level of priority, it could not issue multiple bond classes with the *same* level of priority. Nor are issuers permitted to use interest

---

[1] Alexander W. Roever, "Securities Backed by Automobile Loans and Leases," Chapter 29 in Frank J. Fabozzi (ed.), *The Handbook of Fixed Income Securities* (New York: McGraw-Hill, 2005).

rate derivatives within a grantor trust. This led to the extensive use of the pay-though structures by issues. The most common paythrough structure used being the owner trust.

Moreover, because of the flexibility granted to issuers to manage the cash flows from the collateral when using paythrough structures such as the owner trust, issuers could include performance-related triggers. Because of the reduced credit risk resulting from the inclusion of these triggers, issuers could reduce the cost of credit enhancement.

There are two typical structures used in auto ABS paythough structures.[2] In both structures there are multiple sequential-pay senior classes and a subordinate class. One of the senior classes is a Rule 2a-7 of the Investment Company Act of 1940 eligible money market class. In one typical structure, the senior classes receives all principal until every senior class is paid off. Only after that time is the subordinate class paid any principal. In the other typical structure, once the money market class is paid off, the other senior classes and the subordinate class are paid principal concurrently. However, in this structure, the concurrent payments to the senior classes and subordinate classes require that a performance trigger be reached. If the preformance trigger is breached, the principal distribution rules of the second structure will be the same as that for the first structure.

STUDENT LOAN-BACKED SECURITIES

Student loans are made to cover college cost (undergraduate, graduate, and professional programs such as medical school and law school) and tuition for a wide range of vocational and trade schools. Securities backed by student loans are popularly referred to as SLABS (student loan asset-backed securities).

The student loans that have been most commonly securitized are those that are made under the Federal Family Education Loan Program (FFELP). Under this program, the government makes loans to students via private lenders. The decision by private lenders to extend a loan to a student is not based on the applicant's ability to repay the loan. If a default of a loan occurs and the loan has been properly serviced, then the government will guarantee up to 98% of the principal plus accrued interest.

Loans that are not part of a government guarantee program are called *alternative loans*. These loans are basically consumer loans, and the lender's decision to extend an alternative loan will be based on the

---

[2] Roever, "Securities Backed by Automobile Loans and Leases."

ability of the applicant to repay the loan. Alternative loans are securitized in increasing amounts.

Congress created Fannie Mae and Freddie Mac to provide liquidity in the mortgage market by allowing these government-sponsored enterprises to buy mortgage loans in the secondary market. Congress created the Student Loan Marketing Association (Sallie Mae) as a government-sponsored enterprise to purchase student loans in the secondary market and to securitize pools of student loans. Sallie Mae is a major issuer of SLABS, and its issues are viewed as the benchmark issues. Other entities that issue SLABS are either traditional for profit issuers (e.g., the Key Corp Student Loan Trust) or nonprofit organizations (Michigan Higher Education Loan Authority and the Florida Educational Loan Marketing Corporation). The SLABS of the latter typically are issued as tax-exempt securities and therefore trade in the municipal market.

Collateral

There are different types of student loans under the FFELP, including subsidized and unsubsidized Stafford loans, Parental Loans for Undergraduate Students (PLUS), and Supplemental Loans to Students (SLS). These loans involve three periods with respect to the borrower's payments-deferment period, grace period, and loan repayment period. Typically, student loans work as follows. While a student is in school, no payments are made by the student on the loan. This is the *deferment period*. Upon leaving school, the student is extended a *grace period* of usually six months when no payments on the loan must be made. After this period, payments are made on the loan by the borrower.

Prepayments typically occur due to defaults or loan consolidation. Even if there is no loss of principal faced by the investor when defaults occur, the investor is still exposed to contraction risk. This is the risk that the investor must reinvest the proceeds at a lower spread and, in the case of a bond purchased at a premium, the premium will be lost. Consolidation of a loan occurs when the student who has taken out loans over several years combines them into a single loan. The proceeds from the consolidation are distributed to the original lender and, in turn, distributed to the bondholders. Loan consolidation allows student borrowers to achieve lower rates and longer terms. Student loan consolidation was very popular during the 2001–2005 period, and lead to prepayment rates during those years that were considerably higher than anticipated when the deals were priced.

Structures

Structures on student loan floaters have experienced more than the usual amount of change since 2000. The reason for this is quite simple.

The underlying collateral—student loans—is exclusively indexed to 3-month Treasury bills, while a large percentage of securities are issued as LIBOR floaters. This creates an inherent mismatch between the collateral and the securities.

Issuers have dealt with the mismatch in a variety of ways. Some issued Treasury bill floaters which eliminates the mismatch, others issued hedged or unhedged LIBOR floaters, while others switched back and forth between the two. Recently, some have issued both Treasury and LIBOR floaters in the same transaction.[3]

It is important to bear in mind that when an ABS structure contains a basis mismatch, it is not only the investor, but the issuer that bears a risk. Student loan deals (like deals in many other ABS classes) have excess spread; that is, roughly the difference between the net coupon on the collateral and the coupon on the bonds.

In mortgage-related ABS, the excess spread is much larger than in the student loan sector, and is used to absorb monthly losses. Because losses in federally guaranteed student loans are relatively small, the vast majority of the excess spread flows back to the issuer. Hence, the Treasury bill/LIBOR-basis risk is of major concern to issuers. When an issuer incorporates a swap in the deal, it not only reduces the risk to the investor (by eliminating the effect of an available funds cap) but reduces risk to the issuer by protecting a level of excess spread. When a cap is purchased, it is primarily for the benefit of the investor, because the cap only comes into play once the excess spread in the deal has been effectively reduced to zero.

The indices used on private and public student loan ABS transactions since the earliest deals in 1993 have changed over time (even though throughout this period, the index on the underlying loans was always 3-month Treasury bills). From 1993 to 1995, most issuers, with the notable exception of Sallie Mae, used 1-month LIBOR, which indicated strong investor preference for LIBOR floaters. By contrast, from Sallie Mae's first deal in late 1995, that issuer chose to issue Treasury bill floaters to minimize interest rate mismatch risk.

SBA LOAN-BACKED SECURITIES

The Small Business Administration (SBA) is an agency of the U.S. government empowered to guarantee loans made by approved SBA lenders to qualified borrowers. The loans are backed by the full faith and credit of the

---

[3] Also in conjunction with the choice of index, issuers have incorporated a variety of basis swaps and/or have bought cap protection from third parties, while some have used internal structures to deal with the risk.

government. Most SBA loans are variable rate loans where the reference rate is the prime rate. The rate on the loan is reset monthly on the first of the month or quarterly on the first of January, April, July, and October. SBA regulations specify the maximum coupon allowable in the secondary market. Newly originated loans have maturities between five and 25 years.

The Small Business Secondary Market Improvement Act passed in 1984 permitted the pooling of SBA loans. When pooled, the underlying loans must have similar terms and features. The maturities typically used for pooling loans are 7, 10, 15, 20, and 25 years. Loans without caps are not pooled with loans that have caps.

Most variable rate SBA loans make monthly payments consisting of interest and principal repayment. The amount of the monthly payment for an individual loan is determined as follows. Given the coupon formula of the prime rate plus the loan's quoted margin, the interest rate is determined for each loan. Given the interest rate, a level payment amortization schedule is determined. This level payment is paid until the coupon rate is reset.

The monthly cash flow that the investor in an SBA-backed security receives consists of:

- The coupon interest based on the coupon rate set for the period.
- The scheduled principal repayment (i.e., scheduled amortization).
- Prepayments.

Prepayments for SBA-backed securities are measured in terms of CPR. Voluntary prepayments can be made by the borrower without any penalty. There are several factors contributing to the prepayment speed of a pool of SBA loans. A factor affecting prepayments is the maturity date of the loan. It has been found that the fastest speeds on SBA loans and pools occur for shorter maturities. The purpose of the loan also affects prepayments. There are loans for working capital purposes and loans to finance real estate construction or acquisition. It has been observed that SBA pools with maturities of 10 years or less made for working capital purposes tend to prepay at the fastest speed. In contrast, loans backed by real estate that have long maturities tend to prepay at a slow speed. All other factors constant, pools that have capped loans tend to prepay more slowly than pools of uncapped loans.

AIRCRAFT LEASE-BACKED SECURITIES

Aircraft financing has gone thorough an evolution over the past several years. It started with mainly bank financing, then moved to equipment trust certificates (ETCs), then to enhanced ETCs (EETCs), and finally to aircraft ABS. Today, both EETCs and aircraft ABS are widely used.

EETCs are corporate bonds that share some of the features of structured products, such as credit tranching and liquidity facilities. Aircraft ABS differ from EETCs in that they are not corporate bonds, and they are backed by leases to a number of airlines instead being tied to a single airline. The rating of aircraft ABS is based primarily on the cash flow from their pool of aircraft leases or loans and the collateral value of that aircraft, not on the rating of lessee airlines.

One of the major characteristics that set aircraft ABS apart from other forms of aircraft financing is their diversification. ETCs and EETCs finance aircraft from a single airline. An aircraft ABS is usually backed by leases from a number of different airlines, located in a number of different countries and flying a variety of aircraft types. This diversification is a major attraction for investors. In essence, they are investing in a portfolio of airlines and aircraft types rather than a single airline—as in the case of an airline corporate bond. Diversification also is one of the main criteria that rating agencies look for in an aircraft securitization. The greater the diversification, the higher the credit rating, all else being equal.

Aircraft Leasing

Although there are various forms of financing that might appear in an aircraft ABS deal—including operating leases, financing leases, loans or mortgages—to date, the vast majority of the collateral in aircraft deals has been operating leases. In fact, all of the largest deals have been issued by aircraft leasing companies. This does not mean that a diversified finance company or an airline itself might not at some point bring a lease-backed or other aircraft ABS deal. It just means that so far, aircraft ABS have been mainly the province of leasing companies. Airlines, on the other hand, are active issuers of EETCs.

Aircraft leasing differs from general equipment leasing in that the useful life of an aircraft is much longer than most pieces of industrial or commercial equipment. In a typical equipment lease deal, cash flow from a particular lease on a particular piece of equipment only contributes to the ABS deal for the life of the lease. There is no assumption that the lease will be renewed. In aircraft leasing, the equipment usually has an original useful life of 20+ years, but leases run for only around 4 to 5 years. This means that the aircraft will have to be re-leased on expiration of the original leases. Hence, in the rating agencies' review, there is a great deal of focus on risks associated with re-leasing the aircraft.

The risk of being able to put the plane back out on an attractive lease can be broken down into three components: (1) the time it takes to re-lease the craft; (2) the lease rate; and (3) the lease term. Factors that can affect releasing include the general health of the economy, the health of the airline industry, obsolescence, and type of aircraft.

Servicing

Servicing is important in many ABS sectors, but it is crucial in a lease-backed aircraft deal, especially when the craft must be remarketed when their lease terms expire before the term of the aircraft ABS. It is the servicer's responsibility to re-lease the aircraft. To fulfill that function in a timely and efficient manner, the servicer must be both well-established and well-regarded by the industry.

As Moody's states, the servicer "should have a large and diverse presence in the global aircraft marketplace in terms of the number of aircraft controlled. Market share drives the ability of a servicer to meet aircraft market demand and deal with distressed airlines."

The servicer is also the key to maintaining value of the aircraft, through monitoring usage of the craft by lessees. If a lessee is not maintaining an aircraft properly, it is the servicer's responsibility to correct that situation. Because of servicers' vital role to the securitization, the rating agencies spend a great deal of effort ascertaining how well a servicer is likely to perform.

Defaults

In addition to the risk from needing to re-lease craft, rating agencies are also concerned about possible defaults. Because of protections under Section 1110 of the U.S. Bankruptcy Code, and international statutes that favor aircraft creditors, there is relatively little risk of losing an aircraft. There are, however, repossession costs, plus the loss of revenues during the time it takes to repossess and restore the aircraft to generating lease income.

The rating agencies will "stress" an aircraft financing by assuming a default rate and a period of time and cost for repossessing the aircraft. A major input into base default assumptions is the credit rating of airline lessees. For this part of the review, the ABS rating analyst does rely on the corporate rating of the airline.

While there is little risk of not recovering the aircraft in event of a default, the rating agencies do carefully review the legal and political risks that the aircraft may be exposed to, and evaluate the ease with which the aircraft can be repossessed in the event of a default, especially if any of the lessees are in developing countries.

Enhancement Levels

In aircraft ABS, as in every other ABS sector, the rating agencies attempt to set enhancement levels that are consistent across asset types. That is, the risk of not receiving interest or principal in a aircraft deal rated a particular credit level should be the same as in a credit card or home equity deal (or, for that matter, even for a corporate bond) of the same rating. The total enhancement ranges from 34% to 47%.

Since the early deals, there has been a change in enhancement levels. Early deals depended largely on the sale of aircraft to meet principal payments on the bonds. Since then, aircraft ABS has relied more on lease revenue. Because lease revenue is more robust than sales revenue, the enhancement levels have declined. To understand why a "sales" deal requires more enhancement than a "lease" deal, consider the following. If an aircraft is sold during a recession, the deal suffers that entire decline in market value. On the other hand, if a lease rate declines during a recession, the deal sustains only the loss on the re-lease rate.

FRANCHISE LOAN-BACKED SECURITIES

Franchise loan securities are a hybrid between the commercial mortgage-backed securities (CMBS) and ABS markets. They are often backed by real estate, as in CMBS, but the deal structures are more akin to ABS. Also, franchise loans resemble Small Business Administration (SBA) loans and CDOs more than they do consumer loan-backed ABS securities. Greater reliance is placed on examining each franchise loan within the pool than on using aggregate statistics. In a pool of 100 to 200 loans (typical franchise loan group sizing) each loan is significant. By contrast within the consumer sector, any individual loan from a pool of 10,000 loans (as in home equity deals) does not represent as large a percentage, thus is not considered quite as important.

Franchise loans are similar to SBA loans in average size, maturity and end use. But whereas most SBA loans are floating rate loans indexed to the prime rate, most securitized franchise loans are fixed rate; if they are floating, they are likely to be LIBOR-linked. Franchise loans are used to fund working capital, expansion, acquisitions and renovation of existing franchise facilities.

The typical securitized deal borrower owns a large number of units, as opposed to being a small individual owner of a single franchise unit. However, individual loans are usually made on a single unit, secured either by the real estate, the building, or the equipment in the franchise.

The consolidation within the industry and the emergence of large operators of numerous franchise units has improved industry credit performance. A company owning 10 to 100 units is in a better position to weather a financial setback than is the owner of a single franchise location.

Loans can also be either fixed or floating rate, and are typically closed-end, fully amortizing with maturities of 7 to 20 years. If secured by equipment, maturities range from 7 to 10 years. If they are secured by real estate, maturities usually extend 15 to 20 years. Interest rates range from 8% to 11%, depending on maturity and risk parameters.

Security Characteristics

Because franchise loan collateral is relatively new to the ABS market, and deal size is small, most of these securitized packages have been issued as a 144a private placement (Rule 144a of the Securities Act of 1933 governing private resales of securities to institutions). Issuers also prefer the 144a execution for competitive reasons, because they are reluctant to publicly disclose details of their transactions.

Deals typically range from $100 to $300 million, and are customarily backed by 150 to 200 loans. Average loan size is around $500,000, while individuals loans may range from $15,000 to $2,000,000.

Most deals are structured as sequential-pay bonds with a senior/subordinate credit enhancement. Prepayments can occur if a franchise unit closes or is acquired by another franchisor. However, few prepayments have been experienced within securitized deals as of this writing, and most loans carry steep prepayment penalties that effectively discourage rate refinancing. Those penalties often equal 1% of the original balance of the loan.

Major Sectors

The vast majority of franchise operations consist of three types of retail establishments: restaurants, specialty retail stores (e.g., convenience stores, Blockbusters, 7-11s, Jiffy Lube, and Meineke Muffler), and retail gas stations (e.g., Texaco and Shell). The restaurant category has three major subsectors: quick-service restaurants (e.g., McDonald's, Burger King, Wendy's, and Pizza Hut), casual restaurants (e.g., T.G.I. Fridays, Red Lobster, and Don Pablo's), and family restaurants (e.g., Denny's, Perkins, and Friendly's).

A "concept" is simply another name for a particular franchise idea, since each franchise seeks to differentiate itself from its competitors. Hence, even though Burger King and Wendy's are both QSRs specializing in sandwiches, their menu and style of service are sufficiently different that each has its own business/marketing plan—or "concept." For example, Wendy's has long promoted the "fresh" market, because the firm mandated fresh (not frozen) beef patties in their hamburgers, and helped pioneer the industry's salad bars. Burger King is noted for its "flame broiled" burgers, and doing it "your way."

In addition to segmenting the industry by functional types, it is also segmented by credit grades. For example, Fitch developed a credit tiering system based on expected recoveries of defaulted loans. Tier I concepts have a much lower expected default level than Tier II concepts, and so on. Many financial and operational variables go into these tiered ratings, including number of outlets nationwide (larger, successful concepts benefit from better exposure, national advertising, and the like); concept "seasoning" (especially if it has weathered a recession); and viability in today's competitive environment. (Yesterday's darlings may have become over saturated, or unable to respond to changing tastes or trends by revamping and updating!)

Risk Considerations

There are several risk factors to be aware of when comparing franchise loan pools, and the following are some of the most important.

Number of Loans/Average Size

High concentrations of larger loans represent increased risk, just as in any other pool of securitized loans.

Loan-to-Value Ratio

LTVs can be based on either real estate or business values. It is important to determine which is being used in a particular deal in order to make a valid comparison with other franchise issues. Note that when business value is used to compute LTV, it is common for a nationally recognized accounting firm to provide the valuation estimate.

Fixed Charge Coverage Ratio

The fixed charge coverage ratio (FCCR) is calculated as follows:

$$\text{FCCR} = \frac{\text{Adjusted free cash flow less occupancy costs}}{\text{Occupancy costs plus debt service}}$$

Typical FCCRs range from 1.00 to 3.00, and average around 1.5. A deal with most unit FCCRs below 1.5 would be viewed as having greater risk than average, while one with most FCCRs above 1.5 would be perceived as having less risk than average.

Diversification

As in all ABS sectors, a primary risk factor is the degree of diversification. In a franchise loan deal, important areas for diversification include franchise owner, concept and location.

A typical franchise pool includes loans to 10 to 15 franchisees, each having taken out loans on 5 to 20 individual units. A large concentration of loans to any single franchise operator might increase deal risk. However, such concentration is sometimes allowed, and rating agencies will not penalize severely if that particular franchisee has a very strong record and the individual franchise units have strong financials. It might even be better to have a high concentration of high-quality loans than a more diverse pool of weaker credits.

Concept diversification is also important. Franchise loans extend for 10 to 20 years, and a profitable concept today may become unprofitable as the loans mature.

It is not as important that pooled loans include representation across several major sectors (such as more than one restaurant subsector, or loans from all three major groups). Many finance companies specialize in one or two segments of the industry, and know their area well. Thus a deal from only one of the major sectors does not add any measurable risk as long as there is diversification by franchisee and concept.

Geographical diversification is also important, as it reduces risk associated with regional economic recessions.

Control of Collateral

A key factor in the event of borrower (franchisee) default is control of the collateral. If a franchise loan is secured by a fee simple mortgage, the lender controls disposition of collateral in a bankruptcy. However, if that collateral is a leasehold interest (especially if the lessor is a third party and not the franchisor), the lender may not be able to control disposition in the event of default.

RATE REDUCTION BONDS

The concept of *rate reduction bonds* (RRBs)—also known as *stranded costs* or *stranded assets*—grew out of the movement to deregulate the electric utility industry and bring about a competitive market environment for electric power. Deregulating the electric utility market was complicated by large amounts of "stranded assets" already on the books of many electric utilities. These stranded assets were commitments that had been undertaken by utilities at an earlier time with the understanding that they would be recoverable in utility rates to be approved by the states' utility commissions. However, in a competitive environment for electricity, these assets would likely become uneconomic, and utilities would no longer be assured that they could charge a high enough rate to recover the costs. To compensate investors of these utilities, a special tariff was proposed. This tariff, which would be collected over a specified period of time, would allow the utility to recover its stranded costs.

This tariff, which is commonly known as the *competitive transition charge* (or CTC), is created through legislation. State legislatures allow utilities to levy a fee, which is collected from its customers. Although there is an incremental fee to the consumer, the presumed benefit is that the utility can charge a lower rate as a result of deregulation. This reduction in rates would more than offset the competitive transition charge. In order to facilitate the securitization of these fees, legislation typically designates the revenue stream from these fees as a statutory property right. These rights may be sold to an SPV, which may then issue securities backed by future cash flows from the tariff.

The result is a structured security similar in many ways to other ABS products, but different in one critical aspect: The underlying asset in a RRB deal is created by legislation, which is not the case for other ABS products.

In the first quarter of 2001 there was a good deal of concern regarding RRBs. The sector came under intense scrutiny as a result of the financial problems experienced by California's major utilities. Yet despite the bankruptcy motion filed by Pacific Gas and Electric (PG&E) in 2001—a bellwether issuer of RRBs—rating agencies maintained their triple-A ratings on California's existing RRB issues. This is not the first time the RRB sector had found itself in turmoil. Over much of 1998, the sector was roiled by a movement in California to overturn the existing legislation that had been created specifically for RRB securitization. This put existing RRB issues in jeopardy. However, the ultimate result— a voter initiative was defeated—proved to be positive for this product. The ability of this asset class to retain its rating despite a significant credit crisis at an underlying utility, as well as a serious challenge to the legislation that allows for the creation of these securities, speaks volumes for the soundness of the structures of RRB deals.

Structure

As noted above, state regulatory authorities and/or state legislatures must take the first step in creating RRB issues. State regulatory commissions decide how much, if any, of a specific utility's stranded assets will be recaptured via securitization. They will also decide upon an acceptable time frame and collection formula to be used to calculate the CTC. When this legislation is finalized, the utility is free to proceed with the securitization process.

The basic structure of an RRB issue is straightforward. The utility sells its rights to future CTC cash flows to an SPV created for the sole purpose of purchasing these assets and issuing debt to finance this purchase. In most cases, the utility itself will act as the servicer because it collects the CTC payment from its customer base along with the typical electric utility bill. Upon issuance, the utility receives the proceeds of the securitization (less the fees associated with issuing a deal), effectively reimbursing the utility for its stranded costs immediately.

RRBs usually have a "true-up" mechanism. This mechanism allows the utility to recalculate the CTC on a periodic basis over the term of the deal. Because the CTC is initially calculated based on projections of utility usage and the ability of the servicer to collect revenues, actual collection experience may differ from initial projections. In most cases, the utility can reexamine actual collections, and if the variance is large enough (generally a 2% difference), the utility will be allowed to revise the CTC charge. This true-up mechanism provides cash flow stability as well as credit enhancement to the bondholder.

Enhancement Levels

Credit enhancement levels required by the rating agencies for RRB deals are very low relative to other ABS asset classes. Although exact amounts and forms of credit enhancement may vary by deal, most transactions require little credit enhancement because the underlying asset (the CTC) is a statutory asset and is not directly affected by economic factors or other exogenous variables. Furthermore, the true-up mechanism virtually assures cash flow stability to the bondholder.

As an example, the AAA rated bonds of Detroit Edison Securitization Funding 1 issued in March 2001 were structured with 0.50% initial cash enhancement (funded at closing) and 0.50% overcollateralization (to be funded in equal semi-annual increments over the terms of the transactions). This total of 1% credit enhancement is minuscule in comparison to credit cards, for example, which typically require credit enhancement at the AAA level in the 12% to 15% range for large bank issuers.

Unique Risks

RRBs are subject to risks that are very different from those associated with more traditional structured products (e.g., credit cards, HELs, and so on). For example, risks involving underwriting standards do not exist in the RRB sector because the underlying asset is an artificial construct.

Underwriting standards are a critical factor in evaluating the credit of most other ABS. Also, factors that tend to affect the creditworthiness of many other ABS products—such as levels of consumer credit or the economic environment—generally do not have a direct effect RRBs. Instead, other unique factors that must be considered when evaluating this sector. The most critical risks revolve around the legislative process and environment plus the long-term ability of the trust to collect future revenues to support the security's cash flows.

CHAPTER 7

Structured Finance Default and Recovery Rates

In the previous two chapters, we looked at the various types of structured finance collateral. In this chapter, we look at default and recovery rates on structured finance collateral. The first section describes some of the difficulties in calculating structured finance defaults and recoveries. We then detail the S&P and Moody's default-and-recovery methodologies and their results, including our methodology for combining their results. In the final section, we consider the best way to use this default and recovery information for *high-grade* structured finance-backed CDOs (SF CDOs). These are SF CDOs made up of AA and AAA assets where the constant annual default methodology does not always make complete sense.

To summarize—Exhibit 7.1 is our best estimate of historical defaults and recoveries based on studies by both S&P and Moody's. In the exhibit, we have turned the rating agencies' 5-year cumulative default rates into constant annual default rates that are more familiar to CDO investors. The exhibit also shows *recovery rates* on structured finance tranches. As with default rates, these are shown to vary with the tranche's original rating and its structured finance subsector. These historical results are useful as a starting point in estimating credit losses in a structured finance portfolio. They are also useful in evaluating default and recovery stress tests in the cash flow modeling of SF CDOs.

Exhibit 7.1 shows the superb performance of CMBS and RMBS with respect to both default frequency and default severity. CMBS and RMBS default rates average about half that of corporate default rates. In the higher rating categories, CMBS and RMBS default recoveries are also significantly higher than those of corporates. Meanwhile, the per-

EXHIBIT 7.1   UBS Estimated Historic Constant Annual Defaults/Recoveries

	ABS	CMBS	RMBS & HEL	All SF	Corporates
Aaa	0.03%/87%	0.00%/na	0.03%/97%	0.03%/92%	0.05%/80%
Aa	0.69%/73%	0.00%/na	0.05%/82%	0.15%/77%	0.07%/40%
A	0.47%/55%	0.08%/87%	0.10%/68%	0.23%/62%	0.15%/44%
Baa	1.79%/45%	0.28%/50%	0.49%/56%	0.86%/53%	0.59%/41%
Ba	5.32%/42%	1.24%/54%	1.22%/52%	1.78%/49%	2.62%/41%
B	11.89%/34%	2.21%/47%	2.81%/43%	3.26%/43%	6.02%/36%

Source: Moody's Investors Service, Standard & Poor's, UBS calculations.

formance of ABS was ruined by high defaults in some sub-sectors, namely health care receivables, franchise loans, and manufactured housing. Still, the poor performance of ABS and the superior performance of CMBS and RMBS average out such that on a default frequency and default severity basis, the default performance of structured finance assets compares favorably to that of corporates. In the next chapter, we tie these results in with CDO ratings methodology and performance.

It is important to emphasize that we care more about *future* default rates than *past* default rates in examining structured finance portfolios and SF CDOs. Moreover, there is a great deal of variability in the credit quality of assets with the same rating. Even so, it is important to understand what has happened to an asset class in the past when trying to predict its future. With such an understanding, one can then consider today's economic conditions, underwriting standards, debt burdens, interest rate environment, and all the other variables that will affect defaults in the future.

STRUCTURED FINANCE VERSUS CORPORATE DEFAULT RATES

Rating transition and default studies are necessarily pictures taken of a rear-view mirror. But the nature of structured finance makes it hard to even get an accurate picture of what is behind in the past. One reason is the level of detail necessary in a structured finance study. In a corporate bond rating transition or default study, the unit of study is the corporate entity. But for structured finance, the object being examined is the specific tranche issued by a specific special purpose entity, which is one of many sponsored by a particular corporate entity. The sheer number of these tranches, each with their own unique credit characteristics, makes the creation of default databases difficult.

Furthermore, the occurrence of a structured finance default is often ambiguous. A missed coupon may occur unseen by outsiders to the deal and it may be rectified later. It may also be certain *now,* judging from the state of the special purpose entity's collateral portfolio, that a tranche will eventually default *later* in its life. Likewise, it is often hard to determine default losses or recoveries until the transaction has completely run its course.

Also, corporate entities continue their existence even as their individual debts are issued and retired. Corporate default studies combine the histories of these various debts at the level of the issuer. However, for structured finance, each debt has an independent credit life and experience. The treatment of withdrawn ratings has a bigger affect upon structured finance default rates than corporate default rates.

The heterogeneity of structured finance assets means that broad categories are made up of assets with disparate performance. For example, within the Moody's ABS category, as shown in Exhibit 7.2, health care, franchise loan, and manufactured housing securitizations have had the highest lifetime default rates. A "lifetime" default rate is simply the number of defaulted tranches divided by the number of tranches issued, without any regard to the length of time the tranches have been outstanding. Note that defaults are weighted by the number of tranches, so small speculative-grade tranches count equally with large investment-grade tranches. Thus, when the individual types of deals are aggregated into a broad category, a distorted picture emerges of the performance of the whole and of the parts.

Defaults of structured finance tranches are often directly linked to the originators and servicers of their underlying assets. In fact, overall

EXHIBIT 7.2   Moody's Lifetime Material Impairment Rates within ABS 1993–2003, by Number of Tranches

Health care receivables	37.5%
Franchise loans	32.4%
Manufactured housing	28.2%
Equipment and aircraft leases	3.2%
Home equity loans	2.0%
Autos and trucks	1.4%
Credit cards	0.9%
Others	0.0%
All ABS	4.0%

Source: Moody's Investors Service.

structured finance defaults are driven to a large extent by the idiosyncratic problems of these corporate sponsors. For example, 17% of all ABS defaults are traceable to problems at Conseco/Greentree, a manufactured housing originator. Even more dramatically, 62% of all RMBS defaults are traceable to Quality Mortgage. With past defaults so much a function of one-off corporate problems, predicting future default rates is tenuous. Are we going to have more or fewer Conseco/Greentrees and Quality Mortgages?

With this prelude and caveats, we approach the historical reports of S&P and Moody's with a healthy degree of skepticism about what they can tell us about the future. Nevertheless, as mentioned before, we would like to at least have a clearer picture of the rearview mirror.

S&P RATING TRANSITION STUDIES AND THE MATRIX MULTIPLYING APPROACH

S&P publishes average 1-year rating transition matrices for ABS, CMBS, and RMBS showing how ratings change over a year.[1] We reproduce S&P's rating transition matrix for RMBS (including home equity loan-backed transactions) in Exhibit 7.3. The matrix shows, for example, that on average after one year, 88.1% of BBB-rated RMBS remain BBB. On the other hand, 0.6% of BBB are upgraded to AAA and 0.1% are downgraded to D, S&P's rating for securities that have defaulted on their payment of interest or principal. We use rating transition to D as our proxy for default. S&P's 1-year rating transitions for RMBS averages experience from 1978 through 2003. Their ABS rating transitions are based on experience from 1982 through 2003 and their CMBS rating transitions are based on experience from 1985 through 2003.

To compute 5-year transition-to-D rates from S&P data, we "multiply" transition matrices. For example, we look at the average 1-year matrix to see where BBB RMBS ratings transition to after one year. We then put this vector of ratings and percentages back into the transition matrix to see where ratings transition to after *two* years. We continue this process until we transition the ratings five times to arrive at cumulative *5-year* transitions for RMBS originally rated BBB.

[1] Erkan Erturk et al, *Rating Transitions 2003: U.S. ABS Performance and Outlook*, Standard & Poor's, January 20, 2004, Table 10. Joseph Hu and Roy Chun, *Rating Transitions 2003: Resilient U.S. CMBS Endure Stressed Real Estate Fundamentals*, Standard & Poor's, January 9, 2004, Table 8. Robert B. Pollsen et al., Rating Transitions 2003: *Another Record Year of Credit Performance for U.S. RMBS*, Standard & Poor's, January 9, 2004, Table 11.

EXHIBIT 7.3 One-Year Average Rating Transition Matrix for RMBS & HELs

Rating at Beginning of Year	Rating at End of Year									
	AAA	AA	A	BBB	BB	B	CCC	CC	C	D
AAA	99.8%	0.1%								
AA	8.2%	90.1%	1.4%	0.2%	0.1%	0.1%				
A	3.1%	6.9%	88.5%	1.1%	0.2%	0.1%	0.2%			
BBB	0.6%	3.9%	5.0%	88.1%	0.8%	1.1%	0.3%			0.1%
BB			3.3%	9.0%	84.3%	1.3%	1.1%	0.4%		0.6%
B				1.7%	5.3%	88.0%	2.7%	0.3%		2.0%
CCC							52.5%	13.6%	3.4%	29.9%
CC		0.6%		2.2%				75.3%		22.6%
C										100.0%
D										100.0%

Source: Standard & Poor's.

The advantage of this approach over other methods is that it uses all available rating data and prevents average transition-to-D rates from being greater over shorter periods of time than they are over longer periods of time. On the other hand, the results will not pick up the serial correlation of rating changes; that is, the fact that when a rating is downgraded it is more likely to be downgraded again than credits that were not downgraded. This may cause an underestimation of transition-to-D rates.

RESULTS OF MULTIPLYING S&P RATING TRANSITION MATRICES

In Exhibit 7.4, we show the results of multiplying average 1-year rating transition matrices to arrive at 5-year transition-to-D rates and compare the results to S&P's 5-year corporate default rates.[2] The exhibit shows that within structured finance, ABS has the highest transition-to-D-rates (hereafter "default rates") by far. The ABS BBB default rate is 10 times that of BBB CMBS and RMBS (13.64% for ABS versus 1.15% for CMBS versus 1.32% for RMBS). The AAA ABS default rate is the only one similar to that of CMBS and RMBS (0.03% for ABS versus 0.00% for CMBS and RMBS). ABS default rates are also the only structured finance default rates higher than corporate default rates. Between RMBS and CMBS, CMBS has lower investment-grade default rates and RMBS has lower speculative-grade default rates. But both CMBS and RMBS default rates are lower than corporate default rates. Meanwhile, overall structured finance default rates are similar to those of corporates.

EXHIBIT 7.4   S&P 5-Year Transition-to-D Rates and 5-Year Corporate Default Rates

	ABS	CMBS	RMBS & HELs	All SF	Corporates
AAA	0.03%	0.00%	0.00%	0.06%	0.10%
AA	1.47%	0.01%	0.04%	0.18%	0.31%
A	3.14%	0.25%	0.45%	1.11%	0.65%
BBB	13.64%	1.15%	1.32%	3.53%	3.41%
BB	40.65%	10.93%	5.28%	9.68%	12.38%
B	76.02%	14.66%	14.02%	21.12%	26.82%

Source: Standard & Poor's and UBS calculations.

[2] Brooks Brady and Diane Vazza, *Corporate Defaults in 2003 Recede From Recent Heights*, Standard & Poor's, January 27, 2004, Table 2.

S&P ON STRUCTURED FINANCE LOSS GIVEN DEFAULT

An S&P study has also shed light on *loss given default* (LGD) for structured finance securities; that is, the amount of principal credit losses a security experiences once it has defaulted.[3] S&P shows the amount of *realized principal loss*, which is the amount of principal that the structure has already written off as lost on a particular defaulted tranche. That research report also shows the defaulted tranche's *remaining principal*, which is the amount of principal not written down or repaid and therefore still outstanding and at risk of loss. In Exhibit 7.5, we sum the amount of realized principal loss and half of remaining principal as an estimate of LGD. The exhibit shows LGD by rating category and shows increasing LGD as one descends rating categories. Exhibit 7.5 shows that ABS defaults have been more severe than either CMBS or RMBS defaults.

S&P CONSTANT ANNUAL DEFAULT AND RECOVERIES

To make the S&P default and LGD more relevant to CDO investors, we take the 5-year default rates of Exhibit 7.4 and LGDs of Exhibit 7.5 and present a schedule of historic constant *annual default rates* (CDRs) and recoveries in Exhibit 7.6. In Exhibit 7.6, CDRs are just the 5-year default rates of Exhibit 7.4 divided by five and recovery rates are just one minus the LGDs of Exhibit 7.5. These historic CDRs and recoveries can be used to assess the robustness of assumptions underlying CDO cash flow model results.

EXHIBIT 7.5   S&P Loss Given Default (Realized principal loss + half of remaining principal)

	ABS	CMBS	RMBS & HELs
AAA	23%	na	2%
AA	50%	na	26%
A	50%	na	42%
BBB	64%	43%	47%
BB	76%	53%	59%
B	67%	57%	63%

Source: Standard & Poor's and UBS calculations.

---

[3] Erkan Erturk and Thomas G. Gillis, *Recovery Proxies for Defaulted U.S. Structured Finance Securities*, Standard & Poor's, October 31, 2003, Tables 3, 4, and 5.

EXHIBIT 7.6 S&P Implied Constant Annual Defaults/Recoveries

	ABS	CMBS	RMBS & HELs	All SF	Corporates
AAA	0.01%/77%	0.00%/na	0.00%/98%	0.01%/88%	0.02%/na
AA	0.29%/50%	0.00%/na	0.01%/74%	0.04%/62%	0.06%/na
A	0.63%/50%	0.05%/na	0.09%/58%	0.22%/54%	0.13%/na
BBB	2.73%/36%	0.23%/57%	0.26%/53%	0.71%/49%	0.68%/na
BB	8.13%/24%	2.19%/47%	1.06%/41%	1.94%/37%	2.48%/na
B	15.20%/33%	2.93%/43%	2.80%/37%	4.22%/38%	5.36%/na

Source: Standard & Poor's and UBS calculations.

MOODY'S MATERIAL IMPAIRMENT STUDY

Moody's presents rates of structured finance *material impairments*.[4] A "material impairment" is a payment default that has gone uncured *or* a downgrading to the Ca or C rating categories. A rating of Ca or C in the absence of a payment default may indicate that the structured finance tranche is still paying its coupon, but the condition of the underlying collateral is such that an eventual default on interest or principal is almost certain. Alternatively, the presence of an uncured payment default in the absence of a Ca or C rating may indicate that the payment default is small or expected to be cured.

About half of all material impairments so defined are payment defaults of tranches rated above Ca or C. Thus, with such ratings, Moody's has not taken a public stand that the payment default is severe or is going to continue. In fact, a large percentage of structured finance payment defaults subsequently cure, maybe about 20% to 30%. Thus, we view Moody's material impairment category as an *expansive* definition of default.

Another part of Moody's methodology was to deduct half of all withdrawn ratings when calculating default rates. So, if two ratings out of a cohort of 100 ratings were withdrawn over the year, those defaulting over the year would be compared to a denominator of 99 rather than 100 or 98. But if next year two more ratings are withdrawn, defaults are compared to a denominator of 97. This splits the difference between counting withdrawn ratings as nondefaults and eliminating them completely from the default statistics and thereby increasing default rates. But since a lot of

---

[4] Jian Hu, Richard Cantor, and Alexandra Neely, *Default & Loss Rates of Structured Finance Securities: 1993–2003*, Moody's Investors Service, September 2004, in particular Figures 23 and 25.

structured finance tranches mature every year and have their ratings withdrawn, this treatment increases calculated structured finance defaults above actual defaults. This effect is compounded as tranches season.

We report Moody's structured finance material impairments rates (hereafter "default rates") based on their "original issue cohort " methodology. Moody's forms cohorts of similarly rated tranches *issued* in the same year. Defaults within these cohorts are then tracked as a group going forward. In contrast, Moody's also performs a "rolling cohort" methodology that creates cohorts of similarly rated tranches each year from both new and seasoned issues. Default rates for structured finance tranches, from the same exact dataset, are about twice as high using the rolling cohort method as they are using the original-issue method.

Moody's points out that the reason for the divergence in results between the two impairment measurement methodologies is because marginal defaults among structured finance tranches tend to increase until three years after original issuance, after which they then decline. This pattern of default insures that the rolling cohort method produces higher default rates than the original-issue cohort method. This is because under the rolling cohort method, defaults in later years in the life of a tranche are weighted into the default rate of earlier years.

Under these circumstances, and considering that new issues make up most of a new SF CDO's portfolio, we feel that the original cohort method provides a better estimate of future structured finance default rates. In Exhibit 7.7 we show Moody's 5-year material impairment rates for structured finance tranches, using the original cohort methodology, along with the rating agency's calculation of 5-year corporate default rates.

Moody's presents impairment rates (hereafter default rates) for ABS and RMBS several ways, with home equity loans (HELs) and manufac-

EXHIBIT 7.7 Moody's 5-Year Material Impairment Rates and 5-Year Corporate Default Rate

	ABS without Mfd. Housing	CMBS	RMBS & HELs	All SF	Corporates
Aaa	0.26%	0.00%	0.33%	0.27%	0.40%
Aa	5.42%	0.00%	0.48%	1.33%	0.40%
A	1.55%	0.52%	0.57%	1.23%	0.81%
Baa	4.24%	1.64%	3.56%	5.10%	2.52%
Ba	12.58%	1.49%	6.95%	8.15%	13.85%
B	42.86%	7.44%	14.06%	11.46%	33.39%

Source: Moody's Investors Service.

tured housing variously excluded and included in the broader ABS and RMBS categories. To make Moody's results as comparable as possible to S&P's, we show Moody's data with HELs out of ABS and in RMBS. This conforms to S&P's presentation. Unfortunately, to do so, we also must also show ABS without manufactured housing.

Like S&P's results, Exhibit 7.7 shows that within structured finance, ABS has the highest default experience. If we had been able to include manufactured housing and exclude HELs, the ABS default rate would be even higher. Unlike the S&P results, CMBS consistently has lower default rates than RMBS. Except in some of the investment-grade RMBS categories, CMBS and RMBS default rates are lower than corporate default rates. As a whole, structured finance investment-grade default rates are higher than corporates while structured finance speculative-grade default rates are lower than corporates.

As we mentioned, Moody's presents default rates for ABS with and without manufactured housing defaults. We worked through Moody's various presentations to determine the *minimum* default rate these deals have experienced and present our results in Exhibit 7.8. Comparing Exhibits 7.7 and 7.8, we can tell that default rates for A, Baa, Ba, and B manufactured housing tranches were higher than for any other subset of structured finance transactions isolated by Moody's.

COMPARING AND RECONCILING STRUCTURED FINANCE DEFAULT RATES

We reported S&P transition-to-D rates in Exhibit 7.4 and Moody's material impairment rates in Exhibit 7.7. Unfortunately, there are sometimes big differences between the two sets of numbers, as shown in

EXHIBIT 7.8 Moody's 5-Year Minimum Impairment Rates for Manufactured Housing

	Manufactured Housing
Aaa	n.a.
Aa	>2.19%
A	>1.63%
Baa	>6.48%
Ba	>24.51%
B	>47.48%

Source: Moody's Investors Service, UBS calculations

EXHIBIT 7.9   Moody's 5-Year Material Impairment Rates Minus S&P 5-Year Transition-to-D Rates

	ABS	CMBS	RMBS & HELs	All SF	Corporates
Aaa	0.23%	0.00%	0.33%	0.21%	0.30%
Aa	3.95%	−0.01%	0.44%	1.15%	0.09%
A	−1.59%	0.27%	0.12%	0.12%	0.16%
Baa	−9.40%	0.49%	2.24%	1.57%	−0.89%
Ba	−28.07%	−9.44%	1.67%	−1.53%	1.47%
B	−33.16%	−7.22%	0.04%	−9.66%	6.57%

Source: Moody's Investors Service, Standard & Poor's, UBS calculations.

Exhibit 7.9, where we subtract S&P default rates from Moody's default rates. In the exhibit, positive numbers mean that Moody's has a higher default rate in that sector and rating and negative numbers mean S&P has a higher default rate.

The ABS category has the largest negative differences at least partly caused by the exclusion of manufactured housing in the Moody's ABS default rates we report. If we could add back manufactured housing defaults into the Moody's ABS default rates, those rates would increase and the negative differences in ABS default rates would diminish.

Other potential causes of discrepancies in Exhibit 7.9 are myriad, besides the fact that for S&P we are estimating defaults by multiplying rating transition matrices while Moody's is using the combination of uncured payment defaults and Ca and C downgrades as their measure of material impairment. Beside these obvious differences, there are also differences in the universe of securities the two agencies rate, differences in the agencies' ratings, differences in the agencies' downgrade practices, and differences in how the two studies deal with withdrawn ratings.

One interesting consideration is how these default rates would be affected if we could isolate debt rated by both agencies. In our opinion, a rating agency is typically excluded from rating structured finance transactions when its rating requirements are significantly tougher than other rating agencies. Eliminating the more conservative rating agency therefore makes a tranche more prone to default than it would otherwise be. It seems to us that a default study based on joint Moody's and S&P ratings would produce lower default rates than default studies based on the ratings of either single rating agency.

Taking this view to the extreme, one would say that default rates for jointly rated tranches would be no higher than the *lowest* of each single-rating agency default study. We do not pursue this because we think the methodological differences in the studies by the two rating agencies are more important than the difference between the study results. Still, we think there must be a significant pickup in credit quality when credits in a portfolio are jointly rated by Moody's and S&P, or when each credit in a portfolio is examined as the lower of the two rating agencies' ratings.

We think the difference between S&P and Moody's default rates is due to differing methodologies. S&P's downgrade-to-D rate may miss some defaults that were not recognized by the rating agency. Our own multiplication of rating transition matrices may underestimate downgrades over multiple years by not recognizing the serial correlation of downgrades (i.e., downgraded credits are more likely to be downgraded again than credits that have not been downgraded). Moody's count of tranches experiencing an uncured payment default does not take into account that recent and small payment defaults might be cured. Moody's treatment of withdrawn ratings also increases default rates.

MOODY'S ON STRUCTURED FINANCE HISTORICAL LOSS RATES

Moody's has built a model to predict loss given default (LGD) based on RMBS (including HEL) experience using variables such as tranche size, seniority, seasoning, and principal payments. We present Moody's findings in Exhibit 7.10, which show, like S&P's results, that the higher the RMBS tranche's original rating, the smaller its LGD as a percent of the tranche's original balance. Again, this is no doubt due to the seniority of higher rated tranches and the amortization of those tranches prior to a default. Moody's LGDs for RMBS are smaller than the ones we calcu-

EXHIBIT 7.10   Moody's Estimated RMBS & HEL Loss Given Default as Percent of Original Balance

	Mean	SD
Aaa	2.3%	1.4%
Aa	7.2%	6.7%
A	16.7%	20.6%
Baa	35.2%	26.2%
Ba	34.1%	26.5%
B	52.2%	27.4%

Source: Moody's Investors Service.

lated from S&P by assuming that half of outstanding principal was destined to be lost. Overall, the Moody's model shows that RMBS LGDs are small, even down to the Ba original rating level, compared to the LGD of senior unsecured corporate bonds, which has averaged 74% since 1982.[5]

Applying their LGD model to RMBS, ABS, and CMBS, Moody's determined historical loss rates—the multiplication of default rates and LGD. They also computed loss rates on corporate bonds using bond-specific data. We reproduce Moody's results in Exhibit 7.11. What is striking in the exhibit is how favorable structured finance credit performance becomes when compared to corporates on a default rate and LGD measure. In Exhibits 7.4 and 7.7, where we focused on default rates, ABS looked quite poor in comparison to corporate bonds. The most unfavorable comparison from Moody's default rates in Exhibit 7.7 was between Aa ABS with a 5.42% default rate and Aa corporates with a 0.40% default rate. However, after factoring in LGD, and assuming that Aa ABS losses are similar to Aa RMBS, the loss rate on Aa ABS is 0.27% while the loss rate on corporates is 0.24%. In other words, Aa ABS are 14 times more likely to default than Aa corporates, but after LGD is considered, Aa ABS losses are about equal to Aa corporates. For CMBS, RMBS, and across all structured finance combined, expected losses have generally been much less than for corporates.

In Exhibit 7.12 we work through Moody's various presentations to determine the *minimum loss rate* that manufactured housing transactions have incurred. Similar to our findings on manufactured housing default rates, we can determine by comparing Exhibits 7.11 and 7.12 that manufactured housing loss rates are at least among the highest of any other subset of structured finance transactions isolated by Moody's.

EXHIBIT 7.11   Moody's 5-Year Loss Rates

	ABS without Mfd. Housing	CMBS	RMBS & HEL	All SF	Corporates
Aaa	0.01%	0.00%	0.01%	0.01%	0.08%
Aa	0.27%	0.00%	0.05%	0.10%	0.24%
A	0.61%	0.07%	0.12%	0.38%	0.45%
Baa	1.96%	0.94%	1.42%	2.16%	1.49%
Ba	5.05%	0.59%	2.59%	3.24%	8.20%
B	28.01%	3.66%	7.22%	5.96%	21.39%

Source: Moody's Investors Service.

---

[5] Praveen Varma, et al., *Recovery Rates on Defaulted Corporate Bonds and Preferred Stocks, 1982–2003*, Moody's Investors Service, December 2003, Figure 2.

EXHIBIT 7.12　Moody's 5-Year Minimum Loss Rates for Manufactured Housing

	Manufactured Housing
Aaa	0.00%
Aa	>0.13%
A	>0.52%
Baa	>2.68%
Ba	>9.99%
B	>26.09%

Source: Moody's Investors Service, UBS calculations.

EXHIBIT 7.13　Moody's Implied Constant Annual Defaults and Recoveries

	ABS w/o Mfd. Housing	CMBS	RMBS & HEL	All SF	Corporates
Aaa	0.05%/96%	0.00%/na	0.07%/97%	0.05%/96%	0.08%/80%
Aa	1.08%/95%	0.00%/na	0.10%/90%	0.27%/92%	0.08%/40%
A	0.31%/61%	0.10%/87%	0.11%/79%	0.25%/69%	0.16%/44%
Baa	0.85%/54%	0.33%/43%	0.71%/60%	1.02%/58%	0.50%/41%
Ba	2.52%/60%	0.30%/60%	1.39%/63%	1.63%/60%	2.77%/41%
B	8.57%/35%	1.49%/51%	2.81%/49%	2.29%/48%	6.68%/36%

Source: Moody's Investors Service, UBS calculations.

MOODY'S CONSTANT ANNUAL DEFAULT AND RECOVERIES

We take the Moody's 5-year default rates shown in Exhibit 7.7 and the recovery assumptions embedded in Exhibit 7.11 and present a schedule of historic constant annual default rates (CDRs) and recoveries in Exhibit 7.13. The CDRs in Exhibit 7.13 are just the 5-year default rates of Exhibit 7.7 divided by five. The recovery rates of Exhibit 7.13 are just the loss rates of Exhibit 7.11 divided by the default rates of Exhibit 7.7. Again, as we said with respect to the S&P data in Exhibit 7.6, this presentation may be useful to SF CDO investors assessing the robustness of assumptions underlying CDO cash flow model results.

We mentioned before that we thought Moody's default study might overestimate default rates by including all uncured payment defaults in its definition of a default. As some of those payment defaults will eventually be cured, this tends to overstate defaults. But Moody's incorporates these minor defaults into their estimate of LGD and therefore the LGD estimates are lower than they would otherwise be. So the possible overestimation of default rates is factored into the estimation of LGD. This has very practical implications for the default modeling of structured finance portfolios. It would be overly optimistic to lower Moody's default rate figures because they include minor defaults that will likely be cured yet still use Moody's LGD figures that incorporate small default losses on these minor defaults.

BLENDING S&P AND MOODY'S STUDIES

Following the principle that "the average of two estimates is better than either single estimate," we averaged S&P's and Moody's results in Exhibit 7.1. In the averaged results, the familiar patterns of Exhibits 7.6 and 7.13 hold true. ABS generally has the highest default rates. All structured finance or corporates have the second highest or third highest default rates, depending on the rating category. RMBS generally has the next highest default rates and CMBS generally has the lowest default rates.

In Exhibit 7.1, Moody's high recoveries are lowered by averaging them with S&P's data, where we assumed that half of outstanding principal was also destined to be lost. Still, across the board, structured finance recoveries are quite high and always higher than corporate recoveries in the investment grades.

APPLYING CDRs AND RECOVERIES TO SF CDOs

We suggest that CDO investors use historic results from S&P (Exhibit 7.6), Moody's (Exhibit 7.13), or blended from S&P and Moody's experience (Exhibit 7.1) to assess the robustness of assumptions underlying SF CDO cash flow model results. We think these average historical results provide "base case" default and recovery scenarios from which to assess the impact of economic, underwriting, and other conditions upon future default and recovery rates.

It is a little odd to assign default rates measured in basis points to portfolios where the smallest asset might be 1% of the total portfolio. For example, a reasonable CDR based on historic results for an A rated or better CMBS or RMBS is 0.10% per year or less. Exhibit 7.1 shows a 0.05% CDR for AA RMBS, for example. It is not clear how one should interpret cash flow results based on such default assumptions. In spite of all the uncertainties in predicting future defaults, one thing we know for certain is that 1/10th or 1/20th of a credit is not going to default!

Instead of defaulting small fractions of a high grade (AA and AAA collateral) SF CDO portfolio, many investors like to examine the cash flow results of a tranche if specifically zero, one, two, three or more credits default. This avoids the problem of fractional defaults, but creates its own difficulties: when are defaults assumed to occur and how does one assess the likelihood of a certain number of defaults occurring?

With respect to default timing, Moody's shows that most structured finance defaults occur in the third year after a security's issuance. Specifically, if tranches initially rated Aaa default, they do so four years after issuance, on average. Defaulting tranches rated below Aaa default three years after issuance, on average.

To evaluate the probability of a particular number of credits in a portfolio defaulting, one can use the binomial distribution. For example, suppose that we are looking at a portfolio comprised of 100 CMBS and RMBS assets rated A. When we look at the historical five-year default rates for these assets in Exhibits 7.4 and 7.7 from S&P and Moody's, we see a distribution of default rates from 0.25% to 0.57%. After considering this information and other factors, we might decide that our base case assumption is that these assets have a 0.5% default probability over their life.

The binomial formula for the probability of a certain number of defaults in a portfolio of a certain size is

$$\{N \text{ choose } D\} \times P^D \times (1 - P)^{(N - D)}$$

where

P = default probability
N = number of credits in portfolio
D = number of defaults in portfolio

The notation {N chose D} means that given N and D, the number of unique combinations of defaulting credits that can assembled. For example, in a portfolio of 100 credits, there are 100 unique ways that one credit can default, namely each of the 100 credits can default. For a portfolio of 100 credits, there are 4,950 unique *pairs* of credits that can default.

The application of the binomial formula in this specific example leads to the default probabilities in Exhibit 7.14. The exhibit shows that given a portfolio of 100 credits, each with a 0.5% probability of default, the most likely outcome, at 61% probability, is zero defaults. The next most likely outcome, at 30.44% probability, is one default. From there, higher numbers of defaults in the portfolio become less and less likely.

EXHIBIT 7.14   Probability of Defaults in a 100-Asset Portfolio Where Individual Asset Default Probability = 0.5%

Number of Defaults	Probability
0	60.58%
1	30.44%
2	7.57%
3	1.24%
4	0.15%
5	0.01%
6	0.00%

With Moody's information on default timing and the output of the binomial distribution, we can look at a cash flow run of the SF CDO defaulting one credit in the portfolio in three or four year's time, mindful that according to our assumptions that scenario has a 30% chance of occurring. We can look at the cash flow results of two credits defaulting, mindful that that scenario has an 8% chance of occurring, and so forth.

We have skipped over a couple of difficult questions. First, in a heterogeneous portfolio, which credit does one assume defaults? The biggest? The lowest rated? The highest yielding? Generally, this will not be the same credit, as single risk limits in a high-grade SF CDO are usually stricter for lower-rated credits than for higher-rated credits. All we can suggest is that an investor tailor default scenarios to the specific attributes of the SF CDO portfolio and test the sensitivity of cash flow results to different assumptions.

Another problem ignored so far is the effect of default correlation, the phenomena that credits either default together or do not default together, is going to cause more extreme results than depicted in Exhibit 7.14. In that example, default correlation would create a higher probability of zero defaults and a higher probability of more than one default.

Unfortunately or fortunately, the hypermathematical approaches to default correlation for corporate credits are so far unavailable to structured finance portfolios and their investors. Our practical advice is that investors examine SF CDO portfolios for similarities in the credits that might cause them to default together if they default at all. Obviously, there will be concentrations of real estate-related assets, which have to be evaluated on whether their credit enhancement levels are sufficient to protect against the ebbs and flows of default losses among underlying credits. Given that many structured finance defaults have been originator- and servicer-driven, we think that is a prime factor to focus upon.

CONCLUSION

After a preliminary discussion on SF default rates, we summarized S&P and Moody's results on structured finance rating migrations, material impairments, and loss given default. In Exhibit 7.1, we combined the two rating agencies' results in terms of constant annual default rates and recoveries. Finally, we addressed the cash flow stress testing and assessment of high-grade SF CDOs with collateral portfolios comprised of AA and AAA credits.

CHAPTER 8

Structured Finance Cash Flow CDOs

Structured finance CDO (SF CDO) deals have become an increasingly important part of a fast growing market. In 2005, SF CDOs comprised 41% of the $200 billion cash CDO origination. The deals are of two varieties—mezzanine structured finance paper (16% of total 2005 CDO origination) and high-grade structured finance deals (25% of total 2005 origination). Mezzanine deals employ primarily BBB and A rated collateral, while high-grade deals use mostly AA and AAA collateral. SF CDO deals have used almost the entire spectrum of structured finance products discussed in Chapters 5 and 6. The deals that contain large amounts of mortgage-related collateral tend to rely more heavily on subprime mortgages rather than prime and Alt A structures, as there is considerably more negative convexity in the latter.

In this chapter, we look at structured finance cash flow CDOs. Many investors consider structured finance cash flow CDOs to be very different from high-yield cash flow CDOs. In fact the cash flows deals are structured very similarly to corporate counterparts. We first look at the similarities and differences between cash flow deals backed by structured finance assets versus those supported by high-yield corporate assets. We showed in Chapter 7 that the default and recovery experience of the underlying structured finance collateral has been more favorable than its corporate counterpart. We will argue that by using the same criteria to rate all types of CDOs, rating agencies impose an extra burden on CDOs backed by structured finance collateral. Finally, we discuss several unique features of structured finance collateral and its implications for CDO structuring.

SF CDOs VERSUS HIGH-YIELD CDOs

There are many similarities between the cash flow CDOs backed by structured financial assets and those backed by high-yield assets. The reasons are:

1. They are structured similarly.
2. The rating methodology is similar.
3. Both share similar protections via overcollateralization and interest coverage tests.

However, there are minor differences that generally stem from the fact that the credit quality of a SF CDO is much higher than in a high-yield CDO, which permits lower equity levels in SF CDO structures. The two effects should offset, theoretically producing similar expected losses at each rating level.

Deal Structure

In a cash flow CDO, ability to service the rated notes is based on the interest and principal cash flows of portfolio assets. Both high-yield and SF CDO deals typically have a 5- to 10-year average life, and an 8- to 14-year expected maturity.

One small difference is that structured finance deals tend to have very long legal final maturities compared to high-yield deals. The legal final reflects the underlying legal final of the last cash flow in the portfolio. For example, the manager of a structured finance cash flow CDO deal done in mid-2005, with a 5-year revolving period, must be able to purchase a 30-year structured finance product at the end of the revolving period. That creates a 2040 legal final. By contrast, in a high-yield deal the longest securities that can be purchased are 12 to 14 years. This will be discussed further in this chapter when we look at extension risk.

Liability structure is very similar in all cash flow deals, regardless of the underlying assets. It consists of senior notes, mezzanine notes, and equity. If the underlying assets are fixed and the liabilities are floating, interest rate swaps are used in both cases. One major difference is that credit quality (average rating) of the structured finance assets tends to be considerably higher, which allows less equity in SF CDO structures than in high-yield CDO structures.

A typical 100% high-yield deal will have an average rating of B1 to B2, and equity will average 13% to 15% of the deal amount. By contrast, a typical mezzanine SF CDO deal will have average credit quality of Baa2, with equity averaging only 4% to 6% of the deal and a high-grade SF CDO deal will have equity averaging only 1% of the deal. This is shown in Exhibit 8.1.

There are more Aaa bonds in SF CDOs than in high-yield deals due to the better quality collateral. In a 100% high-yield bond deal containing Aaa, Baa, and unrated tranches, Aaa rated bonds will constitute 73% to 75% of the deal, equity will be 13% to 15%, with the remainder in Baa rated bonds. In a high-yield loan deal, Aaa rated bonds will be 75% to 80% of the deal, Baa rated bonds 10% to 15%, and equity 8% to 10%. In a mezzanine SF deal, Aaa rated bonds will be 78% to 83%, equity will be 5%, and mezzanine bonds will represent the remainder. In a high-grade deal, the Aaa rated bonds will be over 90% of the deal.

It should be noted that SF CDO deals generally have multiple classes of Aaa and mezzanine bonds. Most deals have a senior and a junior Aaa rated bond. In the mezzanine SF CDO structure, if the total size of the Aaa piece is 78% of the deal, the senior Aaa will comprise approximately 55% of the deal, and the junior Aaa will comprise 23% of the deal. In a high-grade deal, if the total size of the Aaa piece is 92% of the deal, the senior Aaa will comprise approximately 84% and the junior AAA 8%. There are generally AA, A, and BBB mezzanine bonds. In the mezzanine SF deals, the mezzanine bonds are about 18% of the deal, with a AA tranche of about 8% of the deal, while the A and BBB tranches will be about 5% apiece. In the high-grade deal, the mezzanine bonds are about 7% of the deal; the AA tranche will be about 4% of the deal, the A rated tranche will be about 2%, and the BBB rated tranche will be about 1%.

Another consequence of the higher credit quality on the SF CDO is that overcollateralization and interest coverage tests on the SF CDO are lower than on the high-yield deals. For example, in mezzanine SF CDO deals, subordinate overcollateralization triggers are in the range of 100 to 105, much lower than the 105 to 112 on CDOs backed by high-yield bonds. Again, this is a natural consequence of the higher quality of the underlying collateral and the lower equity requirements.

EXHIBIT 8.1 Liability Structure of Cash Flow Deals

	High-Yield Bond Deal	High-Yield Loan Deal	Mezzanine SF Deal	High-Grade SF Deal
Aaa	73–75	75–80	78–83	91–93
Mezzanine	10–14	10–15	13–16	6–8
Equity	13–15	8–10	4–6	1

While the basic structure of SF CDOs and corporate bond-backed CDOs are similar, there are six major areas in which the two types of CDOs differ:

- The default and severity experience of structured finance collateral is better than that of corporate bonds. The SF CDOs are given no credit for this.
- The diversity scores for structured finance collateral are lower than for corporate bond-backed deals. This requires extra subordination at each level.
- Loss curves for structured finance collateral are less front loaded than either high-yield losses or the losses assumed in the loss distribution tests.
- When a corporate bond defaults, it defaults. In structured finance collateral, tranches are susceptible to being "written down" in part. These bonds are eliminated from the overcollateralization (OC) tests and interest coverage (IC) tests, and are valued conservatively
- Mortgage related collateral exhibits negative convexity.
- The legal final on structured finance collateral is different from the average life of the securities, posing a unique set of extension risk considerations.

In the remainder of this chapter, we discuss the implications of each of the points above, and what it means to the CDO. It is important to realize that the first three differences relate to the rating methodology, and the last three differences relate to the unique features of structured finance collateral.

RATING AGENCIES ON STRUCTURED FINANCE CDOs

In the previous chapter, we showed that the ratings experience of structured finance collateral was superior to that of corporate debt. That is, CMBS and RMBS default rates average about half of corporate default rates. In the higher rating categories, CMBS and RMBS recovery rates are also significantly higher than corporates. Meanwhile the performance of ABS was ruined by high defaults in some subsectors, namely health care receivables, franchise loans, and manufactured housing. The poor performance of ABS and the superior performance of CMBS and RMBS average out such that on a default frequency and default severity basis, the default performance of structured finance assets compares favorably with that of corporates. Despite this more favorable experience, the rating agencies treat SF CDO collateral like equally rated corporate debt with respect to credit quality.[1]

Perhaps this conservatism is due to the short history of the structured finance market. However, we must also realize that the rating agencies seek to present their ratings as common measures of credit quality across the corporate, public, sovereign, structured finance debt markets, and even across different jurisdictions around the world. They could not market their opinions that way if they admitted, for example, that a structured single-A had the same credit quality as a corporate triple-A.

In any event, Moody's treats structured finance collateral as if it had the same combination of default probability and default severity potential as corporate debt. This means that SF CDO tranches benefit from the same protective credit enhancement requirements that are demanded on corporate debt collateral that has historically had higher default rates and greater default severity.

As we shall see, the rating agencies also tend to treat SF CDOs conservatively with respect to the assessment of their *collateral diversity* and response to *collateral distress*.

Collateral Diversity

The diversity of a CDO collateral pool is an important rating consideration and it bears directly on the amount of credit enhancement a CDO tranche must have to achieve a particular rating. Rating agency treatment of diversity in a SF CDO adds a conservative bias to their ratings of SF CDO tranches. Diversity refers to the *default correlation* of assets in the CDO's portfolio, or the propensity of CDO assets to default at the same time.

Suppose we know that each asset in a CDO's portfolio has a 10% probability of default over the lifetime of the CDO. Does that mean that exactly 10% of the portfolio will default, or does it mean that there is a 10% chance that 100% of the portfolio will default? In both scenarios, there is a 10% probability of default. But the first scenario illustrates extreme *negative* default correlation while the second displays extreme *positive* default correlation.

As seen by this example, positive default correlation creates wide swings in a portfolio's experienced default rate. In our example of extreme positive default correlation, 90% of the time no assets default and 10% of the time all assets default. The credit quality and rating consequences are obvious. If defaults are so correlated that 10% of the time the whole portfolio defaults, then credit enhancement will have to

---

[1] Jeremy Gluck and Helen Remeza, *Moody's Approach to Rating Multisector CDOs*, Moody's Investors Service, September 15, 2000.

address the significant probability that the entire portfolio will default. At the other extreme, if defaults are so negatively correlated that 10% and only 10% of the portfolio will ever default, the CDO only has to protect against the 10% defaults that are bound to occur.

So in a rational rating world, CDO portfolios with high positive default correlation must have extra credit enhancement against their inbred potential for very high defaults. With respect to the diversity of SF CDOs, the rating agencies hold the view that defaults among structured finance tranches are *more* correlated than corporate defaults.

The magic and mysteries of default correlation, and the methods used by the rating agencies to assess it in SF CDO portfolios, are discussed in other chapters of this book. For our purposes here, it is important to understand that not only are the classes of structured finance collateral assumed to be more correlated than in the corporate world, but there are fewer types of collateral. This tends to produce deals with much lower diversity scores. For example, in the corporate world, the typical Moody's diversity score (the method Moody's uses to quantify a portfolio's diversity) is usually a minimum of 40 to 50 for a corporate debt-backed portfolio. For a SF CDO, the diversity score is typically a minimum of 10 to 20.

The lower diversity score on SF CDOs raises the required credit enhancement, perhaps by as much as 40%. But typically the weighted average rating factor (WARF) for a SF CDO is lower (the average rating quality of the SF CDO assets is higher) than for a corporate investment grade bond-backed CDO. A SF CDO with a WARF of 400 to 500 might require 4% equity while an investment grade bond-backed CDO with a WARF of 600 might require only 3% equity. And, do not forget, the structured finance assets have higher credit spreads and historically lower default rates than corporate debt. The higher required equity comes from the rating agency's conservative view of structured finance diversity.

Is Greater Diversity Necessarily a Good Thing?

As a result of a methodology which rewards diversity, many CDOs have tried to increase their diversity score by adding smaller and newer subsectors of the ABS market. In fact, most of the downgrades among SF CDOs have related to the reach for diversity.

The lowest Diversity Score (D-score) structured finance portfolios, from 8 to 10, are comprised of CMBS and REITs. Higher diversity SF CDOs, scoring from 10 to 12, obtain their extra D-score by adding RMBS to CMBS and REITS. Finally, the highest diversity, from 15 to 20, is obtained by adding other types of structured finance assets to RMBS and CMBS assets.

In order to make the point that the highest diversity score CDOs are the most likely to experience problems, we introduce a score developed by UBS: Past and Predicted Par Loss Score, This score, simply referred to as the *P-scores*, measures the change in CDO collateral par that has already occurred and the change in CDO collateral par that is expected to occur. Clearly, if a CDO has suffered a 10% diminution of collateral asset par, it has 10% less collateral par to support the debt tranches. If the default probability of the remaining collateral asset portfolio has risen 10%, the CDO is expected over the course of its life to lose another 10% of collateral par.

Mathematically, the P-score is

$$\text{P-score} = [1 - ((1 - \text{Par Deterioration}) \times (1 - \text{WARF Deterioration}))]$$

Thus, if collateral par has been reduced 10% and the remaining par has a 10% greater change of defaulting then

$$\text{P-score} = [1 - ((1 - 0.1) \times (1 - 0.1))] = 19$$

The higher the P-score, the greater the change in par that has already occurred and is predicted to occur. Negative P-scores mean change for the better; that is, the CDO either has more collateral par, better-rated collateral or both. This simple measure turns out to be a good indicator of the economic health of a CDO.

We have found that more diverse SF CDOs experienced a wider dispersion of P-scores. Exhibit 8.2 shows for each of the deals issued in 2000 and 2001 where the P-score stood at the end of 2002. Note that every deal with a low D-score also has a low P-score (and low P-scores are good). Most high D-score SF CDOs also had low P-scores. However, high P-scores (which are bad) are found only in SF CDOs with high D-scores.

The unavoidable conclusion from this analysis is that straying away from the three traditional SF CDO assets can (but need not) lead to higher levels of asset collateral defaults and downgrades. In fact, all the SF CDOs that have performed poorly had the same problem—they purchased "off-the-run" structured finance securitizations such as mutual fund fees, franchise loans, aircraft loans, and manufactured housing to gain "points" for diversity and to get more spread. These assets have experienced defaults and rate downgrades greatly out of line with other equally rated structured finance assets. This does not mean deals with "off-the-run assets" should be avoided. Rather, CDO investors should embrace, not penalize low diversity deals. And CDO investors need to look at a cash structured finance portfolio and make sure that the portfolio manager has a well thought out reason for including off-the-run assets, and is not just reaching for yield and diversity.

EXHIBIT 8.2   D-Score versus P-Scores

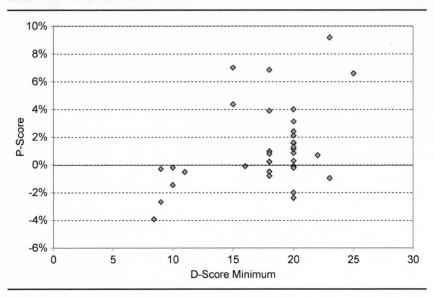

Timing of Credit Losses

Let us look at the disadvantage created by the rating agencies' assumptions regarding the timing of credit losses. Briefly, the rating agencies utilize a loss distribution curve more front loaded than historical loss experience on structured finance collateral would suggest. Losses on ABS, RMBS, and CMBS bonds have different distributions than those on investment-grade and high-yield corporates. Yet, the same loss distribution tests are applied to all CDO collateral categories. And while the approach may be appropriate for high-yield and other types of CDOs, it certainly penalizes SF CDO transactions.

Moody's Approach

As explained in Chapter 2, Moody's approach to rating cash flow CDOs involves several steps. These include developing a diversity score; calculating a weighted average rating factor; using the binomial distribution to determine the probability of a specific number of defaults; and finally, calculating the impact of those defaults on bonds within the CDO structure. One element needed to calculate that impact is a distribution of defaults and losses across time. It is this distribution defaults and losses that we are addressing.

Moody's stresses the tranches via the six different loss distributions shown in Exhibit 2.9 of Chapter 2, and a tranche must pass each test.

The agency's basic approach assumes 50% of the losses will occur at a single point in time, and that remaining losses are evenly distributed over a 5-year period. This single 50% loss is assumed to occur at a different point in each of the six tests. For example, Test 1 assumes that the single 50% loss occurs at the beginning of the deal. Tests 1, 2, and 3 are the hardest for SF CDO structures to pass and for that reason really determine ratings on the CDO tranches. In fact, actual SF CDO losses are more akin to those set up in Tests 4 and 5. If these latter two tests were the toughest criteria used by the rating agency, then a lower cost structure could be used for the SF CDO tranches. The result might be that some receive a higher rating because it is easier for an SF CDO tranche to pass Tests 4 and 5. A similar argument does not apply to corporate and high-yield CDOs; their losses are more front-loaded, and the general CDO rating approach (emphasizing diversity scores) is designed for those securities.

Structured Finance Collateral Default and Bond Loss Curves

We now show that typical loss curves for ABS and MBS collateral are less front-loaded than either high-yield losses or the losses assumed in Moody's loss distribution tests. To illustrate, Exhibit 8.3 shows default

EXHIBIT 8.3   SF CDO Collateral Default and Loss Curves (% occurring in each year)

	Defaults				Avg. Collateral Defaults	Avg. Collateral Losses	BBB SF Bond Losses	Spec.- Grade Corp. Losses
Year	MH	Jumbo WL	CMBS	Home Equities				
1	7	5	3	3	4.5	0.0	0.0	13.2
2	19	14	9	12	13.5	4.5	0.0	13.5
3	22	20	13	23	19.5	13.5	4.5	12.7
4	19	18	14	25	19.0	19.5	13.5	11.5
5	13	15	14	15	14.3	19.0	19.5	10.6
6	9	11	15	10	11.3	14.3	19.0	9.2
7	5	8	13	8	8.5	11.3	14.3	8.1
8	3	5	8	4	5.0	8.5	11.3	7.6
9	3	3	7	0	3.3	5.0	8.5	6.7
10	0	1	4	0	1.3	3.3	5.0	6.8
Total	100	100	100	100	100.0	—	—	—

curves for four types of collateral found frequently in SF CDOs.[2] This can be compared with the last column in Exhibit 8.3, which shows default timing curves on speculative-grade corporate bonds.

Defaults on mortgage-related collateral typically increase for several years, level off, and then decline. Peak defaults usually occur between Years 3 and 5. There are several reasons why there are few defaults in the first year or two. For example, in the residential sector, most home-owners cannot receive a loan unless they meet strict underwriting criteria. Once a homeowner passes that credit scrutiny, it typically takes a while for their financial position to deteriorate to the point where a default becomes a real possibility.

Also, when comparing loss curves in Exhibit 8.3, bear in mind that these only tell when losses occur, not their magnitudes. For example, in certain market environments, home equity deals can easily generate total losses of 4% to 5%, whereas jumbo whole loans produce losses of only 25 to 30 basis points. That is a ratio of 15 or 20 to 1. Of course, to offset those higher loss rates, home equity deals carry much greater credit enhancement in the form of excess spread, overcollateralization, and either subordinated bonds or monoline insurance.

As shown in Exhibit 8.3, defaults in the CMBS sector are distributed over a longer period than in residential loans, and peak defaults come a little later. The manufactured housing (MH) curve in Exhibit 8.3 is a little more front-loaded than other mortgage-related curves. Buyers of manufactured houses typically have less disposable income than site-built home buyers, and if financial difficulty (sickness, divorce, death, and the like) develops they are less able to maintain payments than the average homeowner. This means that manufactured housing losses occur somewhat faster than in other sectors.

We calculated an aggregate default curve from the individual curves presented in Exhibit 8.3. This involved taking a simple average of the four curves on the assumption that each type of collateral appears in CDO deals in roughly the same percentages. The resulting aggregate default curve is then converted into a loss curve by pushing each period's defaults forward one year.

In both the jumbo and home equity sectors, this is a good approximation of how long it takes to move a defaulted loan from foreclosure to liquidation. It admittedly can be longer in some states, and shorter in others. In the CMBS market, the time from default to liquidation can be longer than in the residential mortgage market (roughly 1.5 to 2 years). In con-

---

[2] The CMBS results are based on Howard Esaki, Steven L'Heureux, and Mark Synderman "Commercial Real Estate Defaults: An Update," *Real Estate Finance* 16 (Spring 1999), pp. 80–86.

trast, in manufactured housing and some other sectors that are often included in ABS CDOs, default-to-liquidation periods are shorter than one year. Hence, using a 1-year period for an overall average seems to be a good approximation. The collateral loss curve generated from this approach peaks in Years 4 and 5. The collateral default curve appears as column 5 in Exhibit 8.3 and the collateral loss curve appears as column 6.

Once a collateral loss curve is developed, the question remains of how these losses filter through into losses on the structured bonds. Excess spread, overcollateralization, and other subordinated bonds stand between collateral losses and the bonds that go into a CDO. This protective structuring clearly pushes the bond loss curve out further than the collateral loss curve.

Estimating a bond loss curve for each collateral type requires an enormous number of calculations across many scenarios. In lieu of doing this for the collateral types in our example, we illustrate by showing how long it would take a BBB home equity tranche to experience a loss of principal under various stress scenarios. We selected the BF1 (BBB) class from Saxon 2000–3. That deal had an original WAC of 11.36% and a WAM of 238 months. A loss curve is then used that would produce total cumulative losses of 4.5% over the life of the deal. This is in line with losses experienced on most home equity deals originated today. Collateral characteristics are quite similar to loans created over the several prior years at the time of the analysis, which, on average, have total losses trending towards the 4% to 5% level. We distributed the losses using the standard loss curve we use for stressing home equity bonds. This is a more conservative (i.e., more front-loaded) distribution than the one used in Exhibit 8.3.

The BBB bond did not get hit until losses reached 250% of the base loss curve (i.e., until cumulative losses reached 11.25%), and that initial hit did not occur until 53 months (4.4 years). Once the peak loss period was past, excess spread became positive again and the bond recovered its lost principal. When the loss curve was raised to 300% of the base loss curve (i.e., total cumulative losses reached 13.5%) the BBB bond was hit at 37 months (3.1 years). For a deal to experience losses three times the "normal" curve, the economy must experience an extreme recession. That is very low probability event.

This exercise suggests that actual bond losses, as opposed to collateral loses, extend from around three years out to five or six years, with very few losses occurring in Years 1 or 2.

While a full distribution of bond losses has not been developed here, we believe a conservative approach is to simply move the collateral loss curve in Exhibit 8.3 forward one year to represent a bond loss curve. This gives no bond losses in Years 1 and 2 and very few in Year 3, which agrees with our BBB bond example and our understanding of how infrequently structured BBB bonds experience problems in the first several years.

It is important to realize that all three of the points we have made so far—the fact that structured finance collateral experiences less defaults and lower default severity for any given rating level, diversity scores on the deals are lower, and defaults on structured finance collateral are more back loaded—all relate to the rating methodology. In particular, the ratings for SF CDOs deals have been more conservative than for high-yield bond deals.

We now turn our attention to the unique features of SF CDO collateral—defining "distress," extension risk and negative convexity.

Defining Distress for SF CDO Collateral

The identification of a collateral default in a SF CDO also adds a conservative feature to SF CDOs. Identifying a corporate debt default in a corporate debt-backed CDO is usually pretty straightforward. The issuer is typically in bankruptcy or has missed an interest or principal payment. When corporate debt defaults in a corporate debt-backed CDO, its par is taken out of overcollateralization tests and its coupon is taken out of interest coverage tests. This may cause the corporate-backed CDO to withhold cash flow from one or more subordinated tranches and instead pay down its most senior tranche. This protective measure lowers leverage and protects senior debt tranches.

Unlike corporate debt collateral, structured finance tranches are susceptible to being "written down" in part as well as in whole. This happens as losses have occurred in the underlying assets of the structured finance collateral pool and those losses are allocated to specific deal tranches. Such a written down tranche in a SF CDO would be penalized in the calculation of the SF CDO's overcollateralization and interest coverage tests. First, the written down portion of the tranche and its associate interest are eliminated for the SF CDO's overcollateralization and interest coverage tests. But second, the unwritten down portion of the structured security is multiplied by the lower of market value or a conservative rating agency recovery assumption in the tests. Redirection of cash flow to the senior SF CDO tranche might then occur. This treatment is conservative because, unlike a defaulted corporate bond, the unwritten down structured finance tranche is still performing. The structured security might also be written back up over time because of the effects of excess spread in the structured finance transaction.

STRUCTURED FINANCE ASSETS' NEGATIVE CONVEXITY

Thus far, we have talked about similarities in determining expected defaults among rating methodologies. There is still a nagging concern that we missed something. It is the property of negative convexity, which is potentially a problem for structured finance assets but not for high-yield assets. In most discussions of structured finance products, negative convexity is front and center.[3] Should investors in SF CDOs be concerned with negative convexity?

There is no reason for concern. First there are no structured finance cash flow deals to date that employ more than 50% residential MBS assets. As indicated at the outset of this chapter, most of the assets used for these deals are CMBS, ABS, or REIT debt. As explained when we reviewed CMBS in Chapter 5, these assets have excellent call protection, and most have yield maintenance provisions, which make investors whole in the event of early redemption. Similarly, REIT debt is typically either a noncall bullet security or call-protected by yield maintenance provisions. ABS backed by residential mortgages such as home equity loans and manufactured housing have much less negative convexity than residential mortgage paper.

Moreover, subordinated residential mortgage paper tends to have better call protection than does the underlying collateral. Subordinated mortgage paper typically has a 5-year lockout and a shifting interest structure for the next five years. This paper does not actually receive a pro rata share of prepayments until Year 10.

Finally, investors should realize that high-yield bonds and loans backing CDOs do not have absolute call protection. High-yield bonds with a 10-year maturity typically have a lockout for 3 to 5 years, and then are callable at a premium, which declines over time. By Year 7, the paper is typically callable at par. Loans are generally floating rate, with little call protection. If spreads narrow, borrowers often refinance.

EXTENSION RISK

Extension risk often arises in discussing SF CDOs. SF CDOs might have a "legal final" maturity of 30 years but an "expected final" maturity of

---

[3] In an option-free bond or a bond whose call option value has very little value, the price performance of a bond is such that for a large change in interest rates, the price appreciation is greater than the price depreciation. For example, for a 100 basis point change in interest rates, the price appreciation might be 20% while the price decline might be only 14%. A bond that exhibits this characteristic is said to exhibit "positive convexity." A bond that exhibits a characteristic whereby for a large change in interest rates the gain is less than the loss is said to be "negatively convex." A concern of an investor when acquiring a bond that exhibits negative convexity is that when interest rates decline, the price performance of that bond will be inferior to that of an otherwise similar duration bond that exhibits positive convexity.

10 or 12 years. The earlier maturity is based on the successful auction of assets in the SF CDO portfolio at the expected final date. If proceeds from the sale of SF CDO assets at the expected final date would not be enough to repay all outstanding debt tranches, no sale is made, the assets are retained, and the SF CDO continues on. Auctions are held every three to six months until aggregate bids on the SF CDO's assets are enough to retire all outstanding debt tranches.

Extension risk comes from the possibility that successive auctions fail to attract high enough bids. Even though almost all SF CDO tranches are floating rate instruments, many investors have maturity restrictions or cash flow considerations, so they view any extension of their investment beyond the expected maturity as a bad thing.

Extension Risk in Perspective

So what are the chances an SF CDO will extend, and how bad can it be? We will base our observations on a hypothetical, but broadly characteristic, CDO. Suppose that two-thirds of a SF CDO portfolio is made up of assets that can extend and that SF CDO tranches are scheduled to mature at 10 years. Given very slow prepayment rates, where actual prepayments are half that of pricing prepayment speeds, and rating agency expected default rates on underlying assets, the AAA tranche might be paid down to 38% of its original balance at year 10. Given that the AAA tranche was originally 82% of the SF CDO's capital structure, over half of the CDO's debt tranche principal has been amortized.

The effect of this is to decrease equity's leverage in the transaction. Equity's share of the SF CDO's capital structure would double in this scenario from 4% to 8%. This would mean that the hurdle for retiring the SF CDO's debt tranches is an average asset price of 92%. Note that at this point, the remaining weighted average life of the SF CDO's assets is quite short, so it is more likely the auction is successful.

But if a clearing price is never reached on the serial auctions, the AAA tranche will still completely retire in 16 years under these assumptions. And its average life extends only one and a half years, from eight years to nine and a half years. Not that all investors would see extension as a bad thing. After the expected final maturity, if the auction fails to clear, SF CDO debt tranches coupons are often increased or "stepped up." Some triple-A tranches step up, often 50 basis points. Almost all subordinated tranches step up, usually by considerably more than 50 basis points.

Extension Risk versus Default Risk

Many investors confuse default risk and extension risk. It is clear that severely poor collateral performance will cause the SF CDO to fail its auction test and extend. But extension due to default is not a phenomena limited to SF CDOs. Any security, whether a corporate bond or loan or corporate debt-backed CDO, will probably extend if it defaults. In the corporate debt world, a default often involves a debt restructuring, which leads to the issuance of a replacement security that might incorporate a lower coupon, lower par, and a longer maturity.

For the reasons enumerated above, SF CDO tranches are less likely to default than corporate debt and corporate-backed CDOs. Also, a defaulted SF CDO tranche is likely to recover more than corporate debt. So with respect to default risk or extension risk associated with default risk, an SF CDO tranche is a happier story than corporate debt or corporate debt-backed CDOs. The unique risk of extension in a SF CDO, as distinct from default risk, is limited to the extension risk of an otherwise healthy security.

And the extension of a SF CDO tranche can be positive. This is because at the end of the life of the corporate bond-backed CDO, the asset manager is required to sell the collateral for whatever he or she can get. In the SF CDO, the asset manager is able to hold the collateral if he or she thinks higher recoveries are likely. Meanwhile, the SF CDO investor always has the option of selling the extended offending tranche. Thus, the asset manager is no worse off and probably better off than in the case of the corporate bond-backed CDO.

CONCLUSION

Many investors view CDOs backed by structured finance asset collateral as completely different in character from CDOs backed by high-yield collateral. In fact, the CDO structures are similar and the rating methodology is very similar. However, there are a number of differences in the underlying collateral which impact the CDO structure and performance:

- The mezzanine SF CDO has a higher WARF than high-yield bond deals. The high-grade SF CDO has a much higher WARF than high-yield bond deals. This means that these CDOs have less equity and more AAA tranches than deals with corporate bonds with a lower WARF.
- The rating agencies are conservative in their rating of SF CDOs for a number of reasons: (1) structured finance collateral has less defaults at any given rating level than equivalently rated corporate debt; (2) the loss curves on structured finance collateral are more back-loaded than their corporate bond counterparts, and the front-loaded stress tests are

the same; and (3) the rating agencies make it very hard to achieve high diversity scores in SF CDO deals. The diversity scores on SF CDO deals are much lower than corporate deals. This means, all things being equal, more equity is necessary for any given WARF score.

■ Structured finance collateral can be written down "in part." The methodology for dealing with this is very conservative.

■ Structured finance collateral has long legal final maturities and negative convexity. These features must be evaluated within the deal structure. The step-up features if the deals experience extension risk are very favorable for debt holders, substantially mitigating the risk. The amount of very negatively convex RMBS collateral in a given deal is very limited.

Other Types of Cash CDOs

Emerging Market CDOs

Many portfolio managers have invested a substantial amount of time and energy in understanding CDO structures. Most have become comfortable with CDO deals backed by both structured finance collateral and high-yield bank loans. However, these same portfolio managers are still quite uneasy about any CDO backed primarily by sovereign emerging markets bonds, as they believe that all emerging market debt is tainted by high default experience.

In this chapter, we shed some light on the differences that matter between emerging markets and high-yield deals. The picture that "emerges" (pun intended!) may surprise you—positively, that is—for the following reasons:

- There have actually been few defaults on U.S. dollar denominated sovereign Emerging Market (EM) bonds. The negative bias of many investors against EM CDOs is because they do not fully appreciate the differences between EM sovereign bank loans and EM sovereign bonds.
- Rating agencies are far more conservative in their assumptions when rating emerging markets deals than in rating high-yield deals, as performance data on EM bonds is far more limited. So there is an extra credit cushion already built into comparable credit levels.
- EM CDOs generally provide much greater structural protection, as the average portfolio credit quality is higher, resulting in a lower probability of default on the underlying portfolio. Subordination on EM deals is also much higher, hence the equity itself is much less leveraged.

We will examine each of these points in turn and find that EM CDOs are no more risky than high-yield CDOs, and the rated debt often yields much more.

EM SOVEREIGN BOND DEFAULTS

EM debt has developed a bad rap. This tainted reputation stems from the fact that many potential investors do not distinguish between EM sovereign foreign currency bank loans and sovereign foreign currency bonds. In fact, the historical record on EM sovereign foreign currency bonds is very favorable. Sovereigns are far more likely to default on foreign currency bank loans than on foreign currency bond debt.

Let us look at the asset record, compiled in a Standard & Poor's study released in September 2004, which covers both public and private debt.[1] Exhibit 9.1 shows that out of a universe of 202 sovereign issuers, 12.4% of the issuers are currently in default. This includes defaults on foreign currency debt (both bank loans and bonds) as well as on local currency debt. Note that 11.9% of the issuers are in default within the category of total foreign currency debt, which includes both bank loans and bonds. But a separate break-out of just the sovereign foreign currency bonds indicates that most of these issuers are in default only on their bank loans. In fact, Column (6) of Exhibit 9.1 shows that in 2004 only 1.5% of the issuers were in default on their foreign currency bonds! Note that the 1.5% default on foreign currency bonds is even lower than the 2.0% default on local currency debt.

This 1.5% default rate amounts to only five issuers out of 2002 sovereign borrowers (issuers).

Cumulatively, between 1975 and 2004, Standard and Poor's has identified a total of 78 issuers (41.5% of all sovereigns) that defaulted on their foreign currency bond and bank loans. (This constitutes a much smaller percent of all foreign currency debt in default.) Defaults usually took the form of late payments of principal and/or interest on bank loans. By contrast, only 17 issuers defaulted on foreign currency bonds in that same period. In most of these cases, the defaulted bonds had been issued by smaller countries which had little total debt outstanding. The bonds that the countries defaulted on tended to be held by banks, rather than being public issues held by a broad cross sector of investors.

---

[1] See David T. Beers, "Sovereign Defaults Set to Fall Again in 2005," *Standard & Poor's Credit Week* (September 28, 2004), pp. 11–25.

EXHIBIT 9.1 Sovereign Default Rates

Year	Number of Issuers	(Percent of All Sovereign Issuers)				
		All Issuers in Default	New Issuers in Default	All Foreign Currency Debt[a]	Foreign Currency Bonds	Local Currency Debt[a]
1975	164	2.4	1.2	1.2	0.6	1.2
1976	165	3.0	1.2	2.4	0.6	1.2
1977	166	2.4	0.0	1.8	0.6	0.6
1978	169	4.7	2.4	4.1	0.6	0.6
1979	173	6.4	2.3	5.8	0.6	1.7
1980	174	6.9	2.3	5.7	0.6	1.1
1981	176	10.8	6.8	9.7	0.0	1.1
1982	176	16.5	6.3	15.3	0.0	2.3
1983	177	24.9	9.6	23.7	0.0	1.1
1984	178	24.7	1.1	23.6	0.6	1.7
1985	178	25.3	2.8	24.7	0.6	1.1
1986	179	28.5	5.6	27.9	0.6	1.7
1987	179	30.7	3.4	29.1	1.1	2.2
1988	179	30.2	1.7	29.6	1.1	1.1
1989	179	30.2	1.7	29.1	2.2	1.7
1990	178	30.9	2.2	29.8	1.1	2.8
1991	198	27.3	3.0	26.3	1.0	2.0
1992	198	29.3	3.5	28.8	1.5	1.0
1993	200	27.0	0.5	26.5	1.0	1.5
1994	201	24.9	0.5	24.4	1.0	1.5
1995	201	23.4	1.5	21.9	1.0	2.5
1996	201	22.9	1.5	19.9	1.0	3.0
1997	201	17.9	1.5	15.4	1.0	2.5
1998	201	16.9	1.5	14.9	2.0	3.5
1999	201	14.9	1.5	13.4	2.0	3.5
2000	201	15.4	1.5	13.9	2.0	2.5
2001	201	13.4	0.5	12.4	1.0	1.5
2002	202	14.4	2.0	13.9	2.0	2.0
2003	202	13.4	1.5	12.9	2.0	2.0
2004[b]	202	12.4	0.0	11.9	1.5	2.0

[a] Bank debt & bonds.
[b] Through third quarter.
Source: David T. Beers, "Sovereign Defaults Set to Fall Again in 2005," *Standard & Poor's Credit Week* (September 28, 2004), pp. 11–25.

This has been independently confirmed in a 1995 study by Moody's rating service. The Moody's study noted that "a review of worldwide sovereign default experience since World War II shows that when sovereign nations have defaulted on any of their foreign currency obligations . . . they have been more likely to default on bank loans than on sovereign bonds or notes."[2]

WHY THE BETTER TRACK RECORD?

There are four reasons that EM sovereign bonds have a better track record than sovereign bank loans. First, there is a strong disincentive for a sovereign to default on foreign currency bonds: it will restrict capital market access going forward. The consequences of defaulting on (or rescheduling) bank loans has been more predictable, and far less detrimental to a nation's interest than defaulting on its bonds. Defaulting on bonds could essentially bar a country from the international capital markets for a considerable period of time and will result in much higher borrowing costs when that country is finally able to re-enter the market. Most of the developing nations depend on external financing for their growth, and hampering access to capital markets could sacrifice medium-term growth.

Second, more sovereigns have access to cross-border bank financing than have access to bond issuance in the international capital markets. International bond markets have been receptive to issuance by speculative grade rated sovereign credits since the early 1990s. But relative credit sanity has prevailed, as there have been barriers to entry by sovereigns of less credit quality, notably those from sub-Saharan Africa.

Third, it is far easier to renegotiate debt held by a few banking institutions rather than a bond issuance held by large numbers of international investors. For one, identification of creditors in advance is not always easy. By definition, there are a large number of creditors, some of which may have relatively small holdings. All of which makes restructuring more complex. Also, any one of even the smallest creditors can potentially bring legal proceedings against an issuer in a number of jurisdictions, depending on the security's documentation. The possibility of asset attachments is greater, simply because of the number of potential court cases.

The fourth and final major difference between bank loans and bond debt is that banks have multifaceted relationships with borrowers, and usually receive sizeable fees for a variety of services. Banks often keep

---

[2] Vincent Truglia, David Levey, and Christopher Mahoney, *Sovereign Risk: Bank Deposits Versus Bonds*, Moody's Investors Service, Global Credit Research (October 1995).

their long-term relationship with the borrower in perspective when agreeing to reschedule. Bondholders are not relationship-driven, and there are no business consequences for the bondholders in trying to extract the last possible dollar. The net result is this: Sovereign default rates on bonds are much lower than on bank loans. Unfortunately, many investors do not distinguish between the two and keep looking at sovereign debt as a homogeneous category, which clearly, it is not.

CDO RATING DIFFERENCES: EM VERSUS HIGH YIELD

The rating methodology for cash flow CDOs involves looking at the expected loss on the various tranches under various default scenarios, and probability weighting the results. This in turn requires making assumptions on how diversified the collateral is, how likely it is to default, and how much will be recovered if any default occurs. It is much harder for the rating agencies to feel comfortable with the parameters that they are using for EM bonds than U.S. high-yield bonds.

First, consider EM sovereign debt. Default rate statistics on EM sovereign bonds are very limited. Moreover, EM economies are subject to greater economic instability than those of more developed countries. Corporate debt in EM countries is even more problematic for the rating agencies. Clearly, there is generally less publicly available information about companies in EM countries than about issuers in developed countries. Moreover, financial reporting in many foreign countries is often not subject to uniform reporting and disclosure requirements. Finally and most importantly, the actions of local governments are far more likely to affect the ability or willingness of EM corporates to service their debt.

Given the issues that were mentioned above, the rating agencies react by rating EM assets in a more conservative manner than other collateral. As a result, additional levels of credit protection are built into EM CDOs beyond that which is structured into high-yield CDOs. We now review some major differences in those assumptions.

Recovery Rates

The rating agencies typically assume 30% recovery rates for high-yield debt and 50% on bank loans. For sovereign debt, Moody's assumes that base case recovery rates are 30% of the market value, or 25% of par, whichever is lower. For EM corporate debt, Moody's assumes that recovery rates are 20% of market value (15% of par value) if the issuer is domiciled in an investment grade country, and 15% of market value (10% of par value) if the issuer is domiciled in a noninvestment-grade country. Bonds of countries that face unusually adverse political or economic conditions are treated as having a lower recovery rate, which in some cases, can be as low as zero.

In point of fact, historical recovery rates on sovereign bonds have proved far more favorable. A September 1998 Standard and Poor's study showed that since 1975, the recovery rate on foreign currency bonds has been around 75%.[3] It was higher in the majority of cases in which the defaults were cured quickly though the issuance of new debt. It was lower on bonds that remained in default for longer periods of time. Even for bonds that remained in default for longer periods, most of the recovery rates were just under 50%—far higher than the recovery assumptions made by the rating agencies. The 75% overall recovery rate on sovereign foreign currency bonds is well above the 60% recovery rate on foreign currency bank loans.

Moreover, even though the rating agencies are more generous in the recovery rates they assume for U.S. high-yield borrowers than for sovereign borrowers, actual recovery rates for sovereign borrowers have been higher. A Moody's study showed that the recovery rates on senior unsecured U.S. corporate debt in the 1977–1998 period average 51.31%.[4] Compare this with the 75% recovery rate on the sovereign bonds.

Diversity Scores

Each rating agency has its own set of tools for measuring the diversity of underlying collateral. Moody's methodology has become the industry standard. This treatment reduces the pool of assets to a set of homogenous, uncorrelated assets. For CDOs backed by high-yield or bank loans, a diversity score is calculated by dividing the bonds into 1 of 33 industry groupings, and each industry group is assumed to be uncorrelated.

Assumptions are more conservative for EM bonds, reflecting rating agency fears of "contagion." Countries that carry an investment-grade sovereign rating from Moody's are each treated as a separate industry. Bonds from noninvestment-grade EM issuers are grouped into six geographic regions. These are Latin America, the Caribbean, Eastern Europe, Africa, East Asia, and West Asia. The latter includes the Middle East. Each region constitutes a single "industry." All bonds from a region, regardless of the industry they represent, are taken as part of the same group. Thus, the value of including corporate EM borrowers, which

---

[3] See David T. Beers, *Sovereign Defaults Continue to Decline*, Standard and Poor's (September 1998).
[4] C. Keenan, Igor Shtogrin, and Jorge Sobehart, *Historical Default Rates of Corporate Bond Issuers, 1920–1998*, Moody's Investors Service (January 1999).

would customarily be seen as providing greater diversity and reduced risk from that diversification, is discounted entirely. In point of fact, many EM deals include up to 20% of the portfolio in corporate form.

For all regions except Latin America, the diversity score is the standard table used by Moody's, which relies on the assumption that defaults on bonds in the same region or industry have a correlation coefficient of approximately 30%. This is shown in the first two columns of Exhibit 9.2. For example, if there were equal amounts of debt from each of four Caribbean countries, the diversity score is 2.3. That is, the deal would be credited as if there were 2.3 uncorrelated assets. For Latin American it is assumed the correlation is about 60%, and the diversity score is shown in the third column of Exhibit 9.2. If there were four Latin American issuers, the diversity score would be 1.65. Thus, combining four Caribbean issuers and four Latin American issuers in equal amounts would "count" as 3.95 uncorrelated issuers.

To be even more conservative, all bonds from a particular EM country are taken as constituting one issue. Essentially, 100% correlation is assumed within each country. In effect, EM collateral does not receive diversity score "credit" for having multiple corporate issuers or industries. Thus, if one compares the diversity score on a pool of 100% emerging markets collateral with a pool of U.S. high-yield assets with similar industry diversification, the EM collateral would have a substantially lower diversity score.

EXHIBIT 9.2 Moody's Diversity Score Table for CDOs

Number of Companies (Regions)	Diversity Score for Non-Latin America	Diversity Score for Latin America[a]
1.0	1.00	1.00
1.5	1.20	1.10
2.0	1.50	1.25
2.5	1.80	1.40
3.0	2.00	1.50
3.5	2.20	1.60
4.0	2.30	1.65
4.5	2.50	1.75
5.0	2.70	1.85
5.5	2.80	1.90
6.0	3.00	2.00

[a] Diversity = 1 + (Standard diversity score − 1) × 0.5
Source: Moody's Investors Service.

Structural Protections

We have thus far focused on how Moody's deals with limited historical experience (by making more conservative assumptions). In practice, these more conservative assumptions mean several forms of additional built-in protection for the CDO buyer. First, the average collateral credit quality is higher on a EM CDO than on a high-yield CDO. Second, subordination levels are also generally higher on an EM CDO than on a high-yield CDO.

Higher Average Credit Quality

The conservative approach used by Moody's means that average collateral credit quality of an EM CDO deal is much higher than on a high-yield CDO. That is, CDO managers will generally choose to include higher credit quality bonds to compensate for the lower diversity scores and the more stringent recovery assumptions. Most EM deals have average credit qualities of Ba2 or Ba3. By contrast, most high-yield deals have an average credit quality of B1 or B2.

This difference is highly significant, as shown in Exhibit 9.3. The exhibit shows Moody's data for the average cumulative default rates by letter rating after 10 years. This groups corporate bonds with a given initial rating, and tracks those bonds through time. Data for the period

EXHIBIT 9.3   Cumulative Default Rates After 10 Years as a Function of Credit Quality, 1920–2004

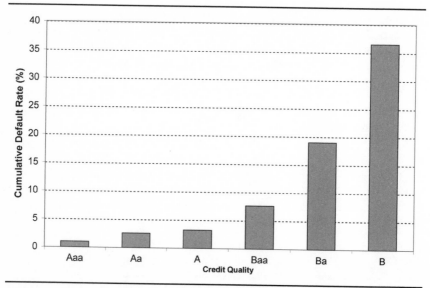

Source: Moody's Investors Service.

1920 to 2004 are included. The exhibit is used to highlight cumulative default rates after 10 years, as that roughly corresponds to the average lives of CDO deals. The findings show that default rates tend to rise exponentially as credit letter ratings fall. Of the bonds that started out life with a Baa rating, 7.63% had defaulted by the end of 10 years. Bonds with an initial rating of Ba had a cumulative default rate of 19.0%, while bonds initially rated B had a cumulative default of 36.51%. While numbers on sovereign debt are unavailable, the results are indicative that higher rated bonds actually default much less than do their lower-rated brethren. Bottom line: The higher initial portfolio quality on sovereign EM CDOs is highly significant.

Moreover, actual EM portfolio quality may be slightly higher than even that indicated by the overall rating. EM corporate bonds (generally 5% to 20% of the deal) can generally receive a rating no higher than the country in which it is based.[5] This is called the "sovereign ceiling." Thus, if a company is rated Aa2 based on "standalone" fundamentals, but is based in a country rated Ba2, the company itself can generally only receive that same Ba2 rating. This same methodology and rating effect is reflected throughout the overall portfolio.

More Subordination

The more conservative rating methodology also means that the rating agencies require higher subordination levels. In particular, equity tranches are usually much larger on EM deals than in high-yield deals. Exhibit 9.4 shows a representative high-yield deal versus a representative sovereign EM deal, both brought to market at approximately the same time. Note that the equity tranche is 7.9% on the high-yield deal versus 18% on the EM deal. More generally, the investment grade bonds receive much more protection on the EM deal than they do on the high-yield deal. In the EM deal, 22.2% of the deal is subordinated to the investment grade bonds, on the high-yield deal only 11.9% is subordinated.

The yields for each tranche are generally higher on the EM CDO than for the corresponding tranche on the high-yield CDO, in spite of the fact that the rating is as high or higher on the EM debt. The AAA rated bond on the EM deal may be priced at 68 discounted margin (DM), versus 57 DM on a simultaneously priced high-yield deal. The A

---

[5] There have been a few CDOs backed primarily by Asian corporate bonds. These CDOs are "story bonds" driven by local investors, and have taken advantage of brief "windows of opportunity." This chapter focuses on CDOs backed by diversified sovereign EM bonds. In practice, the rating agencies criteria is such that it has never been economic to include more than 20% EM corporate bonds in a sovereign EM deal.

EXHIBIT 9.4 Comparison of Emerging Market and High-Yield Deal Structure

Class	Ratings Moody's/S&P/D&P	Amount ($m)	Percent of Deal	Percent Sub	Current Pricing Info
Representative Emerging Market Deal					
A1	Aaa/AAA/NR	163.00	68.6%	31.4%	+68 DM
A2	A2/A/NR	22.00	9.3%	22.2%	+250/10yr Trsy
Mezz.	Ba1/NR/NR	10.00	4.2%	18.0%	+800/10yr Trsy
Equity	NR	42.74	18.0%	—	—
Total		237.74			
Representative High Yield Deal					
A1	Aaa/AAA/AAA	344.50	68.2%	31.8%	+57 DM
A2	NR/A–/A–	79.00	15.6%	16.2%	+225/10yr Trsy
Mezz. 1	NR/NR/BBB–	22.00	4.4%	11.8%	+360/10yr Trsy
Mezz. 2	NR/NR/BB–	20.00	4.0%	7.9%	+700/10yr Trsy
Equity	NR	39.79	7.9%	—	—
Total		505.29			

Note: DM = discounted margin, Trsy = Treasury note.

rated EM tranche is priced at +250/10-year Treasury, versus +225/10-year Treasury for a lower rated (A–) tranche of the high-yield deal. This translates into roughly a 50 basis point differential, as the credit quality differential is worth 25 basis points. The Ba1 mezzanine bond in the EM deal is priced at +800/10-year, versus +700/10-year for the BB– tranche of the high yield deal. Here the EM investor is receiving a 100 b.p. higher spread, as well as higher credit quality. The equity on the EM deal is the only exception to this. It may yield slightly less than on high-yield deals, as the equity is far less leveraged. The difference in the leverage can be seen by the fact that the EM equity is 18% of the deal versus 7.9% of the high-yield deal.

CONCLUSION

It is unfortunate that many investors may be reluctant to look at CDOs backed by EM collateral because of general misimpressions about the collateral. In this chapter, we have shown that there have been few actual defaults on sovereign EM bonds, which is the collateral used to back many EM CDOs. Many investors do not realize this, as they tend to clump together the experiences of both sovereign bank loans and sovereign bonds. Sovereign bank loans have clearly experienced more significant level of defaults. Moreover, when there is a default, the recovery rates are higher on the sovereign bonds than on the bank loans.

Realize that because of the limited history of sovereign bonds, the rating agencies are far more conservative in their ratings. They are particularly harsh in the assumptions they make about recoveries and on diversity characteristics. This more conservative rating methodology means that the average credit quality of bonds is higher in the EM deal. Finally, EM CDOs have more subordination. This extra structural protection is clearly not in the price. EM CDOs trade wider than high-yield CDOs for every rated tranche.

CHAPTER 10

Market Value CDOs

As explained in Chapter 1, there are cash flow and market value collateralized debt obligations. Many investors look suspiciously at the senior and mezzanine tranches of market value CDOs. Their concern is that this deal structure gives the manager the same latitude to manage a portfolio as a hedge fund manager. That view is wrong. It is based on a misconception about how market value CDOs are really structured and the protection they provide investors.

While market value deals are a distinct minority of CDOs, they are the structure of choice for certain types of collateral, where the cash flows are not predictable. It is very difficult to use unpredictable cash flows within the confines of a cash flow structure. Moreover, market value structures may also appeal to managers and equity buyers who like the greater trading flexibility inherent in these deals. Finally, market value transactions also facilitate the purchase of assets that mature beyond the life of the transaction, because the price volatility associated with the forced sale of these assets is explicitly considered.

This chapter provides an overview of the differences between cash flow and market value structures. It also examines the mechanics of market value CDOs, focusing on the advance rates (i.e., the percentage of a particular asset that may be issued as rated debt)—the key to protecting the debt holders. Then we look at some volatility numbers, which indicate how conservative the advance rates used by the rating agencies are.

CASH FLOW VERSUS MARKET VALUE DEALS

Cash flow deals are dependent on the ability of the collateral to generate sufficient current cash flow to pay interest and principal on rated notes issued by the CDO. The ratings are based on the effect of collateral defaults and recoveries on the receipt of timely interest and principal payments from the collateral. The manager focuses on controlling defaults and recoveries. Overcollateralization, as measured on the basis of the par value of the portfolio, provides important structural protection for the bondholders. If overcollateralization tests are not met, then cash flow is diverted from mezzanine and subordinated classes to pay down senior notes, or cash flow is trapped in a reserve account. There are no forced collateral liquidations.

Market value transactions depend upon the ability of the fund manager to maintain and improve the market value of the collateral. Funds to be used for liability principal payments are obtained from liquidating the collateral. Liability interest payments can be made from collateral interest receipts, as well as collateral liquidation proceeds. Ratings are based on collateral price volatility, liquidity, and market value. The manager focuses on maximizing total return while minimizing volatility.

Market overcollateralization tests are conducted regularly. These require that the market value of assets multiplied by the advance rates (discussed later) must be greater than or equal to debt outstanding. If that is not the case, collateral sales and liability redemptions may be required to bring overcollateralization ratios back into compliance. Market value deals have diversity, concentration and other portfolio constraints, albeit fewer than cash flow transactions. For example, in a cash flow transaction if there is a constraint that the asset manager may not hold more than $20 million par value in a particular industry, then if $15 million is currently in the portfolio and the manager would like to invest in $10 million more in that industry, that cannot be done. The manager may only invest in an additional $5 million. In contrast, in a market value transaction, the same manager facing a $20 million constraint could invest an additional $10 million, but when the overcollateralization test is performed, the manager would only receive credit for $20 million, not $25 million.

Exhibit 10.1 summarizes the salient features of cash flow versus market value deals.

THE RATING PROCESS

The credit enhancement for a market value CDO is the cushion between the current market value of the collateral and the face value of the structure's obligations. Within this framework, the collateral must normally be liquidated (either in whole or in part) if the ratio of the market value of the collateral to the debt obligations falls below a predetermined threshold. The liquidated collateral is used to pay down debt obligations, which brings the structure back into compliance.

EXHIBIT 10.1 Comparison of Cash Flow and Market Value CDOs

	Cash Flow Deal	Market Value Deal
Objective	Cash flow deals depend on the ability of the collateral to generate sufficient current cash to pay interest and principal on rated notes issued by the CDO.	Market value transactions depend on the ability of the fund manager to maintain and improve the market value of the collateral.
Rating focus	The ratings are based on the effect of collateral defaults and recoveries on the timely payment of interest and principal from the collateral	Ratings are based on collateral price volatility, liquidity, and market value.
Manager focus	Manager focuses on controlling defaults and recoveries.	Manager focuses on maximizing total return while minimizing volatility.
Structural protection	Overcollateralization is measured on the basis of the portfolio's par value. If overcollateralization tests are failed, then cash flow is diverted from the mezzanine and subordinated classes to pay down senior notes, or cash flow is trapped in a reserve account. There are no forced collateral liquidations.	Market value overcollateralization tests are conducted regularly. The market value of assets multiplied by the advance rates must be greater than or equal to the debt outstanding;[a] otherwise collateral sales and liability redemptions may be required to bring overcollateralization ratios back into compliance.
Diversity and concentration limits	Very strict.	Substantial diversification is required. More is "encouraged" by the structure of advance rates.
Trading limitations	There are limitations on portfolio trading.	There is greater portfolio trading flexibility.
Collateral	Typical cash flow assets include structured finance assets (ABS, CMBS, RMBS) and bank loans.	Typical market value assets include assets eligible for inclusion in cash flow CDOs as well as distressed debt, equities, and convertible bonds.

[a] Advance rate is the percentage of the market value of a particular asset that may be issued as rated debt. Advance rates depend upon the price volatility and quality of price/return data and the liquidity of the assets. Assets with lower price volatility and greater liquidity are typically assigned higher advance rates.

The biggest risk in a market value transaction is a sudden decline in the value of the collateral pool. Thus, the rating agencies focus on the price volatility and liquidity of the assets that may be incorporated into these structures. Volatility and liquidity are reflected in a set of advance rates that are designed to provide a cushion against market risk, and represent adjustments to the value of each asset.

Let us first look at how a market value deal really works. We then take up the methodology used by rating agencies to determine the advance rate. Finally, we look at how conservative those advance rates are relative to the actual price volatility of these instruments.

Advance Rates and Overcollateralization Tests

A market value deal simply requires that the market value of the collateral times the advance rate (the adjustment to the value of the assets to provide a cushion against market risk) be greater than the par value of the liabilities. The rating agencies use a set of advance rates to determine how much rated debt can be issued against the market value of an asset.

Later we learn how advance rates are derived. For now, it important to understand how advance rates are used for the overcollateralization tests. A rating agency assigns an advance rating by asset type. Exhibits 10.2, 10.3, and 10.4 show the asset types used by Moody's, Fitch, and S&P, respectively.

EXHIBIT 10.2   Moody's Asset Types

High-yield bonds
High-yield loans
Distressed bonds
Distressed loans
Distressed equity

Source: Yvonne Fu Falcone and Jeremy Gluck, "Moody's Approach to Market-Value CDOs," Special Report, *Structured Finance* (April 8, 1998).

EXHIBIT 10.3   Fitch Asset Types

High-yield bank loans
BB high-yield bonds
Emerging market bonds
Equity
Distressed debt

Source: Market-Value CBO/CLO Rating Criteria, Fitch (June 1999).

EXHIBIT 10.4   S&P Asset Types

High-yield bond
Distressed bond
Emerging markets bond
Bank loan
Public equity

Source: Erkan Erturk and Soody Nelson, *Structured Market-Value Transactions: A Quantitative Enhancement Approach*, Standard & Poor's (August 1999).

For each asset type there is an advance rate based on the desired rating for the debt issued based on (1) the structure of the transaction and (2) the portfolio composition. For example, Exhibit 10.5 shows Moody's advance rates for a more detailed breakdown of asset type assuming the following:

1. There is only one tranche in the transaction (i.e., there is no subordination, so the only protection is from the advance rates).
2. There is only one asset type in the portfolio.
3. The diversification constraints are as follows:
   a. The maximum allowable investment in one issuer is 5%.
   b. The maximum allowable investment in any one industry is 20%.
   c. The least diversified portfolio consists of 20 issuers and 5 industries.

To see how to use the advance rates in Exhibit 10.5, suppose (1) a portfolio consists of performing high-yield bonds rated B and (2) the deal is carved only into a bond rated A2 and equity (i.e., there is only one rated tranche). As can be seen from Exhibit 10.5, Moody's advance rate would be 0.79. The market value of the deal times the advance rate (0.79 in this case) must be greater than the par value of the liabilities (the A2 rated bonds). So suppose that a deal has assets with a market value of $500 million and liabilities with a par value of $375 million, then the overcollateralization test would involve first calculating the "adjusted market value of the assets." With an advance rate of 0.79 and a market value for the assets of $500 million, the adjusted market value is

$$\text{Adjusted market value} = 0.79 \times \$500 \text{ million} = \$395 \text{ million}$$

The adjusted market value exceeds the par value of the liabilities of $375 million. Therefore, the overcollateralization test is passed.

EXHIBIT 10.5 Moody's Advance Rates for Different Asset Types by Target Rating: Single Tranche Transaction with One Asset Type (20 Issuers and 5 Industries)

Asset Type	Target Rating											
	Aaa	Aa1	Aa2	Aa3	A1	A2	A3	Baa1	Baa2	Baa3		
Performing bank loans valued $0.90 and above	0.870	0.890	0.895	0.900	0.905	0.910	0.915	0.930	0.935	0.940		
Distressed bank loans valued $0.85 and above	0.760	0.780	0.790	0.795	0.810	0.815	0.820	0.830	0.840	0.870		
Performing high-yield bonds rated Baa	0.76	0.79	0.80	0.81	0.83	0.84	0.85	0.87	0.88	0.90		
Performing high-yield bonds rated B	0.72	0.75	0.76	0.77	0.78	0.79	0.80	0.82	0.83	0.85		
Distressed bank loans valued below $0.85	0.58	0.62	0.63	0.64	0.67	0.68	0.69	0.71	0.72	0.74		
Performing high-yield valued below Caa	0.45	0.49	0.50	0.51	0.56	0.58	0.60	0.62	0.64	0.67		
Distressed bonds	0.35	0.39	0.40	0.41	0.47	0.48	0.50	0.54	0.56	0.57		
Reorganized equities	0.31	0.37	0.38	0.39	0.44	0.46	0.47	0.51	0.52	0.54		

Source: Table Yvonne Fu Falcone and Jeremy Gluck, "Moody's Approach to Market-Value CDOs," Special Report, *Structured Finance* (April 8, 1998), p. 9. Reprinted with permission from Moody's Investors Service.

The advance rates are higher for greater diversification. This can be seen by comparing the advance rates in Exhibit 10.6 based on 40 issuers and 10 industries and the advance rates in Exhibit 10.5 based on 20 issuers in five industries.

The advance rates in Exhibit 10.5 and 10.6 are for deals with a single tranche and only one asset type. When there is more than one asset type the advance rates will be different depending on the correlation between the asset types. Specifically, if there is greater diversification within a deal, then the advance rates would be somewhat higher.

To demonstrate how the adjusted market value is computed for a tranche when there is more than one asset type, we will use the advance rates in Exhibit 10.5 *for illustrative purposes only*. The deal has a $375 million rated tranche and $125 million equity. The portfolio composition is shown in Exhibit 10.7. The rating for the tranche is A2, so the advance rates are those shown in Exhibit 10.5 for an A2 rating. Notice that the adjusted market value is $394.9 million which exceeds the $375 million par value of the tranche. Thus, the overcollateralization test is passed.

If a deal has several tranches, then the senior tranches are being provided protection by more than the advance rates.[1] The advance rates will be different from those shown in Exhibits 10.5 and 10.6 and there will be an overcollateralization test applied to each tranche. In the case of a deal with one senior tranche, one subordinated tranche, and an equity tranche, there will be an overcollateralization test for the senior tranche and the subordinated tranche. The former test compares the adjusted market value of the portfolio (based on the advance rates for the senior tranche) to the par value of the senior tranche outstanding. The test is passed when the adjusted market value exceeds the par value of the senior tranche. The overcollateralization for the subordinated tranche compares the adjusted market value (based on the advance rates for the subordinated tranche) to the par value of the subordinated tranche outstanding. If the adjusted market value exceeds the par value of the subordinated tranche, the overcollateralization test is passed.

A Simple Example of Deal Mechanics

In an effort to illustrate deal mechanics, we created a sample CDO using the advance rates in Exhibit 10.5 and looked at the effect of an unrealistically rapid asset value deterioration on this deal. The deal originally consisted of $500 million in assets, with $375 million of bonds rated A2

---

[1] For an explanation of how subordination impacts the advance rates in the Moody's rating methodology, see Exhibit C in Yvonne Fu Falcone and Jeremy Gluck, "Moody's Approach to Market-Value CDOs," Special Report, *Structured Finance* (April 8, 1998), pp, 14–15.

EXHIBIT 10.6 Moody's Advance Rates for Different Asset Types by Target Rating: Single Tranche Transaction with One Asset Types (40 Issuers and 10 Industries)

Asset Type	Target Rating									
	Aaa	Aa1	Aa2	Aa3	A1	A2	A3	Baa1	Baa2	Baa3
Performing bank loans valued $0.90 and above	0.880	0.895	0.900	0.905	0.910	0.915	0.920	0.930	0.935	0.940
Distressed bank loans valued $0.85 and above	0.790	0.805	0.810	0.815	0.820	0.825	0.830	0.840	0.850	0.870
Performing high-yield bonds rated Ba	0.81	0.84	0.85	0.86	0.87	0.88	0.89	0.90	0.91	0.92
Performing high-yield bonds rated B	0.74	0.78	0.79	0.80	0.81	0.82	0.83	0.84	0.85	0.87
Distressed bank loans valued below $0.85	0.62	0.66	0.67	0.68	0.69	0.70	0.71	0.73	0.74	0.76
Performing high-yield bonds rated Caa	0.50	0.56	0.57	0.58	0.61	0.62	0.64	0.67	0.68	0.70
Distressed bonds	0.43	0.47	0.48	0.49	0.52	0.53	0.54	0.58	0.59	0.61
Reorganized equities	0.41	0.45	0.46	0.47	0.49	0.50	0.51	0.54	0.55	0.56

Source: Table A4 in Yvonne Fu Falcone and Jeremy Gluck, "Moody's Approach to Market-Value CDOs," Special Report, *Structured Finance* (April 8, 1998), p. 13. Reprinted with permission from Moody's Investors Service.

EXHIBIT 10.7 Example of Adjusted Market Value Calculation with More than One Asset Type)

	Asset Type ($ millions)	For A2 Rated[a] Advance Rate (%)	For A2 Rated[a] Advance Rate ($)
Performing bank loans valued $0.90 and above	$110	0.91	$100.10
Distressed bank loans valued $0.85 and above	97	0.815	79.06
Performing high-yield bonds rated Baa	106	0.84	89.04
Performing high-yield bonds rated B	84	0.79	66.36
Distressed bank loans valued below $0.85	35	0.68	23.80
Performing high-yield valued below Caa	39	0.58	22.62
Distressed bonds	29	0.48	13.92
Reorganized equities	0	0.46	0.00
Total	$500		$394.90

[a] Assumes advance rates in Exhibit 10.5.

and $125 million of equity (shown in Exhibit 10.8). Initially, the value of the assets times the advance rate is $395 million (in Exhibit 10.8, the column labeled "Adjusted" MV of Assets). This is obviously greater than the $375 million in bonds. The deal has 25% equity to begin ($125 million /$500 million).

We assume that the assets earn 1% per month, and that the value of the assets declines by 3% per month. The net result is that the value of the assets is declining by 2% per month. In addition, the rated debt holders are paid 0.66% per month. For simplicity, we assume all interest payments on the collateral are collected monthly, and the interest payments on the debt are disbursed monthly. After month 3 of declining market prices, the value of the assets is $463.32 million. Applying the 0.79 advance rate, the "adjusted" market value of the assets is $366.02 million, against $375 million of bonds. The structure fails the overcollateralized (market value) test: the adjusted market value of the securities is less than the par value of the bonds. The deal must begin to liquidate.

Let us walk through the process. The shortfall between the adjusted market value of assets and debt is $8.98 million (shown in Exhibit 10.8, the column labeled "Difference"). Since the advance rate is 0.79, each dollar of liquidation is the equivalent of curing only $0.21 of the shortfall. To bring the new adjusted MV of assets into line with the bonds, we must liquidate assets to cure the shortfall. The amount that must be liquidated is determined as follows:

$$\text{Collateral to be liquidated} = [\text{Shortfall}/(1 - \text{Advance rate})]$$

In our example, since the shortfall is \$8.98 million and the advance rate is 0.79:

$$\begin{aligned} \text{Collateral to be liquidated} &= [\$8.89 \text{ million}/(1 - 0.79)] \\ &= \$42.75 \end{aligned}$$

Thus, the new market value of the assets is \$420.56 million, and the new adjusted market value of the assets is \$332.25 million. This is identical to the post liquidation par value of the liabilities.

Assume in the following month that the assets again earn 1%, their value again declines by 3%, and bondholders are again paid 0.66%. There will be another shortfall, this time of \$8.38 million. Thus, \$39.89 million must be liquidated to bring the new adjusted market value of the assets in line with the par value of the bonds.

There are a number of things to note from this example. First, the deal liquidates very quickly in an environment of unfavorable performance. In this simplified example, the par value of the bonds has amortized down to \$154.23 million after 10 months. However, despite a very quick deterioration in market value, the rated debt holders have completely received 100% return of principal and timely payment of interest. Second, there is always a very hefty capital cushion. In this example, the equity before liquidation never drops lower than 19%. By definition, the equity after liquidation must be a minimum of (1 – the advance rate), or 21% in this case.

Market value deals are actually marked-to-market no less frequently than once a week, and the tests are applied at that time. Some are marked-to-market daily. When the test is failed, the excess indebtedness must be repaid within 10 to 15 business days.

Minimum Net Worth Test

In addition to the protection provided by advance rates, rating agencies also require a quarterly minimum net worth test to protect the rated debt. In our example, this requires that 60% of the original equity remains to protect the senior tranche, and 30% to protect the subordinated tranche. If the equity falls below that, noteholders of the senior tranche may vote to accelerate payment of the debt, at which point the asset manager must liquidate assets and fully pay down the debt related

EXHIBIT 10.8 Illustration of Market Value Deal Mechanics (in $ millions)

Assumptions:
1. 3% Drop in market value per month.
2. Assets yield 1% per month.
3. 0.66% income paid per month on A2 bonds).

Month	Market Value of Assets	"Adjusted" MV of Assets[a]	Par Value of Bonds Rated A2	Diff	Liq	New MV of Assets	New AMV of Assets	New Par on Bond	% Equity Before Liq	% Equity After Liq
0	500.00	395.00	375.00	20.00	0.00	500.00	395.00	375.00	0.25	0.25
1[b]	487.53	385.14	375.00	10.14	0.00	487.53	385.14	375.00	0.23	0.23
2	475.30	375.49	375.00	0.49	0.00	475.30	375.49	375.00	0.21	0.21
3	463.32	366.02	375.00	−8.98	42.75	420.56	332.25	332.25	0.19	0.21
4	409.96	323.87	332.25	−8.38	39.89	370.07	292.35	292.35	0.19	0.21
5	360.74	284.98	292.35	−7.37	35.10	325.64	257.25	257.25	0.19	0.21
6	317.43	250.77	257.25	−6.49	30.89	286.54	226.36	226.36	0.19	0.21
7	279.31	220.66	226.36	−5.71	27.18	252.13	199.19	199.19	0.19	0.21
8	245.78	194.16	199.19	−5.02	23.92	221.86	175.27	175.27	0.19	0.21
9	216.27	170.85	175.27	−4.42	21.04	195.22	154.23	154.23	0.19	0.21
10	190.30	150.34	154.23	−3.89	18.52	171.78	135.71	135.71	0.19	0.21

[a] Adjusted MV of assets = MV of assets × 0.79
[b] To illustrate calculations:

Market value of assets	= +500 million × 0.97	=	+485 million
	+500 million × 0.01	=	+5 million
	−375 million × 0.66%	=	−2.475
		=	487.53

211

to the test that has failed. In the simple 1-bond CDO shown in Exhibit 10.8, assume that the rating agency requires a 50% minimum net worth. This would mean that if the equity falls below $62.5 million ($125 million × 50%), the noteholders could vote to liquidate the deal. In this example, this would happen at the end of month 6, where, after the adjustments required to pass the overcollateralization (market value) test, the value of the equity would be $60.18 million ($286.54 million – $226.36 million).

HOW ADVANCE RATES ARE DERIVED

Advance rates are the crucial variable in market value deals. It is useful to look more closely at how these are derived. Advance rates are actually a combination of three factors: price volatility of the securities, correlation among securities, and liquidity. It is interesting to look at how Moody's and Fitch, the two rating agencies that have rated the bulk of the market value transactions, view each of these variables.

Both Moody's and Fitch use historical volatility as the basis for deriving volatility estimates. This volatility is then stressed depending on the length of the historical record and the desired rating of the CDO tranche. Because there is a very complete record for the returns on high-yield bonds (that is, high-quality information collected over a large number of years) only a relatively small stress factor is applied to the historical volatility for this instrument. At the other end of the spectrum, a relatively large stress factor is applied to distressed instruments, especially reorganized equities. The higher the desired rating, the greater the stress factor, which reflects the fact that higher rated tranches are expected to hold up under greater standard deviations of stress. Fitch is very explicit on that final point. A security rated A must be able to sustain market value declines three times as large as needed for the security to obtain a single-B rating. For an AAA rating, the security must be able to sustain market value declines five times as large as would be needed to obtain a B rating.

The choice of market value correlations is problematic. Historical correlations are useful, but correlations often rise sharply during periods of crisis. Thus, Moody's uses correlations that are higher than those prevailing during "normal" periods, but not as high as those observed during the most stressful periods. Moody's assumes correlation of 0.55 between firms within the same industry, and 0.40 among those in different industries.

For most securities, the bid-ask spread is small relative to ordinary price volatility. However, market value transactions lend themselves to using less liquid assets that also have irregular cash flows. For these securities, liquidity can become a key consideration, especially during periods of financial stress. Both Moody's and Fitch make assumptions as to what losses would be during periods of market stress. So, for performing high-yield bonds, Moody's assumes a 5% liquidity "haircut," while for distressed bonds, its "crewcut" is 10%. For performing bank loans the haircut is 7%, while for distressed bank loans it is increased to 12.5%. Reorganized equities get scalped at 20%.

So these three factors—price volatility, correlation among securities and liquidity together—account for the advance rates shown in Exhibits 10.5 and 10.6.

Are Advance Rates Conservative?

To test how conservative advance rates actually are, we look at monthly performance for a readily available set of data—high-yield bonds. We used the performance of Citgroup's High-Yield Bond Index (available on Yield Book). This data cover January 1989 to October 2005.

We use monthly observations because the market values are evaluated at least weekly, and a portfolio normally has 10 to 15 business days to liquidate assets to correct the deficiency. Thus, if the portfolio passes the test one period, and then the market value of the portfolio deteriorates, it could take a maximum of just over four weeks to find and correct the deficiency (1 week maximum until the next test, 15 business days to correct the deficiency). This suggests that monthly intervals are the correct benchmark period for looking at how conservative advance rates are.

The index includes all publicly traded domestic debt with a fixed-rate coupon, a minimum maturity of one year, and a maximum credit quality of Ba1. The index excludes payment-in-kind (PIK) bonds, and Eurobonds.

There are 202 observations in the period investigated. Exhibit 10.9 shows the 1-month returns as a histogram. The monthly return distributions are similar in that they are both representative of the market, and their returns are usually close. Note from this histogram that there was only 1 month in which the total return on the Citigroup index was less than −8% (the worst single month was July 2002 at −8.81%).

The worst three months on the indices were May, June, and July 2002. The Citigroup index was down 1.24% in May, 8.81% in June, and 4.52% in July 2002.

We showed earlier that the advance rates are meant to correspond to one-month price changes. However, the advance rates are more severe than the worst three-month period in the history of the market. Clearly, the advance rates are very conservative.

EXHIBIT 10.9   Monthly Return Distribution—Citigroup High Yield Index[a]

One-Month Return Range	Yield Book
−9 to −8	1
−8 to −7	1
−7 to −6	1
−6 to −5	1
−5 to −4	2
−4 to −3	4
−3 to −2	5
−2 to −1	18
−1 to 0	20
0 to 1	49
1 to 2	59
2 to 3	27
3 to 4	8
4 to 5	0
5 to 6	2
6 to 7	2
7 to 8	1
8 to 9	1
9 to 10	0
10 to 11	0
11 to 12	0
Total Observations	202
Mean	0.73

[a] Monthly returns since 1/1989–10/2005.

Further Evidence of Conservative Aspect of Advance Rates

Want proof of the extent of conservatism in the rating methodology? Market value CDOs have been one of the best performing types of CDOs. Downgrades have been minimal. Many investors will find that particularly surprising in light of asset price volatility over the past decade. Clearly, part of the answer is that the vast majority of CDOs have been of the cash flow variety. However, another part of the answer is that the advance rates are so conservative that price volatility in recent years is well within the range anticipated by the advance rates.

CONCLUSION

Many CDO investors have steered away from the debt in market value deals, believing that purchasing the debt is like making an investment in a hedge fund. As a result, market value deals trade at similar or slightly wider spreads than cash flow deals launched at the same time. The protections built into market value deals are quite powerful from the bondholder's point of view.

Five

Synthetic CDOs

CHAPTER **11**

Introduction to Credit Default
Swaps and Synthetic CDOs

In this chapter we describe the basic workings of credit default swaps (CDS) and synthetic CDOs. These products have grown tremendously since 1996 in terms of both trading volume and product evolution. Specifically, the volume of outstanding credit CDS rose from $20 billion in 1996 to $2.3 trillion in 2005. In 1997, $1 billion of synthetic CDOs had been created (including funded, unfunded, and CDS index tranches); by 2005 there were over $1 trillion of synthetic CDOs outstanding.

In terms of product evolution, CDS have developed from highly idiosyncratic contracts taking a great deal of time to negotiate into a standardized product traded in a liquid market offering competitive quotations on single-name instruments and even indices of credits worldwide. Synthetic CDOs have evolved from vehicles used by commercial banks to offload commercial loan risk to customized tranches where investors can select the names they are exposed to, the level of subordination that protects them from losses, and the premium they are paid (although not all three simultaneously).[1] Finally, the rise of standardized tranches on CDS indices has increased trading liquidity, thereby allowing long-short strategies based on tranche seniority or protection tenor.

CREDIT DEFAULT SWAPS

The *dramatis personae* of a CDS are: a *credit protection buyer*, a *credit protection seller*, a *reference obligor*, and *reference obligations*. What tie

---

[1] An investor can pick two and the third follows as a consequence.

219

these parties together are *notional amount, credit events, physical settlement,* and *cash settlement.*

The protection buyer buys credit protection from the protection seller in a dollar-amount size called the "notional amount." The protection buyer pays the protection seller a fee based on a number of basis points per annum times the notional amount. These payments are paid by the protection buyer quarterly for the life of the CDS. The most liquid CDS maturity is five years.

A reference obligor "credit event," should it occur, triggers a payment from the protection seller to the protection buyer. Basically, a credit event is a bad thing that happens to the reference obligor, such as the reference obligor filing for bankruptcy. The payment from the protection seller to the protection buyer is effected in one of two ways.

In "physical delivery," the protection buyer selects a reference obligation of the reference obligor and delivers it to the protection seller. Usually, any senior unsecured (or any secured) obligation of the reference obligor is a qualified reference obligation. The protection buyer can deliver a par amount of a reference obligation equal to the notional amount of the CDS. The protection seller must then pay the protection buyer par for the reference obligation.

In "cash settlement," the market value of the reference obligation is determined by dealer polling. The difference between the reference obligation's par and its market value is paid in cash by the protection seller to the protection buyer. This arrangement is illustrated in Exhibit 11.1.

EXHIBIT 11.1   Credit Default Swap Payment Flows
A. Initial Flows

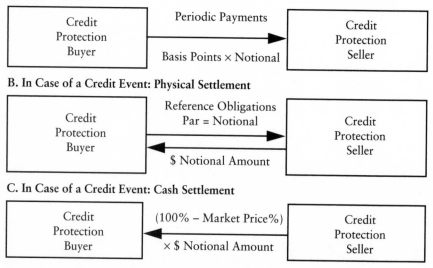

B. In Case of a Credit Event: Physical Settlement

C. In Case of a Credit Event: Cash Settlement

The protection seller under a CDS is said to be the *seller* of the CDS, but he is also *long* the CDS and *long* the underlying credit. The logic behind selling protection and being long the CDS is that the protection seller is in the same credit position as someone who owns, or is long, a bond. Both investors root against default. Of course, there is a major difference between being long a bond and long a CDS. To be long a bond, one must pay its market price. To be long a CDS, one must simply promise to pay future credit event losses.[2]

CDS divorce the assumption of credit risk from the requirement to fund a purchase. One result is that CDS democratize the assumption of credit risk. A leveraged investor with a relatively high cost of funds (e.g., LIBOR + 200) could never profitably purchase a bond with a relatively low coupon (e.g., LIBOR + 100). However, as a credit protection seller, the high cost funder could profitably assume credit risk for a payment of 80 basis points a year.

The credit protection seller's position is also more purely a credit position than if it actually owned a bond, as a bond's market value is much more affected by interest rate movements than is a CDS. Because reference obligations usually include all of the reference obligor's senior unsecured obligations, the CDS is independent of the maturities, prepayments, and calls of the reference obligor's particular bonds or loans.

Conversely, the protection buyer under a CDS is said to be the buyer of the CDS, but short the CDS and short the underlying credit. A CDS allows the protection buyer to short a credit without the operational and practical difficulties of shorting a cash bond. The separation of credit risk and funding that a CDS achieves also allows low-cost funders to fund a bond without taking on the bond's credit risk. A party with a low cost of funds (e.g., LIBOR + 5) could profitably purchase a bond with a relatively high coupon (e.g., LIBOR + 100). The low cost funder could then insulate itself from credit risk by buying protection for 80 basis points a year and achieve a spread of 15 basis points (LIBOR + 100 minus LIBOR + 5 minus 80 basis points). This is the analog to a high cost funder assuming credit risk without funding a bond.

CDS documentation evolved from interest rate swap documentation and some strange vestigial terminology remains. Interest rate swaps have fixed rate payers and floating rate payers for very obvious reasons. More opaquely, the protection buyer in a CDS is referred to as the "fixed rate payer" and the protection seller the "floating rate payer."

---

[2] And sometimes back up that promise with collateralization.

Credit Default Swap Documentation

CDS can be customized in any manner to which both parties agree. This flexibility has been both a strength and a weakness as the market developed. To put a framework around these debates, the International Swaps and Derivatives Association (ISDA) has created CDS definitions so that market participants have a common language in which to negotiate.[3] For example, ISDA defines six different corporate credit events.

So, while the preferred set of credit events is still open to debate, market participants can express their preferences to each other in short hand. For example, they can say that they would like credit events to include "Restructuring" or "Modified Restructuring" or "Modified-Modified Restructuring" or no restructuring whatsoever. Each of these terms in quotes has a specific, detailed ISDA definition readily understood by market participants. Parties are also free to modify existing definitions.

The development of credit derivative definitions is one of the reasons for the dramatic growth of the CDS market. ISDA also provides a confirmation template that organizes the defined terms into a short, easily understandable, and comparable document. The orderly settlement of Argentina, Enron, and WorldCom credit events, based on standard ISDA documentation, added considerably to the credibility of the documentation and to the CDS product itself.

Credit Events

The essential part of a CDS is the specific circumstances considered to be *credit events*. The triggering of a credit event is what causes the protection seller to make a protection payment to the protection buyer. Negotiations between the protection seller and protection buyer determine which specific circumstances will be recognized as credit events in a particular CDS. ISDA defines six possible credit events:

- Bankruptcy
- Failure to Pay
- Obligation Default
- Obligation Acceleration
- Repudiation and Moratorium
- Restructuring

The broader the definition of a credit event, the easier it becomes for a protection payment to be triggered. But the market consensus over the

---

[3] www.isda.org has useful information about credit derivatives and their documentation.

years has been to exclude some credit events and to tighten the definitions for the rest. Parties now generally agree to exclude Obligation
Default and Obligation Acceleration in nonemerging market corporate
CDS. The logic is that these situations do not always rise to the severity
intended to trigger a protection payment. And if the situation of the
underlying credit is severe, Failure to Pay will follow shortly anyway.

Similarly, the Bankruptcy definition has been tightened. In the 1999
ISDA definitions, the Bankruptcy definition contained the phrase
"action in furtherance of bankruptcy." In practice, the market discovered this phrase to be vague. If, for example, a debtor under financial
stress hires an attorney to help it understand the bankruptcy process,
does that mere consultation qualify as an "action in furtherance of
bankruptcy"? This ambiguity was resolved when the phrase was
stricken from the Bankruptcy definition.

Because Repudiation and Moratorium are only applicable to sovereign credits, this leaves three remaining credit events common in most
corporate underlying CDS: Bankruptcy, Failure to Pay, and Restructuring. "Bankruptcy" is the voluntary or involuntary filing of bankruptcy.
"Failure to Pay" is the failure of the reference obligor to make principal
or interest payments on one or more of its obligations. Alas, "Restructuring" has been the focus of a great deal of concern and debate.

The Restructuring Debate

Restructuring refers to relaxing the terms of a debtor's loan or bond
obligations to take into account the debtor's weakened credit situation.
Debt maturities might be extended, coupons lowered, principal reduced,
or debt seniority might even be reduced. Restructuring debt is seen as a
less disruptive and less costly alternative to the bankruptcy process.
While it definitely inflicts a credit loss, the issue in the CDS market is
whether, and how, restructuring should be included as a credit event
capable of triggering a protection payment.

Restructuring as a credit event is a concern to credit protection sellers.
One reason is that it can give the protection buyer an unintended "cheapest-to-deliver" option. When a credit is in bankruptcy, all same-seniority
debt trade similarly, regardless of coupon or maturity. This is because the
bankruptcy court is apt to treat all debt of the same seniority identically
with respect to the distribution of cash or new securities from the bankrupt estate. But this is not the case in a restructuring, where the coupon
and maturity of certain obligations issued by the reference entity may
remain unaffected by the restructuring. The buyer of protection could find
it economically advantageous to search out the cheapest trading debt to
purchase and deliver to the protection seller in exchange for par.

Another concern about restructuring is the possible manipulation of the process by bank lenders that have bought credit protection that includes restructuring. The issue is that if a bank controls the restructuring process, and has purchased protection that covers restructuring, the bank has no economic incentive to limit the diminution of the restructured loan. Such a bank could oversee the restructuring of its loan, allow its terms to be slashed, present that loan to the protection seller for a payment of par, and even provide separate new funding to the troubled credit at a higher point in its new capital structure.

On the other side of the issue have been banks, chiefly in Europe, that view restructuring as a legitimate way to work out a problem loan, and thus desire credit protection to cover this eventuality. The regulators of these banks have been reluctant to give capital relief for credit protection that excludes restructuring risk.

Different approaches have been implemented to address the concerns of both protection sellers and protection buyers. As mentioned, there are four standard ISDA definitions dealing with restructuring: "Restructuring," "Modified Restructuring," "Modified-Modified Restructuring," and the elimination of restructuring entirely. Modified Restructuring and Modified-Modified Restructuring limit the maturity of deliverable reference obligations in different ways, thus constraining the protection buyer's cheapest-to-deliver option.

Settlement Options

The last CDS feature we will describe in this summary is how the amount the protection seller must pay to the protection buyer is calculated if a reference obligor credit event occurs. The vast majority of CDS, about 86% of those outstanding, use *physical settlement*. In physical settlement, the protection buyer transfers a reference obligation to the protection seller in exchange for its par in cash. The par amount transferred is the notional amount of the CDS. Afterwards, as owner of the reference obligations, the protection seller is free to take whatever steps it thinks best to recover the maximum value possible from the reference obligation, including working out or selling the obligations.

If reference obligations have different market values, the protection buyer has what is referred to as the "cheapest-to-deliver option." This is the choice of finding and delivering the least expensive reference obligation to the protection seller in exchange for par.

In *cash settlement*, which is used in about 11% of outstanding CDS, the value of the reference obligation is determined in the market by a specified mark-to-market auction process. Typically, quotations are obtained from qualified dealers and their average calculated. The protection seller pays the difference between the par amount of the reference obligation and the mark-to-market value of the reference obligation. If the protection buyer owned the reference obligation, it remains the protection buyer's asset.

Finally, *fixed amount settlement* is just what it sounds like: the protection seller pays a certain dollar amount to the protection buyer and there is no attempt to determine a recovery value for the reference obligation. This rare method, only used in about 3% of outstanding CDS, has typically been used by corporations buying protection on trade receivables, which are not readily transferable and which cannot easily be marked-to-market.

Growth of the CDS Market

First introduced in the mid-1990s, the CDS product took a long time to take hold. Until 1998, more time was spent on PowerPoint presentations about CDS to potential participants than on actual transactions. But take hold CDS did, and the remarkable growth of the single-name CDS market is its most dramatic feature according to statistics reported by the British Bankers' Association (BBA).[4] Estimates of outstanding notional have grown from $20 billion in 1996, to $1.4 trillion at the end of 2003, and the prediction for 2006 is $2.8 trillion.

The rise of the CDS market paralleled that of more sophisticated approaches to credit risk management. Application of modern portfolio theory to debt portfolios raised interest in the CDS product, and in turn, the CDS product made new credit risk management strategies practical. The CDS product also made it possible to separate the funding of a loan or bond from the assumption of its credit risk. Banks are still adapting to a new financial world order where they are the *originators*, but not necessarily the *holders,* of credit risk. And the bond market often looks to the CDS market for cues on credit quality and spreads.

CDS Underlyings

The CDS market has evolved from its heavy focus on sovereign risk in the mid-1990s to being much more focused on corporate credit risk. In 1996, sovereign risk made up 54% of the CDS market. According to the BBA, corporate underlyings in 2005 compose 64% of the market, fol-

---

[4] All of our credit default swap market statistics are from the British Bankers' Association *BBA Credit Derivative Report 2003/04.* This annual survey of CDS market participants covers, among other topics, market size, the market shares of various participants, and opinions about market issues. The BBA web site is at www.bba.org.uk.

lowed by financial firms at 22%, emerging market sovereigns at 7%, non-emerging market sovereigns at 5%, and 2% for "all other."

The CDS market is also heavily focused on low investment-grade risk. Data reported by the BBA indicates 65% of CDS reference A and BBB rated entities, 19% reference AAA and AA rated entities, 13% reference BB and B rated entities, and 3% reference below B rated entities. The notional amount of all rating categories have been growing, but underlyings that are speculative grade increased relative to those that are investment grade in the period from 2004 to 2005.

Other Aspects Of The CDS Market

Most CDS contracts have an original tenor of five years. This is reflected in the tenors of outstanding CDS, as shown in Exhibit 11.2, where tenors shorter than five years are mainly the result of the passage of time since the original contract was created.

The number of market participants with sizable CDS portfolios is also growing. In 2005 there were about 19 CDS dealers and users with over $50 billion notional amount in various credit derivatives. Exhibit 11.3 shows the estimated breakdown of notional across different types of market participants. The 51% share of protection buying by banks is not predominately driven by banks buying protection on loans they have originated. Most of their CDS portfolio reflects activity as CDS dealers, with other CDS entered into to eliminate credit exposures brought about by their activities in letters of credit and fixed income and equity derivatives.

CDS Indices

The desire of market participants to go long or short a portfolio of underlying names at the same time led to the establishment in 2003 of

EXHIBIT 11.2   Remaining Tenor of Outstanding Credit Default Swaps

Tenor	Share
Under 1 year	7%
1–3 years	17%
3–5 years	37%
5 years	21%
5–7 years	10%
7–10 years	6%
Over 10 years	2%

EXHIBIT 11.3   Market Share of CDS Participants

	Sellers	Buyers
Banks	38%	51%
Security firms	16%	16%
Hedge funds	15%	16%
Monoline insurers	10%	2%
Re-insurers	7%	3%
Pension funds	4%	3%
Mutual funds	4%	3%
Other insurance companies	3%	2%
Corporates	2%	3%
Government/export credit agencies	1%	1%

Source: British Bankers' Association.

rival CDS indices, Trac-X and iBoxx. These indices merged in early 2004, deepening the liquidity of the consolidated indices. New indices and subindices have since been added. Exhibit 11.4 arranges current indices by geographic concentration, gives the proper name of the main index, describes the composition of the main index, and outlines subindices.[5]

These broad indices are available in maturities from one to ten years, with the greatest liquidity at 5-, 10-, and, to a lesser extent, 7-year maturities. A new index series is created every six months. At that time, the specific composition of credits in each new series is determined and a new premium level determined for each maturity. Premiums on indices are exchanged once a quarter on the 20*th* of March, June, September, and December. Over the life of the index, the index's premium remains fixed. To compensate for changes in the price of credit protection, an upfront payment is exchanged. This upfront payment can be regarded as the present value of the difference between the index's fixed premium and the current market premium for the index.

Each name in an index is equally weighted in the indices. For the North American indices, only Bankruptcy and Failure to Pay are credit events even though Modified Restructuring is commonly a credit event in the North American market. For the European indices, Bankruptcy, Failure to Pay, and Modified-Modified Restructuring are credit events.

---

[5] www.mark-it.com has details on the composition of indices and subindices.

EXHIBIT 11.4 Credit Default Swap Indices

Geographic Concentration	Main Index Name	Main Index Composition	Subindices
North America investment grade	Dow Jones CDX NA IG	125 corporate names	5 Industries: Consumer, Energy, Financials, Industrials, and Technology/Media/Telecom High Volatility
North American high yield	Dow Jones CDX NA HY	100 corporate names	BB rated B rated High Beta
Europe	Dow Jones iTraxx Europe	125 corporate names	9 Industries: Autos, Consumer, Consumer Cyclicals, Consumer Non-Cyclicals, Energy, Senior Financials, Subordinate Financials, Industrials, and Technology/Media/Telecom Largest Corporates Lower Rated (aka Crossover) High Volatility
Japan	Dow Jones iTraxx CJ Japan	50 corporate names	3 industries: Capital Goods, Financials, Technology High Volatility
Asia ex-Japan	Dow Jones iTraxx Asia ex-Japan	50 corporate and sovereign names	3 Geographies: China and Taiwan, Korea, and the rest of ex-Japan Asia
Australia	Dow Jones iTraxx Australia	25 corporate names	None
Emerging market	Dow Jones CDX EM	15 sovereign names	None
Emerging market diversified	Dow Jones CDX EM Diversified	40 sovereign and corporate names	3 Geographies: Asia, EEMEA, Latin America

Indices are static and as credit events occur, protection sellers make protection payments to protection buyers, and the notional amount of the index then decreases. It is important to realize that CDS index trades are bilateral agreements. There is no exchange and only recently have there been attempts to centralize the determination of protection payments. Otherwise, protection payments are subject to individual physical settlements.

We will see later how these indices have also contributed to synthetic CDOs, our next topic.

SYNTHETIC CDOs

To motivate the use of synthetic CDOs, we start with an example of a bank seeking credit protection on loans it has made. Instead of wishing to protect itself against a *single* loan credit exposure, a bank may wish to protect itself against credit exposure to a $1 billion *portfolio* of a hundred $10 million loans. Of course, the bank could enter into one hundred $10 million CDS, each referencing a single credit. But it might instead decide to create a *synthetic CDO*. How would that work? We will describe a synthetic CDO that strictly follows the CDS methodology we have already described.

Our illustrative bank could divide the $1 billion of credit risk it wishes to buy protection on into a number of "basket" swaps that *serially* assume the risk. For example, the protection seller (also known as the CDO investor) of the *first* basket swap might assume the *first* $35 million of protection payments on any of the 100 loans in the $1 billion portfolio. The CDO investor would not have any responsibility for portfolio losses exceeding $35 million.

A *second* basket swap would assume portfolio protection payments exceeding $35 million, but the CDO investor's responsibility would end at losses over $45 million ($35 million is the tranche's "attachment point" and $45 million is its "detachment point" or "exhaustion point"). The CDO investor in the second basket is therefore on the hook for, at most, $10 million of losses. An illustrative division of the loan portfolio's credit risk into first, second, third, and higher loss tranches is summarized in Exhibit 11.5.

In Exhibit 11.5, we label the various basket swaps A through F, show their attachment and detachment points in percentage and dollar terms, and show the total dollar amount for which they are at risk. In market parlance, the F tranche of our example would be the CDO's *equity* or *first loss tranche*. We have estimated the rating and pricing of

EXHIBIT 11.5   An Illustrative $1 Billion CDO

Tranche	Attachment/ Detachment Percentage	Attachment/ Detachment ($ million)	Total Amount at Risk ($ millions)	Indicative Rating	Indicative Pricing (basis points)
A	13%–100%	130 to 1,000	870	AAA	15
B	7.5%–13%	75 to 130	55	AA+	90
C	6.5%–7.5%	65 to 75	10	AA	175
D	4.5%–6.5%	45 to 65	20	A	275
E	3.5%–4.5%	35 to 45	10	BBB	550
F	0%–3.5%	10 to 35	35	NR	NA

the various tranches as if the underlying loan portfolio was of BBB credit quality. The rating of the tranches reflects rating agency judgment about the probability and severity of a protection seller having to make a protection payment. With 3.5% subordination below it, the Class E tranche is rated BBB. With 13% subordination, the Class A tranche is rated AAA. Tranching the loan portfolio's credit risk into different seniorities and credit ratings tailors the risk to investors' preferences for particular levels of risk and return.

The synthetic CDO illustrated in Exhibit 11.5 is thus the combination of single-name CDS technology and the tranche technology of a cash CDO.

Morphing a Basket Swap CDO Into a Cash Investment CDO

To simplify our discussion, we have described our illustrative synthetic CDO as a series of basket CDS with attachment and detachment points and a notional amount. In market parlance, these are *unfunded* CDO tranches. In practice, many synthetic CDO investors (protection sellers) prefer to purchase a cash instrument that looks more like a regular debt instrument.

One way to accomplish this is for the bank seeking protection to issue a note that *embeds* the terms of the basket CDS. In such a format, the CDO investor buys a cash instrument, the note. Protection losses on the underlying referenced portfolio do not require further payments from the note buyer/protection seller. Rather, the amount of principal due back to the CDO investor is reduced by the reference portfolio's protection losses. This credit-linked note (CLN) is an example of a *funded* CDO tranche and it is illustrated in Exhibit 11.6.

Besides satisfying investors who want a cash investment, this arrangement eliminates any concern about the protection seller's ability to make

EXHIBIT 11.6   Flows in a Credit-Linked Note

A. Initial Flows

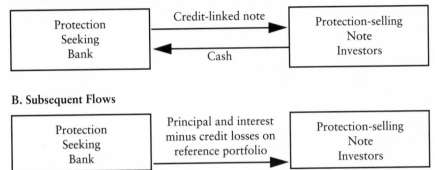

B. Subsequent Flows

payments for reference portfolio protection losses. Essentially, the funded synthetic CDO investor has *prepaid* its potential payment obligation by buying the note. However, the CDO investor now has the credit risk of the bank as regards the return of principal under the note. The note's coupon should therefore reflect both the credit risk of the underlying reference portfolio and the credit risk of the protection-buying bank.

We have also described a synthetic CDO as a series of bilateral agreements between a bank and CDO investors. In practice, it is often convenient to form a special purpose vehicle (SPV) to act as intermediary between protection selling CDO investors and the protection-seeking bank. In our example, the SPV would sell protection to the bank seeking protection and the SPV would simultaneously buy protection from CDO investors via the tranched basket CDS described previously.

If a CDO investor desires a cash investment, the SPV will take funds received from the investor and purchase highly rated assets. As protection losses hit a particular CDO tranche, the SPV will liquidate these assets and make payments to the protection-seeking bank. This will require the CDO to have invested in highly liquid assets with little market risk, such as repurchase agreements collateralized by Treasury securities.

Alternatively, the CDO can be structured so that it does not make protection payments until the end of its life. In that case, the CDO would purchase assets that were maturity-matched to the unwinding of the CDO. Principal from maturing assets, such as AAA asset-backed securities, would be used to pay protection losses to the protection-seeking bank with the residual paid to protection sellers as note principal. The CDO would still buy highly rated assets, but it could purchase assets that were less liquid and had more market value risk because these assets would never be sold. This is illustrated in Exhibit 11.7.

EXHIBIT 11.7   Flows in a Funded Synthetic CDO
A. Initial Flows

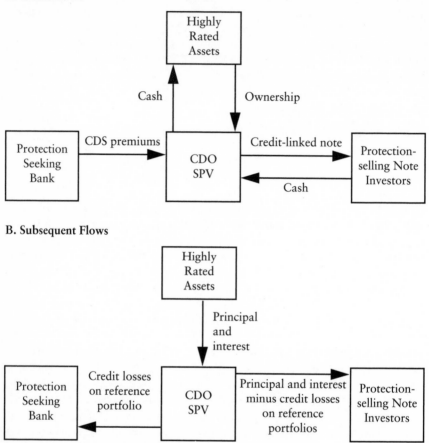

B. Subsequent Flows

Where is the CDO in a Synthetic CDO?

Our pedagogical route first described a synthetic CDO as a series of basket CDS entered into between a bank seeking credit protection and a series of counterparties offering credit protection. Then, we explained how any of the basket swaps could be incorporated into a CLN issued by the bank. Someone might argue that the term "CDO" is being stretched here and that these swaps are simply a series of bilateral transactions that do not rise to the title of "CDO." Certainly, there is no separate legal corporate entity that one can point to and call "the CDO" in these structures. Perhaps one should refer to these structures as "virtual CDOs." But they certainly combine the credit transfer mechanism of CDS with the tranching format of cash CDOs.

But finally, we describe the use of an SPV in the CDO structure, as close as one can come to a "bricks and mortar" CDO. As we shall see, particularly in Chapters 12 and 13, CDS, CLNs, bilateral agreements, and SPVs are all put together in various ways to create CDO structures. We refer to the overall structure comprising all these elements as a synthetic CDO. This seems a more useful definition than focusing solely on SPVs in the structure.

The Evolution Of Synthetic CDOs

We have also explained our illustrative synthetic CDO in the context of a bank trying to hedge credit risk that it had accumulated through its lending activity; in other words, a synthetic CDO done for *balance sheet* purposes, designed to reduce required economic or regulatory capital. These were, in fact, the first kind of synthetic CDOs.

Later, however, *arbitrage synthetic CDOs* were created, where the impetus came from investors seeking credit exposure and compensation for credit risk. In an arbitrage synthetic CDO, an asset manager or investor typically approaches a CDS dealer with the names, rating, or geographical specifications of a portfolio they wish to become exposed to on a first loss basis. Together, the investor and the dealer create an acceptable portfolio from risks the dealer already has, or can obtain, through the CDS market. The CDS dealer then places the senior tranches of the CDO with other investors. These were typically static portfolio CDOs.

In the typical *managed synthetic CDO,* the CDO sells credit protection to a number of different dealers under the direction of an asset manager until a portfolio of risk is created. Some of these CDOs incorporated cash flow diversion mechanisms based on coverage tests, as commonly done in cash CDOs. This type of structure was flawed and for this reason cash flow diversions are now rarely incorporated into synthetic CDOs.

Single-tranche CDOs are notable for what they are not: the placement of a complete capital structure complement of tranches, from equity to super senior. Instead, a protection seller enters into one specific CDO tranche with a CDS dealer in isolation. This creates an imbalanced position for the CDS dealer, as it might have, for example, bought protection on the 3% to 7% tranche of a synthetic CDO comprised of 150 underlying investment-grade names. The CDS dealer will sell protection on these names in the single-name CDS market, varying the notional amount of protection it buys from name to name in a process called *delta hedging.*

While we have our doubts about the reliability of delta hedging, because CDS dealers believe in its efficacy,[6] protection sellers enjoy great flexibility in choosing the terms of the single tranche CDO. Protection sellers can choose the portfolio they wish to reference and the attachment and detachment points of the tranche they wish to sell protection on. These factors will imply a price for that protection. Or the protection seller can start with a premium in mind and negotiate the other terms to create a transaction that supplies that premium.

Finally, the CDS indices described earlier have been sliced into *standardized tranches* that are traded. For example, the Dow Jones CDX NA IG is divided into tranches with respective attachment and detachment points of 0% to 3%, 3% to 7%, 7% to 10%, 10% to 15%, and 15% to 30%. Trading of these "standard" tranches is pretty liquid for maturities of 5-, 7-, and 10-years.

Structural Factors Affecting a Synthetic CDO's Price

Structural factors, such as attachment and detachment points, tranche width, and the timing of tranche premiums, affect tranche pricing. There are three points to remember about attachments points, detachment points, and tranche width:

- For the same width, the tranche with the lowest attachment point is riskier and should have a higher premium.
- For tranches with the same attachment point, a tranche with a larger width will have a higher premium by dollar amount, but a lower premium as a percent of notional.
- For tranches with the same detachment point, a tranche with a larger width will have a higher premium by dollar amount and a higher premium as a percent of notional.

For the intuition behind these points, imagine a CDO with 100 tranches, each referencing 1% of the underlying portfolio. The 0% to 1% tranche is the riskiest, followed by the 1% to 2% tranche, then the 2% to 3% tranche, until finally one gets to the least risky 99% to 100% tranche. If such a CDO was offered, its tranches should have premiums corresponding to their risk, i.e., the 0% to 1% tranche should have the highest premium and the 99% to 100% tranche the lowest premium. The *dollar amount premium* of a 0% to 2% tranche should equal the sum of dollar amount premiums of the 0% to 1% and 1% to 2% tranches. The *premium as a percent of notional* of a 0% to 2% tranche

---

[6] Any losses dealers incur in delta hedging do not affect the terms or economics of the single tranche CDO or the single-tranche CDO buyer.

should equal the *average* premium as a percent of notional of the 0% to 1% and 1% to 2% tranches. These simple insights provide the grounds for the three statements above.[7]

The timing of payments to protection sellers is an issue with funded CDO tranches. For example, the principal on the CDO note can be immediately written down as credit events occur. If so, further interest and premium payments would thereafter be based on a lower principal amount. Alternatively, CDO tranches might never be written down and the protection seller might receive all interest and premium payments, even if they do not receive all note principal at maturity.

For the same running premium, it is obviously better for the protection seller if principal is not written down. Therefore, protection sellers should require a higher premium if principal write-downs occur over the life of the CDO. But how should one quantify the appropriate difference in premiums? The more likely credit losses are to occur, the greater the difference should be between immediate write-down and no write-down premiums. Obviously, the more risky reference credits are or the more junior a CDO tranche is, the more likely write downs are to occur.

Also, the sooner credit events are expected to occur, the greater the difference should be between immediate write-down and no write-down premiums. This is because the sooner write-downs occur, the sooner cash flow will be diminished under the immediate write-down method. To size the correct difference in premiums under the two methods, one

---

[7] The excruciating details are explained here. For the same width, the tranche with the lowest attachment point is riskier and should have a higher premium. A CDO's 0% to 3% tranche is riskier than the same CDO's 1% to 4% tranche because the 0% to 1% part of the 0% to 3% tranche is riskier than the 3% to 4% part of the 1% to 4% tranche. The 0% to 3% tranche should therefore command a higher premium, both as a dollar amount and as a percent of notional.

For tranches with the same attachment point, a tranche with a larger width will have a higher dollar amount premium, but a lower percent of notional premium. The dollar amount premium of the 0% to 4% tranche is the premium of the 0% to 3% tranche plus the premium of the 3% to 4% tranche. At the same time, the percent of notional premium of the 0% to 4% tranche is less than that of the 0% to 3% tranche. This is because the percent premium of the 3% to 4% tranche is less than the percent premium of the 0% to 3% tranche.

For tranches with the same detachment point, a tranche with a larger width will have a higher dollar amount premium and a higher percent of notional premium. The dollar amount premium of the 0% to 4% tranche is premium of the 1% to 4% tranche plus the premium of the 0% to 1% tranche. At the same time, the percent of notional premium of the 0% to 4% tranche is greater than that of the 1% to 4% tranche. This is because the percent premium of a 0% to 1% tranche is greater than the percent premium of the 1% to 4% tranche.

needs to model the timing of reference obligor credit events and tranche write-downs.

With upfront premium payments, the issue of principal write-downs is not relevant. But what should the relationship be between an upfront premium payment and a running premium payment? The present value of the running premium payment stream should equal the upfront payment. In calculating the present value of the running payment, however, one must factor in the risk that the protection buyer will default. This can be accounted for by adding the protection buyer's credit spread to the interest rate used to discount running premium payments.

Synthetic CDO Advantages

The advantages of synthetic CDOs are such that almost all CDOs backed by investment-grade corporate debt, as well as a growing number of CDOs backed by structured finance assets, are synthetic. Synthetic CDOs enjoy a number of advantages over their cash counterparts:

- The unfunded nature of super-senior tranches allows the CDO to buy cheap loss protection. This lets the synthetic CDO provide a higher spread to its equity tranche.
- It is often easier to access credits in the synthetic market than in the cash market.
- CDS often trade cheaper than the cash bonds of the same name, meaning that the premium on a CDS is often greater than the cash bond's spread above LIBOR or swap rate.

We look at each of these points in turn.

Cheap Unfunded Super-Senior Tranches

Recall from Exhibit 11.5 that a great proportion of a synthetic CDO's liabilities are of AAA quality. The exact proportion depends on the credit quality of the CDO's underlying reference credits. The better the credit quality of the CDO's reference credits, the greater the size of the AAA tranche in the CDO's liability structure.

A synthetic CDO's AAA tranche is usually divided into two parts: a "super-senior AAA" equal to 60% to 90% of the total AAA tranche and a "junior AAA" equal to the remainder of the total AAA tranche. The super-senior AAA tranche is senior to a tranche that is also rated AAA, so the super senior's credit risk can be considered to be even better than AAA.

A synthetic CDO typically buys super-senior credit protection from CDO investors in unfunded form, even if its other tranches are funded. Buying protection in unfunded form has historically had significant cost advantages to the CDO. Unfunded super-senior protection has varied between 5 and 20 basis points over recent years while funded AAA CDO tranches have varied between 25 and 70 basis points over LIBOR. The difference to the equity tranche (which typically gets all residual CDO cash flows) is significant. Assuming the equity tranche is 3.5% of the CDO's liabilities, an improvement of 21 basis points in the cost of half the CDO's purchase of protection adds 3% $[(0.21 \times 0.5)/0.035]$ to equity's internal rate of return.

Easier and Faster Access to Credits

In cash CDOs with bonds or loans as collateral, collateral availability can be an issue. For example, if the CDO asset manager is striving to obtain collateral that fits a given industry bucket, but which is unavailable, the CDO's collateral ramp-up period may be extended or else the manager may have to make due with credits it otherwise would not have purchased. In synthetic CDOs, the manager can often access names in the CDS market that are unavailable in the cash market. This seems to also be true in the evolving market for CDS on ABS and MBS. Because of easier access to credits, ramp-up periods on synthetic CDOs can be quite short in comparison to cash CDOs.

CDS Can Be Cheaper Than Cash Bonds

The final economic advantage of synthetic deals we will discuss is that selling synthetic credit protection can be more rewarding than buying the underlying cash bond. That is, CDS premiums are often greater than the same name's cash bond spread to LIBOR or spread to the swap rate. In general, the difference is larger the further down the credit spectrum one descends.

To quantify this, we looked at CDS premiums and bond spreads for 20 BBB credits from January 2005 to November 2005. The 20 credits were selected based on bond and CDS liquidity, and their ratings ranged from BBB+ to BBB–. In Exhibit 11.8, we take the average of the credits' five-year cash bond spread and subtract their average five-year CDS premium.[8] In cases where there was no 5-year cash bond, we used an interpolated spread. The positive numbers in Exhibit 11.8 indicate that the CDS premium was greater than the cash bond spread. In 2005, this was normally the case. The average difference, in favor of CDS, was 5 basis points.[9]

---

[8] Data for the analysis were obtained from the UBS Credit Delta System.

[9] For more detail on the basis between cash and CDS, see Stephen Antczak, Tommy Leung, and Yina Luo, "Basis Package Relative Value," in *Journal of Structured Finance*, Fall 2004.

EXHIBIT 11.8   BBB Cash Spread to Swaps Minus CDS Premium

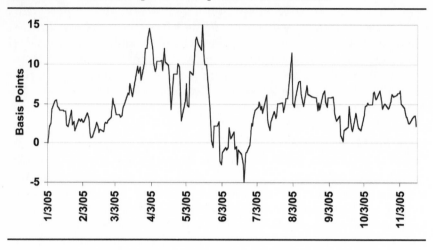

The differences between the cash and credit default swap markets reflect the fact that CDS and cash bonds embed slightly different risks. Two of these differences call for higher pricing on credit default swaps, while one implies lower pricing.

First, restructuring is generally a more severe event in the CDS market (on CDS where restructuring is defined as a credit event) than in the cash market. This is because, as we discussed in our explanation of restructuring, it triggers the protection buyer's cheapest-to-deliver option to increase protection payments.

Second, in the CDS market, loss is measured against par: the protection buyer pays par for a defaulted reference obligation or pays the difference between par and market quotation on a defaulted reference obligation. In the cash market, loss is usually measured from the price of the defaulted obligation, which might have been less than par.

Third, and on the opposing side implying lower pricing on CDS, there is counterparty risk in a CDS, because protection buyers are counting on the performance of protection sellers. In higher-rated credits, this effect is more important than the restructuring and default issues. It also explains why CDS on highly rated entities sometimes have higher premiums than the cash spread. However, in most CDOs, reference obligors are rated A or lower, so this effect is less important.

In addition to the structural differences between cash and CDS, there are transitory influences that are quite important in determining relative pricing at any given point. In particular, reinsurers can be quite active as sellers of credit protection. Because they are high-cost funders, they prefer credit default swaps to cash instruments, and, when active, they push down the premium on CDS. When there is a demand to buy credit protection for hedging purposes, CDS premiums will widen to the cash bond, because it is difficult to short cash instruments. Other transitory influences include the supply/demand for structured portfolio investments such as CDOs, as well as the presence of convertible bond investors looking for arbitrage opportunities around the conversion date.

Rating Agency Considerations

Each rating agency uses a different approach in rating synthetic CDO transactions, but they all rely on historical default and recovery data. There is a considerable amount of such information on bonds and loans. However, the application of these data to the frequency and severity of credit events on CDS is not straightforward. Factors that are unique to CDS that affect both the frequency and severity of losses include: (1) the use of restructuring as a credit event; (2) the presence of the cheapest-to-deliver option; and (3) the latitude in timing the enforcement of a credit event.

CONCLUSION

Our overview of CDS and synthetic CDOs in this chapter has shown a market of fast growth and rapid innovation. Only actively traded since 1996, single-name credit default swaps have spawned a number of different instruments: full capital structure synthetic CDOs, single-tranche synthetic CDOs, CDS indices, and tranches based on CDS indices. The rise of these instruments has inspired and facilitated new approaches to the assumption and management of credit risk.

CHAPTER 12

Synthetic Balance Sheet CDOs

The first synthetic CDOs were initiated by U.S. and European banks in 1997 for balance sheet purposes. The motivation was to achieve regulatory capital relief without forcing the banks to sell loans they had originated. Instead, synthetic balance sheet CDOs allowed sponsoring banks to purchase credit protection on loans they continued to own, which reduced banks' credit risk and required capital.

A synthetic CDO's ability to delink the credit risk of an asset from the ownership of an asset affords banks substantial flexibility in balance sheet management. In this chapter, we look at synthetic balance sheet CDOs, focusing on their structure, capital efficiencies, and funding benefits. We highlight the difference between fully funded and partially funded synthetic balance sheet CDOs. We begin by summarizing the problems associated with *cash* balance sheet collateralized loan obligations (CLOs).

CASH CLOs FOR BALANCE SHEET MANAGEMENT

Cash (as opposed to synthetic) balance sheet CLOs were the first CDOs to address the balance sheet management needs of commercial banks. In a cash CLO, a bank sells a pool of loans to a special purpose vehicle (SPV, more commonly referred to simply as "the CLO").

A bank gains a huge capital advantage by using a balance sheet CLO. If a bank holds loans directly in portfolio, it must hold risk-based capital equal to 8% of the loans. (Loans are a 100% risk weight asset, and as bank capital must equal 8% of risk-weighted assets, required capital for a loan is 8% times 100% or 8%.) But if the bank sells loans to a cash CLO, it can greatly reduce its required capital.

EXHIBIT 12.1   Structure of a Cash Balance Sheet CLO

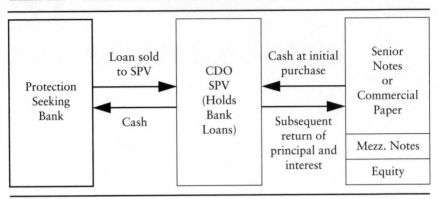

We have set out a typical cash balance sheet CLO structure in Exhibit 12.1. Note that the bank sells its loans to the CLO, which buys these loans with the cash proceeds of the notes it has issued. The notes are credit tranched. The senior notes (or commercial paper) are sold at a very tight spread. The mezzanine notes are sold in the marketplace to insurance companies, money managers, banks, and bank conduits. The originating bank generally buys the CLO's equity tranche. The retention by the bank of a first loss position in the CLO's liabilities is equivalent to an insurance deductible, and this arrangement partially ensures that the originating bank will be motivated to service the loan portfolio correctly and help prevent losses. For a portfolio of investment-grade loans, senior notes will make up about 92% of the CDO's capital structure, mezzanine notes 4%, and equity about 4%.

From the point of view of the originating bank, the capital implications of this cash CLO structure are far more favorable than holding the same loans outright. When banks sponsor a cash balance sheet CLO, they are required to hold the lesser of the following: (1) the capital charge of the underlying loans, which would be 8%, as stated earlier; or (2) 100% of the CLO liabilities they retain. If 100% of the liability is the smaller number, as it generally will be in a CLO structure, the institution is said to be subject to "low-level recourse" requirements. In this case, the bank has retained the CLO's equity tranche, which is 4% of the underlying loans. The 100% capital charge on the 4% equity piece creates a 4% capital requirement. This is precisely one half of the 8% capital required if the bank held those same loans outright. This is shown in Exhibit 12.2, which we will refer to throughout this chapter.

EXHIBIT 12.2 Comparison of Capital Charges

Alternative	Equity Retained	Capital Charge Methodology	Capital Charge Incurred
Hold loans on balance sheet	n.a.	100% risk weight, 8% risk-based capital (RBC) requirement	8%
Cash balance sheet CLO	4%	Low-level recourse requirement: lesser of the capital charge on the unlevered amount or 100% of bank liability.	100% of 4% equity retained = 4%
Fully funded synthetic CDO	1%	Low-level recourse requirement on equity. 20% risk weight on credit default swap if swap is with OECD institution. 0% risk weight if swap is directly with CDO and fully collateralized with 0% RBC securities (cash or cash substitutes or Treasuries).	If credit default swap is with an OECD institution: 100% of 1% equity + (20% × 8%) on swap = 2.6% If credit default swap is collateralized with 0% RBC securities: 100% of 1% equity + 0% on swap = 1%
Partially funded synthetic CDO	1% (10% junior credit default swap, 90% senior default swap, always with OECD institution)	For U.S. banks, the super-senior piece always receives a 20% risk weight regardless of whether it is retained or laid off. Treatment on equity and junior credit default swap is the same as above.	If junior credit default swap is with OECD institution: 100% of 1% equity + (20% × 8% on swaps) = 2.6% If junior credit default swap is collateralized with 0% RBC securities: 100% of 1% equity + (0% × 10% junior swap) + (20% × 8% × 90% on super-senior swap) = 2.44%

243

Bank Problems Using Cash CLOs

From the bank's point of view, cash CLOs go a long way toward more efficient capital utilization. However, two problems still remain. First, there is a funding issue. Second, there is the question of confidentiality.

With respect to the first problem, most banks are low-cost funders. Between the noninterest-bearing deposits they hold and their ability to borrow at LIBOR, most commercial banks borrow money at an average cost that is below LIBOR. It does not pay to transfer high-quality assets from a low-cost funder such as a bank to a higher-cost funder such as a cash CLO. The higher-cost funder cannot profitably fund higher-rated assets.

Exhibit 12.3 shows us why. Assume that a high-cost funder borrows at LIBOR + 30, while a low-cost funder borrows at LIBOR − 5. Further assume a high-quality asset (such as an investment-grade loan) pays LIBOR + 35 and the cost of protection on this credit risk is 20 basis points per annum. So, after netting out credit risk, the asset yields LIBOR + 15. The high-cost funder could only finance this asset at a deficit of 15 basis points, while the low-cost funder can carry the same asset at a surplus of 20 basis points.

That difference in funding costs is important because cash CLO financing is relatively expensive. AAA CLO tranches have sold for LIBOR + 25 to LIBOR + 70 in recent years. Lower-rated tranche cost more, of course. Thus, a bank efficiently managing its regulatory capital by moving loans to a cash CLO has to accept an inefficient means of financing those loans.

However, on the positive side, CLO funding is *term funding*, which is more advantageous than short-term funding that must be *rolled* over and might become more expensive. This might be of benefit to some banks. CLO funding is also nonrecourse funding because cash CLO liability holders have no recourse back to the originating bank. This might be an advantageous situation for speculatively rated loans.

The second disadvantage of the CLO structure is one of confidentiality. If a loan is transferred into a CLO, borrower notification is always

EXHIBIT 12.3   Transferring AAA Risk from Low-Cost Funder to High-Cost Funder

	Low-Cost Funder	High-Cost Funder
Yield on high-quality asset	LIBOR + 35	LIBOR + 35
Less funding cost	LIBOR − 5	LIBOR + 30
Less cost of laying off the credit risk	20 bps	20 bps
Net excess return	20 bps	−15 bps

EXHIBIT 12.4   Comparison of Bank Balance Sheet Management Techniques

Option	Achieve Capital Relief?	Achieve Confiden- tiality?	Wide Range of Assets Allowed?	Achieve Favorable Loan Funding?	Achieve Unfunded Super-Senior Economies?
Leave assets on balance sheet	No	Yes	Yes	Yes	NA
Cash CLO	Yes	No	No	No	NA
Fully funded synthetic CDO	Yes	Yes	Yes	Yes	No
Partially funded synthetic CDO	Yes	Yes	Yes	Yes	Yes

required and borrower consent is often required. Borrowers do not always understand why their bank has sold their loan, so customer relationships understandably put an impediment on a bank's willingness to sell or transfer a customer's loan. These disadvantages are shown in Exhibit 12.4

A related disadvantage to the cash CLO structure is that the CLO cannot negotiate new terms and conditions for a loan. In order to modify its terms and conditions, the loan must be bought back by the originating bank or exchanged for a new loan from the originating bank. The substitution process adds a substantial hassle factor.

Fully Funded Synthetic CDOs

The first fully funded synthetic CDO was Glacier Finance Ltd, which was done by Swiss Bank in August 1997. A synthetic balance sheet CDO sells credit protection on an underlying reference portfolio of loans to the originating bank in exchange for premium payment. In a *fully funded* synthetic CDO, the CDO issues debt and equity equal to the notional of the reference pool of loans. The CDO's liabilities are tranched in seniority and credit quality from AAA down to equity. There are often two AAA tranches, one more senior than the other. The senior-most AAA tranche is called the "super-senior" tranche and, because it is senior to another AAA tranche, its credit quality is arguably even better than AAA. In synthetic CDOs, just as in the cash CLOs, the originating bank retains a first-loss or equity position in the CDO.

Proceeds from the sale of the CDO's debt and equity are invested in a portfolio of high-quality assets. (Remember, the synthetic CDO does not buy the reference loans.) These assets are usually government securities, repurchase agreements on government securities, or AAA-rated asset-backed securities. Interest on the high-quality assets and credit protection premiums from the originating bank are used to pay interest on the CDO's notes. The mechanics of this are illustrated in panel A. of Exhibit 11.7 in Chapter 11.

The high-quality assets the CDO holds are referred to as the CDO's collateral. This can be confusing because in a cash CLO, the loans the CLO owns would be considered its collateral. In a cash CLO, loan-collateral credit losses cause the CLO to be unable to pay its liabilities. In a synthetic CDO, highly rated collateral ensures that the CDO will be able to pay default loss on the underlying reference loan portfolio to the originating bank.

Using an example can make this clearer. Assume the CDO has issued four tranches: $95 of AAA tranche, $2 of BBB tranche, $2 of BB tranche, and $1 of unrated equity. Moreover, assume $2 of loans experience a "credit event," and that the payout on the credit event is $1. The trustee would liquidate $1 of the high-quality collateral the CDO owns to pay default losses to the originating bank.

Alternatively, the trustee could wait for the natural maturity of the collateral, which is timed to coincide with the maturity of the CDO. When principal comes in from the collateral at its maturity, $1 is directed to the originating bank to pay for default losses. Synthetic CDOs can be structured relying on either the immediate liquidation of collateral or on the natural maturity of the collateral. This determines when the originating bank is paid default losses.

In either case, the $1 equity tranche would be completely written down, interest payments to it would cease, and it will never receive any principal. If these were all the losses that arose in the course of the transaction, the AAA through BB tranches would receive all principal and interest due. If an additional $2 of loans in the portfolio experience a credit event, also compensated at 50%, the trustee would liquidate an additional $1 of collateral (or wait for the maturity of the collateral) and then pay default losses to the originating bank. The principal on the BB tranche would be written down by $1.

The BB tranche would thereafter receive interest only on its remaining $1 of principal. If no further default losses occur, it would receive only $1 of principal.

Fully Funded Swap Arrangements

The originating bank is the protection buyer, and the CDO is the protection seller. Usually, the two parties enter into a CDS directly, but sometimes another Organisation for Economic Co-operation and Development (OECD) bank steps in between the originating bank and the CDO. This second scenario is illustrated in Exhibit 12.5. Back-to-back swaps have the economic effect of mitigating the risk for the intermediating bank, and as

EXHIBIT 12.5 Intermediary Bank in a Synthetic CDO Structure

A. Initial Flows

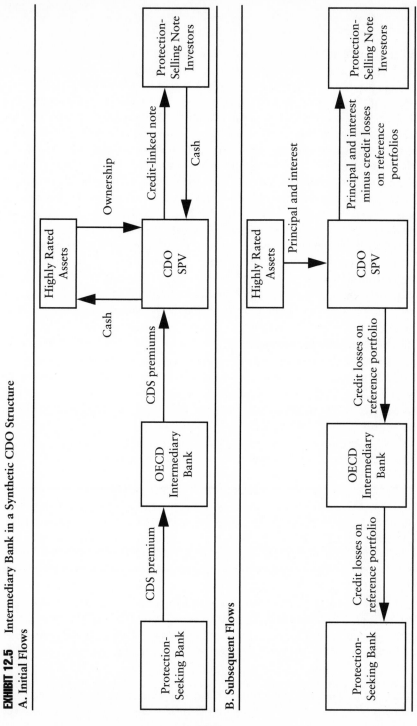

B. Subsequent Flows

before, they leave the originating bank as the protection buyer and the CDO as the protection seller. Although these structures are conceptually similar, they have different implications for required regulatory capital.

If the swap is done directly between the originating bank and the CDO, capital treatment for the originating bank will depend entirely on the risk weight of the CDO's collateral. That is, if the CDO's collateral is cash, cash substitutes, or Treasury securities, the risk weight of the swap is 0%. If the CDO invests in AAA-asset-backed securities, the risk weight of the swap is 100%. The introduction of an intermediary OECD bank changes the risk-based capital treatment for the originating bank. The risk weight of the swap is 20% under Bank for International Settlement (BIS) guidelines because it is with an OECD bank.

Thus, when setting up the synthetic CDO, the originating bank must decide whether it is more favorable to do the following: (1) limit the collateral account to 0% risk weight assets, which will constrain the choice of high quality collateral that can be used; or (2) introduce an OECD bank as intermediary and incur capital charges on a 20% risk-weighted asset.

Fully Funded Capital Requirements

The equity that is retained by the originating bank will always carry a 100% risk weight. Assume this equity portion is 1%, as is shown in Exhibit 12.2. Additional capital requirements depend on whether or not there is an intermediary bank. Without the presence of an intermediary bank, and if the CDO invests entirely in 0% risk-weighted assets, the capital charge on the swap is 0%, as mentioned above. Thus, the total capital charge on the CDO would just be the retained equity of, in our example, 1%.

If there is an intermediary OECD bank, the risk-based capital requirement on the swap is 20% of 8% (equaling 1.6%) of the notional amount of the credit default swap. Thus, if a bank entered into a fully funded synthetic CDO with a 1% first-loss position, the capital requirement is 100% of the first-loss piece, plus the risk-based capital requirement on the credit default swap. This would mean a capital charge of 2.6%.

U.S. Bank regulators allow for even lower capital charges for U.S. banks.[1] The regulators (the Federal Reserve and Office of the Comptroller of the Currency) describe two approaches and require banks to use the higher of the two.

---

[1] This is outlined in a document entitled *Capital Interpretation, Synthetic Collateralized Loan Obligations* (November 15, 1999). This document is available on the Federal Reserve web site.

The first approach is to hold capital dollar for dollar against the first loss position. On a 1% first loss position, this would be a 1% capital charge.

The second approach would be to have the transaction treated as a direct credit substitute, and assessed an 8% capital charge against its face value of 1%. The swap, if collateralized by Treasury securities at the CDO, would have no capital charge. If guaranteed by an intermediary bank, the swap would be assigned a 20% risk weight. Thus, under this approach, using our example, the capital charge would be $(0.08 \times (0.01 + 0.2))$ or 1.68%. Because this is higher than the 1% charge under the first approach, it would be the applicable charge.

Fully Funded Advantages and Disadvantages

It is useful now to focus on the advantages of the synthetic fully funded CDO over the cash CLO, as shown in Exhibit 12.4. First, the capital treatment is favorable. Second, the structure is confidential with respect to the bank's customers. Customers need not be notified that their loan has been sold, as the loan clearly stays with the bank. For banks, this point is particularly important, because selling a loan is looked at by many as compromising a customer relationship. It is true the names in the reference pool must be provided to the protection seller, but the names need not be publicly disclosed. Third, the bank has the flexibility to use the credit protection as a hedge for any senior obligation of the reference entity (including not only loans, but also bonds, derivatives, receivables, and so on). Fourth, the loans stay on the originating bank's balance sheet, so they are funded efficiently.

However, the disadvantage of a fully funded synthetic CDO over a partially funded synthetic CDO (discussed next) is that a funded senior tranche is more expensive than if the same risk was sold (i.e., the CDO bought credit protection) in pure unfunded credit default swap form.

PARTIALLY FUNDED SYNTHETIC CDOs

The first partially funded synthetic CDO was BISTRO (Broad Index Secured Trust Offering), which was done by JPMorgan in December 1997. The building blocks are the same in a partially funded structure, but the CDO only issues notes from 5% to 15% of the notional amount of the reference portfolio. The CDO buys protection on the remaining notional of the reference portfolio through an unfunded credit default swap. Partially funded synthetic CDOs deliver the advantage of a fully funded synthetic CDO at less cost. As a result, partially funded synthetic

CDOs have become more common than fully funded synthetic CDOs for both balance sheet synthetic CDOs and arbitrage synthetic CDOs.

The structure of a partially funded synthetic CDO is very similar to that of a fully funded CDO. The originating bank buys protection on a portfolio of corporate credit exposures via a credit default swap, either directly or indirectly, from the CDO. This is shown in panel A. of Exhibit 12.6. Thus, the originating bank is the protection buyer, and the CDO is the protection seller. As in a fully funded transaction, there may or may not be an intermediary OECD bank that sells credit protection to the originating bank and buys credit protection from the CDO.

In BISTRO CDOs, there was generally an intermediary bank, while in most other partially funded CDO structures, the credit default swap is done directly between the bank and the CDO. The partially funded structure in which there is an OECD intermediary is shown panel B. of Exhibit 12.6. As with cash CLOs and fully funded synthetic CDOs, the originating bank typically holds the equity issued by the partially funded synthetic CDO.

The CDO purchases government securities, repurchase agreements on government securities or other high-quality assets, which it funds through the issuance of notes. Those notes are credit tranched, and sold into the capital market. However, in departure from the fully funded structure, the CDO issues a substantially smaller amount of notes, and purchases substantially less high-quality assets, than the notional amount of the reference portfolio. This is shown in Exhibit 12.6.

Typically, the note issuance will amount from 5% to 15% of the notional amount of the reference portfolio. Thus, only the first 5% to 15% of losses in a particular portfolio are collateralized by the CDO, which leaves the larger super-senior risk uncollateralized.

In a partially funded synthetic balance sheet CDO, the risk on the super-senior piece can be laid off via a second credit default swap, often referred to as the "super-senior credit default swap," again shown in Exhibits 12.6. And the swap on the funded portion of the transaction is often referred to as the "junior credit default swap."

The advantage for the originating bank is that the super-senior credit default swap is cheaper than a funded note issued by the CDO. What we mean is that the spread above LIBOR for a funded super-senior note is greater than the premium on a super-senior credit default swap exposed to the same risk, historically, about 10 basis points or more.

Partially Funded Capital Treatment

In a partially funded CDO, the super-senior risk is often afforded the same capital treatment whether or not the risk is laid off on another

EXHIBIT 12.6 Partially Funded Synthetic CDO
A. Swap Directly Between Originating Bank and SPV

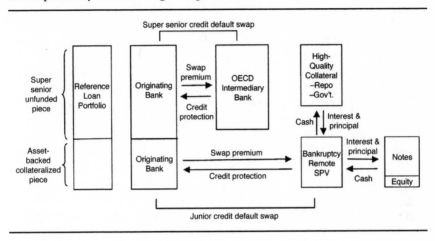

B. OECD Bank Intermediating Swap

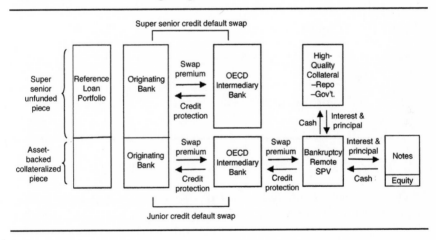

OECD bank. If the risk is laid off via a credit default swap with another OECD bank, the originating bank will be afforded a 20% risk weight. If the risk is not laid off, but is instead retained by the originating bank, the bank may still qualify for a 20% risk weight.

On November 15, 1999, the Federal Reserve issued a set of capital interpretations on synthetic CLOs, which apply to U.S banks.[2] These

---

[2] Capital Interpretations, Synthetic Collateralized Loan Obligations.

guidelines allow the retained super-senior risk to receive a 20% risk weight, as long as a number of conditions are met including the presence of a junior tranche rated Aaa or AAA from a nationally recognized statistical rating agency (NRSRO, meaning Moody's, S&P, Fitch, and DBRS). Prior to this interpretation, if the risk of the super-senior piece was not laid off, there was no capital relief, and its risk weight was 100%. For European banks, the treatment varies jurisdiction by jurisdiction.

The regulatory capital charge on the equity tranche and the junior credit default swap follows the same rules as on the fully funded CDO, and these are summarized in Exhibit 12.2. If the junior swap is done directly with the CDO, and the CDO is collateralized with 0% risk weight assets, then the junior swap has a 0% risk weight. The capital charge on would be 100% of the first loss piece (the equity portion), plus the capital charge on the super-senior credit default swap.

Assume again a 1% first loss piece and that the junior credit swap is for 10% of the transaction amount (which means that the super-senior portion is 90% of the notional amount). The credit charge on the super-senior swap is

(20% risk weight) × (8% capital charge) × (90% of the notional amount)
= 1.44%

Thus, the total capital charge is 2.44% (1% on equity + 1.44% on the super-senior swap).

If an OECD bank serves as the protection seller to the originating bank on the junior default swap, the 20% capital charge would apply to 100% of the notional loan amount. Thus, the capital charge would be 20% of 8% or 1.6%. The total capital charge on the transaction would be

(Capital charge on the swaps) + (Capital charge on the equity) = 2.6%

Under U.S. bank regulation, the capital charges would be somewhat lower. If the junior credit default swap was collateralized by Treasuries, the capital charge would be 8% on the 1% first-loss position (direct credit substitute rule) plus 8% × 20% on the 90% super-senior price, for a total of 1.52%. This is obviously higher than for a dollar-for-dollar charge on the 1% piece that is retained.

If an OECD bank acts as the protection seller on the credit default swap, the direct credit substitute rule would apply on the 1% first-loss piece, and a 20% risk-based capital requirement would apply on 100% of the notional amount, for a total capital charge of 1.68%.

This partially funded structure has several advantages. It allows banks to reduce the risk on a large number of on-balance sheet assets.

Confidentiality concerns are also mitigated, as is a funding advantage (because only 5% to 15% of the loans are funded). Finally, favorable regulatory capital treatment is achieved, as shown in Exhibit 12.4. As a result, partially funded synthetic balance sheet transactions have become the norm.

CONCLUSION

Bank balance sheet CDOs are almost always done in synthetic rather than cash form. The risk of the loan is transferred to the synthetic CDO, and ultimately to the parties that have sold credit protection to the CDOs, but the loan itself remains at the bank. The relationship between the bank and its borrower is therefore undisturbed and the bank continues to fund the loan. In practice, the CDO's purchase of credit protection is cheaper in unfunded credit default swap form than in funded note form.

CHAPTER 13

Synthetic Arbitrage CDOs

In this chapter, we discuss synthetic arbitrage CDOs. As explained in detail in Chapter 11, a synthetic CDO does not actually own the portfolio of assets on which it bears credit risk. Instead, it gains credit exposure by selling protection via credit default swaps. In turn, the synthetic CDO buys protection from investors via the tranches it issues. These tranches are responsible for credit losses in the reference portfolio that rise above a particular attachment point; each tranche's liability ends at a particular detachment or exhaustion point. Unlike balance sheet synthetic CDOs discussed in Chapter 12, the motivation in an arbitrage synthetic CDO is investors' desire to assume tranched credit risk in return for spread.

Issuance of synthetic arbitrage CDOs got under way in earnest in 2000, but exploded the next year to about $60 billion, including both funded and unfunded tranches. By 2005, synthetic arbitrage issuance was over $500 billion, if one counts in the standard tranches of credit default swap indices.

Synthetic arbitrage CDOs come in the following forms:

- The oldest are *full-capital structure CDOs* that include a full complement of tranches from super senior to equity. These CDOs have either static reference portfolios or a manager who actively trades the underlying portfolio of credit default swaps (CDS).
- *Single-tranche CDOs* are newer, and are made possible by dealers' faith in their ability to hedge the risk of a CDO tranche through single-name CDS. Single tranche CDOs often allow CDO investors to substitute credits and amend other terms over the course of the CDOs' life.
- *Standard tranches of credit default swap indices* are the most liquid type of CDOs. These instruments allow long-short strategies that appeal to certain types of investors.

In this chapter, we will outline the features of these types of synthetic arbitrage CDOs.

FULL-CAPITAL STRUCTURE SYNTHETIC ARBITRAGE CDOs

Full capital structure synthetic arbitrage CDOs come in many forms. The best way to explain the differences is to focus on two CDO types that represent the range of structural variations.

The first has a static reference portfolio of 100 investment-grade names which we will refer to as CDO #1. The second, which we refer to as CDO #2, is managed with roughly the same underlying credit quality as CDO #1. Salient features of each of the two CDOs, including capital structures and spreads, are shown in Exhibit 13.1.

Static versus Managed

Synthetic arbitrage CDOs can be done as static pools or as managed transactions. The advantage to static CDOs is that the investor can examine the proposed portfolio before closing and know that the portfolio will not change. The investors can ask that certain credits be removed from the portfolio or can decide not to invest in the CDO at all. There are also no ongoing management fees.

The disadvantage to a static deal becomes apparent if an underlying credit begins to deteriorate, because no mechanism exists for the CDO to rid itself of the problem credit, which remains in the portfolio and may continue to erode.

Over time, the balance of static versus managed synthetic full-capital structure arbitrage CDOs has changed, shifting from 80%/20% in favor of static portfolios in 2001 to 80%/ 20% in favor of managed portfolios in 2005. Investor preferences have changed partly because of the poor performance of many investment-grade corporate credits in 2001 and 2002. In those years, 13 once-investment-grade names defaulted, and many of those credits happened to be overrepresented in static CDO portfolios.

Capital Structure

Observe from Exhibit 13.1 that static synthetic CDO #1 has much higher equity (3% versus 1.6%) and no coverage tests. The higher equity percentage is a reflection of the absence of coverage tests. The key to understanding the smaller size of the equity tranche in CDO #2 is the structure of its interest waterfall.

First, the trustee fee, the senior default swap fee, and the senior advisory fee are all paid out of the available collateral interest and CDS

EXHIBIT 13.1 Synthetic CDO Spectrum

		Deal #1		Deal #2	
Amount		$1 billion reference pool 100 reference entities		$1 billion reference pool 100 reference obligors	
Management		Static		Managed	
Class	Capital Structure	Amount ($ million)	Spread (bps)	Amount ($ million)	Spread (bps)
	Super Senior	870	6	890	6
Class A	AAA	50	50	30	48
Class B	AA	30	90	30	85
Class C	A	5	175	14	125
Class D	BBB	15	400	20	275
Class E	Equity	30		16	
Coverage Test		None		Cash collateral Class A+B+C+D	>111%
Final maturity		5 years		5 years	
Write-down provisions		Immediately upon default		At end of life of deal	
Swap settlement		Cash		Physical	

premium receipts. Next, interest is paid to the various note holders, from Class A to Class D, in order of their seniority. Then, a coverage test is conducted. If the coverage test is passed, remaining funds are used to pay the subordinate advisory fee, and the residual cash flow goes to equity holders.

But if the coverage test is failed, cash flow is trapped in a reserve account. Cash in the CDO's reserve account is factored into the coverage test, helping the CDO to meet its required ratio. If the coverage test comes back into compliance, future excess cash flows can be released to the subordinate advisory fee and to equity holders. At the CDO's maturity, cash in the reserve account becomes part of the principal waterfall and helps to pay off tranches in order of their seniority.

Despite the different proportions of equity in the two CDOs, the credit protection enjoyed by rated tranches in each CDO is about equal. This is so because credit protection is measured not only by the amount of subordination below a tranche, but also by how high credit losses can be on the underlying portfolio before the tranche's cash flows are affected. In this case, the rated tranches from both CDOs can survive approximately the same level of default losses; the lower amount of equity in CDO #2 is compensated for by its coverage test and cash trap mechanism.

Settlement on Credit Default Swaps

Note in Exhibit 13.1 that CDO #1 uses cash settlement on the reference pool of assets, while CDO #2 uses physical settlement. There are advantages and disadvantages to both. Cash settlement is simple and final, thus one generally sees cash settlement in static deals. With physical settlement, the CDO has to deal with the defaulted debt that has been delivered to it. In a managed CDO, however, the manager can decide whether to sell the debt immediately or hold it in hope of realizing a higher market value later. Physical settlement tends is more common than cash settlement in managed deals.

Equity Cash Flows and the Timing of Write-Downs

In CDO #1, equity is paid a fixed coupon, and thus has no claim on the residual cash flows of the CDO. Equity holders receive interest only on the outstanding equity balance. In CDO #2, the equity holders have a claim on all residual cash flows of the CDO.

The timing of write-downs is very different for the two CDOs. In CDO #1, there is a cash settlement whenever a credit event occurs. Thus, when a credit event occurs (1) that credit is removed from the pool, (2) the CDO pays default losses, and (3) the lowest tranche in the

CDO is written down by the amount of default losses. If equity is written down to zero, further losses are written down against the next most junior tranche and so on, moving up the CDO's capital structure.

By contrast, when a credit event occurs in CDO #2, physical settlement occurs. The security can be sold, but there is no write-down until the end of the deal. At that time, the principal cash flows go through the principal waterfall, paying off first the Class A note holders and then those in Class B, C, and D. After note holders are paid, remaining funds go to the equity holders.

Because of these structural differences and investor taste, the BBB and lower classes in CDO #1 generally sell wider than they do in CDO #2. In Exhibit 13.1, the BBB tranche is shown at LIBOR + 400 in CDO #1; it is only LIBOR + 275 in CDO #2. In CDO #1, the write-downs are immediate, and there is no way to recoup losses by better performance later in the deal's life. Moreover, if any of the classes (including the equity) incur losses, their interest is reduced accordingly.

How "Arbitrage" Are Synthetic Arbitrage CDOs?

We have called the CDOs discussed "arbitrage" CDOs. We now look at that label more closely. In some synthetic CDOs, particularly in static portfolio CDOs, the selection of underlying credits is constrained by the availability of risk at the specific bank putting together the CDO.

What do we mean by this? We said earlier that potential equity investors in a synthetic CDO go to a bank with a list of credits on which they want to sell first loss protection. In practice, the final selection of the portfolio depends upon names that the bank either is exposed to already or can become exposed to quickly.

If the bank has an imbalance in its single-name CDS book (which was caused by having sold more protection on a particular name than it has purchased), it will be interested in buying protection on that name from an "arbitrage" CDO. Sometimes the bank's desire to buy credit protection on a particular name derives from exposures built up in other activities. For example, the bank might be exposed to a certain counterparty on interest rate and currency derivatives. In that case, the bank may be interested in buying protection from a CDO. Sometimes the bank can sell protection on a particular name, thereby creating the need to buy protection from a CDO.

The issue of the availability of credit exposure gives these "arbitrage" CDOs a certain balance sheet feel. This is less true in the case of managed synthetic CDOs, where the manager can offer to sell credit protection to a number of banks. Another "arbitrage" synthetic CDO with a balance sheet favor is the CDO driven by a bank's desire to lay off the credit risk of a bond portfolio it owns. The bank thereafter becomes the funder of the bond portfolio without being the owner of its credit risk.

SINGLE-TRANCHE CDOs

Single-tranche CDOs are notable for what they are not: the placement of a complete capital structure complement of tranches, from equity to super senior. Instead, a protection seller enters into one specific CDO tranche with a CDS dealer in isolation.

This arrangement creates an imbalanced position for the CDS dealer. For example, it might have bought protection on the 3% to 7% tranche of a synthetic CDO comprising 150 underlying investment-grade names. The CDS dealer will sell protection on these names in the single-name CDS market, varying the notional amount of protection it buys from name to name, in a process called *delta hedging.*

While there are concerns with using delta hedging, because CDS dealers believe in its efficacy, protection sellers enjoy great flexibility in choosing the terms of single tranche CDOs.[1] Protection sellers can choose the portfolio they wish to reference, as well as the attachment and detachment points of the tranche they wish to sell protection on. These factors will imply a price for that protection.

Alternatively, the protection seller can start with a premium in mind and then negotiate other terms to create a transaction furnishing that premium. Because there are only two parties to the transaction, execution can be quicker than it would be with a full-capital structure CDO encompassing many constituencies.

The single-tranche synthetic CDO can also provide flexibility over its life. As reference credits in the underlying portfolio either erode or improve in credit quality, the value of the CDO changes. If, for example, reference credits have all been severely downgraded, the value of credit protection increases because it is more likely there will be default losses. A protection seller of such a single-tranche CDO might be willing to pay a fee to terminate the CDO early rather than be exposed to default losses later.

Single-tranche CDO investors can go back to the original dealer to reverse out of a trade, or they can reverse the trade with another dealer. If investors have sold protection to dealer A, for example, they can buy

---

[1] Any losses dealers incur in delta hedging do not affect the terms or economics of the single-tranche CDO.

protection on the exact terms from dealer B. This would leave them with offsetting trades. In many cases, dealers will allow the investor to step out of the trades completely, and the two dealers will face each other directly.

Many single-tranche synthetic CDOs have a feature where terms of the CDO are adjustable over its life. Recall the example where underlying credits have severely deteriorated. Protection sellers might be allowed to replace a soured credit with a better one for a fee. Or, instead of paying a fee, the terms of the CDO tranche might change. In exchange for getting rid of a troubled underlying credit, the attachment point might be decreased, or the detachment point might be increased, or the premium might decrease.

STANDARD TRANCHES OF CDS INDICES

Now let us look at our last type of synthetic arbitrage CDO. The tranches of the CDS indices described in Chapter 11 are quoted and traded like liquid synthetic CDO tranches. As shown in Exhibit 13.2, the Dow Jones CDX.NA.IG is divided up into 0% to 3%, 3% to 7%, 7% to 10%, 10% to 15%, and 15% to 30% tranches. For the investment-grade indices, equity tranches require an upfront payment from the protection buyer to the protection seller. After that, a fixed 500 bps per annum is exchanged. For the high-yield index, the first two tranches require upfront payments but have no running fee. The higher tranches of the indices trade solely on their running fees. Exhibit 13.2 gives details of tranche structure for various CDS indices.

Investors in standard tranches often engage in various forms of long/short trades. They might sell protection on an equity or first-loss tranche and buy protection on a more senior tranche of the same index. (In market parlance, they are said to be long the equity tranche and short the more senior tranche.) Being long a tranche can be confusing to some investors because one has *sold* protection on it, but the situation is analogous to being long a bond. When one is long a bond or long a CDO tranche (having sold protection), an investor abhors a default and does not want interest rates, credit spreads, or CDS premiums to rise or widen.

Another popular long/short trade is to sell protection on a tranche in a longer maturity and then to buy protection on the same tranche from the same index in a shorter maturity. Hedge funds are big participants in long/short strategies.

EXHIBIT 13.2   Standard Tranches of CDS Indices

CDX NA IG

	Attachment/ Detachment Points	Upfront Payment	Running Premium
Tranche 1	0%–3%	Yes	500 bps
Tranche 2	3%–7%	No	Yes
Tranche 3	7%–10%	No	Yes
Tranche 4	10%–15%	No	Yes
Tranche 5	15%–30%	No	Yes

iTraxx Europe, iTraxx Asia (ex Japan), iTraxx Japan

	Attachment/ Detachment Points	Upfront Payment	Running Premium
Tranche 1	0%–3%	Yes	500 bps
Tranche 2	3%–6%	No	Yes
Tranche 3	6%–9%	No	Yes
Tranche 4	9%–12%	No	Yes
Tranche 5	12%–22%	No	Yes

CDX NA HY

	Attachment/ Detachment Points	Upfront Payment	Running Premium
Tranche 1	0%–10%	Yes	No
Tranche 2	10%–15%	Yes	No
Tranche 3	15%–25%	No	Yes
Tranche 4	25%–35%	No	Yes
Tranche 5	35%–100%	No	Yes

CONCLUSION

Synthetic arbitrage CDOs incorporate ever-evolving structures that have rapidly gained acceptance in the market. Based on the actual amount of credit risk transferred, synthetic structures are more important than those using cash collateral.

One reason for this is the cheap price of unfunded credit protection on super-senior tranches. The economics of synthetic deals are further enhanced by the ability to more easily and quickly ramp-up a portfolio and execute a CDO. Finally, selling protection via credit default swaps is often more rewarding than assuming credit risk through a cash bond.

Synthetic CDO structures are varied. Some synthetic CDOs are static, while others are managed. Some employ standard synthetic architecture (i.e., writing down from the bottom of the capital structure first, no cash traps, and cash settlement). Others employ some aspects of cash flow CDO architecture (i.e., no write-downs until the end of the life of the deal, less equity compensated by cash trapping-coverage tests, and physical settlement).

The rise of single-tranche CDOs affords greater flexibility to investors, including ease and speed in execution and the chance to amend the CDO's terms later in its life. Standard tranches of CDS indices are the most liquid type of synthetic CDO; they also provide investors with the chance to put on various long-short positions to assume customized risks.

CHAPTER 14

A Framework for Evaluating Trades in the Credit Derivatives Market

As discussed in Chapter 11, the markets for credit default swap (CDS) and synthetic collateralized debt obligation (CDO) have grown tremendously, both in terms of trading volume and product evolution. In terms of product evolution, CDSs have developed from highly idiosyncratic contracts, taking a great deal of time to negotiate, into a liquid market offering competitive quotations on single-name instruments and even indices of credits. Synthetic CDOs have evolved from vehicles used by commercial banks to offload commercial loan risk to customized tranches where investors can select underlying credits. And the rise of standard tranches of CDS indices has blurred the distinction between credit default swaps and synthetic CDOs.

As a result of these instruments, credit trades offered to participants in the credit derivatives market every day involve assessing trade-offs, such as the following two examples:

- Is it better to sell credit protection on a single BBB rated corporate name or on the BBB rated tranche of a synthetic CDO?
- Is it better to sell credit protection on a portfolio of BB names or on the equity tranche of a CDO comprised of A-rated names?

These examples offer us the chance to analyze risk to a single credit, a portfolio of credits, and a tranche of a CDO. They also allow us the opportunity to compare risk to credits with the same underlying rating and to credits with different underlying ratings.

In this chapter, we describe an empirically driven methodology that uses historical default and loss-given-default data to answer these types of questions. Specifically, we show how the single-name, portfolio, and tranched positions mentioned would have performed had they been entered into in 1970, 1971, and so on. We begin by examining the historical default rate and loss given default data available to investors. Then we discuss the considerations that go into making a model that uses this data to arrive at a historic perspective. Next, we show historic pro forma results for the positions mentioned above. Finally, we discuss the advantages and limitations of this approach and the type of empirical research that would help improve the analysis.

ASSESSING SINGLE-NAME AND CDO TRANCHED EXPOSURES

Suppose one is offered the choice of selling credit protection via two different 5-year credit derivatives. Both reference BBB rated credits, but one is based on exposure to a single credit while the other is based on tranched exposure to 100 credits. The two choices are:

- Sell credit protection for five years on a single BBB rated corporate for 82 basis points via a single-name CDS.
- Sell credit protection for five years on 100 underlying BBB corporates for 325 basis points and be responsible for default losses that occur on the 5% to 7% synthetic CDO tranche.[1]

Below we describe the available data to assess these two trades.

Historical Default Rates

What historical data do we have at our disposal to see how these two choices would have fared in the past? Exhibit 14.1 shows the results of studies from Moody's,[2] S&P,[3] and Fitch[4] with respect to the average 5-year historical default rate of BBB/Baa corporates.

---

[1] All market prices herein were realistic at the time this chapter was written.

[2] Exhibits 17 and 18 in David T. Hamilton, *et al.*, *Default and Recovery Rates of Corporate Issuers, 1920–2004*, Moody's Investors Service (January 2005).

[3] Table 11 in Diane Vazza, Devi Aurora, and Ryan Schneck, *Annual Global Corporate Default Study: Corporate Defaults Poised to Rise in 2005*, Standard and Poor's (January 2005).

[4] Charlotte L. Needham, Mariarosa Verde, and Stephanie K. Mah, *Fitch Ratings Corporate Finance 2004 Transition and Default Study*, Fitch Ratings (May 17, 2005), p. 8.

EXHIBIT 14.1 Average BBB/Baa 5-Year Default Rates

Fitch 1990–2004	3.45%
Moody's 1920–2004	3.40%
Moody's 1970–2004	2.08%
S&P 1981–2004	3.25%
Average of studies	3.05%

Source: Fitch Ratings, Moody's Investors Servic, and Standard & Poor's.

The Fitch study averages results over one decade, the S&P study over two decades, and the Moody's studies over three and eight decades, respectively. In the bottom row of the Exhibit 14.1, we calculated the average of these average 5-year BBB/Baa default rates as 3.05%.

These average default rates are not very useful for analyzing credit derivatives, especially CDO tranches. According to any of the default rates in Exhibit 14.1, default losses would never rise to a level that would affect a 5% to 7% CDO tranche, even if there were zero recoveries and loss given default was therefore 100%.

For the CDO tranche, the fluctuation around the average default rate matters a lot. The wider the fluctuation, the more often the default rate will rise to a level where it affects the 5% to 7% CDO tranche. Default rate fluctuation has two sources:

1. Default rates vary from time to time, even among credits with the same rating.
2. Default rates differ among portfolios created at the same time, again even if they contain credits with the same ratings.

Rating Cohort and Portfolio Defaults

Exhibit 14.2 shows how default rates have varied over time. The exhibit shows the 5-year default rate for BBB/Baa *rating cohorts*. A "rating cohort" comprises all corporates with the same senior unsecured rating at a particular time. BBB and Baa rating cohorts were formed at the beginning of every year from 1970 through 2000, and their defaults were tracked over the next five years.

For example, the 1.43% default rate for 1970 in the Moody's time series indicates that of all corporates with senior unsecured ratings of Baa at January 1, 1970, 1.43% of them defaulted within five years up to January 1, 1975. At the opposite end of the exhibit, the 4.02% default rate at 2000 in the S&P time series indicates that of all corporates with senior unsecured ratings of BBB at January 1, 2000, 4.02% defaulted within five years up to January 1, 2005.

EXHIBIT 14.2   Five-Year BBB/Baa Rating Cohort Default Rates

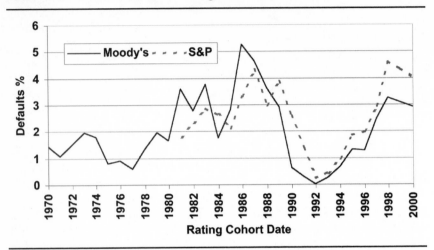

Source: Moody's Investors Service and Standard & Poor's.

EXHIBIT 14.3   Number of Defaults in 100-Name Portfolio, Default Probability = 1%

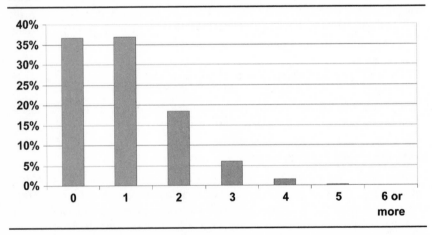

   The 5-year default rates of Moody's Baa rating cohorts have varied from 0.00% to 5.26%, while the S&P BBB rating cohorts have varied from 0.25% to 4.59%. This gives us perspective on the fluctuation of default rates over time. However, default rates also fluctuate among portfolios created at the same time because of the simple workings of chance.

   When 100-name portfolios are created in an environment where there is, for example, a 1% default rate, each portfolio will not experience exactly one default. Using the binomial distribution, Exhibit 14.3 shows the probability that zero, one, two, or more defaults will occur out of a 100-name portfolio if the general population-wide default rate is 1%. As one would expect, the most likely possibility is one default out of 100 names. But there also are decreasing probabilities for two, three, four, and even more defaults.[5]

Default Timing

The time-fluctuation default rates shown in Exhibit 14.2 and the portfolio-fluctuating default rates in Exhibit 14.3 provide a lot more detail than the average default rates of Exhibit 14.1. With Exhibits 14.2 and 14.3, we can begin to imagine how the 5% to 7% CDO tranche could be touched by defaults. This could happen because the default rate of a particular rating cohort is high or because the default rate of a particular portfolio of credits within a rating cohort is high.

However, this default data is still inadequate for our purposes. We need to know more about the timing of defaults within the 5-year period because this greatly influences the valuation of credit derivatives. If defaults happen early in the life of a credit derivative, the seller of protection receives fewer or smaller premium payments and makes default loss payments sooner. That reduces the present value of the credit protection seller's position relative what its present value would be if the same defaults occurred later in the life of the credit derivative.

Exhibits 14.4 and 14.5 show the timing of default rates by focusing on Baa *marginal default rates* using Moody's default experience. "Marginal default rates" are the default rates that occur within the first year, within the second year, within the third year, and so on. The exhibits show the wide variability of marginal default rates. First-year marginal default rates for Baa credits range from 0.00% to 1.33% and fifth-year marginal defaults range from 0.00% to 1.65%.

---

[5] Those familiar with techniques for looking at default risk in credit portfolios will notice that we are doing things unusually. The common practice is to assume a single unvarying default rate and some level of positive default correlation (actually positive correlation of changes in asset values) to create default rate fluctuations in a portfolio. But we vary default probability and accept the zero default correlation assumption of the binomial distribution. Regardless of how one feels about the dominant credit modeling approach, we have an advantage in performing this historical analysis, because we know the default rate for each rating cohort in each year from 1970 through 2000. Looking back in time at each rating cohort, we are not so much dealing with default *probabilities* as with default *rates*. Given that a particular rating cohort of hundreds of names experienced a particular default rate, the default rate experienced by a *randomly drawn* subset of 100 names from the rating cohort is an independent or uncorrelated process and the binomial distribution is appropriate. We assess the assumption that synthetic CDO portfolios are randomly drawn from the credit population near the end of this chapter.

EXHIBIT 14.4   Baa Marginal Default Rates

	1st	2nd	3rd	4th	5th
1970	0.27%	0.00%	0.00%	0.87%	0.30%
1971	0.00%	0.00%	0.80%	0.27%	0.00%
1972	0.00%	0.73%	0.25%	0.26%	0.27%
1973	0.46%	0.23%	0.48%	0.24%	0.52%
1974	0.00%	0.47%	0.25%	0.51%	0.53%
1975	0.00%	0.00%	0.26%	0.53%	0.00%
1976	0.00%	0.27%	0.29%	0.00%	0.31%
1977	0.28%	0.29%	0.00%	0.00%	0.00%
1978	0.00%	0.00%	0.00%	0.00%	1.32%
1979	0.00%	0.30%	0.00%	1.30%	0.34%
1980	0.00%	0.00%	0.96%	0.33%	0.34%
1981	0.00%	0.61%	1.27%	0.67%	1.03%
1982	0.31%	0.00%	1.01%	1.05%	0.37%
1983	0.00%	1.16%	0.41%	1.71%	0.47%
1984	0.36%	0.00%	0.41%	0.46%	0.51%
1985	0.00%	1.20%	0.00%	0.51%	1.08%
1986	1.33%	0.00%	1.68%	0.88%	1.38%
1987	0.00%	1.05%	0.37%	1.56%	1.65%
1988	0.00%	0.33%	0.70%	1.45%	1.16%
1989	0.59%	0.63%	0.65%	1.04%	0.00%
1990	0.00%	0.62%	0.00%	0.00%	0.00%
1991	0.27%	0.00%	0.00%	0.00%	0.00%
1992	0.00%	0.00%	0.00%	0.00%	0.00%
1993	0.00%	0.00%	0.25%	0.00%	0.00%
1994	0.00%	0.20%	0.00%	0.22%	0.22%
1995	0.00%	0.00%	0.00%	0.42%	0.87%
1996	0.00%	0.00%	0.17%	0.54%	0.56%
1997	0.00%	0.14%	0.60%	0.61%	1.13%
1998	0.12%	0.36%	0.50%	1.03%	1.21%
1999	0.10%	0.53%	0.78%	1.27%	0.37%
2000	0.38%	0.49%	1.35%	0.45%	0.24%

Source: Moody's Investors Service.

EXHIBIT 14.5   Distribution of 5-Year Baa Defaults

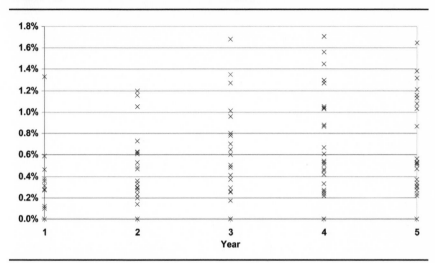

Source: Moody's Investors Service.

EXHIBIT 14.6   Senior Unsecured Loss Given Default

Moody's Issuer Weighted	51.56%
Moody's Par Weighted	49.70%
S&P Ultimate	50.25%
Average of studies	50.50%

Source: Moody's Investors Service and Standard & Poor's.

Loss Given Default

Of course, default rate is only half of the credit loss equation. Exhibit 14.6 shows the results of rating agency studies of loss given default (default loss severity, or one minus recovery as a percent of par) for senior unsecured bonds.[6] Over various periods and subject to different calculation methods, all of the studies come close to the 50.50% average.

Yet, just as with default rates, there is a great deal of variability in loss given default from year to year. This is illustrated in Exhibit 14.7,

---

[6] The Moody's data are from David T. Hamilton and Richard Cantor, *Rating Transitions and Defaults Conditional on Watchlist, Outlook and Rating History*, *Moody's Investors Service* (February 2004). The S&P data are from David Keisman, "Recovery Trends and Analysis," PowerPoint presentation, Standard and Poor's (March 24, 2004).

EXHIBIT 14.7   Yearly Loss Given Default

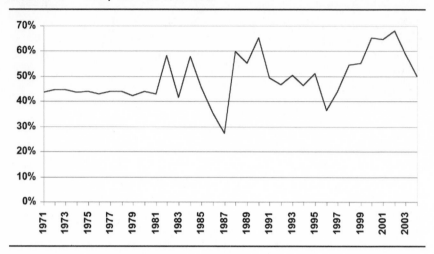

which shows average loss given default year-by-year.[7] It is also important to understand that within any particular year, loss given default varies from one defaulted credit to another. On average, the standard deviation of loss given default among defaulted corporates within the same year has been 25%.

The Historical Credit Model

Assume in our original problem a $100 notional for both trades. We now have the ingredients for our historical exploration of these two credit derivative opportunities:

- Five years of marginal default rates for Baa corporates beginning each year from 1970 through 2000, as shown in Exhibit 14.4.
- Loss given default rates for each year 1970 through 2004, as shown in Exhibit 14.7, and the additional information that the standard deviation of loss given default within any year is around 25%.

For the 1970 Baa rating cohort, we used marginal default rates of 0.27%, 0.00%, 0.00%, 0.87%, and 0.30% as shown in Exhibit 14.4. We

---

[7] Loss given default for 1982 through 2003 are actual senior unsecured bond prices one month after default. Loss given defaults from 1970 through 1981 were estimated via a regression using Moody's all-corporate default rate. This regression was Loss given default = 41.7% + 5.8 × All corporate default rate and had an adjusted R-square of 26%.

further divide each yearly marginal default rate into two, so that we can determine defaults in the first six months and last six months of each year. Given the default rate, the binomial distribution determines how many defaults occur in each 6-month period. For each default, loss given default is determined first by looking at the average loss given default for that particular year. These are 57%, 43%, 44%, 44%, and 43% for the years 1970 through 1974. Each particular loss given default is simulated using these average yearly loss given defaults and a 25% standard deviation and normal distribution. Premium payments and credit loss payments were tracked and cash flows were present valued at a 5% discount rate.

Exhibit 14.8 shows the results of our modeling. There is no contest. The expected present value of the 5% to 7% CDO tranche across all 31 rating cohorts from 1970 through 2000 is $14.04, while the expected present value of the single-name CDS is only $2.67. The $11.37 difference is caused by both the *pricing* of the two alternatives and by their *expected losses*. The CDO's premium is 325 basis points, which creates a $14.22 present value if there are no default loss payouts. Meanwhile, the premium for the CDS is only 82 basis points, which creates a $3.59 present value if there are no default loss payouts. So right away, the CDO starts with a $10.63 advantage. Moreover, expected default loss payouts are less for the CDO than for the CDS: specifically, $0.18 for the CDO, and $0.92 for the CDS.

What if one simply puts more notional at risk in the CDS trade? In Exhibit 14.9, we show our model's results after increasing the notional amount of the single-name CDS trade to $527. The average present value of each alternative becomes $14.04.

EXHIBIT 14.8   Present Values of Two BBB-Underlying Trades

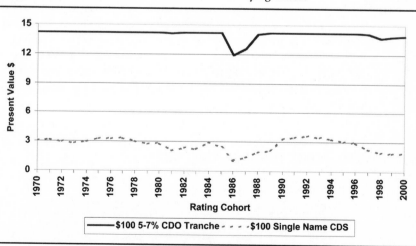

EXHIBIT 14.9 Present Value of Two BBB-Underlying Trades

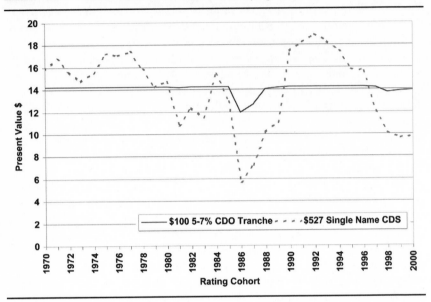

Obviously, the extreme downside of the two trades is now very much different. It is only possible to lose $100 in the CDO trade, but it is theoretically possible to lose $527 in the CDS trade. More practically, the volatility of CDS trade becomes obvious. Year-by-year, the average present value of the CDO ranges from $11.94 to $14.22; meanwhile, the average present value of the CDS ranges from $5.76 to $18.90.

Moreover, within each rating cohort there is greater variability of returns in the CDS trade than in the CDO trade. In Exhibit 14.10 we also show the average present value of the two trades minus one standard deviation.[8] Under this stress, the $527 single-name CDS usually has a negative present value. Clearly, using historical defaults and recovery and the assumed pricing, the 5% to 7% CDO tranche is a much less risky than the single-name CDS.

ASSESSING CDO EQUITY VERSUS A BASKET SWAP

In our second example, we suppose that an investor is offered a different choice of selling credit protection via two different 5-year credit

---

[8] The standard deviation we are referring to is of the results of simulations for each particular rating cohort. It reflects the variability of portfolios formed at the same time.

EXHIBIT 14.10   Present Value of Two BBB-Underlying Trades

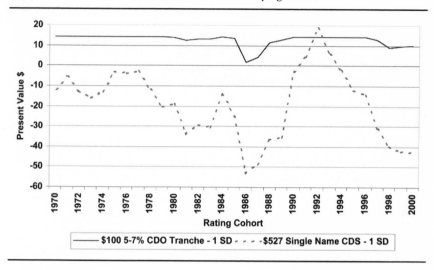

derivatives—CDO equity and a basket swap. Both are first loss positions, but one is based on exposure to an undivided portfolio while the other is based on tranched exposure to a higher-rated portfolio. The two choices are:

- Sell credit protection for five years on a portfolio of 100 BB corporate names for 350 basis points via a basket CDS, "BB basket."
- Sell credit protection for five years on 100 A-rated corporates for 35% upfront and 500 basis points per annum, being responsible for any default losses that occur on the 0% to 3% synthetic CDO tranche, "CDO equity."

We again assume $100 notional for both trades. We still make use of the yearly loss given default data displayed in Exhibit 14.7 and the 25% interyear standard deviation of loss given default. But now, we use marginal default rates for BB and A rating cohorts from 1970 through 2000. These data are shown graphically in Exhibits 14.11 and 14.12. Note the difference in scale on the exhibit's vertical axis.

Exhibit 14.13 shows the expected present values of the CDO equity and BB basket alternatives for each rating cohort from 1970 through 2000. Again, there is no contest between the two alternatives. The average of the CDO equity series is $49.14 versus $10.08 for the BB basket, giving CDO equity a $39.06 advantage. The CDO begins with a pricing advantage, because—in the absence of any default loss payout—the

EXHIBIT 14.11 Yearly A Rating Marginal Default Rates

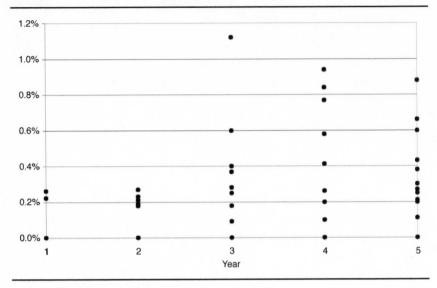

Source: Moody's Investors Service.

EXHIBIT 14.12 Yearly BB Marginal Default Rates

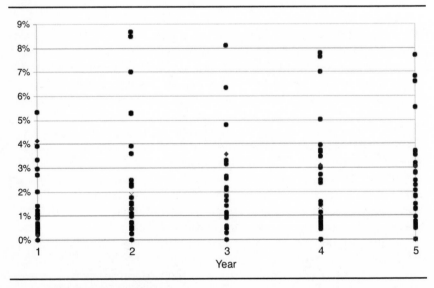

Source: Moody's Investors Service.

EXHIBIT 14.13 $100 A Equity versus $100 BB Basket

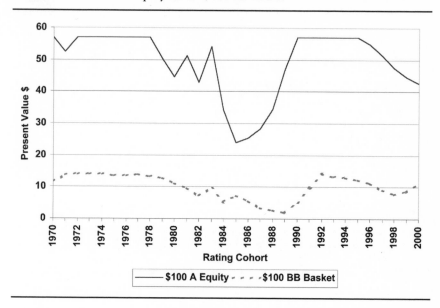

present values of the CDO and BB basket are $56.88 and $15.32, respectively. The slightly higher expected loss on CDO equity versus the BB basket, $7.74 versus $5.24, is not enough to overcome the advantage with which the CDO begins.

In Exhibit 14.14, we again equalize the expected present value of the two trades, this time by inflating the notional of the BB basket to $488. Now, both trades have an expected present value of $49.14. Besides having a higher theoretical worst-case potential loss because of its higher notional, the BB basket shows more volatility year-to-year. The CDO ranges from $23.73 to $56.88 while the BB basket ranges from $9.62 to $69.14. Finally, in Exhibit 14.15, we show average present values minus one standard deviation. Again, the basket trade is more volatile than the CDO equity trade. Our conclusion is that the CDO equity trade is more attractive than the BB basket trade.

Methodological Caveats

Our analysis assumes that the credits we looked at are about as default-prone as any other credit of the same rating. In other words, we assume no adverse (or verse) selection bias in the choice of credits. We are assuming that the creators of these trades have not gone through Moody's ratings and picked the worst (or best) credits out of each rating

EXHIBIT 14.14 $100 A Equity versus $488 BB Basket

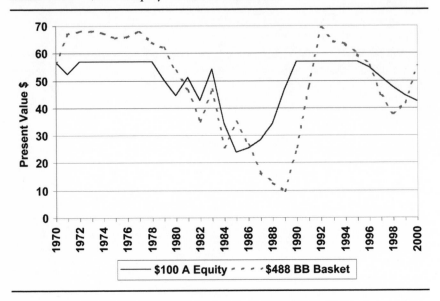

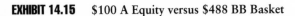

EXHIBIT 14.15 $100 A Equity versus $488 BB Basket

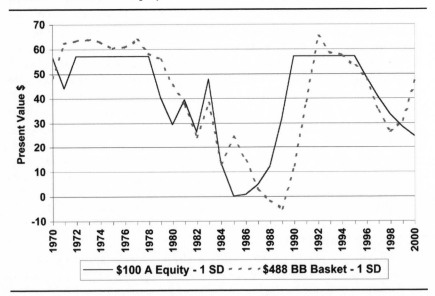

category. We also assume that the CDOs are about as diverse (e.g., by industry) as the entire rating cohort.

Finally, our analysis focuses on long-term buy-and-hold results. We do not address short-term mark to market volatility, especially price volatility that is not the result of defaults and recoveries. We focus solely on the present value of cash flows and note that ultimately market values must reflect actual cash flows. We also do not address the working capital cost of collateralization or the cost of economic capital to support trades.

Caveats and Wishes

Our methodology yields immediate insights from history. By no means, however, do we believe that we provide the final answer to the challenge of analyzing tranched credit risk if for no other reason than that an accurate view of the past is unavailable. In this chapter, we relied upon default studies based on credit ratings knowing that there is a great deal of variability in the credit quality of corporates that carry the same rating. In the past, this has lead to adverse selection in some synthetic CDO portfolios, where the worst credits of a particular rating are selected as reference entities.

We would prefer that default studies were performed on more homogeneous groups of corporate credits. That way, variability in default rates over time would be less a function of the variability in name credit quality and misratings and more attributable to economic and underwriting factors.

There are numerous avenues that researchers could pursue to develop more credit-homogeneous cohorts and thus better default studies. For example, each quarter Moody's shows how bond spreads rank the credit quality of corporates better than do ratings.[9] A default study based on relative bond spread, instead of on rating, would better stratify credits and help us to make better predictions about the future. Moody's has already done a default study incorporating rating outlooks, rating watches, and prior rating changes, in addition to the credit's current rating.[10] This study shows that the predictive power of ratings is refined with this additional information. A long-term default study using these variables would also give the market a better view of the past to apply to the future.

---

[9] For example, Richard Cantor and Christopher Mann, *The Performance of Moody's Corporate Bond Ratings: September 2004 Quarterly Update*, Moody's Investors Service, October 2004.

[10] David T. Hamilton and Richard Cantor, *Rating Transitions and Defaults Conditional on Watchlist, Outlook and Rating History*, Moody's Investors Service, February 2004.

Finally, statistical default modeling based on the Merton model or structural model, financial statement variables, spreads, or combinations of these variables has the potential to form more homogeneous credit cohorts and thus eliminate misratings as a source of default rate fluctuation over time. It would also help our predictions if these models were applied more to the prediction of *absolute default rate* rather than to the *relative default propensity* of particular credits. All these methods, and others we have not thought of, would give us a better credit view of a portfolio.

The second reason why our method is not the final answer to the problem of tranched credit analysis is that even with a perfect view of the past, one always has to determine the applicability of history to the current situation. We have more modest goals for our methodology than those who approach portfolio credit risk like a physics problem whose solution is calculable to an infinite number of decimal places. We simply want to know what has happened in the past before we try to predict what will happen in the future. The question that naturally follows from this is "What part of the past is most applicable to the future?" An informed opinion depends on an assessment of current economic conditions and underwriting standards.

CONCLUSION

We applied a historical perspective to the analysis of a single credit, a portfolio of credits, and a CDO tranche, as well as to credits with the same and different underlying ratings. We asked, and answered, the question: "What would have happened if we had done this trade in 1970, 1971, 1972 ... 2000?" In the matchup between the BBB CDO tranche and the single-name BBB CDS, the CDO unambiguously would have performed better. In the matchup between the CDO equity tranche and the BB basket swap, the results were more ambiguous, but were favorable to the CDO equity.

In our analysis we used only actual data on marginal defaults and yearly loss given default. We think this brings a much needed dose of reality to the analysis of credit portfolios.

Structured Finance Credit Default Swaps and Synthetic CDOs

Until 2005, there was only a trickle of synthetic CDOs based on structured finance underlyings. Synthetic CDOs were almost always based on corporate credit. That changed in 2005 when Wall Street dealers released a series of templates for transacting single-name credit default swaps on structured finance underlyings (SF CDS). This jump-started the market for SF CDS, which in turn breathed life into the market for synthetic SF CDOs.

Not that documentation issues are settled. A group of end users, headed by monoline insurers, have proposed their own, very different, template for trades. This has lead to different varieties of SF CDS and synthetic SF CDOs. In this chapter, we look at SF CDS documentation issues and how they affect synthetic SF CDOs.

With respect to SF CDS documentation, we cover:

■ The differences between corporate and structured finance credit.
■ The evolution of SF CDS documentation.
■ The competing dealer and end user templates.
■ The SF CDS terms which best replicate the economics of owning a cash SF bond.

With respect to synthetic SF CDOs, we cover:

■ Manager's new found flexibility in accessing credit risk.
■ The creation of new SF CDO structures.
■ The effect on SF CDO credit quality.

DIFFERENCES BETWEEN CORPORATE AND STRUCTURED FINANCE CREDIT

Two differences between corporate credit and structured finance credit drive the structure of their respective credit default swaps. Unfortunately, these differences generally work against SF CDS. We explain these differences and the hurdles they present to the SF CDS market and later describe the various attempts made in the SF CDS market to overcome these obstacles.

Difference #1: Generality versus Specificity

The first difference is the *generality* of corporate credit risk versus the *specificity* of structured finance credit risk. In the corporate market, the focus is on the corporate entity (e.g., GM) with less emphasis placed on the credit's individual obligations (e.g., the 4⅜% of 2008). In the structured finance market, the focus is very specific: a particular tranche from a particular securitization of a particular originator (e.g., the Class M7 of Home Equity Loan Trust 2005-AB4 originated by Countrywide).

In corporate CDS, the usual practice is for all senior unsecured obligations to be Reference Obligations.[1] So corporate obligations may be retired and new ones created, but the corporate CDS overarches them all and has its own maturity. The corporate CDS market runs on the assumption that it does not much matter which senior unsecured obligation is tendered for Physical Settlement or marked to market for cash settlement. The model here is bankruptcy, where all senior unsecured debts are supposed to be treated the same in that their eventual recovery (in cash or new securities) is the same regardless of maturity or coupon. Credit Events that allow for differences in the value of reference obligations, such as Restructuring, are the source of concern, controversy, and remediation.[2]

Things could not be more different with SF CDS. This is because each tranche in a structured finance securitization (SF securitization)

---

[1] Capitalized terms in this chapter refer to ISDA-defined credit default swap terms.

[2] As explained in Chapter 11, the definition of a Restructuring Credit Event has been modified twice and it is often eliminated altogether as a Credit Event in the U.S. market. The problem is that Restructuring creates a "cheapest to deliver" option. What is a cheapest to deliver option? If, after a restructuring credit event, the reference obligor's bonds trade at different levels, it behooves the protection buyer to deliver the reference obligation with the lowest market value. The existence of a cheapest to deliver option argues against the case we have made that corporate CDS are obligor rather than obligation focused. But the efforts to eliminate the cheapest to deliver option argue that the market sees this as a problem. Indeed, the cheapest to deliver option impeded the corporate CDS market's growth.

intentionally has its own distinct credit quality from that of other tranches. This is reflected in the different ratings on tranches. For example, it is not uncommon for a home equity loan-backed securitization to issue tranches in every investment-grade rating category from AAA down to BBB−; and each securitization is backed by its own unique pool of assets. SF CDS follow credit reality and focus on the specific tranche. SF CDS maturity and amortization follow the maturity and amortization of the Reference Obligation.

Difference #2: Clarity versus Ambiguity

The second difference between corporate credit and structured finance is the *clarity* of a corporate credit problem versus the *ambiguity* of a structured finance credit problem. The model in the corporate market is that a corporation fails to pay interest or principal on an obligation, cross defaults with its other obligations occurs, and pretty soon the corporation is filed into bankruptcy (if the corporate does not file for bankruptcy first). These events are dramatic, easily discernable, and severe.

In contrast, a credit problem at a SF securitization can be subtle. For example, a SF securitization should never go into bankruptcy. In essence, the expense, delay, and uncertainty of bankruptcy are unnecessary evils as securitization documentation already encompasses the possibility that cash flows from collateral may not be enough to pay liabilities. In essence, a SF securitization comes with a prepackaged insolvency plan that eliminates the need for judicial interference.

Furthermore, the flexibility of a SF tranche's cash flows is such that the existence or extent of a credit problem is ambiguous. Problems may be minor, they may resolve themselves, or they may not rise to the same level of distress as a defined Credit Event in a corporate CDS. For example:

- Many SF tranches are structured to defer interest payments if collateral cash flow is insufficient due to delinquencies and defaults. Later, if collateral cash flow recovers, deferred interest is made up.
- Many RMBS and mortgage ABS tranches are structured to defer interest payments if collateral cash flow is insufficient due to interest rate caps on underlying collateral. Many mortgages have restrictions on how fast homeowner interest rate and payments can rise. These restrictions might cause an interest rate mismatch with the securitization's tranches. If so, the *available funds cap* causes tranches to defer interest, as they would if the shortfall in collateral cash flow had been caused by defaults. Later, if collateral cash flow recovers, deferred interest is made up.

EXHIBIT 15.1   Differences Between Corporate Credit and Structured Finance Credit

	Corporate Credit	Structured Finance Credit
Generality	All of a corporation's senior unsecured debt is affected in the same way by the corporation's bankruptcy.	Each tranche of a securitization has its own individual credit quality.
Clarity	A corporation's inability to make an interest payment is a significant event.	Missed payments might be small and might reverse.

- Many SF securitizations call for the writedown of tranche principal in the case of collateral losses. From that point forward, interest and principal payments are based on the lower written down amount. However, some of these writedowns are reversible and in practice are reversed as collateral performance stabilizes or improves. Moody's calculates that 19% of such structured finance impairments have been cured.[3]
- Some SF securitizations do not use the writedown process. Tranche principal is not considered defaulted until some far off legal final maturity. So there is no official early acknowledgment of a principal default.
- Each SF tranche has an expected maturity based on underlying collateral maturities and prepayments. However, this expected maturity could be violated due to either slower than expected collateral prepayments or higher than expected collateral losses.

We summarize the differences between corporate credit and structured finance credit in Exhibit 15.1. The *specificity* of structured finance credit risk (as opposed to the *generality* of corporate credit risk) and the *ambiguity* of a structured finance credit problem (versus the *clarity* of a corporate credit problem) hamper SF CDS, as we discuss next.

DIFFICULTIES IN SF CDS

The differences between corporate and structured finance credit generally work against the creation of structured finance CDS. Or more accurately, the differences work against creating SF CDS in the image of corporate CDS.

---

[3] See Figure 6 (p. 9) in Jian Hu et al., *Default & Loss Rates of Structured Finance Securities: 1993–2004*, Moody's Investors Service, July 2005.

The following two consensuses drive the corporate CDS market:

1. A Credit Event triggering a payment from the protection seller to the protection buyer should be the result of a significant credit problem.
2. The settlement process should represent credit losses rather than market value risks such as the difficulty of valuing a defaulted obligation.

The ideal corporate CDS combination is therefore a Bankruptcy Credit Event and a Physical Settlement. Bankruptcy is ideal because it indicates a severe credit problem. Physical Settlement is ideal because if the credit problem is minor, the value of the Reference Obligation delivered should be high. Furthermore, the protection seller can decide to hold the reference obligation or sell it when the seller sees fit. Therefore, the protection payment is not subjected to noncredit risks associated with the market value polling process.

Structured finance credits lack anything as clear cut as bankruptcy. Interruptions in interest payments are incremental and reversible. So are principal writedowns and some SF securitizations do not even have principal writedowns. It violates CDS market consensus to trigger a Credit Event because of an interest deferral or principal writedown that is small and could very well be reversed later. On the other hand, it seems unfair to force a protection buyer to wait for a far-off legal final maturity before calling a Credit Event.

The small size of underlying SF tranches presents settlement problems. Typically, SF CDS are written on tranches in the BBB to A range of the securitization. For a subprime MBS securitization, these tranches make up only 5% to 10% of the deal's total capital structure. In a $1.6 billion securitization, these tranches are in the range of $10 to $20 million each. These small sizes would make it very difficult for a protection buyer (other than someone who already owned the tranche) to make Physical Settlement. Contrast this to the corporate CDS market where any unsecured debt of the reference obligor is deliverable.[4] The small sizes of SF tranches (not to mention the difficulty of analyzing SF credit) would also make dealer polling especially arbitrary.

So now we will look at three attempts to create SF CDS documentation to overcome these problems:

---

[4] Not that it is always easy to find a corporate reference obligation to deliver. The notional of CDS on a corporate name might be a multiple of its outstanding debt. There are reports of "squeezes" where protection buyers have to overpay to get deliverable reference obligations. But the situation is better than in the structured finance market.

1. Traditional SF CDS circa 1998 to 2004 based on corporate CDS.
2. The dealer mixed pay-as-you-go and physical settlement template.
3. The end user pure pay-as-you-go template.

Traditional SF CDS and "Hard" Credit Events

The circuitous route of SF CDS documentation begs the question as to whether we have gotten where we are today via random mutation or intelligent design. We will stay away from that controversy. Suffice it to say that SF CDS has been around, as the basis for the first synthetic SF CDOs, since 1998. Underlying Reference Obligations in these CDOs were usually in the AAA and AA rating categories. These early synthetic SF CDOs were often done for balance sheet purposes, in that the party buying protection from the CDO owned the underlying SF tranches and achieved a reduction in required capital by sponsoring the CDO. Other SF CDS of this era were driven by low-cost funders buying individual SF tranches and laying off their credit risk via single-name SF CDS. The reference obligations of these trades were also usually highly rated.[5]

As explained in Chapter 11, the International Swap and Derivatives Association (ISDA) published corporate CDS definitions in 1999, produced three supplements in 2001, and published new corporate CDS definitions in 2003. As corporate CDS definitions became more known and accepted, early SF CDS participants began to use the corporate CDS template with modifications to accommodate structured finance credit. Over time, certain versions of these structured finance modifications became, if not standard, at least well known and understood in the market. These SF CDS followed corporate CDS Credit Events, with significant modifications, and corporate CDS settlement, without modification. Typical Credit Events for a synthetic SF CDO were:

- CDS "Failure to Pay," a version of the corporate
- "SF Failure to Pay Principal"
- "SF Failure to Pay Interest"
- "Distressed Downgrade"

The corporate CDS definition of Failure to Pay includes the situation in which a SF tranche had not paid its principal by its legal final

---

[5] Both the SF CDO and the single-name underlying SF CDS were made possible by a "negative basis." A bond's basis is its CDS premium minus its spread above LIBOR. If this is a negative number, it means that an investor can purchase the bond, buy credit protection via a CDS, and enjoy a LIBOR plus net coupon. This would appeal to any investor with a cost of funds close to LIBOR. The negative basis trade investor is being paid to fund the bond without taking its credit risk.

maturity. It would also include the situation where a SF tranche, which is not allowed by its terms to defer interest, has in fact missed an interest payment.

SF Failure to Pay Principal would encompass a principal writedown, so long as at least one other condition was met:

- The terms of the SF tranche not allow written down principal to ever be written back up.
- The terms of the SF tranche not allow interest to be paid on the written down principal, even if principal is written back up.
- The SF tranche is downgraded to some rating, such as Ca or below by Moody's or CCC– or below by S&P.

SF Failure to Pay Interest would encompass a missed interest payment, so long as at least one other condition was met:

- The terms of the SF tranche not allow for unpaid interest to be paid at a later date.
- The terms of the SF tranche not allow interest to be paid on deferred interest.
- The SF tranche is downgraded to some rating, such as Ca or below by Moody's or CCC– or below by S&P.

A Distressed Downgrade would be a downgrade to C by Moody's and/or D by S&P. Note that the discrepancy in rating between the two agencies is because Moody's does not have a D rating (a C rating is Moody's lowest.)

Other Credit Events were occasionally used. "Bankruptcy" was sometimes included as a Credit Event, even though the chance of a SF securitization becoming bankrupt was next to nil. "Mathematical Impossibility" or "Under Collateralization" or "Implied Writedown" was based on the impossibility of collateral cash flow being sufficient to pay principal and interest on a SF tranche. This might be determined by taking the par amount of collateral, deducting the par of more senior tranches, and then comparing the remainder to the par of the SF tranche. Normally, a threshold level of undercollateralization was required to trigger a Credit Event. More sophisticated cash flow modeling approaches were also employed to test for under collateralization.

Rating Agency Concerns

Within the list of acceptable Credit Events, one notes the caution exercised in determining an allowable Credit Event. For a SF tranche whose terms allow principal write-ups and interest to be paid on deferred interest, it normally took a rating agency downgrade to trigger a Credit Event. These terms were driven by two parties: (1) the rating agencies who rated SF CDOs; and (2) the monoline bond insurers who were often the protection seller on AAA synthetic SF CDO tranches and single-name SF CDS trades.

One concern rating agencies had was with the applicability of their ratings on the SF CDO's collateral. If a SF security allows reversible writedowns and catch-ups of deferred interest, the rating of the security would not address the probability of those events. In rating a SF security with those terms, the rating agency would focus solely on the security's ability to provide *eventual* payment of principal and interest. Because eventual payment is easier for the security to achieve than timely payment, a security rated for eventual payment would achieve a higher rating than the same security rated for timely payment.

If a failure to make timely payment is a Credit Event in a SF CDO, and the rating of the security only addresses eventual payment, the rating does not address the probability of a Credit Event.[6] The same goes with the triggering of an available funds cap. Because the rating agencies did not feel they could assess the interest rate risk (or because deal structurers did not want them to!) of some structures, they neatly removed that risk from their analysis. So again, if the triggering of the available funds cap is a Credit Event, the security's rating does not address the probability of such a Credit Event. As the rating agencies base their CDO ratings in part on ratings of the CDO's underlying collateral, their analysis falls apart if their collateral ratings do not address the risk of Credit Events.

The rating agencies also felt that their ratings could not address the risks inherent in the cash settlement process. For example, Moody's noted "performing tranches of structured finance transactions are generally illiquid, while distressed tranches are even more illiquid."[7] The rating agencies were not confident that their recovery assumptions would prove valid in a dealer polling process.

Meanwhile, monoline insurance companies are bound by statute to only guarantee the scheduled interest and principal amortization of the bonds they guarantee. Although they usually reserve the right to accelerate payment, they cannot legally bind themselves to immediate payout. The

---

[6] This is akin to a gymnastic judge's score being multiplied by the wrong difficulty factor. Not helpful? Then just read the sentence again.

[7] See, for example, Yuri Yoshizawa, *Moody's Approach To Rating Synthetic Resecuritizations*, Moody's Investors Service, October 29, 2003, which lays out rating agency concerns very well. Proving that nothing financial is truly new under the sun, Yoshizawa suggested "partial settlement," or Pay As You Go Settlement, as a positive solution to the ambiguity of Credit Events in a SF CDS.

reason is the inherent liquidity strain such a requirement would impose upon the insurer. In essence, monoline insurance payments are "pay as you go," with an acceleration option owned by the insurance company.

It is understandable that protection sellers only want significant problems to count as Credit Events. It is also understandable that protection sellers do not want the uncertainty of dealer polling. Yet it also seems unfair for protection buyers to have to wait for the legal final maturity of a SF security or be dependent upon rating agency downgrades before they collect protection payments on obviously impaired securities. Out of such concerns, the idea arose to supplement hard Credit Events and hard settlement with milder forms of both.

Pay As You Go, The Dealer Template

The innovation of Pay As You Go CDS (PayGo CDS) is softer and reversible Credit Events (called "Floating Amount Events") and partial, reversing settlements (Pay As You Go Settlement). Also, the CDS template eliminates cash settlement and the risks of dealer polling.

Under PayGo, if a SF security experiences an Interest Shortfall, the protection seller pays the protection buyer the amount of the shortfall. The payment is made even if the interest on the SF security is by its terms deferrable. But if the SF security later catches up on interest payments, the protection buyer returns the payment to the protection seller. A SF security can, of course, suffer multiple interest shortfalls and therefore a PayGo SF CDS could suffer multiple interest shortfall events.

Interest Shortfall, as a Floating Amount Event, is more easily triggered than the equivalent problem as a Credit Event in traditional SF CDS. A traditional SF CDS would ignore the non-payment of deferrable interest (i.e., a SF security with a PIK feature) unless the missed coupon was accompanied by a severe downgrade. But the payment of only the SF security's missed coupon is a mild settlement event in contrast to physical or cash settlement of the entire notional amount that would occur in a traditional SF CDS. Moreover, the PayGo settlement is reversible should the SF security catch up on deferred interest. (There's more to say about Interest Shortfall, but we will "defer" that discussion for now.)

In PayGo terminology, the kinder, gentler Credit Events are "Floating Amount Events" and the payments from the protection seller to the protection buyer are "Floating Amounts." Reversing payments from the protection buyer to the protection seller are "Additional Fixed Amounts." They are "additional" to the premium payments the protection buyer already pays the protection seller.

One can guess how the PayGo concept is applied to Principal Writedowns. The protection seller pays the protection buyer the amount of

Principal Writedown. The SF CDS continues on with a smaller notional amount reflecting the partial settlement of the CDS. If the writedown is later reversed, the protection buyer returns the written down amount to the protection seller.

Again, the PayGo event is more easily triggered than a Credit Event in a traditional SF CDS. A traditional SF CDS would ignore a principal writedown that was reversible unless it was accompanied by a severe downgrade. Again the partial settlement of just the SF security's written down amount is a mild settlement event and it is reversible should the principal be written back up. A SF security can, of course, suffer multiple writedowns and therefore a PayGo SF CDS could suffer multiple writedown events. Premiums from the protection buyer to the protection seller would be based on the written down notional amount of the SF CDS.

The partial and fluid nature of the settlements is in contrast to the binary and severe nature of hard Credit Events and hard settlement and appropriate for minor credit problems. However, this is a big problem: the PayGo template allows the protection buyer to force a Physical Settlement of the CDS' entire notional amount upon a writedown. And unlike traditional SF CDS, this does not require that a ratings downgrade accompany the writedown.

The PayGo treatments of Interest Shortfall and Writedown are at odds with each other. For Interest Shortfall, the innovation is a more sensitive trigger (because of the removal of the rating downgrade requirement) but a less severe settlement (because of the partial and reversible nature of the Pay As You Go Settlement). For writedown, the same applies, *but only if the protection buyer chooses to call a writedown a Floating Amount Event.* If the protection buyer chooses to call a writedown a Credit Event, it triggers Physical Settlement of the entire notional amount of the CDS. In Exhibit 15.2, we show the ways interest shortfall and writedown can be classified and settled.

The PayGo template documents the protection buyer's option by defining writedown as both a Floating Amount Event (with Pay As You Go Settlement) and as a Credit Event (with Physical Settlement). We show the PayGo template scheme of Floating Amount Events and Credit

EXHIBIT 15.2 Different Treatments of Interest Shortfall and Writedown

Event	Classification	Settlement
Interest Shortfall	Floating Amount Event	Pay As You Go
Writedown	Floating Amount Event or Credit Event	Pay As You Go or Physical Settlement

EXHIBIT 15.3 Floating Amount Events, Credit Events, and Buyer's Choice

Floating Amount Event and Pay As You Go Settlement	Protection Buyer's Choice: Pay As You Go Settlement or Physical Settlement	Credit Events and Physical Settlement
Interest Shortfall	Writedown	Distress Ratings Downgrade
	Failure To Pay Principal	Maturity Extension

Events in Exhibit 15.3. In the exhibit, Interest Shortfall is shown as a Floating Amount Event with Pay As You Go Settlement. Writedown is shown as being, at the option of the protection buyer, either a Floating Amount Event with Pay As You Go Settlement or a Credit Event with Physical Settlement.

Failure to Pay Principal is both a Floating Amount Event and a Credit Event. For the vast majority of SF securities, this event is going to come at the security's legal final maturity or at the exhaustion of the SF securitization's collateral portfolio. Having Failure to Pay Principal be both a Floating Amount Event and a Credit Event allows the protection buyer to receive a settlement amount whether or not the protection buyer owns the SF security.

Distress Ratings Downgrade and maturity extension are purely Credit Events in the PayGo template and are designated as optional events. Distressed Ratings Downgrade is a holdover from the traditional SF CDS. Maturity Extension covers the rare situation in which the legal final maturity of a SF tranche has been extended.

PayGo and Interest Shortfalls

In determining that an interest shortfall has occurred, there is no differentiation between Interest Shortfalls that are due to defaults and losses in the underlying SF security's collateral portfolio or Interest Shortfalls that are due to the workings of the SF security's available funds cap.

We mentioned the available funds cap in our discussion of the ambiguities of a SF credit problem. Many RMBS and mortgage ABS tranches are structured to defer part of their interest payments if collateral cash flow is insufficient due to interest rate caps on underlying loan collateral. Collateral cash flow may become insufficient, even if the collateral portfolio is performing well, because many mortgages have restrictions on how fast homeowner interest rates and payments can rise. The available funds cap (AFC) limits the amount of interest the SF security is required to pay in cash and creates an interest deferral that is payable in future periods. Later, as underlying collateral resets to higher coupons, these deferred amounts may be paid.

Since deferral is part of the SF security's structure, the rating agencies do not rate the timely payments of these amounts, only their eventual payment. In fact, it is the rating agency's difficulty in assessing interest rate mismatches between SF collateral and a SF security that causes the carve-out of timely interest. Yet, structured finance investors expect uncapped interest rate payments and consider an interest deferral to be a significant credit problem. Protection buyers want this eventuality to be covered by SF CDS.

PayGo SF CDS present three options for sizing the protection seller's payment under an Interest Shortfall: No Cap Applicable, Variable Cap, and Fixed Cap.

1. *Under No Cap Applicable*, the protection seller pays the protection buyer the full amount of the Interest Shortfall. If no interest whatsoever is paid on the reference obligation, this could be as high as the obligation's LIBOR index and coupon spread. This payment, like all Interest Shortfall payments to the protection buyer, is netted against the CDS premium payment the protection buyer pays the protection seller.
2. *Under Variable Cap*, the protection seller's payment is limited to the reference obligation's LIBOR index plus the CDS premium. This can be less than the No Cap Applicable amount if the premium on the CDS is less than the coupon spread on the reference obligation.
3. *Under Fixed Cap* or "premium squeeze to zero," the protection seller's payment to the protection buyer is limited to the CDS premium. The net amount, then, can never be a payment from the protection seller to the protection buyer. The market convention is to elect Fixed Cap.

PayGo and Step Up

Many SF securitizations have an expected maturity many years previous to the legal final maturity. The expected maturity takes into account expected collateral prepayments and defaults as well as a potential cleanup sale of collateral when the portfolio gets small. The view of rating agencies and investors regarding a SF security's cleanup call is analogous to their view of PIK risk and AFC risk. The rating agencies do not feel they can assess the future level of prepayments or a sale of remaining collateral years in the future. Therefore, their rating does not address payment of the SF security by its expected maturity. Investors, on the other hand, expect the expected maturity and consider extension risk to be a significant credit problem. It is common for the terms of a SF security to require an increase in coupon (a step-up) if the security should extend beyond its expected maturity.

The PayGo CDS template offers counterparties a chance to choose Optional Early Step-Up. If elected, the premium on the SF CDS steps up when the reference obligation steps up. However, the protection buyer has five business days to cancel the SF CDS. If Optional Early Step-Up is not elected, the SF CDS ignores the expected maturity of the SF tranche.

Pay As You Go, The End User Template

The dealer template we have been discussing is the result of a schism within the ISDA committee that had been charged with developing a SF PayGo CDS template. The other half of the committee is comprised of end users, most notably monoline insurers, and they put forward their own proposal in September 2005.

The biggest difference between the dealer template and the end user template is the elimination of Credit Events and Physical Settlement in the end-user document. The end-user template is purely Pay As You Go Settlement. This affects the Writedown event the most. Recall that under the dealer template, the protection buyer has the option to take the writedown amount, or force Physical Settlement of the entire notional amount of the SF CDS. In the end user template (also called the monoline template), the protection buyer can only receive the writedown amount.

Obviously, the removal of the Physical Settlement option appeals to protection sellers and not to protection buyers. Protection sellers cannot be faced with a sudden liquidity requirement to fund the purchase of the reference obligation at par. Protection buyers lose an option to opportunistically choose the settlement of their choice. But it does seem that the end user version better honors the pragmatism of creating sensitive floating payment events that trigger incremental and reversible settlements.

However, another end user change reduces the sensitivity of Floating Payment Events. This is the end user abolishment of Implied Writedown for SF securities that do not have a codified writedown process within their structure. If the amount of collateral in a securitization is insufficient to pay a reference obligation in full, it seems inequitable to delay the recognition of the event until the legal final maturity of the SF security.

The end-user template does not allow the protection buyer to cancel the CDS at the SF tranche's expected maturity. It is a principle of financial guaranty insurance that the insured not be able to cancel its policy when it determines it is not needed. Furthermore, any step-up in coupon must be passed through to the protection seller.

The final significant change in the end user template is the elimination of Interest Shortfalls due to the actions of an available funds cap. The view here seems to be that this is an interest rate risk rather than a credit risk.

Just Like Buying A Cash SF Bond?

Investors are concerned about the fidelity of SF CDS to a cash position in the SF reference obligation. From the protection seller's point of view, what set of Floating Amount Events, Credit Events, and settlement mechanisms best replicate the economic experience of owning the underlying reference SF obligation?

The too easy answer is a SF CDS structure that triggers Physical Settlement at the first sign of trouble. Obviously, the protection seller will get the cash instrument's cash flows if it buys the cash instrument as it essentially does in Physical Settlement. What we are looking for is the economic equivalence of a cash bond in *synthetic* form. So any Physical Settlement, as envisioned in the dealer template, is automatically disqualified. One should use the strict pay as you go settlement of the end user template to create a truly synthetic experience.

However, if a SF security is irrevocably impaired, there is no point in delaying the recognition of that economic fact. Therefore, the prohibition against Implied Writedown in the end user document should be shunned in favor of the dealer template flexibility on this point.

Owning a cash bond means having its available funds cap risk. Therefore, the protection seller should choose the Variable Cap under the dealer template and shun the end user template, which eliminates protection payments for interest shortfalls due to an available funds cap.

Owning a cash bond also means receiving the coupon step-up if the SF security is not repaid by its expected maturity. Therefore, the SF CDS should follow the end user template and cause the coupon step-up to be passed through to the protection seller.

SF CDS EFFECT ON SF CDO MANAGEMENT

The single-name SF CDS market has been a liberating experience for SF CDO managers.

Since 2003, the SF CDO market has been hampered by a relative scarcity of CDO assets, particularly in mezzanine tranches (rated BBB to A), where new issue sizes are small. Simply put, the demand for CDO liabilities has been greater than the supply of cash CDO assets. This has been extremely frustrating to SF CDO managers, who would sometimes do a considerable amount of credit work on a bond and get an insultingly small allocation. It has not been unheard for a manager to receive $1 million of a bond when they put in an order for $5 million. Good managers have been unable to scale up the size and frequency of their CDO offerings solely because of small asset allocations.

.SF CDS has opened up access to SF credits by allowing CDO managers to sell credit protection to security firms, macrohedge funds, and mortgage hedge funds. SF CDS has already multiplied the supply of credit risk to SF CDOs. We expect an increasing amount of credit risk to be available to SF CDOs via SF CDS. This is advantageous to SF CDO managers for a number of reasons:

- SF CDO managers can do credit work on new issues, perhaps get only a small allocation in the new issue cash market, but sell protection via SF CDS in a size that is a multiple of their cash allocation.
- SF CDO managers have also become less beholden to the new issue pipeline and can select credits from older vintages. Seasoned issues (particularly 2004 issues) are much more readily accessed via CDS than in the secondary cash market. For cash flow reasons, SF CDS is also an advantageous way for a SF CDO to access bonds from earlier vintages that might be trading at a premium.[8]
- Decoupling from the new issue cash market allows SF CDO managers to be pickier about credits and focus more intently on and be more discriminating about collateral attributes, structural features, originators, and servicers.
- Finally, the SF CDS market allows managers to short credits they do not like. Therefore, the analysis leading to a "no-buy" decision is not wasted. SF CDS allows them to express a negative view about a credit other than by simply not buying it.

TWO NEW TYPES OF SF CDOs

SF CDS have produced two new types of mezzanine SF CDOs. Both are driven by the efficiency of their unfunded super-senior tranche, which is generally equal to about 70% of their capital structure. SF CDOs have been able to buy credit protection in unfunded form at a savings of

---

[8] SF CDS sometimes trade with an upfront exchange when the market value of the reference obligation is not trading at par. For example, if the reference obligation is trading at a premium, the protection seller would pay the protection buyer the difference between market value and par. Then, the protection premium paid by the protection buyer to the protection seller is closer to the reset spread of the reference obligation. When CDOs sell protection via single-name SF CDS, they generally choose not to make the upfront exchange and instead set the protection premium closer to the reference obligation's discount margin. With a lot of SF collateral trading at a premium, this means that the CDO does not pay an upfront exchange and instead accepts a lower protection premium.

about 10 basis points to funded tranches. And while some super-senior protection providers have raised their prices in the face of strong demand, the economics of unfunded issuance are still advantageous.

New hybrid SF CDOs are backed by a mixture of 30% to 40% cash assets and 60% to 70% SF CDS. These CDOs almost naturally evolved from cash transactions, as CDO managers discovered they could buy a new issue cash SF security and subsequently access more of the same risk via the SF CDS market. In some of these CDO, the manager has the ability to call for additional cash funding from super-senior tranche holders. This allows the manager to opportunistically shift into cash collateral if cash spreads become attractive. The manager can also pay off the funding if it wants to shift back into SF CDS.

The other new form of SF CDO structure is 100% synthetic and sources credit risk completely through SF CDS. These CDOs are much different than older synthetic SF CDOs that contained higher-rated assets in the AAA to AA range and were done for balance sheet motivations. Issuance of fully synthetic mezzanine SF CDOs accomplished this year is already greater than any year's issuance of the older type of fully synthetic SF CDOs.

EFFECTS OF SF CDS ON CDO CREDIT QUALITY AND SPREADS

SF CDS is arguably a better credit risk for the CDO than its cash equivalent. This is because the common practice is for the CDO to sell protection under the Fixed Cap or "premium squeeze to zero" option. As such, the CDO's payment to the protection buyer for an interest shortfall due to the working of an available funds cap is limited to the amount the protection buyer pays to the CDO as CDS premium. The implicit LIBOR component of coupon survives AFC risk. Furthermore, gains from short credit positions in the CDO are treated as principal and flow through the principal waterfall structure. It's important to note that the rating agencies do not take these benefits into consideration when they rate a synthetic SF CDO. Therefore, there is no offsetting compensation in the CDO structure and the effect is an increase in CDO debt credit quality.

Another result of SF CDS is that SF CDOs now take considerably less than the 6 to 9 months to ramp up that they previously did. Ramp-up periods are now only a few weeks. Because of this, we expect a higher correlation between asset spreads and CDO liability spreads. In the past, dealers could not tighten CDO liabilities if assets tightened over ramp-up. Now, CDO asset volatility will quickly translate into CDO debt spread volatility.

CONCLUSION

In this chapter, we contrasted structured finance credit with corporate credit in order to highlight the unique problems in developing SF CDS. The specific nature of SF credit, at a tranche-by-tranche level of detail, makes Physical Settlement difficult and Cash Settlement extremely problematic. The subtle and reversible nature of SF credit problems calls for the flexibility provided by pay as you go settlement. Dealers and end users have both offered their visions of SF CDS. We picked and chose among their terms to get a set that best replicated the economics of owning a cash SF security.

SF CDS have given SF CDO manager's a new way to access credit risk and freed them from the tyranny of the new issue market. Hybrid and fully synthetic SF CDOs have proven popular with managers and investors. Finally, we have shown that SF CDS has positive effects on SF CDO credit quality.

Default Correlation

CHAPTER 16

Default Correlation: The Basics

Default correlation measures whether credit risky assets are more likely to default together or separately. For example, default correlation answers the following question: If 10 bonds each have a 10% probability of default, does that mean: (1) One and only one is definitely going to default? Or (2) is there a 10% chance *all* of them will default and a 90% chance *none* of them are going to default? If the answer is "in between," where in between?

Default correlation is essential to understanding the risk of credit portfolios, including CDOs, and is the subject of this chapter. Along with *default probability* and *loss in the event of default*, default correlation determines the credit risk of a portfolio and the economic capital required to support that portfolio

In this chapter, we look closely at the definition of default correlation, discuss its drivers, and explain it relevance for CDO investors. We then provide pictorial representations of default probability and default correlation and present mathematical formulas relating default correlation to default probability. The difficulty of the problem becomes evident when we show that pairwise default correlations are not sufficient to understand the behavior of a credit risky portfolio and introduce "higher orders of default correlation." In the next chapter, we continue our discussion of default correlations where we cover empirical results and problems related to default correlation, as well as our opinion on proposed solutions to the problem of incorporating default correlation into credit analysis.

DEFAULT CORRELATION DEFINED

Default correlation is the phenomenon that the likelihood of one obligor defaulting on its debt is affected by whether or not another obligor

301

has defaulted on its debts. A simple example of this is if one firm is the creditor of another: if Credit A defaults on its obligations to Credit B, we think it is more likely that Credit B will be unable to pay its own obligations. This is an example of *positive* default correlation. The default of one credit makes it *more* likely the other credit will default.

There could also be *negative* default correlation. Suppose that Credit A and Credit B are competitors. If Credit A defaults and goes out of business, it might be the case that Credit B will get Credit A's customers and be able to get price concessions from Credit A's suppliers. If this is true, the default of one credit makes it less likely the other credit will default. This would be an example of negative correlation.

Default correlation is not normally discussed with respect to the particular business relationship between one credit and another. And the existence of default correlation does not imply that one credit's default directly causes the change in another credit's default probability. It is a maxim of statistics that correlation does not imply causation. Nor do we think negative default correlation is very common. Primarily, we think positive default correlation generally exists among credits because the fortunes of individual companies are linked together via the health of the general economy or the health of broad subsets of the general economy.

Drivers of Default Correlation

The pattern of yearly default rates for U.S. corporations since 1920 is notable for the high concentrations of defaults around 1933, 1991, and 2001. A good number of firms in almost all industries defaulted on their credit obligations in these depressions and recessions. The boom years of the 1950s and 1960s, however, produced very few defaults. To varying degrees, all businesses tend to be affected by the health of the general economy, regardless of their specific characteristics. The phenomena of companies tending to default together or not default together is indicative of positive default correlation.

Defaults can also be caused by industry-specific events that only affect firms in those particular industries. Despite a favorable overall economy, low oil prices caused 22 companies in the oil industry to default on rated debt between 1982 and 1986. Bad investments or perhaps bad regulation caused 19 thrifts to default in 1989 and 1990. At the turn of the 21st century, numerous dot coms defaulted due to the correction of "irrational exuberance." Again, the phenomena of companies in a particular industry tending to default together or not default together is indicative of positive default correlation.

There are other default-risk relationships among businesses that do not become obvious until they occur. The effect of low oil prices rippled through the Texas economy affecting just about every industry and credit in the state. A spike in the price of silver once negatively affected both film manufacturers and silverware makers. The failure of the South American anchovy harvest in 1972 drove up the price of alternative sources of cattle feed and put both Peruvian fishermen and Midwest cattle ranchers under pressure. These default-producing characteristics hide until, because of the defaults they cause, their presence becomes obvious.

Finally, there are truly company-specific default factors such as the health of a company's founder or the chance a warehouse will be destroyed by fire. These factors do not transfer default contagion to other credits. Recent defaults brought on by corporate fraud are also considered to be company-specific events. For example, the default of Parmalat did not widen the credit default swap premiums of other industrial companies.

Defaults are therefore the result of an unknown and unspecified multifactor model of default that seems akin to a multifactor equity-pricing model. Default correlation occurs when, for example, economy-wide or industry-wide default-causing variables assume particular values and cause widespread havoc. Uncorrelated defaults occur when company-specific default-causing variables cause trouble for individual credits.

Why We Care About Default Correlation

Default correlation is critical in understanding and predicting the behavior of credit portfolios. It directly affects the risk-return profile of investors in credit risky assets and is therefore important to the creditors and regulators of these investors. Default correlation also has implications for industrial companies that expose themselves to the credit risk of their suppliers and customers through the normal course of business. We support these assertions with an example.

Suppose we wish to understand the risk of a bond portfolio and we know that each of the 10 bonds in the portfolio has a 10% probability of default over the next five years. What does this tell us about the behavior of the portfolio as a whole? Not much, it turns out, unless we also understand the default correlation among credits in the portfolio.

It could be, for example, that all the bonds in the portfolio always default together. Or to put it another way, if one of the 10 bonds default, they all default. If so, this would be an example of "perfect" *positive* default correlation. Combined with the fact that each bond has a 10% probability of default, we can make a conclusion about how this portfolio will perform. There is a 10% probability that *all* the bonds in the portfolio will default. And there is a 90% probability that *none* of the bonds will default. Perfect positive default correlation, the fact that all the bonds will either default together or not default at all, combines with the 10% probability of default to produce this extreme distribution, as shown in Exhibit 16.1.

At the other extreme, it could be the case that bonds in the portfolio *always* default separately. Or to put it another way, if one of the 10 bonds defaults, no other bonds default. This would be an example of "perfect" *negative* default correlation. Combined with the fact that each bond has a 10% probability of default, we can make a conclusion about how this portfolio will perform: there is a 100% probability that *one* and only one bond in the portfolio will default. Perfect negative default correlation, the fact that when one bond defaults no other bonds default, combines with the 10% probability of default to produce this extreme distribution, as shown in Exhibit 16.2.

EXHIBIT 16.1   Extreme Positive Default Correlation

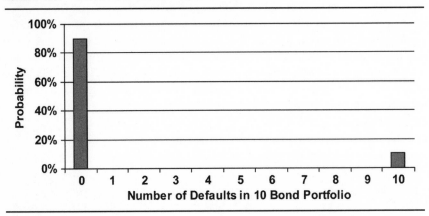

EXHIBIT 16.2   Extreme Negative Default Correlation

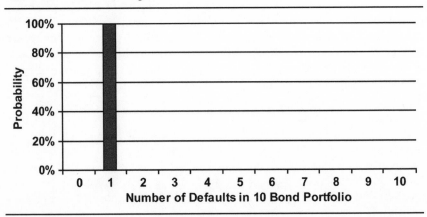

The difference in the distributions depicted in Exhibits 16.1 and 16.2 has profound implications for investors in these portfolios. Remember that in both cases, the default probability of bonds in the portfolio is 10% and the expected number of defaults is one. But one knows with *certainty* the result of the portfolio depicted in Exhibit 16.2: One and only one bond is going to default. This certainty would be of comfort to a lender to this investor. The lender knows with certainty that nine of the bonds are going to perform and that par and interest from those nine performing bonds will be available to repay the investor's indebtedness.

The investor in the portfolio depicted in Exhibit 16.1 has the greatest uncertainty. Ninety percent of the time the portfolio will have no defaults and 10% of the time every bond in the portfolio will default. A lender to an investor with this portfolio has a 10% risk that *no* bonds in the portfolio will perform.

A complete analysis of the risk of these two example portfolios would depend on the distribution of default recoveries. But it is obvious that the portfolio depicted in Exhibit 16.1 is much more risky than the portfolio depicted in Exhibit 16.2, even though the default probabilities of bonds in the portfolios are the same. The difference in risk profiles, which is due only to default correlation, has profound implications to investors, lenders, rating agencies, and regulators. Debt backed by the portfolio depicted in Exhibit 16.1 should bear a higher premium for credit risk and be rated lower. If this is a regulated entity, it should be required to have more capital.

DEFAULT PROBABILITY AND DEFAULT CORRELATION

In the sections to follow, we show default probability and default correlation pictorially (with the help of Venn diagrams), present the basic algebra of default correlation, and then delve into the deficiency of pairwise correlations in explaining default distributions.

Picturing Default Probability

Suppose we have two obligors, Credit A and Credit B, each with 10% default probability. The circles A and B in Exhibit 16.3 represent the 10% probability that A and B will default, respectively. There are four possibilities depicted in the exhibit:

1. Both A and B default, as shown by the overlap of circles A and B.
2. Only A defaults, as shown by circle A that does not overlap with B.

EXHIBIT 16.3   Credit A and Credit B Default Probability, Pictorially

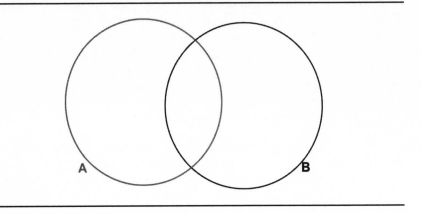

3. Only B defaults, as shown by circle B that does not overlap with A.
4. Neither A or B default, as implied by the area outside both circles A and B.

Recall that we defined positive and negative default correlation by how one revises their assessment of the default probability of one credit once one finds out whether another credit has defaulted. If, upon the default of one credit you revise the default probability of the second credit *upwards*, you implicitly think there is *positive* default correlation between the two credits. If upon the default of one credit you revise the default probability of the second credit *downwards*, you implicitly think there is *negative* default correlation between the two credits.

Exhibit 16.3 is purposely drawn so that knowing whether one credit defaults does not cause us to revise our estimation of the default probability of the other credit. The exhibit pictorially represents no or *zero default correlation* between Credits A and B, neither positive or negative default correlation. In other words, knowing that A has defaulted does not change our assessment of the probability that B will default.

Here is the explanation. Recall that the probability of A defaulting is 10% and the probability of B defaulting is 10%. Suppose A has defaulted. Now, pictorially, we are within the circle labeled A in Exhibit 16.3. No or zero correlation means that we do not change our estimation of Credit B's default probability just because Credit A has defaulted. We still think there is a 10% probability that B will default. Given that we are within circle A, and circle A represents 10% probability, the probability that B will default must be 10% of circle A or 10% of 10% or 1%. The intersection of circles A and B depicts this 1% probability. This leads to a very simple general formula for calculating the probability that both A and B will default when there is no or zero default correlation.

Recall the phrase in the above paragraph that the overlap of A and B, or the space where both A and B default is "10% of 10% or 1%." What this means mathematically is the probability of both Credits A and B defaulting (the joint probability of default for Credits A and B) is $10\% \times 10\%$ or 1%. Working from the specific to the general (which we label Equation 1), our notation gives us the following:

$$10\% \times 10\% = 1\%$$

$$P(A) \times P(B) = P(A \text{ and } B) \tag{16.1}$$

where

$P(A)$	=	the probability of Credit A defaulting (10% in our example)
$P(B)$	=	the probability of Credit B defaulting (10% in our example)
$P(A \text{ and } B)$	=	the probability of both Credits A and B defaulting

The $P(A \text{ and } B)$ is called the *joint probability* of default for Credits A and B (1% in our example). This is the general expression for joint default probability assuming zero correlation.

Now that we have calculated the joint probability of A and B defaulting, we can assign probabilities to all the alternatives in Exhibit 16.3. We do this in Exhibit 16.4. We assumed that the default probability of Credit A was 10%, which we represent by the circle labeled A in

EXHIBIT 16.4   Default Probabilities, Pictorially

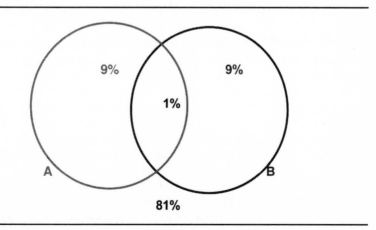

Exhibit 16.4. We have already determined that the joint probability and Credit A and Credit B defaulting, as represented by the intersection of the circles labeled A and B, is 1%. Therefore, the probability that Credit A will default and Credit B will not default, represented by the area within circle A but also outside circle B, is 9%. Likewise, the probability that Credit B will default and Credit A will not default is 9%. The probabilities than either or both Credit A and Credit B will default, the area within circles A and B, adds up to 19%. Therefore, the probabilities that neither Credit A nor Credit B will default, represented by the area outside circles A and B, is 81%.

These results are also shown below throwing some "nots," "ors," and "neithers" into the notation.

P(A) = 10%
P(A and B) = 1%
P(A not B) = P(A) − P(A and B) = 10% − 1% = 9%
P(A or B) = P(A) + P(B) − P(A and B) = 10% + 10% − 1% = 19%
P(neither A or B) = 100% − P(A or B) = 100% − 19% = 81%

P(A not B) means that A defaults and B does not default. P(A or B) means that either A or B defaults and includes the possibility that *both* A and B default. "Neither" means neither A or B defaults.

Picturing Default Correlation

We have pictorially covered scenarios of joint default, single default, and no-default probabilities in our two credit world *assuming zero default correlation*. Exhibit 16.4, showing moderate overlap of the "default circles" has been our map to these scenarios. There are, of course, other possibilities. There could be no overlap, or 0% joint default probability, between Credit A and Credit B, as depicted in Exhibit 16.5 Or there could be *complete* overlap as depicted in Exhibit 16.6. The joint default probability equals 10% because we assume that Credit A and B each have a 10% probability of default and in Exhibit 16.6 they are depicted as always defaulting together. (Note that we draw the circles in Exhibit 16.6 a little offset so you can see that there are two of them. Otherwise, they rest exactly on top of each other.)

Recall that Exhibit 16.5 depicts perfect *negative* default correlation since if one credit defaults we know the other will not. Exhibit 16.6 depicts perfect *positive* default correlation because if one credit defaults we know the other one will too. Unfortunately, our equation (16.1) does not take into account the situations depicted in Exhibits 16.5 and 16.6. That formula does not help us calculate joint default probability in

EXHIBIT 16.5   No Joint Probability

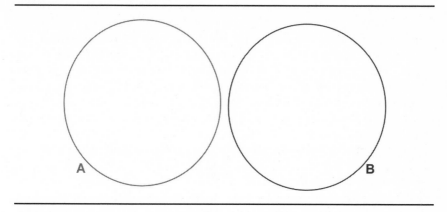

EXHIBIT 16.6   Maximum Joint Probability

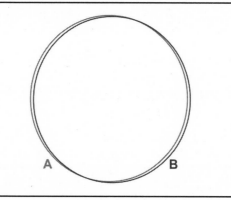

either of these circumstances or in any circumstance other than zero default correlation. Which leads us to the next part of this section.

Calculating Default Correlation Mathematically

With the Venn diagrams under our belt, we can become more precise in understanding default correlation with a little high school algebra. What we are going to do in this section is mathematically define default correlation. Once defined, the equation will allow us to compute default correlation between any two credits given their individual default probabilities and their joint default probability. Then we will solve the same equation for joint default probability. The reworked equation will allow us to calculate the joint default probability of any two credits given their individual default probabilities and the default correlation between the two credits.

What we would like to have is a mathematical way to express the degree of overlap in the Venn diagrams or the joint default probability of the credits depicted in the Venn diagrams. As shown earlier we have no overlap depicted in Exhibit 16.5, "moderate" overlap depicted back in Exhibit 16.4, and complete overlap depicted in Exhibit 16.6. One way is to refer to the joint probability of default. It's 0% in Exhibit 16.5, 1% in Exhibit 16.4, and 10% in Exhibit 16.6. All possible degrees of overlap could be described via the continuous scale of joint default probability running from 0% to 10%. However, this measure is tied up with the individual credit's probability of default. A 1% joint probability of default is a very high default correlation if both credits have only a 1% probability of default to begin with. A 1% joint probability of default is a very negative default correlation if both credits have a 50.5% probability of default to begin with. We would like a measure of overlap that does not depend on the default probabilities of the credits.

This is exactly what default correlation, a number running from –1 to +1, does. Default correlation is defined mathematically as

$$\text{Default correlation (A and B)}$$
$$= \frac{\text{Covariance(A, B)}}{\text{Standard deviation(A)Standard deviation(B)}} \qquad (16.2)$$

What we are going to do now is to delve more into the equation (16.2) and better define default correlation between Credits A and B.

The *standard deviation* in the formula is a measure of how much A can vary. A, in this case, is whether or not Credit A defaults. What this means intuitively is how certain or uncertain we are that A will default. We are very certain about whether A will default if A's default probability is 0% or 100%. Then we know with certainty whether or not A is going to default. At 50% default probability of default, we are most uncertain whether A is going to default.

The term for an event like default, where either the event happens or does not happen, and there is no in between, is *binomial* and the probability is defined by a probability distribution called a binomial distribution. The standard deviation of a binomial distribution is

$$\text{Standard deviation(A)} = \{P(A) \times [1 - P(A)]\}^{1/2} \qquad (16.3)$$

In the example we have been working with, where the default probability of A is 10%, or $P(A) = 10\%$, the standard deviation of A is

$$\text{Standard deviation(A)} = (10\% \times 90\%)^{1/2} = 30\%$$

All the possible standard deviations of a binomial event, where the probability varies from 0% to 100%, are shown in Exhibit 16.7. Above 10% probability on the horizontal axis we can see that the standard deviation is indeed 30%. The exhibit also illustrates the statements we made before likening standard deviation to the uncertainty of whether or not the credit is going to default. At 0% and 100% default probability, where we are completely certain what is going to happen, standard deviation is 0%. At 50% default probability, where we are least certain whether the credit is going to default, standard deviation is at its highest.

The *covariance* of A and B is a measure of how far the actual joint probability of A and B is from the joint probability that we would obtain if there was zero default correlation. Mathematically, this is simply *actual joint probability of A and B* minus the *joint probability of A and B assuming zero correlation*. Recall from equation (16.1) that the joint probability of A and B assuming zero correlation is $P(A) \times P(B)$. Therefore the covariance[1] between A and B is

$$\text{Covariance(A, B)} = P(A \text{ and } B) - P(A) \times P(B) \qquad (16.4)$$

In our earlier example, we worked out that the joint probability of default, assuming zero default correlation, is 1%. From Exhibit 16.5,

EXHIBIT 16.7 Standard Deviation and Default Probability

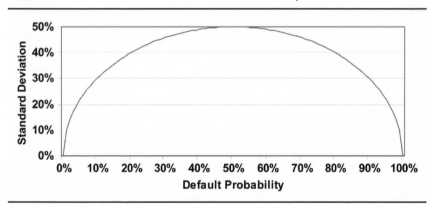

---

[1] Covariance is more formally defined as the Expectation$(A \times B)$ – Expectation$(A) \times$ Expectation(B). When we define default as 1 and no default as 0, equation (16.4) is the result.

EXHIBIT 16.8   Covariance and Joint Probability

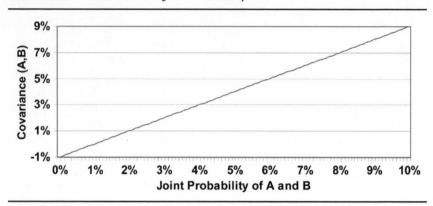

we know that given perfect negative default correlation, the actual joint probability can be as small as 0%. From Exhibit 16.6, we know that given perfect positive default correlation, the actual joint probability can be as high as 10%. Exhibit 16.8 depicts the relationship between joint default probability and covariance graphically.

Substituting equations (16.3) and (16.4) into equation (16.2) we get

$$\text{Correlation(A and B)}$$
$$= \frac{P(A \text{ and } B) - P(A) \times P(B)}{\{P(A) - [1 - P(A)]\}^{1/2} \times \{P(B) - [1 - P(B)]\}^{1/2}} \qquad (16.5)$$

Now, finally, we can define mathematically the default correlation we saw visually in Exhibits 16.4, 16.5, and 16.6. In Exhibit 16.4, the joint default probability of A and B, P(A and B) was 1% simply because we wanted to show the case where the default probability of one credit does not depend on whether another credit had defaulted. The product of A's and B's default probabilities, P(A) × P(B), is 10% × 10%, or 1%. Moving to the denominator of equation (16.5), the product of A's and B's standard deviations, $\{P(A) \times [1 - P(A)]\}^{1/2} \times \{P(B) \times [1 - P(B)]\}^{1/2}$ is 9%. Putting this all together, we get

$$\text{Correlation(A and B)} = \frac{1\% - 1\%}{9\%} = 0.00$$

Similarly, for Exhibit 16.5, where the joint default probability is 0%, default correlation is −0.11. In Exhibit 16.6, where joint default

EXHIBIT 16.9   Default Correlation and Joint Default Probability

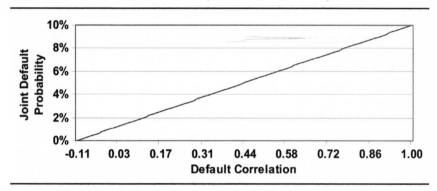

EXHIBIT 16.10   Default Correlation, Joint Default Probability, and Underlying Default Probability

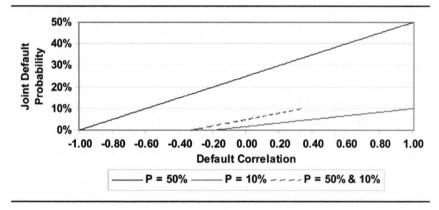

probability is 10%, default correlation is +1.00. In our example, as the joint default probability moves from 0% to 10%, default correlation increases linearly from –0.11 to +1.00, as shown in Exhibit 16.9.

Theoretically, correlation can range from –1.00 to +1.00. But for binomial events such as default, the range of possible default correlations is dictated by the default probabilities of the two credits. With 10% probability of default for both credits, the possible range of default correlation is reduced to the range from –0.11 to +1.00. If both credits do not have the same default probability, they cannot have +1.00 default correlation. Only if the default probability of both credits were 50% would it be mathematically possible for default correlation to range fully from –1.00 to +1.00.

Exhibit 16.10 shows the relationship between default correlation and joint default probability when the individual default probability of both credits is 50%, when the individual default probability of both credits is 10%, and when the individual default probabilities of credits are 10% and 50%, respectively.

Note that as described, default correlation in the case where the default probability of both credits is 50% ranges from +1.00 to –1.00. Also, note the slope of the two lines. The same increase in default correlation has a bigger effect on the joint probability of default when individual default probabilities are 50% than when individual default probabilities are 10%.

We will see in Chapter 17 that equation (16.5) allows us to calculate historic default correlations from empirical default data. For now we rearrange equation (16.5) to solve for the joint probability of default. Then we can calculate the joint default probability of A and B given their individual probabilities of default and their default correlation.

$$
\begin{aligned}
&P(A \text{ and } B) \\
&= \text{Correlation}(A \text{ and } B) \times \{P(A) \times [1 - P(A)]\}^{1/2} \qquad (16.6) \\
&\quad \times \{P(B) \times [1 - P(B)]\}^{1/2} + P(A) \times P(B)
\end{aligned}
$$

Default Correlation in a Triplet

As this point, readers familiar with the concept of correlation for continuous variables like stock returns or interest rates are apt to find some surprises. We have already seen in Exhibit 16.9 how the range of default correlation can be restricted. Many people are used to looking at portfolio risk in the context of Markowitz's portfolio theory which relies on the variance-covariance matrices.[2] In that framework, if you have an estimate of the standard deviation of the return for each security, and the correlation of the return of each pair of securities, you can explain the behavior of the entire portfolio. Not so with a binomial variable such as default. We illustrate the difference in this section.

Instead of the two-credit world we have focused on, suppose we have three credits, A, B, and C, each with a 10% probability of default. Also suppose that the default correlation between each pair of credits is zero. As we have discussed before, this means that the joint probability between each pair of credits is 1%. We illustrate this situation in Exhibit 16.11.

Now we are eager to understand the behavior of all three credits together. We seem to have a lot of information: each credit's default probability and the default correlation between each pair of credits. What

---

[2] Harry M. Markowitz, "Portfolio Selection," *Journal of Finance* (March 1952), pp. 77–91.

EXHIBIT 16.11   Pairwise Joint Default Correlation

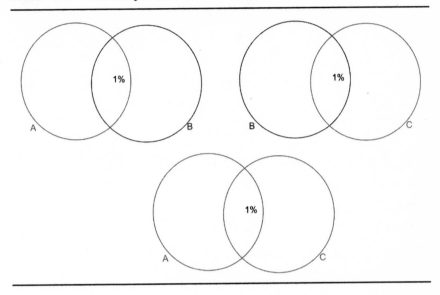

does this tell us about how defaults will occur among all three credits? Not much, it turns out. One might jump to the conclusion that if the pairs AB, BC, and AC all are zero default correlated, the default correlations between the *pair* AB and the single credit C, or the *pair* BC and the single credit A, or the *pair* AC and B must also all be zero default correlated. Since the zero default correlation joint default probability of any pair is 10% × 10% or 1%, the zero default correlation triple joint probability of default is 1% × 10% or 0.1%. In general, the triple joint default probability assuming zero pairwise and zero triplet default correlation is

$$P(A \text{ and } B \text{ and } C) = P(A) \times P(B) \times P(C)$$
$$= 10\% \times 10\% \times 10\% = 0.1\%$$

Once we know that P(A and B and C) = 0.1%, we can figure out that P(A and B not C) is 0.9% and that P(A not B not C) is 8.1%. This is illustrated pictorially in Exhibit 16.12. Exhibit 16.13 shows the probabilities of all possible default outcomes under the heading "0.00 Triplet Default Correlation."

There is no reason why just because *pairs* of credits have zero default correlation that the default correlation between a *pair* and a *third* credit must also be zero. Exhibit 16.14 and 16.15 show the extremes of possible correlation. (Note the switch from circles to rectan-

EXHIBIT 16.12   Zero Pairwise and Zero Triplet Default Correlation

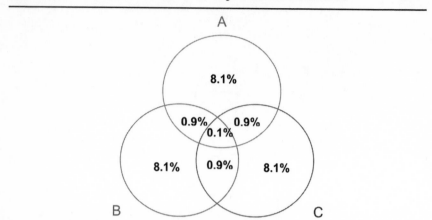

EXHIBIT 16.13   Default Probabilities Under 0.00 Pairwise Default Correlation and Various Triplet Default Correlation

Number of Defaults	−0.03 Triplet Default Correlation	0.00 Triplet Default Correlation	0.30 Triplet Default Correlation
0	73.0%	72.9%	72.0%
1	24.0%	24.3%	27.0%
2	3.0%	2.7%	0.0%
3	0.0%	0.1%	1.0%

EXHIBIT 16.14   Zero Pairwise and Positive Triplet Default Correlation

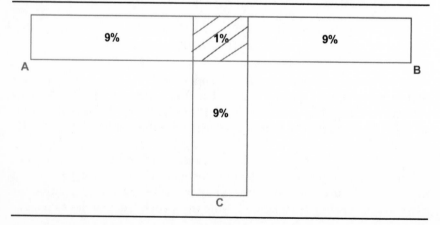

EXHIBIT 16.15   Zero Pairwise and Negative Triplet Default Correlation

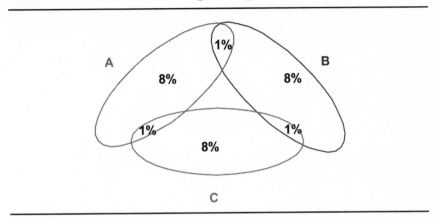

gles and ovals in these Venn diagrams to show the overlapping probabilities clearly.)

In Exhibit 16.14, whenever two credits default, the third credit joins them in default and there is no situation where only *two* credits default. Exhibit 16.13 shows the probabilities of all possible default outcomes under the heading "0.30 Triplet Default Correlation." There is a 1% probability that all three credits default, 0% probability that two credits default, 27% probability that one credit will default and 72% probability that no credits will default.

This sounds like positive default correlation: if you know that any two credits have defaulted, your estimate of the default probability of the third credit increases from 10% to 100%. We can solve for the triplet default correlation by treating the default of A and B as *one* event and comparing that event to the default of C. Using equation (16.5), and substitution in AB for A and C for B we have

Correlation(AB and C)

$$
= \frac{P(AB \text{ and } C) - P(AB) \times P(C)}{\{P(AB) \times [1 - P(AB)]\}^{1/2} \times \{P(C) \times [1 - P(C)]\}^{1/2}}
$$

$$
= \frac{1\% - 1\% \times 10\%}{\{1\% \times [1 - 1\%]\}^{1/2} \times \{10\% \times [1 - 10\%]\}^{1/2}} = 0.30
$$

But this triplet default correlation of 0.30 occurs while all *pairwise* default correlations are zero.

In Exhibit 16.15, in contrast, there is no situation where all three credits default. In this case, if you know that two credits have defaulted, your estimate of the default probability of the third credit decreases from 10% to 0%. This sounds like negative default correlation. In this situation, the triplet default correlation is –0.03. Exhibit 16.13 shows the probabilities of all possible default outcomes under the heading "–0.03 Triplet Default Correlation." There is a 0% probability that all three credits default, 3% probability that two credits default, 24% probability that one credit will default and 73% probability that no credits will default.

Note that the expected number of defaults in each triplet correlation scenario is the same. In the zero triplet correlation scenario, the expected number of defaults is 24.3% × 1 + 2.7% × 2 + 0.1% × 3 or 0.3. In the positive triplet correlation scenario, the expected number of defaults in the portfolio is 27% × 1 + 1% × 3 or 0.3. In the negative triplet correlation scenario, the expected number of defaults in the portfolio is 24% × 1 + 3% × 2 or also 0.3.

Note also that the probability of any two credits defaulting at the same time in any of the triplet default scenarios is 1%. In the –0.03 triplet correlation scenario, the 3.0% probability of two defaults divides into a 1% probability of any pair of credits defaulting. In the positive triplet correlation scenario, the probability of *all* three credits defaulting at the same time is 1%. Which means that the probability of each possible pair of credits defaulting is also 1%. In the zero triplet correlation scenario, the 2.7% probability of two defaults divides into a 0.9% probability of any pair of credits defaulting. Also in the 0.00 triplet correlation scenario, the probability of *all* three credits defaulting at the same time is 0.1%. Which adds another 0.1% of probability and brings the total probability of any pair of credits defaulting to 1.0%.

So in all three triplet-correlation scenarios, the defaults of pairs AB, BC, and AC each have a 1% chance of occurring. This is proof that pairwise default correlation is 0.00. But the sad truth is that knowing pairwise default correlations does not tell you everything you would like to know about the behavior of this three credit portfolio. This makes default correlation computationally very difficult.

Pairwise and Triplet Default Correlation

In Exhibit 16.16 we show the range of triplet default correlation for the whole range of pairwise default correlation, given that the default probability of each of the three credits is 10%. That is, for any point on the horizontal axis giving a possible pairwise default correlation, we show the *minimum* triplet default correlation can be and the *maximum* triplet default correlation can be.

EXHIBIT 16.16   Range of Triplet Default Correlation

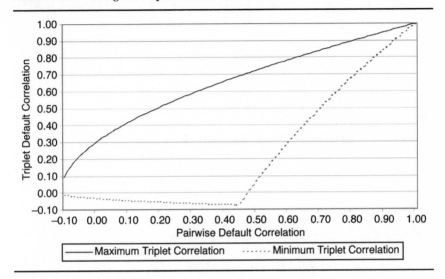

EXHIBIT 16.17   Default Probabilities with Minimum Triplet Default Correlation

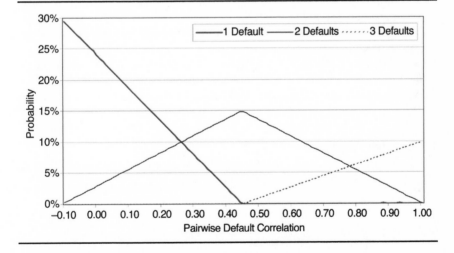

The effects of varying triplet default correlation are show in Exhibits 16.17 and 16.18. In Exhibit 16.17, we show the probabilities of one, two, and three defaults given triplet default correlation is as *low* as it can be (given pairwise default correlation). In Exhibit 16.18, we show the probabilities of one, two, and three defaults given triplet default correlation is as *high* as it can be (given pairwise default correlation).

EXHIBIT 16.18   Default Probabilities with Maximum Triplet Default Correlation

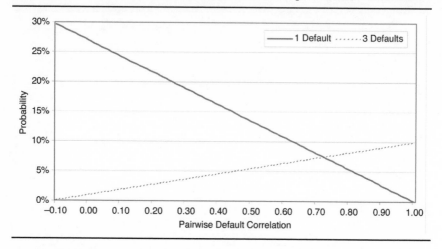

Comparing Exhibits 16.17 and 16.18, the probability of extreme default results is greater with maximum triplet default correlation than it is in the minimum triplet default correlation case. In Exhibit 16.17, two defaults is the most probable outcome under a wide range of pairwise default correlations. In Exhibit 16.18, two defaults never occur. This harkens back to Exhibits 16.1 and 16.2, where there was a wide range of default results with positive default correlation and a narrow range of default results with negative default correlation. Given pairwise default correlation, low triplet default correlation works to create a stable number of defaults and high triplet default correlation works to create a wide range in the number of defaults.

Group Default Correlation

We wanted to make sure that higher-orders of default correlation were also important for large portfolios. So we consider a 100-credit portfolio where each credit has a 10% probability of default. We computed the probabilities of zero to 100 credits defaulting under three correlation scenarios:

- Zero pairwise default correlation and zero higher correlations.
- Zero pairwise default correlation and maximum negative higher correlations.
- Zero pairwise default correlation and maximum positive higher correlations.

EXHIBIT 16.19   Default Probabilities in a 100-Credit Portfolio

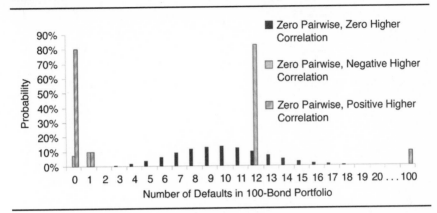

The results are shown in Exhibit 16.19 and show the extreme distribution of the positive higher correlation portfolio and the very stable distribution of the negative higher correlation portfolio relative to the zero higher correlation portfolio. Again, our conclusion is that pairwise default correlations do not give us all the information we need to understand the behavior of a portfolio.

Intuitively, increasing higher-level default correlation seems logical. Assuming that positive pairwise default correlation exists, the first default in the portfolio will cause us to revise our estimation of the default probability of remaining credits in the portfolio upwards. It seems logical that if a *second* credit defaults, we would want to again revise our estimation of the default probabilities of remaining credits upwards. This is the effect of higher-order positive default correlation. As more and more credits default, we think it more likely that remaining credits will also default.

CONCLUSION

In this chapter, we provide a not overly mathematical guide to default correlation. We defined default correlation and discussed its causes in the context of systematic and unsystematic drivers of default. We used Venn diagrams to picture default probability and default correlation; and provide mathematical formulas for default correlation, joint probability of default, and the calculation of empirical default correlation. We emphasized higher orders of default correlation and the insufficiency of pairwise default correlation to define default probabilities in a portfolio comprised of more than two credits.

CHAPTER 17

Empirical Default Correlations: Problems and Solutions

In the previous chapter, we provided the basic foundation for under-standing default correlation. In this chapter, we explore the determina-tion of historical default correlations and the problems inherent in empirical default correlation. We then compare different approaches of incorporating default correlation into portfolio credit analysis. Finally, we recommend the approach that makes the most direct use of historical data and is easiest to understand.

EMPIRICAL RESULTS

With enough data—and one very strong assumption that we discuss in detail later—we can calculate *historic default correlations*. The default correlation formula was given in the previous chapter (equation (16.5)) and is reproduced below as equation (17.1):

Correlation(A and B)

$$
= \frac{P(A \text{ and } B) - P(A) \times P(B)}{\{P(A) \times [1 - P(A)]\}^{1/2} \times \{P(B) \times [1 - P(B)]\}^{1/2}} \tag{17.1}
$$

To compute, say, the default correlation of two B-rated companies over one year, we set P(A) and P(B) in equation (17.1) for the default correlation equal to the historic average 1-year default rate for B-rated companies. The remaining variable in equation (17.1) is the joint proba-bility of default, P(A and B). We compute P(A and B) by first counting

323

the number of companies rated B at the beginning of a year that subsequently defaulted over that particular year. We then calculate all possible *pairs* of such defaulting B rated companies. If X is the number of B rated companies defaulting in a year, the possible pairs are

$$\frac{X \times (X - 1)}{2}$$

We next calculate all possible pairs of B rated companies, whether or not they defaulted, using the same formula, $[Y \times (Y - 1)]/2$, where Y is the number of B rated companies *available* to default. The joint default probability of B rated companies in a particular year is

$$\frac{[X \times (X - 1)]/2}{[Y \times (Y - 1)]/2}$$

The average of this statistic is taken over available years in the dataset to determine P(A and B).

Now, having all the terms in equation (17.1), we can solve for the default correlation between two B rated credits A and B. In a similar manner, it is possible to calculate default correlations over longer periods and between groups of credits of different ratings, for example the default correlation between Aa and Ba credits over five years.

Default correlations between all combinations of Moody's rating categories for time periods from 1 to 10 years were computed elsewhere.[1] The data used included 24 years of default data covering the years 1970 through 1993, including industrial companies, utilities, financial institutions, and sovereign issuers. We reproduce the results for historic default correlations in Exhibit 17.1.

We conclude the following from the results reported in Exhibit 17.1:

- Default correlations increase as ratings decrease.
- Default correlations initially increase with time and then decrease with time.

We believe that default correlations increase as ratings decrease because lower-rated companies are relatively more susceptible to problems in the *general economy* while higher-rated companies are relatively more susceptible to *company-specific* problems. Low-rated companies,

---

[1] Douglas Lucas, "Default Correlation and Credit Analysis," *Journal of Fixed Income* (March 1995), pp. 76–87.

EXHIBIT 17.1 Historic Default Correlations

1-Year Default Correlations × 100

	Aaa	Aa	A	Baa	Ba	B
Aaa	0					
Aa	0	0				
A	0	0	0			
Baa	0	0	0	0		
Ba	0	0	0	0	2	
B	0	1	0	1	4	7

2-Year Default Correlations × 100

	Aaa	Aa	A	Baa	Ba	B
Aaa	0					
Aa	0	0				
A	0	0	0			
Baa	0	0	0	0		
Ba	0	1	1	1	6	
B	0	1	1	2	10	16

3-Year Default Correlations × 100

	Aaa	Aa	A	Baa	Ba	B
Aaa	0					
Aa	0	0				
A	0	1	1			
Baa	0	0	0	0		
Ba	0	2	2	1	9	
B	0	2	3	3	17	22

4-Year Default Correlations ×100

	Aaa	Aa	A	Baa	Ba	B
Aaa	0					
Aa	0	0				
A	0	1	1			
Baa	0	1	1	0		
Ba	0	2	3	3	13	
B	0	2	4	5	22	27

5-Year Default Correlations ×100

	Aaa	Aa	A	Baa	Ba	B
Aaa	0					
Aa	0	0				
A	0	1	1			
Baa	0	1	1	0		
Ba	0	3	4	3	15	
B	0	4	6	7	25	29

Exhibit 17.1   (Continued)

6-Year Default Correlations ×100

	Aaa	Aa	A	Baa	Ba	B
Aaa	0					
Aa	1	1				
A	1	1	1			
Baa	0	1	1	0		
Ba	1	3	4	3	15	
B	1	4	7	7	25	29

7-Year Default Correlations ×100

	Aaa	Aa	A	Baa	Ba	B
Aaa	0					
Aa	1	0				
A	1	1	2			
Baa	0	1	1	0		
Ba	2	2	4	3	13	
B	3	3	9	8	24	30

8-Year Default Correlations ×100

	Aaa	Aa	A	Baa	Ba	B
Aaa	1					
Aa	1	0				
A	1	1	2			
Baa	1	1	1	0		
Ba	3	3	5	2	10	
B	6	5	11	7	23	37

9-Year Default Correlations ×100

	Aaa	Aa	A	Baa	Ba	B
Aaa	1					
Aa	1	0				
A	2	1	2			
Baa	2	1	1	0		
Ba	4	3	5	2	8	
B	8	6	12	6	20	39

10-Year Default Correlations ×100

	Aaa	Aa	A	Baa	Ba	B
Aaa	1					
Aa	2	1				
A	2	2	2			
Baa	2	1	1	0		
Ba	4	3	4	2	8	
B	9	8	9	6	17	38

Source: Exhibit 6 in Douglas Lucas, "Default Correlation and Credit Analysis," *Journal of Fixed Income* (March 1995).

being closer to default already, are more likely to be pushed into default because of an economic downturn. As economic conditions affect all low-rated credits simultaneously, defaults among these credits are likely to be correlated. In contrast, defaults of highly rated companies, besides being rare, are typically the result of company-specific problems. As these problems are by definition isolated to individual credits, they do not produce default correlation.

With respect to default correlation increasing and then decreasing with the time period analyzed, we note that default correlations peak at five and six year periods for rating pairs Baa/Ba, Baa/B, Ba/Ba, and Ba/B. However, default correlations peak at nine years for rating pairs A/B and B/B.

We note that over arbitrarily short time periods, defaults are necessarily uncorrelated. Imagine a database whose column headings are the names of credits and whose rows represent time intervals, perhaps four-year intervals. The entry in a particular cell is 1 if the credit defaulted in that time interval and 0 otherwise. Ones in the same row indicate that credits defaulted together in that time interval and indicate the presence of positive default correlation. If a shorter time period is used, fewer ones will appear in the same row, lowering perceived default correlation. At some arbitrarily short period of time, no more than one 1 will appear in a row and there will be no evidence of positive default correlation.

The decrease in default correlation that occurs in most rating categories over longer time periods may be caused by the relationship of the time period being studied to the average business cycle. If the time period studied covers the entire ebb and flow of the business cycle, defaults caused by general economic conditions average out over the period, thus lowering default correlation. We think that default correlation is maximized when the time period tested most closely approximates the length of an economic recession or expansion.

Just as the pairwise default correlations in Exhibit 17.1 can be calculated, so to can higher-order default correlations. Rather than demonstrate this, we instead turn to a discussion of the reliability of empirically observed default correlations.

PROBLEMS WITH HISTORICAL DEFAULT CORRELATIONS

Implicit in our discussion on empirical default correlation is the idea that wide swings in default rates are indicative of positive default correlation while small swings or steady default rates are indicative of low or even negative default correlation. We illustrate this concept explicitly in Exhibit 17.2

EXHIBIT 17.2   Simulated Annual Default Rates Under Different Default
Correlations

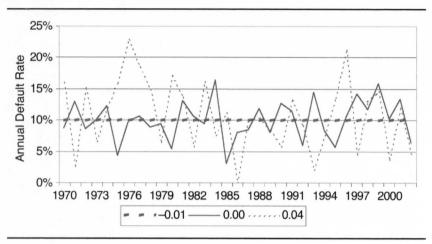

The exhibit depicts annual default rates for three 100-credit portfolios
assuming 10% default probability per year for each credit and pairwise
default correlations of –0.01, 0.00, and 0.04, respectively. The dashed
line, steady at exactly 10%, is produced with perfect negative default correlation, in this case –0.01. The solid line that ranges between 3% and
16% was produced with 0.00 default correlation. Finally, the most volatile series, the dotted line, which varies between 0% and 23%, was produced with default correlation of 0.04. This shows that a little bit of
default correlation can cause substantial swings in experienced defaults.

However, the default rates of the most volatile series in Exhibit 17.2
could have been produced by *varying default probability* instead of
default correlation. Suppose that over the time period shown in Exhibit
17.2, annual default probability averaged 10%, but varied from year to
year. For example, maybe in 1976 the default probability of credits in
the portfolio was 22% and in 1986 it was 1%. In this case, high and
low experienced default rates are caused by varying default probability,
not positive default correlation. In any particular year, given that year's
specific default probability, default correlation could be zero.

For another perspective on our inability to distinguish varying
default probability from default correlation, consider our discussion at
the outset of the previous chapter. We said the variability in annual corporate default rates since 1920 was evidence of default correlation. Our
implicit assumption was that the long-term average of the series, 1%,
was the year-in and year-out annual default probability. Of course, we
do not directly observe default probability, we only observe default

results. But it seems logical that credit analysts in 1934 and 1952 would have had vastly different expectations of future defaults. Put another way, their respective estimates of U.S. corporate default probability would have been very different.

The assumption in calculating default correlation is that default probability is constant for each rating class. This turns out to be unsupportable. Varying default probability, a simple and plausible alternative explanation of fluctuating default rates, puts into question all our work deriving empirical default correlations in the previous part of this section. It puts into question all consideration of default correlation. We cannot be sure whether the variability in default rates from year to year or over longer periods is due to default correlation or changing default probability.

Pragmatic scrutiny of credit ratings and the credit rating process suggests to us instead that ratings are more *relative* than *absolute* measures of default probability and that default probabilities for different rating categories change year-to-year. It is a hard enough job to arrange credits in an industry in relative order of credit quality. It seems to us very difficult to assess credit quality against an absolute measure like default probability and then calibrate this measure across different industries. In fact, the rating agencies themselves say that ratings are relative measures of credit quality.[2]

If ratings are relative measures of credit quality, or if for any reason the probabilities of default for different rating categories change over time, this would mean that the historically derived default correlations presented in Exhibit 17.1 are based on an inaccurate assumption and overstate true default correlation. But more importantly, default correlation is just not the right way to look at or think about experienced default rates.

Another perspective on the idea of varying default rates is shown in Exhibit 17.3. Here we have rearranged the annual default rates of the positively correlated series in Exhibit 17.2 so that the default rates are in strict order from lowest to highest. In the calculation of default correlation, assuming a constant 10% annual default probability, the *order* of default rates does not make a difference. This series would still have default correlation of 0.04.

On average, it is true that the annual default rate is 10%. But looking at this time series, some simple rules to explain and predict default rates present themselves. First, "defaults this year will be what they were last year." Second, "defaults this year will be what they were last

---

[2] Jerome Fons, Richard Cantor, and Christopher Mahoney, *Understanding Moody's Corporate Bond Ratings and Rating Process*, Moody's Investors Service, May 2002.

EXHIBIT 17.3   Time-Correlated Default Rates

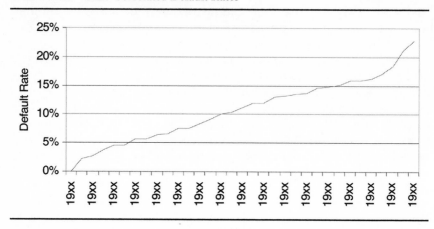

year *plus* the change in default rate between last year and the previous year." Yet, our method of calculating default correlation would not pick up the "memory," or *time series correlation*, of default rates. This suggests another type of correlation, along the dimension of time, which also seems important to our understanding of defaults.

The indistinctiveness of default correlation and changing default probability will drive our conclusions as we assess different default correlation methodologies in the next section.

PROPOSED SOLUTIONS

Given the importance of default correlation in evaluating credit portfolios, it is not surprising that a lot of effort has been given to incorporating default correlation into the analysis of credit risky portfolios. The goal of various approaches is to create default probability distributions that accurately depict the effect of default correlation upon a credit portfolio. From the default distribution and assumptions about loss in the event of default, one can determine required economic capital against a credit portfolio or the credit risk of a CDO tranche.

The default correlation solutions we highlight in this chapter take very different approaches to the problem. We find no single approach completely satisfying, but certain solutions have strengths in certain applications. We present this survey of default correlation methodologies to help understand the comparative advantages and disadvantages of different methodologies and develop an appreciative, but skeptical, view to them all.

Single-Name and Industry Limits

The effect of default correlation is not a new discovery, despite the new technologies brought to bear on the challenge. Often, the issue of default correlation is discussed and expressed in terms of portfolio *diversity*. Banks and other fixed income investors have an incentive to create low default correlated, or diverse, portfolios. Investors want loss distributions that are more stable rather than distributions that experience wide swings. For example, from the point of view of capital adequacy, a commercial bank with a portfolio like Exhibit 16.2 of Chapter 16 will require less capital than a bank with a loan portfolio like Exhibit 16.1 of Chapter 16. This is because the potential for large credit losses is lower in a less positively default-correlated portfolio. Ideally, a bank would prefer the stable default distribution of the extremely negatively default correlated portfolio in Exhibit 16.2. With that portfolio, future defaults and required capital are known with certainty.

One tool that has been used through the ages to manage default correlation and create less volatile default losses is *exposure limits* or *concentration limits*. In the previous chapter, we discussed industry-specific factors as a cause of defaults and default correlation and cited examples in the oil, thrift, and dotcom industries. The rationale behind industry exposure limits in credit portfolios is that credits within a particular industry are more default-correlated than credits in different industries. Beside industry limits, credit portfolios might have risk limits on obligors from specific countries.

Credit portfolios also have *single-name limits*. Technically, this has nothing to do with default correlation but with *portfolio diversity* or the "law of large numbers." Simply put, the more individual credits there are in the portfolio, the more likely it is that the portfolio's actual credit results will equal the theoretical expectation.[3] Exhibit 17.4 shows the probability of defaults in three portfolios comprised of 10, 40, and 80 credits, respectively. We assume a 10% default probability for each credit in the respective portfolios and zero default correlation. The exhibit shows the probability of 0% of the credits defaulting, as well as the probability of defaults in the ranges of 1% to 10%, 11% to 20%, 21% to 30%, and 31% to 40% of credits in the respective portfolios. In the 10-credit portfolio, the range of defaults is from 0% to 40% of credits in that portfolio. In the 40-credit portfolio, the range of portfolio defaults is from 0% to 30%. Finally, in the 80-credit portfolio, almost all probability is encompassed between 1% and 20% of the portfolio defaulting. This demonstrates that the more credits added to a portfolio, the more stable its potential outcomes become.

---

[3] This is true as long as the portfolio does not have complete positive correlation, which is to say it is almost always true.

EXHIBIT 17.4   Illustration of Law of Large Numbers

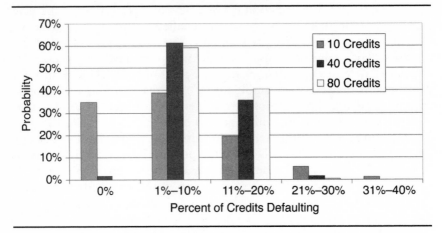

The problem with single-name and industry limits is that there is no way to determine optimum levels. Diversity is good, but how much is enough? This is a relevant question because diversity is not free. Single-name and industry limits require that more individual credits in more industries be included in the portfolio. The cost of reviewing and monitoring credits is expensive. Also, the search for a more diverse portfolio might lead to one that has lower credit quality, resulting in more defaults and greater default severity. Meanwhile, as more and more credits are added to the portfolio, the diversification benefit of adding still more credits diminishes (i.e., the benefit of going from 50 to 60 credits is far less that the benefit of going from 10 to 20), At some point, the cost of diversity exceeds the benefits of diversity. Also, the trade off between single-name, industry, and other limits is not quantified. Is it better to have relatively lower single-name limits and relatively higher industry limits or the opposite?

Rating agencies began to consider portfolio diversity explicitly when they rated CDOs in the mid-1980s. Back then, the rating agencies controlled default correlation risk in CDO portfolios by setting strict limits on industry and single-name concentrations. The rating agencies simply refused to rate any CDO that did not comply with their standards. However, the rating agencies also did not give credit to a CDO for having additional industry or single-name diversity. The issue of the costs and benefits of industry and single-name limits took on more prominence as the CDO market grew in the late 1980s.

Moody's Diversity Score

In 1989, Moody's struggled to handle default correlation and diversity in the rating of CDOs and developed some simple ad hoc rules.[4] To handle nondiversifiable default correlation due to general economic conditions, Moody's stressed historic default rates. For example, Moody's first corporate bond default study, also completed in 1989, had just calculated the historic 10-year B2 default rate to be 29.3%. However, when assessing B2 bonds in a CDO portfolio, the rating agency assumed a 37.9% 10-year default rate, reflecting the average historic default rate plus two standard deviations based on the historic volatility of the 10-year default rate.

To assess single-name and industry concentrations in a CDO portfolio, Moody's developed a single index measurement it christened *Diversity Score*. The measure explicitly quantified the trade-off between industry diversity and single-name diversity in CDO portfolios.

Moody's divided the economy into 32 industries. As shown in Exhibit 17.5, the first name in any industry earned a CDO one diversity

EXHIBIT 17.5 Moody's Diversity Score Calculation

Number of Credits in Same Industry	Diversity Points
1	1.0
2	1.5
3	2.0
4	2.33
5	2.67
6	3.0
7	3.25
8	3.50
9	3.75
10	4.0
11	4.2
12	4.4
13	4.6
14	4.8
15	5.0

---

[4] Douglas Lucas, *Rating Cash Flow Transactions Backed by Corporate Debt*, Moody's Investors Service, September, 1989.

point, the next two in the same industry earned the CDO ½ a point each, the next three ⅓ a point each, the next four ¼ a point each, and finally the next five after that, ⅕ a diversity point each. The CDO's Diversity Score was the sum of all the points accumulated in each of the industries represented in the CDO portfolio. So if a CDO had three credits in each of 10 industries, by Exhibit 17.5 the CDO earned 2.0 diversity points in each of the 10 industries for a Diversity Score of 20. Another ad hoc formulaic adjustment was made to adjust for uneven par amounts in the CDO portfolio.

The idea behind the Diversity Score was that a large number of default-correlated credits behave like a smaller number of uncorrelated credits. In modeling the default distribution of a CDO collateral portfolio, a portfolio with 80 correlated credits with a Diversity Score of 40 would be evaluated as if contained only 40 uncorrelated credits. Intuitively, this is the same as saying that credits in the portfolio always default in pairs. Exhibit 17.4 provides a graphical representation. Instead of the relatively narrow default distribution of the 80-credit portfolio, the CDO collateral portfolio would be considered to have the wider default distribution of the 40-credit portfolio in that exhibit. The wider distribution of defaults would require the CDO to have more credit enhancement to issue its debts, all other things equal.

Moody's Diversity Score became an obligatory concept in CDOs because it was part of Moody's CDO rating methodology. However, the Diversity Score also obtained recognition outside the area of CDOs when applied to other credit risk portfolios. Its appeal was that it explicitly quantified trade-offs between default correlation caused by the general economy, default correlation caused by industry factors, and the effects of single-name diversity. But while these trade-offs were explicitly quantified, they lacked any theoretical or empirical justification. Their appropriateness relied on an intuitive grasp of very unintuitive questions—for example, is a portfolio of 30 names in 30 industries as diversified as a portfolio of 60 names in 10 industries? Should CDOs of these portfolios be required to have the same credit enhancement, all other things equal? For these reasons, some quantification of default correlation was required.

CSFB's Changing Default Probability Model

Analysts at Credit Suisse First Boston (CSFB) made good use of the insight we discussed early in this chapter regarding empirical default correlations and the associated problems with its estimation that there is no objective distinction between changing default probability and default correlation. Their method of incorporating default correlation into credit modeling was to change default probabilities and assume zero default correlation.[5] An illustration will help make their approach clearer.

Let us assume we have a 10-credit portfolio comprised of high risk loans that we believe have a 10% annual probability of default. Our belief in the loan's default probability springs from the fact that over the last 20 years, loans like these have defaulted at an average annual rate of 10%. However, it turns out that there is great variability in their annual default rate, as shown in Exhibit 17.6.

As we state, we do not know whether volatility of annual default rates stems from default correlation or from changes in default probability from one year to the next. The CSFB approach assumes that each annual default rate reflects that year's default probability for these types of loans. Given that assumption, what are the "probabilities of annual loan default probabilities?" Exhibit 17.7 reassembles the default rates of Exhibit 17.6 into a graph showing the historic likelihood of any specific annual default rate. For example, as shown in Exhibit 17.7, there is a 5% probability of a 2% default probability, a 5% probability of a 3% default probability, and so on.

We would like to determine the default probability distribution of a 10-credit loan portfolio. From year to year, we believe the default probability of these credits ranges from 2% to 20%. When the probability of default is 2%, the probability of different numbers of loan defaults is as shown in Exhibit 17.8. The default probability distribution in the exhibit is the result of the 2% default probability, 10 credits in the portfolio,

EXHIBIT 17.6   Hypothetical Annual Default Rates of High-Risk Loans

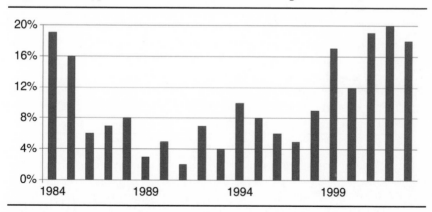

[5] The widely distributed and annotated approach was first documented in Tom Wilde, *CreditRisk+: A Credit Risk Management Framework*, Credit Suisse First Boston, 1997, available at www.csfb.com/creditrisk/.

EXHIBIT 17.7   Historic Probability of Annual Default Rates

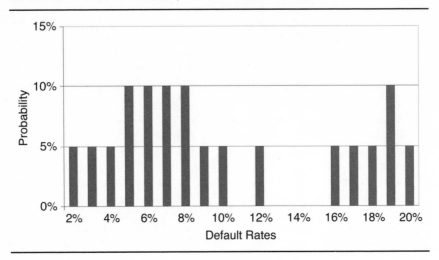

EXHIBIT 17.8   Defaults Given 2% Default Probability

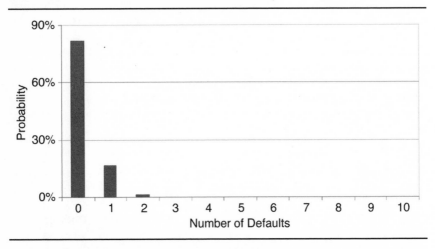

and the assumption of zero default correlation among the credits. As we pointed out in discussing Exhibit 17.4, if there were more credits in the portfolio, the distribution would be tighter. In contrast to the assumption in Exhibit 17.8, Exhibit 17.9 shows the default probability distribution given that annual loan default probability is 20%. Naturally, the probability of more defaults in the 10-credit loan portfolio is higher.

EXHIBIT 17.9   Defaults Given 20% Default Probability

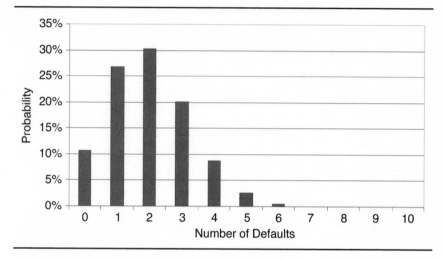

EXHIBIT 17.10   Static versus Varying Default Probability

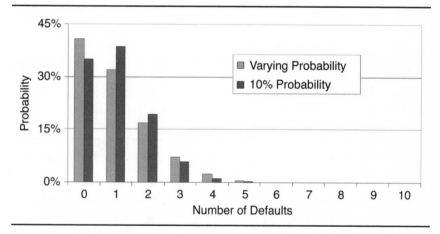

Given that annual default probability is distributed as shown in Exhibit 17.7, what is the default probability distribution allowing annual default probability to vary? This is shown in Exhibit 17.10. For comparison, we show the default probability distribution assuming a constant 10% annual default rate. Varying default probability creates a wider default distribution than assuming a static 10% default probability. This is exactly what we said was the effect of default correlation.

The analysts at CSFB confronted the problem of default probability and default correlation in a unique manner. They avoided altogether the calculation problems associated with default correlation. However, their method is best suited for credits of homogenous quality where a long default history of similar credits is available. The method is ill suited to heterogeneous credits or credits where a long history of default behavior is not available. Likewise, it does not differentiate between individual credits in a portfolio. All credits in the portfolio are assumed to have the same probability of default and the same default correlation with other credits. To take into account a portfolio comprised of debt with different default probabilities and different default correlations, another approach is necessary.

Merton-KMV Default Probability Model

To explain the Merton-KMV approach to estimating default probability, consider the following three quantities:

1. The market value of the firm.
2. The volatility of the market value of the firm.
3. The liabilities of the firm.

A firm is insolvent when its market value is less than its liabilities. Creditors will refuse to refinance its debt or advance working capital, the company will run out of cash, and it will default. A credit is less apt to experience this dire scenario (1) the greater its market value, (2) the less volatile its market value, and (3) the smaller its liabilities.

Implementing Robert Merton's theoretical framework,[6] the partners of KMV (now Moody's KMV) developed a model that estimates the default probabilities of corporate credits. In essence, the model employs the following formula:

$$\frac{\text{Market value of the firm} - \text{Liabilities of the firm}}{\text{Volatility of the market value of the firm}}$$

In this formula, the numerator is the difference in the market value of the firm and the amount of the firm's liabilities. Dividing this dollar amount by the volatility (i.e., standard deviation) of market value standardizes the formula into a number that is comparable between firms. Assuming like normal distributions, the probability of one credit experiencing a two standard deviation decline in market value is the same as

---

[6] Robert C. Merton, "On the Pricing of Corporate Debt: The Risk Structure of Interest Rates," *Journal of Finance* 29 (1974), pp. 449–470.

any other credit experiencing a two standard deviation decline in market value.

There are a myriad of practical obstacles to building this model to estimate relative default probability. For example, how does on quantify the three variables? How does one take into account that not only must the firm be technically insolvent, there must also be a *default trigger,* such as the need to refinance debt or the need for working capital, to precipitate an actual default? KMV made pragmatic decisions to increase the model's ability to rank the relative default probability of credits. For example, KMV research found that weighting long-term debt less than short-term debt in the calculation of a firm's liabilities increased the predictive accuracy of the model. It was also found that the size of the firm affected the probability of default (larger firms default less often) and chose to include this variable as an adjustment to the volatility of the firm's market value. KMV made other adjustments to calibrate modeled default probabilities to historical default rates. In the end, the practical implementation of the theoretical model lost some of the latter's mechanistic and objective beauty, but produced useful means of assessing relative credit quality.

A bonus of KMV's default prediction model is its insight into default correlation.[7] Recall that the default of a firm occurs when its market value sinks below the level of its liabilities. (The firm's liabilities are assumed to remain static in the model.) If one can correlate the volatility of one firm's market value to the volatility of another firm's market value, one discovers something about their default correlation.

For example, suppose the market value of Credit A and Credit B always move in the same direction; that is, both firms' market values increase or both firms' market values decrease. This means that as the market value of the two firms change, those market values either both fall closer to the level of each firm's liabilities or both rise up away from the level of each firm's liabilities. If the relationship between the market value of the two firms is understood, one can calculate the probability that the market values of both firms will decline below the level of their liabilities causing both credits to default.

This approach to default correlation has several wonderful properties. First, since a firm's market value is a continuous variable, it does not have all the problems, referred to in the previous change of handling the binomial default variable. Just as for stock returns, pairwise correlations of firm market values are sufficient to calculate a portfolio's default distribution.

---

[7] Peter Crosbie and Jeffrey Bohn, *Modeling Default Risk*, Moody's KMV, 2002.

EXHIBIT 17.11   Asset Correlations versus Default Correlations

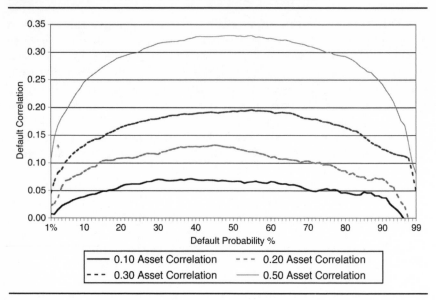

When market values are simulated, the KMV model keeps track of individual credits and when defaults occur. The default results of multiple simulations of firm market value can be used to create a default probability distribution. Finally, the KMV model is credit specific. Individual credits can have different default probabilities and pairwise market value correlations can be specific to each pair of credits in the portfolio.

The KMV approach to default correlation is so entrenched that when most practitioners speak of "default correlation" they are really referring to "market value correlation." But the relationship between the two is not straightforward. As Exhibit 17.11 shows, default correlation (on the vertical axis of the exhibit) is a function of both market value correlation and the individual default probabilities of the two firms. But at any default probability, a particular market value correlation produces a much smaller default correlation between the two credits. Given any particular market value correlation, default correlation is highest at 50% individual credit default probability and lowest at 1% or 99% individual credit default probability.

Of all the variables in the KMV Merton default model, the most critical in arriving at default probability distributions is the correlation of potential market values of firms.

Modeling Firm Market Values

There are at least three methods of predicting a firm's market value volatility and the correlation of one firm's market value to another's. KMV's first method, since discarded, used an econometric model of firm value. Each firm's market value was modeled as a unique function of 18 or so economic and financial variables, including GNP, the level of interest rates, and industry health factors. The steps in determining correlated defaults were to:

1. Simulate a fluctuation in the econometric variables.
2. Calculate a new market value for each of the firms from the values of the econometric variables.
3. Determine which credits' market values had declined below their liabilities and thus defaulted.
4. Repeat many times to form a default probability distribution.

The problem with this approach was that it depended on how well the econometric model captured firms' potential market value changes. The variables in the econometric model itself limited how credits could be market value- and thus default-correlated. With 18 econometric variables, there are only 18 ways credits can be correlated. Surprising connections between credits (such as our anchovy harvest example in the previous chapter) cannot be captured in such a model.

For whatever reasons, KMV abandoned the econometric method and moved to a model of future firm market values that depends on *historic* relationships. KMV now simply looks at the correlation of two firms' *past* market values (which it determines as part of its default probability modeling) to predict a joint distribution of the two firm's *future* market values. This raises the question of whether these market values, which are optimized to help produce good default probability estimates in a statistical model, are also good at estimating default correlation. Competitors of KMV have argued that historic equity price correlations, which are much easier to obtain, are just as good as historic market value correlations in predicting future firm market value correlations. Equity price correlations are certainly more available.

But the larger question is whether the past relationship of the market value of two firms (as calculated by KMV) or equity prices of two firm, is so indicative of their future relationship that default correlations can be determined. It seems to us that the relationship between two firms' market values is unstable and might completely change in the future, especially if one or both of them become more at risk to default. For example, we have seen the market value correlation of Ford and GM vary from 30% to 70% over two years.

Judging Default Correlation Methodologies

Ultimately, there is no objective way to measure the goodness of a default correlation model. First, when comparing the model's estimated default probability distribution to actual default results, we never know whether the model is wrong or whether the actual result is wrong. By a "wrong" actual result, we mean an atypical result from nature (i.e., a 100-year flood or six-sigma event).

Second, if we could determine that a default probability distribution is wrong, we can never be sure why. The distribution could be off because either the default correlations or default probabilities were wrong. We covered the inability to separate the two factors earlier in this chapter. Without the ability to objectively measure the performance of default correlation models, one has to rely on an intuitive view of their reasonableness.

Moody's Diversity Score is a good way to express and enforce diversity requirements upon a CDO manager. It is convenient to have a single measurement that trades off industry diversity and single-name diversity. Our view is that the formula overrewards industry diversity relative to single-name diversity. We would rather have a portfolio of 10 firms in the same industry rather than four firms in four different industries. Moody's Diversity Score would rank these portfolios as equally diverse. The desire of some CDO investors to place a single-name exposure limit on top of a CDO's Diversity Score requirement suggests that others share our view.

That raises the question of whether one needs default correlation modeling to compare diversified credit portfolios. Take two portfolios, each comprised of 50 or more credits pretty evenly dispersed among 15 industries. Given this diversity, how likely is it that one portfolio is much more default correlated than another? Or, if a correlation methodology suggests that one portfolio is more default correlated than another, how likely is it that analysis is correct? In comparing two diversified portfolios, we do not think it can be persuasively argued that one portfolio is better than the other because of its default correlation.

Yet, to analyze the risk of a credit portfolio, we see value in simulating default rates via the CSFB approach and creating a default probability distribution. To be most appropriate to the CSFB approach, credits in a portfolio must be homogenous, we must not be interested in tracking which individual credits default, and we must have a long default history of similar credits. Many credit portfolios generally fulfill these requirements.

On a theoretical level, we have a great deal of sympathy for the view that historical default rate fluctuations are caused by fluctuations in default probabilities rather than the workings of default correlation.

Our view of rating agency ratings, internal bank rating systems, and statistical models of default probability is that they are all better indicators of *relative* default probability than *absolute* default probability. The theory behind CSFB's approach is in harmony with our experience.

We also think the CSFB approach is easy to grasp. For example, the difference between assuming that annual default probability is always 10% versus assuming that annual default probability varies according to a distribution like the one in Exhibit 17.7 is intuitive. One can look at various versions of that exhibit with narrower or wider distributions and easily understand what is being assumed about the volatility of default probability.

Finally, in preferring the CSFB approach over the KMV approach, we note that the efficacy of the CSFB approach could be improved by certain empirical studies. We now have long time series of annual default rates by rating thanks to the rating agencies' default studies. We also have models that predict the *absolute* level of future default rates for speculative grade bonds and loans.[8] But we also know that credits can be grouped into more harmonious credit risk buckets by looking not only at their current rating, but also at their past ratings history, their rating outlook status, and their yield relative to that of other similarly-rated credits. Why could empirical studies not be conducted to determine historical default by *all* these default-predicting variables? Another avenue of study, helpful to this analysis, would be how default rates vary from one year to another and how one year's default rate is affected by the previous year's default rate. In other words, one should look at the time series autoregressive correlation of default rates.

If an analyst is faced with a heterogeneous portfolio or needs to keep track of which credits default or when they default, he has to consider the KMV approach. The approach is appropriate when looking at *nth* to default swaps and other basket swaps with a relatively small number of underlyings.

However, in recommending the KMV approach for this application, we are skeptical about using historic market values or historic equity prices to make fine distinctions in the relationships of particular credits. The volatility of these variables is itself volatile from measurement period to measurement period. Using historic asset or equity data at the firm or even the industry level may create distinctions that are not stable or predictive. And the number of correlation estimates that must be made, one for every pair of credits in the portfolio, increases the chances for errors to affect the predictive ability of the model.

---

[8] For example, Moody's prediction of speculative grade bond defaults and S&P LCD's prediction of speculative-grade loan defaults.

People who see the Merton model of default as immutably true tend to go along with its extension into default correlation. People who see the KMV implementation of the Merton model as a statistically fitted model that provides insight into relative default probability are more skeptical. We are in the later camp.

CONCLUSION

In this chapter we explained the calculation and results of historic default correlation. We showed that default correlations among well-diversified portfolios vary by the ratings of the credits and also by the time period over which defaults are examined. We described two major problems in measuring default correlation and therefore implementing a default correlation solution: (1) There is no way to distinguish changing default probability from default correlation; and (2) the way default correlation is commonly looked at ignores time series correlation of default probability. We feel that these problems in applying default correlation to actual portfolios have not been adequately explored.

We discussed the various ways analysts have attempted to incorporate default correlation into their analysis of credit risky portfolios:

- The antiquated method of industry and single-name exposure limits.
- Moody's ad hoc method of assessing the trade-off between industry and single-name diversity in their Diversity Score.
- The changing-default probability approach of CSFB.
- The historical market value approach of KMV.

In comparing well-diversified portfolios, we wondered whether any default correlation modeling is necessary. Given a certain level of single-name and industry diversity, we doubt that typical portfolios have very different default correlations and we are skeptical of any measurement showing that they do. However, we saw value in creating default probability distributions. We appreciated the CSFB method that focuses on observable default rates and were skeptical of making credit-by-credit distinctions in default correlation based on estimates of historical firm market value.

CDO Equity

CHAPTER 18

Why Buy CDO Equity?

Our four reasons for buying CDO equity are:

1. The nonrecourse term financing that CDOs provide to CDO equity is very beneficial to the equity holders.
2. The cash flow CDO structure is very forgiving to CDO equity holders, providing significant return even when CDO debt holders are destined to receive less than their due.
3. CDO equity holders receive two valuable options that further increase the value of their investment. Basically, these options are to "sell out early" or "wait and see."
4. CDO equity can be used as a *defensive investment strategy* for those investors who are unsure of future economic conditions.

In this chapter, we discuss these reasons for buying CDO equity.

NONRECOURSE TERM FINANCING

CDOs do not just provide financing to CDO equity holders. They deliver *nonrecourse term financing* because CDO equity holders own stock in a company and are not liable for the losses of that company. CDOs provide "term financing" because the financing rate does not change, the financing cannot be withdrawn, and a cash flow CDO cannot be forced to liquidate its assets.

CDO equity is a leveraged position in the assets of a CDO, with the CDO's debt tranches providing the financing for equity holders. CDO equity receives whatever cash flow remains after satisfaction of debt claims. Equity sustains the risk of collateral asset payment delays and credit losses, but also receives the upside if CDO assets generate cash flow in excess of debt tranche requirements. Meanwhile, debt tranche holders only have recourse to the CDO's assets, and cannot make any additional claims against equity holders. CDO equity holders are not at risk for anything beyond their initial investment.

CDO equity holders receive financing that is in place for up to 12, or even 15, years. Moreover, the financing rate is locked in, either at a fixed rate, or more commonly, at a spread above LIBOR. CDO debt is subject to early amortization only if asset quality deteriorates according to objective measures (primarily par value overcollateralization tests). In such cases, principal repayment is due only to the extent the asset portfolio provides cash flow, and asset sales are never required.

If these features of CDO financing seem unremarkable, it is only because they are familiar to CDO debt and equity investors. They are in stark contrast to the terms available in the repo market or in other short-term secured financing arrangements. In those, financing rates can fluctuate and higher levels of security (larger collateral haircuts) can be demanded at the pleasure of the creditor. In fact, financing can be pulled altogether with little warning. Collateral assets are subject to sale by the creditor to meet what are essentially margin calls, and creditors have recourse to the borrower if the collateral is insufficient to extinguish the debt. CDO equity holders avoid all these risks.

The Value of Nonrecourse Financing

To test the value of nonrecourse term financing, we sought out the *worst* historical default experience of U.S. high yield loans. Using S&P LCD data, we examined cumulative default rates *by issuance year cohort* or the *"vintage"* of the loan, as shown in Exhibit 18.1. In the exhibit, we weight the default experience of BB/BB– loans 50% and that of B+/B loans 50% to replicate the asset portfolio of the typical CLO. The highest cumulative default rate in Exhibit 18.1 is the 19.0% five-year rate for loans issued in 2000. Note that the 2000 cohort's average annual default rate is 3.8%, while that of the next highest cohort is 3.0%, and the average for all cohorts 2.1%. From Exhibit 18.1, we can see that the 2000 issuance cohort is the worst performing of any from 1998 through 2002. From other S&P data, we also know that the 2000 issuance cohort is the worst performing cohort as far back as 1995.

Just as default rates vary among issuance cohorts, recovery rates also vary year-to-year. This is illustrated in Exhibit 18.2, which, using Moody's data, shows average yearly recoveries. In the exhibit, recoveries are measured by the average bid quotation for the loan one month after its default.

EXHIBIT 18.1   Cumulative Defaults of Rated High Yield Loans Through December 2004 Weighted 50% BB/BB– and 50% B+/B

Issuance Cohort	Years After Issuance						Annual Average
	1	2	3	4	5	6	
1998	1.6%	5.4%	7.8%	10.1%	13.9%	15.4%	2.6%
1999	2.8%	7.9%	10.2%	10.2%	11.5%	11.5%	1.9%
2000	3.2%	10.9%	16.3%	19.0%	19.0%		3.8%
2001	7.2%	9.4%	11.9%	11.9%			3.0%
2002	2.2%	2.5%	2.5%				0.8%
2003	0.4%	0.7%					0.4%
2004	2.0%						2.0%
Average	2.7%	6.1%	9.7%	12.8%	14.8%	13.5%	2.1%

Source: Steven Miller, Robert Polenberg, and Aditi Mahendroo, *Q2 05 Institutional Loan Default Review*, S&P LCD, July 2005.

EXHIBIT 18.2   Average Annual Loan Recoveries

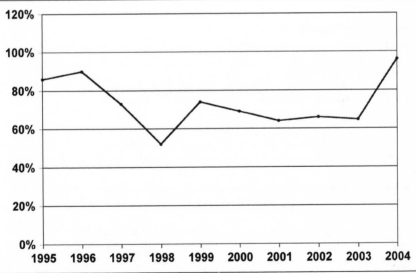

Source: Based on data obtained from Greg M. Gupton, et al., *Bank Loan Loss Given Default*, Moody's, November 2000; and David Hamilton, et al., *Default and Recovery Rates of Corporate Bond Issuers, 1920–2004*, Moody's Investors Service, January 2005.

Now we have the ingredients to recreate the experience of the 2000 loan issuance cohort. But an important aspect of our experiment will be to not merely use the *average* default experience of that poorly performing cohort. Default rates also fluctuate among *portfolios* created at the same time due to the workings of chance. When 50-name portfolios are created in an environment where there is, for example, a 2% default rate, each portfolio will not experience exactly one default. A statistics formula called the "binomial distribution," whose result is shown in Exhibit 18.3, calculates the probability that 0, 1, 2, and more defaults will occur within a 50-name portfolio if the general population-wide default rate is 2%. As one would expect, the most likely possibility is one default out of 50 names. But there also are decreasing probabilities for 2, 3, 4, and even more defaults.[1]

It is also important to understand that *within* any particular year, default recovery varies from one defaulted loan to another. On average, the standard deviation of recovery among defaulted loans within the same year has been 23%. Now, with the annual default rates of the 2000 loan issuance cohort and annual loan recovery rates from 2000 to 2004, we are ready to proceed with our experiment to value nonrecourse term financing.

The Historical Experiment

We decomposed *cumulative* default experience of the 2000 loan issuance cohort into *marginal default rates* in order to accurately represent the timing of defaults over the life of the loans.[2] Annual marginal default rates for the first four years of the 2000 cohort are 2.3%, 7.0%,

---

[1] Those familiar with techniques for looking at default risk within credit portfolios will notice that we are doing things unusually. The common practice is to assume a single unvarying default rate and some level of positive default correlation (actually positive correlation of changes in asset values) to create default rate fluctuations in a portfolio. But here we accept the zero default correlation assumption of the binomial distribution. Regardless of how one feels about the dominant credit modeling approach, we have an advantage in performing this historical analysis, as we know the default rate for the 2000 loan issuance cohort over each year of its existence. Looking back in time at that issuance cohort, we are not so much dealing with default *probabilities* as with default rates. Given that the issuance cohort as a whole experienced a particular default rate, the default rate experienced by a randomly drawn subset of 50 names from the issuance cohort is an independent or uncorrelated process and the binomial distribution is appropriate.

[2] A marginal default rate is the default rate *within* a particular year. The marginal default rate within the fourth year is the four-year cumulative default rate minus the three-year cumulative default rate.

EXHIBIT 18.3 Probability of Number of Defaults Given 2% Default Probability and 50 Loans

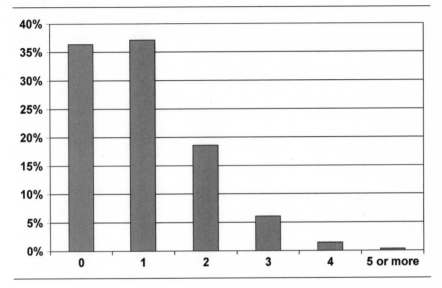

5.6%, and 2.8%, respectively. Given the population default rate each year, the binomial distribution determines the probability of different numbers of defaults in a particular portfolio of loans. We assume a 50-loan portfolio with each loan having $2 of par. For each default, recovery is determined first by looking at the average recovery for that particular year as shown in Exhibit 18.2. Then, the particular recovery is estimated assuming a 23% standard deviation and normal distribution. Recoveries are capped at principal plus accrued interest. Our results are shown in Exhibit 18.4.

The second column of Exhibit 18.4 shows the results of the experiment under the default and recovery assumptions already described. The three rows under Portfolio Results show present value statistics for the loan portfolio. To derive these, we assume that loans yield LIBOR + 226 basis points (what newly issued loans were yielding when we did this experiment), given a portfolio mix of 50% BB/BB– loans and 50% B+/B loans to sync with the typical CLO portfolio and our 2000 issuance cohort assumption. To discount future cash flows, we use LIBOR + 62 basis points (which was the average interest expense of CDO debt tranches).

Discounting the loan portfolio's future cash flows by the cost of their financing allows a useful interpretation of the present value results: the present value (PV) is the amount of debt the leveraged investor can repay, assuming the cost of that debt is LIBOR + 62. So the mean PV of

EXHIBIT 18.4   Recourse and Nonrecourse Investment Results

	2000 Loan Vintage Default Experience	Two Times 2000 Loan Vintage Experience
Portfolio Results		
PV Mean	99.70	93.60
PV SD	2.77	4.39
95% PV Range	93.41 to 104.13	83.86 to 100.94
Recourse Leverage Results		
PV Mean	7.70	1.60
95% PV Range	1.41 to 12.13	−8.14 to 8.94
Probability of Recourse	1.10%	32.64%
Average Size of Recourse	1.57	3.40
Nonrecourse Leverage Results		
PV Mean	7.80	4.03
95% PV Range	1.41 to 12.13	0.00 to 8.94
Probability of Recourse	0.00%	0.00%
Expected Size of Recourse	0.00	0.00

$99.70 indicates that after-default cash flow from the loan portfolio will, on average, be enough to repay $99.70 of debt bearing interest at LIBOR + 62. The standard deviation of the PV is $2.77 and the middle 95th percentile range of PV (from the 2.5th percentile to the 97.5th percentile) is from $93.41 to $104.13.

Moving down the second column of Exhibit 18.4, under Recourse Leverage Results, we show present value results for a *recourse* leverage investment of $8 in the loan portfolio. We assume the investor contributes $8 of equity and borrows $92, again because that is current practice in the CLO market where CLO equity makes up 8% of the CLO's capital structure and debt tranches make up the rest. Most importantly, we assume that if the loan portfolio fails to deliver $92 of present value, the recourse leverage investor must make up the difference.

The $7.70 mean present value in the exhibit indicates that the $8 recourse leverage investment will, on average, yield $7.70 of present value, discounting future cash flows at LIBOR + 62. This is not a very good return to the investor and it is driven by our focus on the awful 2000 loan issuance cohort. Considering the 17.7% cumulative default rate on the loans and the 92% financing of the portfolio, a 30-cent loss is not so bad. The middle 95th percentile range of recourse leverage PV is from $1.41 to $12.13. The 1.10% "Probability of Recourse" is the likelihood that the PV of the loan portfolio will be less than the $92 required to pay off debt holders and the recourse leverage investor will have to make up the difference. The $1.57 "Average Size of Recourse" is the average amount the investor will have to contribute, given that he has to contribute anything over his original $8 investment.

Finally, under Nonrecourse Leverage Results in Exhibit 18.4, we get to the present value statistics for the *non*recourse leverage investor. The mean PV of the investment increases 10 cents from the recourse PV of $7.70 to the nonrecourse PV of $7.80. The middle 95th percentile range of the nonrecourse case is the same as in the recourse case. To emphasize the difference between recourse and nonrecourse borrowing, we show that there is 0% probability of the nonrecourse investor having to make a recourse payment. And the size of the nonexistent payment is $0.00.

The advantage of the nonrecourse investor over the recourse investor is 10 cents of mean PV and the elimination of the 1.1% chance of making a recourse payment that would otherwise average $1.57. But nonrecourse leverage is even more valuable in harsher situations. In the third column of Exhibit 18.4, we recalculate PV statistics assuming twice the default rates of the 2000 issuance cohort.

Naturally, the PV of the loan portfolio falls, specifically from $99.70 to $93.60. The entire amount of this $6.10 decline is reflected in the PV of the recourse leverage investment, whose PV plummets from $7.70 to $1.60. However, the PV of the nonrecourse leverage investment only falls $3.77, from $7.80 to $4.03. Recourse leverage is burdened by the 32.64% chance of having to make a recourse payment, which would average $3.40. Nonrecourse leverage is dramatically better than recourse leverage under these severe default rate assumptions.

We have demonstrated the value of a CDO's nonrecourse leverage over the more typical recourse leverage available from the repo market or other short-term secured financing arrangements. In doing so, we tried to make our assumptions as realistic as possible, using loan spreads, CLO spreads, and the amount of leverage available to CLO equity current as of the time of the analysis. However, we did not consider CLO fees, either up-front fees associated with setting up the structure or ongoing management fees. These, of course, would diminish CDO equity returns. We also assume that the cost of CDO funding remains constant over time. In fact, as debt tranches amortize, the cost of funding changes.

Another assumption we implicitly made was that CDO equity waits until debt holders are repaid in full before receiving any cash flow. But in any realistic collateral default scenario that produces losses on CDO debt, CDO equity will initially receive cash flow. Later, overcollateralization tests become binding and redirect collateral cash flows to pay down debt holders or purchase new assets. So some cash flow will leak out of the CDO structure to equity holders in scenarios where CDO debt holders are not repaid in full. How much flows through depends on the timing of collateral losses and the strictness of the CDO structure in cutting off cash flow to equity holders. We are going to explore this now by looking at INTEX cash flow results of an actual CLO.

THE FORGIVING NATURE OF CDO FINANCING

To demonstrate the leakage of cash flow to equity holders, we picked a typical CLO whose cash flow model is available on INTEX. We compared cash flows of the equity tranche to those of the CDO's lowest debt tranche, a floating rate BB debt, under different default scenarios. Our first test was simply to stress both tranches by increasing constant annual defaults (CDRs) with loan recoveries set at 65% of par. To put results for the BB debt and the equity tranche on the same scale, we priced both tranches in every CDR scenario to yield 15%.[3] Exhibit 18.5 shows the results of this experiment.

Exhibit 18.5 shows that equity immediately begins losing value with increases in CDR. Meanwhile, BB debt remains unfazed until CDR reaches 6%. At 6% CDR, the price for BB debt to yield 15% falls from 76% to 65%, indicating that it has lost a significant amount of value. Yet at 6% CDR, equity is has a "price" of 25%, down a great deal from its 0% CDR price of 111%, but still with positive value. So at 6% CDR, equity has significant value when BB debt is receiving less than its promised principal and interest. From 6% to 10% CDR, BB debt, in fact, loses value at a much faster pace than does equity. After 10% CDR, price deterioration flattens out for both tranches.

The forgiving nature of the cash flow CDO structure to equity holders is even more apparent if defaults are initially delayed. We think a scenario of delayed defaults is also more realistic for newly issued loans. Exhibit 18.6 shows a CDR scenario based on increasing defaults. In the first year, CDR is 0%, in the second year 0.5%, in the third and all future years 1.0%. This will be our base case default scenario and we will adjust it by multiplying it by 0, 1, 2, 3, and so on to create more stressful scenar-

---

[3] Comparing IRRs is inappropriate, particularly when there are negative IRR results and especially when there are negative IRR results for alternatives of different maturities. Which is worse, a –3% IRR for an investment with a 10-year maturity or a –5% IRR for an investment with a six-year maturity?

EXHIBIT 18.5   Equity and BB Debt Priced to Yield 15%

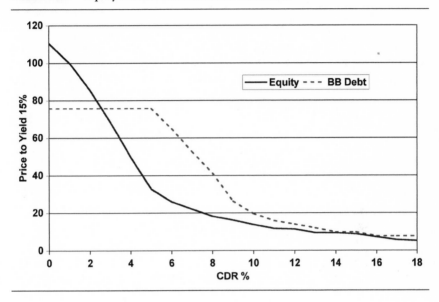

EXHIBIT 18.6   CDR Scenario

Year	CDR
1	0.0%
2	0.5%
3	1.0%
4	1.0%
Thereafter	1.0%

ios. But note that no matter how high a factor we multiply the CDR scenario by, there are never any defaults in the CDO's first year. This allows equity to receive the maximum cash flow possible in its first year.

Exhibit 18.7 shows the results of multiplications of this CDR scenario. Again, we price equity and BB debt to yield 15% in each default scenario. As in Exhibit 18.5, the "price" of equity immediately deteriorates with greater defaults. But at 5.0 times the CDR scenario, the price of equity flattens out significantly. This is because most of equity's value is coming from cash flows in the early years of the CDO. Meanwhile, BB debt maintains its price until 5.75 times the default scenario, after which it rapidly loses price. At 8.75 times the default scenario, the price of the BB tranche actually crosses below the price of equity. So with this

EXHIBIT 18.7   Equity and BB Debt Priced to Yield 15%

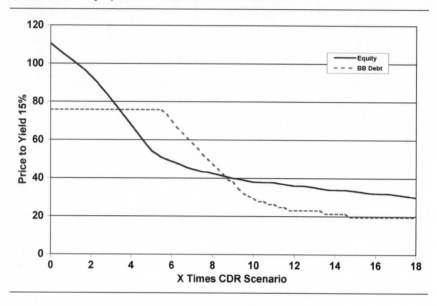

particular CLO in this particular CDR pattern, we have the case where one is better off owning equity in both low and high default scenarios.

A Short Detour for a Trade Idea

The joint performance of equity and BB debt from this CLO suggests a trade, namely, going long equity and shorting BB debt. One logical combination would be to buy $200 of equity and short $100 of BB debt. This has the same initial outlay as buying $100 of equity or $100 of BB debt that we have depicted in Exhibits 18.5 and 18.7. The solid line in Exhibit 18.8 shows the price to yield 15% of this strategy, over different multiplications of the CDR scenario shown in Exhibit 18.6. The light dashed lines in the exhibit are the price to yield 15% of straight $100 long positions in equity and debt as previously shown in Exhibit 18.7. The long-short combination dominates the pure equity and the pure debt strategies from 0% to 4% CDR and above 9% CDR.

CDO OPTIONS

The value of equity is also enhanced by two different call options equity holders have on the CDO's assets. The simplest to understand option is

EXHIBIT 18.8   Long Equity/Short BB Debt Priced to Yield 15%

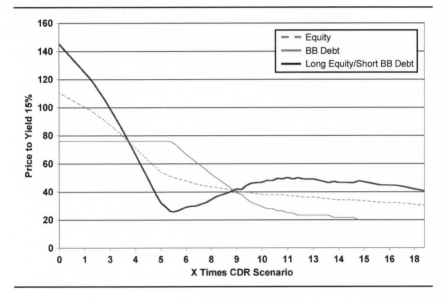

in the market value of the CDO's assets. After a noncall period, CDO assets can be liquidated. To the extent proceeds from the liquidation exceed the cost of repaying debt and other expenses, equity holders benefit dollar-for-dollar. Certainly, if the market value of the CDO assets is less than the cost of unwinding a CDO, equity holders would not want to liquidate assets. And a cash flow CDO is never forced to sell collateral before that collateral's maturity. Nor does the market value of CDO collateral affect CDO equity distributions. Equity holders in a market value-challenged CDO will keep receiving cash flow, provided that overcollateralization tests are not violated.

CDO equity holders also have a call option in the after-default cash flows of a CDO's asset portfolio. If CDO asset cash flow exceeds debt tranche requirements, the equity tranche also gains dollar-for-dollar. And if after-default cash flow is insufficient to satisfy debt tranches, CDO equity "loses" the same amount of return whether the CDO debt service shortfall is $1 million or whether it is only $1. Whereas the strike price of CDO equity's market value option is the amount necessary to retire the CDO's debt and repay the CDO's other senior expenses, the strike price of CDO equity's after-default cash flow option is the cash flow necessary to service CDO debt until overcollateralization tests are failed.

So CDO equity holders have two similar options:

1. On the market value of assets in the CDO portfolio that is exercised by liquidating and unwinding the CDO.
2. On the after-default cash flow of the CDO asset portfolio that is reaped by simply waiting to see how actual defaults and coverage tests interact to produce equity cash flow.

Like all option holders, CDO equity tranche holders are long volatility. They benefit if the underlying has greater market risk and if the underlying has greater after-default cash flow risk. This is because all underlying collateral asset outcomes below the strike price have the same result for the option holder (i.e., the option is worthless). But volatility on the upside creates greater and greater returns for the option holder.

To illustrate the benefit of the volatility of after-default cash flows, we assume that asset spreads over Treasuries are indicative of the asset's risk of credit losses. That is, a spread of Treasuries +100 indicates expected credit losses of 100 basis points. We then compare the one-year after-default cash flow distributions of two CDO portfolios, each consisting of $90 of collateral. One portfolio has a 100 basis point spread over Treasuries (and therefore expected losses of 100 basis points according to our assumption), while the other portfolio has a 500 basis point spread over Treasuries (and therefore expected losses of 500 basis points).

Note that for both portfolios, the expected return is the Treasury return, which we set at 5%. For the 100 basis point spread portfolio, the highest return it can attain (if it experiences zero defaults) is Treasuries + 100 or 6%; which is about $96 with return of principal. For the 500 basis point spread portfolio, the highest return it can attain (in zero defaults) is Treasuries + 500 or 10%; about $99 with return of principal.

Exhibit 18.9 shows the distribution of after-default cash flow of the 100 basis point spread assets in solid bars, and the 500 basis point spread assets in hashed bars. Note the wider distribution of after-default cash flows of the more credit-risky assets (higher probability of large default losses and of higher cash flow). If debt service on CDO debt tranches (which is the strike price of equity's cash flow option) is arbitrarily set at, say, $96 on the scale above, then the equity associated with the low credit risk asset portfolio is worthless. That's because there is zero possibility that the low credit risk assets will generate more than $96 of cash flow. But the 500 basis point spread assets have a 26% chance of generating more than $96 of cash flow. If the value of the cash flows is greater than $96, CDO equity receives the overage, which could be as much as $3 ($99 – $96). In this example, equity's expected cash flow is approximately $0.26.

EXHIBIT 18.9   After-Default Cash Flow Volatility

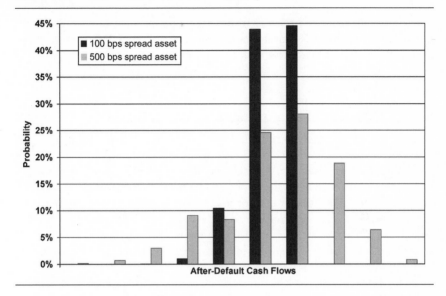

Market value and after-default cash flow optionalities increase the value of CDO equity. A CDO manager would never liquidate a CDO unless there was considerable upside for CDO equity holders. A CDO manager might refrain from selling a credit-deteriorated asset in order to avoid crystallizing a loss and retain a potential upside benefit for equity holders if the credit pulls through. And in fact, some CDO managers have intentionally purchased riskier assets to take advantage of CDO equity's cash flow optionality.

CDO EQUITY AS A DEFENSIVE STRATEGY

As damaging as it may be to our careers as financial analysts, we admit that we do not know what the future may bring. Furthermore, it seems to us that prognostications based on the most careful analysis of past economic experience may prove incorrect in the face of today's potential for dramatic political events. To put it succinctly, politics (at least big-enough politics) trumps economics. Those few who share our uncertainty should consider CDO equity as a defensive investment.

Here is what we mean. Rather than invest $100 in high-yield loans or investment grade ABS on an unlevered basis, the concerned investor should consider purchasing CDO equity that controls $100 of those assets. The remainder can be stored in whatever safe harbor asset one prefers.

The resulting risk profile will not have all the upside potential as if one had dedicated his portfolio completely to the CDO's underlying assets. But the downside risk will be significantly mitigated.

CONCLUSION

We have tried to answer the question "Why buy CDO equity?" with four arguments.

First, nonrecourse term financing is a very good thing. The "heads I win, tails I don't lose everything" bet sets a floor to the downside of leveraged investing. An investor cannot lose more than the initial investment.

Second, the forgiving nature of the cash flow CDO structure further enhances equity holder's return if CDO assets underperform. This feature is especially pertinent when an investor expects a period of continuing low defaults and high recoveries before any CDO asset deterioration.

Third, the ability to sell out early or wait and see gives CDO equity holders flexibility to take advantage of market value appreciation and delay the effects of credit quality deterioration.

Fourth, CDO equity can be used in conjunction with a safe harbor asset as a defensive investment strategy for those who are unsure of future economic conditions.

CHAPTER 19

CDO Equity Returns and Return Correlation

There has been a good deal of research published on historic CDO equity returns, particularly with regard to the monthly volatility of equity returns, their Sharpe ratios,[1] and the correlation of CDO equity returns to the returns of other assets. Unfortunately, the calculation of these variables is so fundamentally flawed that the results that have been reported to investors are useless. The reason is quite simple: The secondary market for CDO equity is undeveloped. As a result, there are no monthly prices for CDO equity. It follows that one cannot calculate monthly CDO equity returns, the monthly volatility of CDO equity returns, or a CDO equity Sharpe ratio. Nor can one correlate monthly CDO equity returns with those of other assets.

In this chapter, we investigate what part of the historic record has any bearing on future CDO equity returns. We conclude that the only historic data that provide insight into the future performance of CDO equity are the default and recovery of underlying CDO assets. Consequently, this limits the usefulness of the historic CDO equity return measures mentioned above, even if they could be calculated reliably.

We then make the most of available default and recovery data to examine the implication to CDO equity created in today's environment with either high-yield loan or structured finance underlying assets. Next, making some simplifying assumptions, we show that the correlation between CDO equity returns and CDO underlying asset returns is a simple function of the levered and nonrecourse nature of CDO equity.

---

[1] The Sharpe ratio is the monthly return on CDO equity minus the risk-free return divided by the standard deviation of monthly CDO equity returns.

An understanding of CDO equity return/CDO asset return correlation can be gained without an appeal to dubious data and calculations. And once we correlate CDO equity returns to the CDO's underlying assets, it is simple to correlate CDO equity returns to the returns of other assets.

Finally, we circle back to the simplifying assumptions we made to correlate CDO equity returns to the returns of other assets. We show that these assumptions *underestimate* CDO equity returns and *overestimate* the correlation of CDO equity returns to those of other assets. Thus, if CDO equity appears to be a good addition to a portfolio based on the assumptions we made earlier, it is in fact a better addition to the portfolio once we relax those assumptions.

FLAWED METHODOLOGIES

Despite the insurmountable obstacle in calculating the measures discussed earlier, some researchers brave onward, employing the following techniques: (1) If they do not have historical mark-to-markets, they interpolate linearly between known points; (2) they adjust the data for statistical anomalies; and (3) they exclude extreme values.

Linear Interpolation

We will first turn our attention to the "linear interpolation" methodologies employed by some researchers. Presumably, these researchers have obtained the initial purchase prices for some number of CDO equity tranches. They also probably have obtained the cash flows of those CDO equity tranches since issuance. Somehow, they also have obtained current CDO equity market values.[2]

Now, what can we say about linear interpolation between the initial sales price of CDO equity and whatever subsequent CDO equity market value our competitors have calculated at whatever particular point in time they have calculated such a market value? Let us see what linear interpolation would produce if applied to a more familiar financial variable. In Exhibit 19.1, we show what the technique of linear interpolation would produce if applied to the Dow Jones Industrial Average from September 1998 to September 2005.

---

[2] We will not ask how these prices have been obtained, but we note that the most defensible market value quotation would be "zero," obtained because either the assets of the CDO have all been liquidated, or the state of the CDO is such that it can be determined with certainty that CDO equity will never receive any future cash flows.

EXHIBIT 19.1 The Dow Jones Industrial Average, Linearly Interpolated

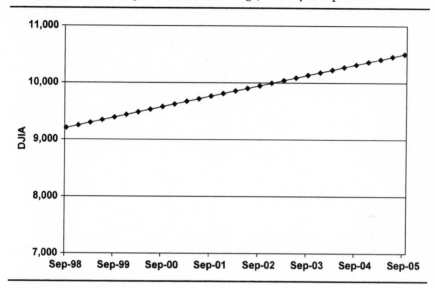

In Exhibit 19.1, we begin with a reading for the Dow of 9,200 in September 1998, end with a reading of 10,500 in September 2005, and draw a straight line between the two points. The resulting pattern may seem unfamiliar to those involved in the equity market over the seven-year time period. But this "interpolated" view of the Dow leads to pretty wonderful results. The monthly variability in the growth of the Dow is zero! Better still, the Sharpe ratio for the Dow, from the time series shown in the exhibit, would be approximately positive infinity.

Applying linear interpolation to CDO equity also would smooth out the rough spots in a time series of the market value of equity, if indeed there were a reliable market value of equity. In fact, we think the only price volatility introduced in the procedure used by some researchers is a result of the misapplication of CDO equity cash flows between those cash flows representing dividends and those cash flows representing the repayment of CDO equity principal.

Statistical Anomalies and Extreme Values

We depart from the field of finance to better illustrate the implication of adjusting for statistical anomalies and excluding extreme values. In Exhibit 19.2, we show the number of lives lost at sea in major ship sinkings between 1900 and 1914. It is an unfortunate but not particularly sensational graph. But what if we include the statistical anomaly and extreme value representing the *Titanic*, as shown in Exhibit 19.3? Then,

EXHIBIT 19.2 Lives Lost at Sea, Excluding Statistical Anomalies and Extreme Values

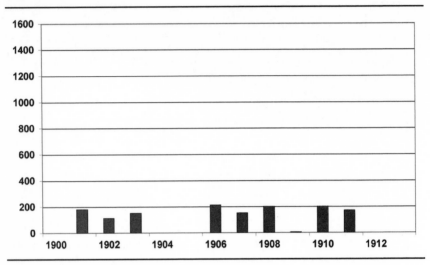

EXHIBIT 19.3 Lives Lost at Sea, Including the *Titanic*

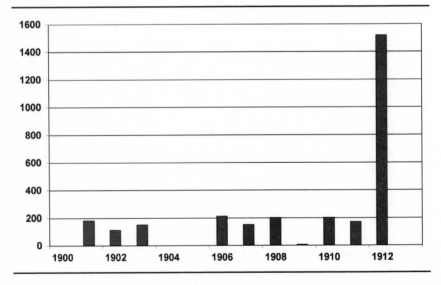

things look pretty sensational and a lot more interesting, which goes to prove that the most interesting things in life are usually anomalies and extremes. A picture of ship disasters misses a lot without the inclusion of the *Titanic*. And, while we do not know exactly what is lost when researchers adjust statistical anomalies and exclude extreme values, we know it is bound to be quite interesting, too.

THE APPROPRIATE LESSON FROM HISTORY

Many CDO research reports have struggled to say something about CDO equity market value volatility, Sharpe ratios, and the correlation of CDO equity returns with the returns of other assets. We have argued that this is impossible because (1) the secondary CDO equity market is not well developed; (2) there are no monthly CDO equity prices; and (3) there are no monthly CDO equity returns. Given these fatal obstacles, it makes no sense to look at CDO equity returns in a mark-to-market context when there is, in fact, no real market and therefore no real marking to it. Past CDO equity returns can be evaluated reliably over the life of CDO equities only after all of their cash flows are known.

What if CDO equity was traded on the New York Stock Exchange, and the bid-ask spread was 0.125%, and we had daily traded prices for every single CDO equity ever issued? In that world, we could compute monthly and even daily price volatility as well as Sharpe ratios and return correlations with other assets. If these computations were available, how much weight should we give them in terms of predicting future CDO equity performance, especially the performance of new and recently created CDO equity? The important question here is, "What can history teach us about future CDO equity returns?"

To answer this question, one first has to think about the determinates of CDO equity returns. These factors are: (1) the collateral's promised yield; (2) the CDO's funding cost; (3) the amount of leverage in the CDO structure; (4) the cash flow structure of the CDO; (5) the influence of the CDO manager; and (6) the collateral's default and recovery performance.

Given that these factors are the determinates of CDO equity returns, which ones are subject to historical analysis? Or to put it another way, of these six factors, for which do we care about past values and for which do we care only about current value? We discuss each below:

1. *The collateral's promised yield or the cash flow from the CDO's portfolio in the absence of collateral defaults.* If the CDO is fully ramped

up,[3] the CDO equity investor need only look at the portfolio's weighted average coupon or weighted average spread. If the CDO is in the process of buying its collateral portfolio, the CDO equity investor would best look at current spreads in the respective collateral markets. The long-term history of collateral spreads does not offer much insight to the CDO equity investor, with the exception of being perhaps an indicator of collateral reinvestment risk.

2. *CDO funding cost or the cost of the CDO's own debt.* Historic CDO spreads do not matter at all to the returns of new CDO equity. We only care about the levels at which CDO debt can be placed today. Old CDO liability spreads do not help us predict returns on new CDO equity.

3. *The amount of leverage in the CDO structure.* Past CDO leverage ratios do not change the fact of current rating-agency and debt-investor requirements. Past leverage ratios do not matter to the future performance of today's CDO equity.

4. *The cash flow structure of the CDO, including overcollateralization tests and equity caps that determine cash distributions to CDO equity holders.* CDO structures today are dramatically different from ones executed 18 months ago and different even from CDO structures executed one year ago. How structures used to be has no effect on how today's structures are going to affect CDO equity returns.

5. *CDO manager influence.* A manager's historic total return performance or default-avoidance performance may help predict future CDO equity returns. But perhaps a stronger factor influencing CDO equity performance is any bias shown to equity or debt investors by the manager in previous CDOs. While managers' historical behavior may be important in predicting CDO equity returns, we view it as a nonquantifiable and nonmodelable factor.

6. *Collateral defaults and recoveries.* Of all the factors influencing CDO equity returns, the one most open to an appeal to history is collateral defaults and recoveries. In analyzing potential CDO equity returns, we should be very interested in the historic average and the historic volatility of default rates and recovery rates. This does not mean that we do not consider today's economic conditions or underwriting standards in estimating future default and recoveries. Past experience, in good times, bad times, and average times is a good place to start when thinking about future collateral defaults and recoveries.

---

[3] The ramp-up period is the period that follows the closing date of the transaction, where the CDO manager finishes buying the CDO's collateral portfolio. This period usually lasts less than one year.

Thus, history makes little difference with respect to most of the factors affecting CDO equity returns. Only current levels matter. Given this, how applicable would historic CDO equity price volatility, Sharpe ratios, and return correlation with other assets be to *new* CDO equity offerings, even if these measures could be reasonably calculated? It seems to us that the measures would be of little guidance to an investor considering a CDO equity purchase today.

LOAN DEFAULTS AND RECOVERIES

In this section, we present the latest loan default and recovery data and show how these data can be incorporated in modeling future collateralized loan obligation (CLO) equity returns. We then do the same for structured finance (SF) CDO equity, using the structured finance default estimates we have developed. After exhausting the historical data, we will come back to the issue of the correlation of CDO equity returns to the returns of other assets. Making some simplifying assumptions, we show that the correlation relationship between CDO equity returns and CDO underlying asset returns is a function of the *levered and nonrecourse nature of CDO equity*. Once we correlate CDO equity returns to the returns of the CDO's underlying assets, it is simple to correlate CDO equity returns to the returns of other assets. Lastly, we examine the simplifying assumptions we made to correlate CDO equity returns to the returns of other assets. We show that these assumptions *underestimate* CDO equity returns and *overestimate* the correlation of CDO equity returns to those of other assets. Thus, if CDO equity appears to be a good addition to a portfolio based on the assumptions we made earlier, it is in fact a *better* addition to the portfolio once we relax those assumptions.

Exhibit 19.4 shows S&P LCD institutional loan defaults by year of origination or "vintage." The percentage of defaulting loans in each vintage is shown in the year they defaulted.

In Exhibit 19.5 we carve up and reassemble the data in Exhibit 19.4 in three ways: (1) *marginal* default rates (i.e., defaults *in* the 1st, 2nd, 3rd, 4th, 5th, and 6th year after issuance); (2) *cumulative* default rates (i.e., defaults *over* 1, 2, 3, 4, 5, and 6 years); and (3) default rate averages weighting the experience of vintage years equally and weighting the experience of vintage years by the number of loans issued in each year. We look at the experience of BB/BB– loans, B+/B loans, and a 50%/50% split of BB and B loans. Finally, we compare the experience of S&P

EXHIBIT 19.4   S&P LCD High-Yield Loan Default Data: Number of Public Filers and Subsequent Defaulters

Year of Origination	Public Filers	1995	1996	1997	1998	1999	2000	2001	2002	2003	2004	1H 2005
1995	27	—	—	—	—	—	1	—	—	—	—	—
1996	66		—	—	—	—	1	—	—	—	—	—
1997	107			—	3	2	10	3	1	—	—	—
1998	188				1	7	11	7	6	4	—	—
1999	165					—	7	13	3	2	2	—
2000	138						—	11	15	2	1	—
2001	114							2	3	—	1	—
2002	167								1	3	2	—
2003	289									—	3	—
2004	435										—	1
Totals	1696	0	0	0	4	9	30	36	29	11	9	1

Source: S&P LCD.

EXHIBIT 19.5   Average Cumulative Default Rates for High-Yield Loans and Bonds, 1998–2004 Issuance Cohorts

	1	2	3	4	5	6	Average
Year-Weighted Cumulative Default Rates							
BBB Corporate Bond	0.4%	1.1%	2.0%	3.1%	4.1%	4.6%	0.8%
BB/BB– Loan	0.9%	3.0%	4.2%	5.3%	7.0%	7.8%	1.3%
BB Corporate Bond	1.4%	4.2%	7.8%	11.0%	13.7%	15.5%	2.6%
B+/B Loan	4.5%	9.6%	13.1%	15.3%	17.8%	19.2%	3.2%
B Corporate Bond	6.3%	14.4%	21.1%	26.9%	30.4%	32.9%	5.5%
Issuer Weighted Cumulative Default Rates							
BBB Corporate Bond	0.3%	1.1%	2.0%	3.1%	4.0%	4.4%	0.7%
BB/BB– Loan	0.8%	2.6%	3.7%	4.4%	5.7%	6.3%	1.0%
BB Corporate Bond	1.4%	4.2%	7.8%	10.8%	13.4%	15.0%	2.5%
B+/B Loan	3.1%	8.1%	11.7%	13.5%	15.9%	17.3%	2.9%
B Corporate Bond	6.1%	14.1%	20.8%	26.3%	29.7%	32.2%	5.4%

Note: Calculations by authors based on data from S&P LCD.

LCD's loan default experience with that of S&P's corporate senior unsecured bond default experience between 1995 and 2003.[4]

In Exhibit 19.6 we show loan and bond recovery experience.[5] Note that we depict loan recoveries two ways: a lower figure providing a loan's average price in the secondary market one month after default, and also the present value of all after-default cash flows. In Exhibit 19.7, we show a time series of the annual average recovery rates of bank loans, again measured by their price in the secondary market one month after default.

EXHIBIT 19.6 Loan and Bond Recoveries 1995–2004

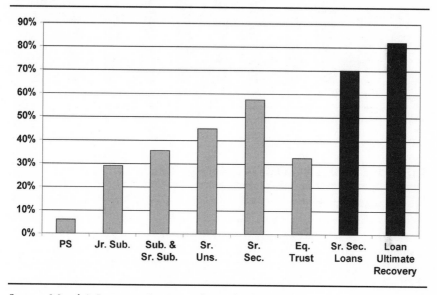

Source: Moody's Investors Service and Standard &Poor's.

---

[4] See Brooks Brady, and Diane Vazza, *Corporate Defaults in 2003 Recede From Recent Highs*, Standard & Poor's, January 27, 2004.
[5] Ultimate loan recovery is from David Keisman, *Recovery Trends and Analysis*, PowerPoint presentation, Standard & Poor's, March 24, 2004. Other recovery data are from Greg M. Gupton, Daniel Gates, and Lea V. Carty, *Bank Loan Loss Given Default*, Moody's, November 2000 and Praveen Varma, Richard Cantor, and David Hamilton, *Recovery Rates on Defaulted Corporate Bonds and Preferred Stocks, 1982–2003*, Moody's Investors Service, December 2003. Moody's annual default studies are from David T. Hamilton, Praveen Varma, Sharon Ou, and Richard Cantor, *Default and Recovery Rates of Corporate Bond Issuers: A Statistical Review of Moody's Ratings Performance, 1920–2003*, Moody's Investors Service, January 2004.

EXHIBIT 19.7   Senior Secured Bank Loan Immediate Recoveries

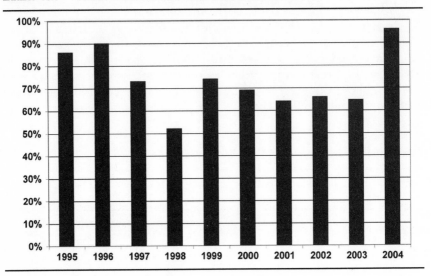

Source: Moody's Investors Service.

CASH FLOW MODELING DEFAULTS AND RECOVERIES

Now that we have assembled loan default and recovery data, what do we do with it? First, we incorporate into a CDO cash flow model all the quantifiable variables we previously discussed that affect CDO equity returns: the collateral's promised yield, CDO liability funding costs, the amount of leverage in the CDO structure, and the cash flow structure of the CDO. These are the variables whose historical trends have no significance in evaluating CDO equity; all we care about is their current values. Now we use our cash flow model and test different historical rates of loan defaults and recoveries to create a sensitivity analysis of CDO equity's internal rate of return (IRR). We show the result for a hypothetical high-yield loan CLO in Exhibit 19.8.

Perhaps a good historical base-case default and recovery scenario is the issuer-weighted average 2.54% annual defaults and the average 71% immediate recovery scenario. This scenario creates a 14% return to equity using the cash flow model of our hypothetical CLO. On the optimistic extreme, the 1995 and 1996 loan vintages have had a 0.72% annual default rate and in 1996 the average recovery amount was 90%. This scenario yields an 18% equity IRR. On the pessimistic extreme, the 2000 cohort not only has had high defaults, but we are annualizing its experience at what is the worst time in the life of a vintage—that is, just before annual

EXHIBIT 19.8   HYL CLO Equity IRRs: Defaults and Recoveries Applied to a Hypothetical Structure

Annual Default Rates	1996 Recovery 90%	Average Recovery 71%	1998 Recovery 52%
95-96 Cohort 0.72%	18	16	16
Yearly average 2.19%	16	15	12
Issuer average 2.54%	15	14	10
1999 Cohort 2.78%	15	12	9
1997 Cohort 3.38%	14	11	8
2000 Cohort 4.96%	13	3	0

defaults normally begin to decline below the average. The annual default rate of the 2000 vintage at this point is 4.96%. We simultaneously use 1998 loan recovery experience, when loans had their worst annual average recovery rate of 52%. This very harsh scenario leads to 0% equity IRR.

In this analysis we have modeled the known CDO equity return inputs (collateral yield, cost of CDO debt, amount of equity leverage, and the CDO's cash flow structure) and tested the major unknown CDO equity return input via different historical default and recovery scenarios. If we were going to continue this analysis, we would now look at the historic default and recovery experience of the manager and try to factor in the effect of its management style on CDO equity returns. We would also look at current economic conditions, loan underwriting standards, and reinvestment risk.

STRUCTURED FINANCE DEFAULTS AND RECOVERIES

In this section, we apply the technique described in the previous section to structured finance (SF) CDO equity. The collateral pools for SF cash flow CDOs have been comprised of almost the entire spectrum of structured finance products in the market. Within the mortgage-related sector, cash flow CDO deals have often used a combination of BBB rated residential mortgage-backed securities (RMBS), commercial mortgage-backed securities (CMBS), and real estate investment trust (REIT) debt.

Studies by the rating agencies have documented defaults and recoveries for structured finance assets, focusing in RMBS, CMBS, and ABS.[6]

---

[6] See, for example, the study by Moody's: Jian Hu and Richard Cantor, "Defaults and Losses Given Default of Structured Finance Securities," *Journal of Fixed Income* (March 2004), pp. 5–24.

These studies are much harder to do than default studies on corporate credits. One aspect is visibility and the level of required detail. A corporate default study looks at obvious events that affect large corporations. A structured finance default study has to look at what is happening at particular tranches in a particular transaction that might be one of many from a particular originator or servicer. Another aspect is the ambiguity of default. A structured finance tranche might have missed interest payments, but also might stand a good chance of getting caught up in full on accrued interest. Or a tranche might be current on interest, but an examination of the transaction makes it obvious that the tranche will not receive full principal. In Chapter 7, we provide the estimates of structured finance default rates reproduced in Exhibit 19.9. In Exhibit 19.10, we present structured finance recoveries as reported in a 2002 study by Standard & Poor's[7] and compare them to corporate bond recoveries.

SF CDO CASH FLOW MODELING

Again, to look at CDO equity returns, we incorporate the current values for the collateral's promised yield, CDO liability funding cost, the amount of leverage in the CDO structure, and the cash flow structure of the CDO into a cash flow model. We then test the effect of various historical default and recoveries on CDO equity returns and show the results in Exhibit 19.11.

EXHIBIT 19.9   Estimated Historic Constant Annual Defaults/Recoveries

	ABS	CMBS	RMBS & HEL	All SF	Corporates
Aaa	0.03%/87%	0.00%/na	0.03%/97%	0.03%/92%	0.05%/80%
Aa	0.69%/73%	0.00%/na	0.05%/82%	0.15%/77%	0.07%/40%
A	0.47%/55%	0.08%/87%	0.10%/68%	0.23%/62%	0.15%/44%
Baa	1.79%/45%	0.28%/50%	0.49%/56%	0.86%/53%	0.59%/41%
Ba	5.32%/42%	1.24%/54%	1.22%/52%	1.78%/49%	2.62%/41%
B	11.89%/34%	2.21%/47%	2.81%/43%	3.26%/43%	6.02%/36%

Note: Calculations by authors based on data from Moody's and Standard & Poor's.

---

[7] Joseph Hu, Robert B. Pollsen, Roy Chun, and Patrick Coyne, *Recoveries of Defaulted U.S. Structured Finance Securities: Inception to June 30, 2002*, Standard & Poor's, September 12, 2002.

EXHIBIT 19.10   Structured Finance and Corporate Bond Recoveries

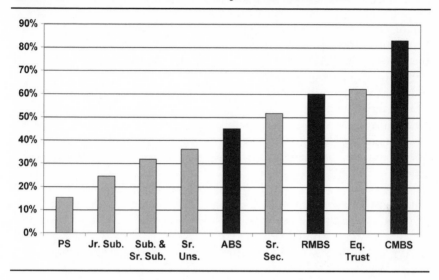

Source: Moody's Investors Service and Standard &Poor's.

EXHIBIT 19.11   SF CDO Equity IRRs: Defaults and Recoveries Applied to a Hypothetical Structure

Annual Default Rates	CMBS Recovery 82%	RMBS Recovery 60%	ABS Recovery 45%	Stress Recovery 25%
CMBS A/BBB 0.09%	17	17	17	16
CMBS BBB 0.14%	17	17	17	16
Resi B&C A/BBB 0.24%	17	17	16	14
Corporates A/BBB 0.33%	16	16	15	13
Resi B&C BBB 0.38%	16	15	14	11
RMBS A/BBB 0.44%	16	15	14	10
Corporates BBB 0.54%	16	15	14	9
RMBS BBB 0.76%	14	13	12	8

In the top row of the exhibit, for example, a CMBS A/BBB default rate of 0.09% per year produces equity IRRs of 16% to 17%, depending on the recovery assumption used. Note that as an extra stress, we use a nonhistorical recovery rate of 25% to further test equity's recovery sensitivity. At the opposite default extreme, using a RMBS BBB default rate of 0.76% per year, as in the bottom row of the exhibit, produces equity IRRs ranging from 8% to 14%.

RETURN CORRELATION AND NONRECOURSE LEVERAGE

There are two things that investors want to know about a particular investment offering. First, does the offering have a favorable return profile? Second, how does the variability of the offering's return fit in with the preexisting portfolio?

We have gone into detail about how to assess the return profile of CDO equity, making use of current values for many important variables, historical values for collateral defaults and recoveries, and cash flow modeling. It turns out that the answer to the second question above, on return correlation, is based on the nonrecourse leverage nature of CDO equity.

CDO equity is basically a leveraged position in the assets of a CDO, with the CDO's debt tranches being the financing for the equity position. CDO equity receives whatever cash flow remains after satisfaction of debt claims. Equity sustains the risk of collateral asset payment delays and credit losses, but also receives the upside if CDO assets generate cash flow in excess of debt tranche requirements. Meanwhile, debt tranche holders only have recourse to the CDO's assets, and cannot make any additional claims against equity holders. CDO equity holders are not at risk for any more than their initial investment.

CDO equity holders receive financing that is in place for up to 12, or even 15, years. Moreover, the financing rate is locked in, either at a fixed rate or more commonly at a spread above a designated floating index (usually LIBOR). CDO debt is subject to early amortization only if asset quality deteriorates according to objective measures (such as overcollateralization tests). In that case, principal repayment is due only to the extent the asset portfolio provides cash flow. Asset sales are never required.

The features of financing available to CDO equity are in contrast to the repo market or other short-term secured financing arrangements. In those, financing rates can fluctuate and higher levels of security (larger collateral haircuts) can be demanded. In fact, financing can be pulled altogether with little warning. Collateral assets are subject to sale by the creditor, and creditors have recourse to the borrower if the collateral is insufficient to extinguish the debt. Leveraged investors in a CDO's assets (also known as. CDO equity holders) avoid all these risks.

Return Correlation Simplified

In Exhibit 19.12 we graph CDO underlying returns and CDO equity returns under the simplifying assumptions that (1) CDO equity does not receive any cash flow until the claims of CDO debt holder are completely satisfied; and (2) CDO equity holders do not take advantage of

EXHIBIT 19.12 Two Regions of CDO Equity Return Correlation

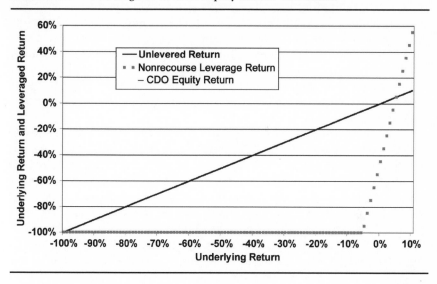

certain *optionalities* inherent in their position. We will relax these assumptions and explain their significance shortly.

The graph's horizontal axis depicts returns on the CDO's underlying assets. In our example, the best case is that the CDO portfolio suffers no defaults and returns its promised yield of 10%. In the worst case, all the assets in the CDO's portfolio default without any recovery and the portfolio's return is –100%. The thin line going up at a 30-degree angle represents the tautology that the return of the underlying CDO assets depends on the return of the underlying CDO assets. Therefore, it also goes from –100% to +10%.

The thick line in Exhibit 19.12, which moves along the bottom of the graph and becomes a rising dotted line at the right of the exhibit, represents CDO equity returns. We assume that equity contributes 10% of the funding for the CDO's asset portfolio and that 90% of the CDO portfolio is funded with CDO debt costing an average of 5%.

There are two distinct regions in Exhibit 19.12 with respect to the return correlation of CDO equity and the CDO's underlying assets. In the right side of the exhibit, when CDO equity return varies between –100% and +55%, there is a strict mathematical relationship based on the excess cash flow from the underlying CDO collateral over that which is necessary to service the CDO's debt. All of this excess goes to CDO equity and every extra dollar of excess cash flow is an extra dollar of return to CDO equity. In this region, at the right of the exhibit, the return correlation between CDO assets and CDO equity is a perfect 1.0.

Between CDO underlying returns of –100% and –5%, CDO equity's return is flatlined at a –100% loss in our example. This is because, as we have said, of the nonrecourse nature of CDO equity. As equity holders in a corporate entity, CDO equity holders are not responsible for the debts of the CDO and can only lose the purchase price of their equity investment. In this region, the return correlation between CDO assets and CDO equity is zero.

The simple, and pretty good, answer to the correlation of CDO equity returns and the CDO asset portfolio is thus: when CDO equity is not completely wiped out, the return correlation is 1.0; and when CDO equity *is* wiped out, the return correlation is zero. These correlations are based on the cash flows of the CDO equity and CDO assets over their lives, as opposed to monthly price movements. We have argued why this is the only reasonable way to look at CDO equity returns.

Having correlated CDO equity returns to the returns of the underlying CDO assets, it is simple to compare the return correlation of the underlying CDO assets to what might be in the investor's portfolio through the traditional practice of using monthly returns, as we show in Exhibit 19.13. So, if CLO equity is firmly in-the-money, its return correlation with the loans in its portfolio is 1.0. The exhibit shows the monthly return correlation of loans to other assets, which is our proxy for the return correlation of CLO equity with those same assets.

Relaxing the Assumption of Strict Equity Subordination

We mentioned making some simplifying assumptions in the above analysis and now it is appropriate to discuss their implications. Our first assumption was that CDO equity holders do not receive cash flow until and unless CDO debt holders are repaid in full. But in any realistic collateral default scenario that produces losses on CDO debt, CDO equity will ini-

EXHIBIT 19.13 Monthly Asset Return Correlations

	HYL	HYB	IGB	S&P	U.S.T
High-yield loans	1.00				
High-yield bonds	0.48	1.00			
Investment-grade bonds	–0.06	0.23	1.00		
S&P 500	0.14	0.51	0.02	1.00	
U.S. Treasuries	–0.11	0.04	0.91	–0.09	1.00

tially receive cash flow. Later, overcollateralization tests become binding and redirect cash flows to paying down debt holders or purchasing new collateral assets. So some cash flow will leak out of the CDO structure to equity holders in scenarios where CDO debt holders are not repaid in full. How much depends on the timing of collateral losses and the strictness of the CDO structure in cutting off cash flow to equity holders.

What this means with respect to the previous analysis is that we have been too pessimistic about CDO equity returns in cases when CDO debt holders are not repaid in full. In fact, rather than flat-lined at –100% in Exhibit 19.12, there would be some return to CDO equity holders in all but the very worse collateral return scenarios. While relaxing our assumption about strict equity subordination messes up the CDO returns we drew in Exhibit 19.12, it does so in a nice way for CDO equity, as it means the equity will get a higher return than we supposed. This is particularly true for CDO equity existing on the cusp of having value or being worthless.

How does relaxing the assumption about CDO equity subordination affect the correlation of CDO equity returns to those of other asset returns? The dependence of CDO equity returns to the strictness of the CDO structure makes CDO equity returns less correlated to any asset return. This is because the strictness of a CDO's structural features is uncorrelated to the returns of financial assets.

Relaxing the Assumption of Nonoptionality

Our second assumption in the above analysis was that CDO equity holders do not take advantage of certain options inherent in their position. In the previous chapter, we discuss the two different options CDO equity holder's have on the CDO's assets:

1. On the market value of assets in the CDO portfolio that is exercised by liquidating and unwinding the CDO.
2. On the after-default cash flow of the CDO asset portfolio that is reaped by simply waiting to see how actual defaults and coverage tests interact to produce equity cash flow.

Market value and after-default cash flow optionalities break up our hold-to-maturity analysis, but again in a positive way for CDO equity. Our assumption, this time about the CDO equity not being able to take advantage of certain optionalities, underestimates CDO equity returns. These optionalities also serve to further uncorrelate CDO equity returns to other assets because their existence and their use is uncorrelated with the return of financial assets.

CONCLUSION

In this chapter, we explained why research about historic CDO equity returns, particularly with regard to the monthly volatility of equity returns, their Sharpe ratios, and the correlation of CDO equity returns to the returns of other assets, is misguided. We described the flaws of a type of CDO equity analysis built on dubious data and methods. We queried whether, even if return data for old CDO equity were available, how applicable they would be to new CDO equity issues.

We proposed what we believe to be an eminently reasonable, unsurprising, and even commonplace method of looking at CDO equity: Model what can be modeled in cash flow analysis, assess the relevance of historic defaults and recoveries, and test their implications in the cash flow model. We provided historic defaults and recoveries for high-yield loans and structured finance assets using rating agency data.

Then, with regard to the correlation of CDO equity returns to CDO underlying asset returns, we offered a novel perspective that takes into account the nonrecourse nature of CDO equity. After relating CDO equity to CDO asset collateral, we used traditional methods (where there are adequate data) to follow the chain of correlations to other assets in the investor's portfolio. Finally, we relaxed assumptions that we made in the analysis of CDO equity returns and return correlation and showed that these assumptions underestimate CDO equity returns and overestimate CDO equity return correlation.

PART Eight

Other CDO Topics

CHAPTER 20

Analytical Challenges in Secondary CDO Market Trading

The secondary CDO market has grown rapidly. Annual par traded totaled approximately $2 billion in 2002, then soared to $14 billion in 2003 (about half of that from Abbey National sales), to $25 billion in 2004, and $30 billion in 2005. More importantly, the secondary market has become an important part of CDO investor thinking, providing a second chance to acquire CDOs and rewarding rigorous analysis.

One reason for the secondary CDO market's growth is the significant increase in resources available for analyzing outstanding CDOs, chiefly the availability of CDO-specific cash flow models. However, potential buyers of secondary CDOs still face challenges when considering a purchase. A very liquid secondary CDO market, trading with the ease of corporate bonds, will probably never be achieved. Cash flow CDOs, with idiosyncratic portfolios, management, and structures, will always be complex and take time to analyze.

In this chapter we first review secondary market developments and pitfalls. Next, we provide a step-by-step guide to evaluating a secondary CDO. We pay particular attention to two popular analytical methods: *net asset value* (NAV) *analysis* and *cash flow modeling*. These two techniques have improved investors' understanding of CDOs and therefore secondary market liquidity. But they must be implemented with care.

We demonstrate that NAV can produce results far from the actual trading level of secondary CDOs. The simple NAV calculation does not address the different cash flow characteristics that CDO tranches can have. In cash flow modeling, the choice of default scenario is vital to the relevance and comparability of results. For structured finance-backed CDOs, we suggest a way to determine default scenarios based on the ratings *and* prices of underlying collateral. For high-yield, corporate-backed CDOs, we review and formalize market practice.

Finally, we recommend the terms *primary* market purchasers should demand on their CDOs to ensure that the bonds have the greatest possible liquidity in the *secondary* market.

IMPORTANT DEVELOPMENTS: SPREAD TIGHTENING, INCREASED ACTIVITY

The dominant credit market trend from 2003 through mid-2005 was spread tightening. CDO assets and CDO liabilities have both been a part of this trend. High-yield bonds, investment grade bonds, leveraged loans, and structured finance assets (ABS, CMBS, and RMBS) have all tightened, as have the liabilities of CDOs holding these assets. To use leveraged loans and CLOs as an example, BB loans tightened over 200 basis points from 2003 through 2005. Over the same period, BBB CLOs tightened 110 basis points while AAA CLOs narrowed 30 basis points. So too have targeted (or pitch book advertised) returns to equity, from a range of 14% to 16% in 2003 to 12% to 14% in 2005.

Secondary CDOs, which traded much wider than new issue CDOs in 2003, had further to tighten, and they did. A *clean* (meaning, a CDO without significant deterioration in its collateral portfolio), seasoned CDO traded like a new issue CDO rated two rating categories lower. For example, a secondary CDO rated AAA traded at the spread of a new issue CDO rated A. By 2005, clean CDOs traded *tighter* than new issues, on the logical rationale that they have a shorter remaining life and should move down the credit curve.

More investors have been attracted to the secondary CDO market, overcoming a barrier that still exists for other investors. We call this the "safety in numbers" theory. Some primary CDO buyers will not consider the secondary market because they feel safer buying into the initial distribution of a CDO, when a number of other investors are also making the same decision. Other primary-only investors feel uneasy about buying something another investor is selling. For a growing number of CDO investors, however these perhaps irrational concerns are overcome by the desire to take advantage of another means of acquiring CDOs. As primary allocations shrink in the face of demand for CDOs, investors who buy into the high yields and rationale of CDOs appreciate a "second chance" to acquire CDOs.

On the supply side of the secondary market, more investors are willing to sell at reasonable prices. First, accounting rule changes have made

CDO holders more willing to sell. To the extent Emerging Issues Task Force (ETIF) 9920 and other mark-to-market accounting treatments create accurate valuations of distressed CDOs, selling is income statement neutral. And if accounting requirements produce punitive CDO valuations, selling may even produce gains. With more trading, sellers and buyers have more comparables and are more willing to sell, knowing the price they are receiving is consistent with the price of other secondary CDOs, a sort of secondary market "safety in numbers" effect. The increase in secondary trading is helping traders and investors develop perspective and create a "relative value matrix" in their heads. By this, we mean an intuitive idea of how CDOs will trade in the market based on credit quality, remaining maturity, manager, and other factors.

A final spur to new entrants is the availability of CDO information and analysis. CDO documentation and trustee reports are now more available from managers and dealers via private web sites and initiatives such as The Bond Market Association's CDO Library. Services such as LoanX, LPC, and IDC supply prices of underlying assets in CDOs. INTEX provides a common platform for investors to test CDO returns under various assumptions about defaults, recoveries, interest rates, and collateral amortization. Vendors such as Risk Metrics, Wall Street Analytics, and Moody's KMV supply cash flow analysis driven by Monte Carlo simulations and default correlation assumptions. In 2003, making a bid in the secondary market often took a week. Today, with these tools, many investors feel comfortable making a bid within hours.

Without doubt, the secondary market received a big boost from the Abbey National liquidation in 2003. The $8 billion of CDO bid lists sparked investor and dealer interest in the secondary market for corporate-backed CDOs. Whereas only three dealers were very active in secondary CDOs in 2002, 8 to 10 dealers in 2005 had committed traders and balance sheet to the product. Despite criticism that bid lists are an inefficient way to sell CDOs, by 2005 they were a common and accepted part of the secondary market. In 2005, bid lists circulated at a rate of about four or five a week, altogether offering about $100 to 200 million of par a week.

Sellers in the secondary market have largely been from the ranks of insurance companies and banks that bought early vintages of CDOs and began selling in the credit market downturn of 2001 and 2002. In many cases, these sellers had been early entrants into primary CDOs who got burnt by high-yield bond CBOs. Many got out too early in the secondary market's development to receive the best price for their positions. More recently, hedge fund buyers of secondary CDOs are selling to reap gains from their positions.

Buyers of senior secondary CDOs include negative basis investors,[1] conduits, and SIVs. But the big influx into the market has been mezzanine and equity tranche buyers. These include hedge funds, structured credit funds, other alternative investors, high net worth individuals, and family offices.

Another development is of *synthetic* secondary trading, where sellers and buyers trade exposure to a CDO in either credit default swap or credit-linked note form. This trading is often related to the shorting of CDO exposure in the context of a long exposure to another CDO tranche. For example, quite a few CDO investors have put on long positions in equity or BB CDO tranches and shorted positions in more senior tranches.

PITFALLS IN SECONDARY CDO TRADING

As with the buying and selling of any financial instrument, the trading of secondary CDOs is not without its pitfalls. The list of hazards we will discuss includes:

- Reliance on inaccurate or incomplete information.
- Over-reliance on net asset value analysis.
- Ignoring the potential for collateral prepayments and CDO calls.
- Inaccurate reinvestment assumptions.
- Ignoring manager behavior.
- Over-reliance on cash flow models.

Reliance on Inaccurate or Incomplete Information

Perhaps the most basic mistake, in terms of being clearly right or clearly wrong, is reliance on inaccurate or incomplete information about a CDO. There are many factual points that can be got wrong about a CDO, chief among them are its portfolio and the priorities of its cash flow waterfall. Obviously, getting these points right is important to the

---

[1] The "basis" of a bond is its credit default swap premium minus its spread above LIBOR in the cash market. Thus, if credit protection on a senior AAA CDO tranche can be purchased for 10 basis points and that tranche's spread above LIBOR is 25 basis points, there is a 15 basis point negative basis $(10 - 25 = -15)$. A "negative basis trade" in a CDO context is when, for example, Party A buys a AAA CDO tranche and Party B sells credit protection on the CDO tranche to Party A. The *funding* of the CDO tranche has therefore been separated from the *assumption of its credit risk*. Typically, a financial institution with a low cost of funds buys the tranche and a monoline insurance company writes the credit default swap.

proper valuation of a CDO. We mentioned before the increased availability of CDO information and analysis as a factor in expanding the secondary market, so there is now little excuse for getting the basics of a CDO wrong.

Overreliance on Net Asset Value Analysis

Briefly, because we address this later in detail when we provide a step-by-step guide to evaluating a secondary CDO, the calculation of a CDO tranche's net asset value begins with the aggregate market value of the CDO's assets. This figure is adjusted by the market value of interest rate hedges. That usually means subtracting the amount by which an interest rate swap is out-of-the-money to the CDO. Finally, the par amount of CDO tranches ranking senior to the tranche in question is subtracted. The result, the net asset value of a particular tranche, is divided by the par amount of the tranche and the percentage is considered by some to estimate the tranche's market value.

NAV analysis says something about the relative quality of assets, in comparison to CDO liabilities, that cannot be evaluated by traditional par value overcollateralization tests. However, the NAV concept is unrealistic in that the CDO is not going to be liquidated unless all of its debt tranches can be fully repaid. But the big problem with NAV analysis is that it does not take into account the cash flow characteristics of a CDO. The best example is that of a non-PIK CDO tranche—that is, one whose coupon comes before any overcollateralization test. While this tranche may have zero NAV, it most likely has a pretty sure interest stream that may have a significant present value.

Ignoring the Potential for Collateral Prepayments and CDO Calls

In 2004 and 2005, some sellers of CDOs ignored the potential for CDO collateral prepayments and CDO calls at great cost to themselves as high yield bond and loan prepayments were much greater than expected. For example, loan repayments (both scheduled amortization and prepayments) reached a record $99 billion (about half the outstanding amount of loans) during one 12-month period in 2004 to 2005.[2] For CBOs and CLOs out of their reinvestment period, significant cash has flowed through to repay CDO debt.

In some cases, senior tranches paid down faster than expected, providing windfalls to investors who purchased tranches at a discount. In

---

[2] *S&P/LSTA Leverage Loan Index: February 2005 Review*, Standard & Poor's, March 9, 2005.

other cases, PIK-ing tranches returned to cash flow status faster than expected, also increasing their value. Sellers, obviously, suffered opportunity costs in letting their CDOs go too cheaply.

Similar to collateral prepayments are opportunistic calls of CDO debt and unwindings of CDOs. As we mentioned before, this cannot be accomplishment without paying all CDO debt holders off in full. According to S&P, at least 40 CDO were called between 2003 and 2005, including 12 emerging market CDOs, six high-yield CBOs, two SF CDOs, and nine CLOs. Investors who sold tranches of these CDOs at less than par before they were called also suffered an opportunity cost.

Inaccurate Reinvestment Assumptions

Modeling CDOs at their initial reinvestment assumption with respect to spread is obviously inaccurate in a declining spread environment. In fact, in the aftermath of dramatic spread tightening, assuming that a CDO can reinvest at all has been a bad assumption for many CDOs violating their minimum weighted average spread (WAS) requirement. Built up cash in CDOs that cannot reinvest can usually be passed out of the CDO even before the end of the CDO's reinvestment period at manager discretion. And cash balances usually *have* to be passed out of the CDO after the CDO's reinvestment period.

Ignoring Manager Behavior

CDO investors ignore manager behavior at their peril. While class warfare may be discredited as the driver of human history, it still is a good model for the way some managers manage their CDOs. Whether a CDO manager is equity friendly or debt friendly determines whether overcollateralization tests are gamed or allowed to fail and thus divert cash flows from subordinate tranches to senior tranches.

Overreliance on Cash Flow Models

Finally, as much as we depend upon them, we list over-reliance upon cash flow modeling as our final secondary CDO pitfall. One problem is the way most cash flow modeling is done, via constant annual default rates. The fact is that some structures don't show their strengths or weaknesses in these rather unrealistic default scenarios. For example, the value of equity caps and turbo amortization only becomes apparent in scenarios where defaults are delayed.

EIGHT-POINT CHECKLIST IN EVALUATING A CDO IN THE SECONDARY MARKET

Exhibit 20.1 lists the eight questions that a CDO investor needs to ask about a secondary offering and the resources available to answer those questions. We address each question in turn.

EXHIBIT 20.1 Eight Secondary CDO Questions

Question	Data and Analysis
1. How has the average credit quality of the collateral portfolio fared?	Initial, minimum, and current Moody's or Fitch weighted average rating factor (WARF).
2. What is the dispersal of collateral ratings?	Percent of collateral at or below particular ratings. For a CDO portfolio that was initially investment grade, the percentage of the portfolio at or below Ba1/BB+, B1/B+, Caa1/CCC+, Ca/CC, and in default.
3. What are the single-name concentrations in the portfolio?	Highest percentage of collateral from the same issue, same issuer, same servicer, and (if CDOs are part of the collateral portfolio) same CDO manager.
4. What are the industry (or collateral type) concentrations in the portfolio?	Breakdown of the portfolio by industry; preferably by industry and rating.
5. How has the CDO's par overcollateralization (OC) fared and is the ratio being manipulated by the CDO's manager?	Initial, minimum, and current OCs. Cumulative debt tranche principal pay downs. OC pattern between payments dates. Collateral trading patterns.
6. What is the liquidation value of the tranche?	Net asset value analysis.
7. How good is the manager?	Performance of the manager's other CDOs, especially older CDOs with the same underlying assets. Comparison of the manager's CDOs to other CDOs of the same underlying assets and vintage. Reports and conversations with the manager.
8. How will the CDO's cash flow structure respond to different levels of defaults, recoveries, interest rates, and collateral prepayments?	Cash flow modeling where CDO collateral cash flow variables are associated with CDO tranche, cash flows and IRRs.

EXHIBIT 20.2   SF CDOs—Three Examples

CDO	Class	Coupon	PIK-able?	Rating History	Offered
A	B-1	8.27%	Yes	A3	75%
B	B	7.38%	No	AA to A+	95%
C	A	L + 50s	No	AAA	92.5%

To make the discussion more realistic and tangible, we look at three actual bonds offered for sale in the secondary market, as shown in Exhibit 20.2.[3] We chose to focus on three structured finance-backed CDOs (SF CDOs) as our examples because this type of CDO presents all the analytical hurdles of corporate-backed CDOs as well as its own unique challenges.[4] When we get to the eighth CDO question in Exhibit 20.1, cash flow modeling, we will address SF CDOs and high-yield, corporate-backed CDOs separately.

How has the Average Credit Quality of the Collateral Portfolio Fared?

The first place to start in evaluating a CDO is the trustee report. These monthly reports contain the results of all cash diversion and collateral quality tests, list the collateral portfolio itself, and detail trading activity over the month. If one can obtain a Microsoft Excel file of the collateral, one can sort the collateral or use pivot tables to analyze the distribution of collateral ratings, industries, and collateral types (RMBS A, manufactured housing, CMBS conduit, etc.). Monthly one- or two-page reports from the CDO's banker highlight the most important collateral tests and sometimes contain graphs that show their trends over time. But these banker summaries do not detail collateral or trading activity.

In the trustee report, Moody's and Fitch's weighted average rating factor (WARF) are measures of the *average* rating of the portfolio. Moody's rating factors for each rating increase at an increasing rate down the rating scale. Thus, Aaa = 1, Aa2 = 20, A2 = 120, Baa2 = 360, Ba2 = 1,350, B2 = 2,720, Caa2 = 6,500, and Ca and C = 10,000. The secret to this scale is that if one divides the rating factors by 10,000, one gets (approximately) the 10-year default rate results of Moody's 1989 corporate bond default study. Thus, an increase in Moody's WARF from 2,720 to 3,490 (B2 to B3 rating) means that the collateral's 10-year default probability has increased (3,490 − 2,720)/10,000 or 7.7% in

---

[3] We disguise the names of these CDOs to cut down on our hate mail.
[4] We estimate that less than 10% of secondary trades involve SF CDOs.

absolute default rate, based on historical patterns of default. From the Moody's and Fitch WARF in the trustee report, we can see how the collateral portfolio's average rating has changed since the CDO's inception.

Using the trustee report for each of the three CDOs we are concerned with, we show their WARF statistics in Exhibit 20.3. We see from the exhibit that of the three CDOs, A has done the best job of maintaining its WARF. Meanwhile, both B and C have suffered about the same deterioration. Note that as B is a static portfolio CDO, there is no WARF trigger.

What is the Dispersal of Collateral Ratings?

Just as important as the drift of the CDO's *average* collateral rating is the *distribution* of collateral ratings. For example, we would like to know whether a decrease in the average rating of the collateral portfolio was caused by many credits being downgraded *slightly* or by a *few* credits being downgraded *severely*. We would consider the second scenario worse as it implies that some credits are close to defaulting. Based on this criterion, C's portfolio is worse than B's portfolio, even though their average WARFs are about the same. Exhibit 20.4 shows that C has twice as many below-investment-grade credits, and more credits rated B1 and below, Caa1 and below, and Ca and below. Meanwhile, A, which has the best *average* WARF, also has the smallest distribution of low-rated credits.

EXHIBIT 20.3   WARF Comparison

	A	B	C
Original WARF	312	432	424
Current WARF	323	834	856
Trigger WARF	360	NA	445

EXHIBIT 20.4   Low-Rated Collateral

	A	B	C
Ba1 and below	12.0%	12.3%	26.0%
B1 and below	4.3%	7.9%	10.6%
Caa1 and below	3.0%	4.4%	7.1%
Ca and below	0.0%	2.1%	3.2%

What are the Single-Name Concentrations in the Portfolio?

CDO diversification requirements limit purchases of collateral assets from the same issue, issuer, and servicer. Unlike ratings, which can drift lower, positions cannot become more concentrated unless the portfolio itself shrinks. A look at single-name concentrations in these three CDOs sparks no concerns.

What are the Industry (or Collateral Type) Concentrations in the Portfolio?

The trustee report also contains a breakdown of collateral into various types of commercial mortgage-backed securities (CMBS), residential mortgage-backed securities (RMBS), and asset-backed securities (ABS). From this breakdown, one can determine how far afield the asset manager has gone to construct the CDO's portfolio. For example, we would like to know the percentages of the collateral portfolio made up of troubled ABS sectors such as manufactured housing, mutual fund 12b-1 fees, aircraft leases, franchise loans, and high-yield bond CDOs. An even more useful table, which only a few trustee reports have, shows industry diversification and ratings *simultaneously*.

In Exhibit 20.5, we have constructed such a table for A using an Excel file of the collateral portfolio. This exhibit is useful because it distinguishes between a manager that has, for example, recently and opportunistically purchased AAA manufactured housing tranches and one who bought BBB rated tranches and held them as they were downgraded to B. In the case of A, the troubled industries of aircraft, manufactured housing, and restaurant and food services (which are actually franchise loans) have all been downgraded since purchase.

Some trustees provide the same information in a different format, giving the *average* rating by industry. We show a sample of their presentation in Exhibit 20.6. A nice feature of the format is the breakout of industry categories between investment grade and speculative grade. We see, in this made-up example, that investment-grade aircraft leases, which make up 5% of the CDO's collateral portfolio, have an average rating of A2, while speculative-grade aircraft leases, which make up 3% of the portfolio, have an average rating of Ba3. If these statistics were merged, we would only know that the *average* rating was somewhere in the Baa rating category.

A visual inspection of the B portfolio tells us that the rating deterioration has been centered on manufactured housing. Caa1 and Ca issues make up 5% of the portfolio. For C, the ratings deterioration of the portfolio is most severe in CMBS conduit; health, education, and child-care franchise loans; and aircraft leases.

EXHIBIT 20.5 CDO A Portfolio, by Rating & Industry

	Cash	Aaa	Aa	A	Baa	Ba	B	Caa	Totals
Cash	1.5%								1.5%
Aircraft lease					6.3%			1.6%	8.0%
CMBS conduit				1.2%	17.1%	4.4%			22.8%
CMBS credit tenant lease		2.1%							2.1%
CMBS large loan					3.4%				3.4%
HEL				4.1%	7.9%	0.9%			12.9%
Manufactured housing				1.3%	2.8%			1.4%	5.5%
REIT diversified					2.3%				2.3%
REIT hotel					2.3%				2.3%
REIT office					3.9%				3.9%
REIT retail					7.7%				7.7%
Residential A mortgage		0.3%	0.2%	3.5%	3.6%	0.5%			8.0%
Residential B/C mortgage			1.3%	1.4%	9.7%	1.8%			14.2%
Restaurant and food services				2.5%	1.6%		1.3%		5.3%
Totals	1.5%	2.4%	1.5%	14.0%	68.6%	7.7%	1.3%	3.0%	100.0%

EXHIBIT 20.6   Sample Trustee Report

Industry	Percent of Portfolio	Average Rating
Aircraft lease, investment grade	5.0%	A2
Aircraft lease, speculative grade	3.0%	Ba3
CMBS conduit, investment grade	2.0%	Baa3
CMBS conduit, speculative grade	9.0%	Caa1

The decline in SF collateral yields and spreads in recent years has hurt SF CDO manager flexibility. Because managers are required to maintain certain weighted average coupons or weighted average spreads in their collateral portfolios, they have been faced with a difficult choice. Managers could seek out misrated collateral satisfying both ratings and coupon/spread requirements. This would benefit equity holders, at least in the short run, as excess spread in the CDO would be maintained. Or managers could terminate the reinvestment period and begin using principal cash flow to pay down the most senior tranche. This would benefit debt tranche holders, at least from a credit perspective.

Instead, some managers have taken a middle ground and built up large cash reserves, waiting for reinvestment opportunities at both the right spread and right credit quality. The low reinvestment rate on cash hurts excess spread and equity holders in the short run, but keeps alive the ability to take advantage of better spreads in the future. From a debt holder perspective, holding cash is neutral—not as good as paying down debt tranches, but definitely not as bad as buying low-priced but high-rated assets. None of the three CDOs we are analyzing have large cash positions. We now turn our attention to CDO collateral par and portfolio trading.

How has the CDO's Par Overcollateralization Fared and is the Ratio Being Manipulated?

Most SF CDOs are still in their revolving or reinvestment period, when principal is returned to debt tranches only if something has gone wrong— usually the violation of par overcollateralization tests. One wants to know whether a CDO is paying principal on its debt tranches early because of the poor performance of its collateral. Even more importantly, one wants to know whether the CDO *should* be making these principal payments, but the manager is avoiding them by engaging in *par-building trades*.

Par-building is the practice of selling higher-priced collateral to purchase more par of lower-priced collateral. This keeps the CDO in compliance with its par overcollateralization tests and avoids cutting off cash flow to lower tranches and to the subordinate manager fee. Otherwise, cash flow would be redirected to pay down the CDO's most senior tranche. The problem with this strategy, from the point of view of a potential debt investor, is that the CDO has not delevered and the credit quality of its low-priced collateral is suspect.

A structural feature unique to SF CDOs mitigates par-loss avoidance. Almost since their inception, the rating agencies have demanded haircuts for low-rated collateral in par OC tests. Thus, even if the loss in par is not realized through a sale, a severely downgraded portfolio still would cause the triggering of OC tests, the diversion of cash flow, and the pay-down of debt tranches.

To detect par-building trades, the first thing to do is compare the original and current outstanding par of the CDO tranches. This will show whether the CDO has *ever* triggered the early amortization of its debt. The second place to look is the pattern of the overcollateralization (OC) ratios over time. If these display a zigzag pattern of declines to or below the OC trigger and then sudden rises, yet the debt tranches have never amortized, it could be that the collateral manager is buying low-priced assets to manipulate the OC ratio into compliance before each payment date. To know for sure, one must look at the trustee's log of trades and the prices at which assets were sold versus the prices at which assets were purchased. A consistent pattern of selling high to purchase low means that the manager is engaging in par-building trades to keep the CDO in compliance with OC ratios.

On the other hand, if the collateral manager is allowing the CDO cash diversion mechanisms to work as intended, the prospective buyer should consider the effect of the diversion of cash flow to senior tranches. The potential investor should note the principal pay-down that would be required to bring the CDO back into OC compliance. Then the potential investor should note how much excess spread is available each payment period to pay down CDO principal. This will give an idea of how fast the CDO will get back into OC compliance, how much senior principal will be repaid early, how long junior tranches will go without cash flow, and how delevered various debt tranches will become.

Let's apply this analysis to the three CDOs in Exhibit 20.1. A has had consistently high OC ratios and has never paid down debt tranche principal. A look at its trades shows that it has purchased collateral consistently at prices close to par. An exception occurred in June 2003, when it purchased $6 million of home equity for 61% and $3.5 million of manufactured housing for 77%. As there was never an issue with passing OC tests, these appear to be opportunistic trades.

B is a static portfolio CDO and has paid down $17.6 million, or 5.7% of its capital structure.

C never has paid down debt tranche principal yet often has been in violation of its OC tests. The OC ratios have a habit of rising right before payment dates. In the month before one recent payment date, the OC ratio rose an amazing 9% to get the CDO into compliance. In a recent trustee report, the manager sold several bonds at an average price 8% higher than the ones it bought. But more often, the manager sells collateral that is being haircut in the OC test because of its low ratings and buys similarly priced collateral that is higher rated. Unfortunately, recently purchased collateral has a knack of being downgraded, and the CDO is in the same position all over again. The best one can say for the management of this CDO is that it will soon be over. The CDO will enter its amortization phase shortly.

Besides looking to see whether the collateral manager is engaging actively in par-building trades, the prospective secondary purchaser should check to see if the collateral manager is avoiding *par-losing trades*. Is the portfolio full of low-rated or low-priced assets? The temptation for the collateral manager is to keep these positions and not realize losses. From the point of view of CDO equity holders, these positions represent upside potential if they do, in fact, perform. Selling them crystallizes the loss and destroys the possibility of this upside. Thus, it is very tempting for collateral managers to hold on to these positions.

For the three CDOs that we are comparing, C has the most low-rated collateral, B the second most, and A the least, as we discussed previously and showed in Exhibit 20.2.

What is the Net Asset Value of the Tranche?

The idea behind net asset value (NAV) analysis is simple. The value of a particular CDO tranche is related to its *liquidation value* or the market value of the CDO's collateral *minus* the obligations of the CDO to parties senior to the particular CDO tranche. In theory, this calculation is easy, as shown in Exhibit 20.7 and the points below:

- Value all the CDO's collateral assets and aggregate the results.
- Add the amount in the principal proceeds account.
- Subtract (or perhaps add, but in the interest rate environment at the time of this analysis, most probably subtract) the market value of swaps and add the market value of caps the CDO currently has with its interest-rate hedging counterparty.
- Subtract the outstanding par of any tranches senior to the particular tranche of interest.
- Divide the result by the par amount of the tranche of interest to get tranche's NAV or "liquidation" price.

EXHIBIT 20.7   Net Asset Value Analysis ($ millions)

	B	C
Collateral debt securities	274.6	230.8
Cash in principal proceeds account	0.2	0.0
Swap and cap	−25.2	−37.7
Subtotal	249.6	193.1
Senior tranche principal	198.4	0.0
Available for tranche	51.1	193.1
Tranche size	54.0	197.5
Tranche net asset value	94.7%	97.8%

The NAV approach does not claim to be entirely realistic, as the liquidation of collateral is not going to happen in CDOs employing the cash flow credit structure unless that liquidation supplies enough cash to repay all seniorities of CDO debt. Also, future cash flows from the CDO's collateral portfolio are probably going to be greater than that indicated by their market prices. This is particularly the case with low-rated collateral. But the idea behind the NAV approach is that market prices relate to credit risk, future default losses, and, ultimately, future cash flows. A higher NAV should make one tranche more attractive to another, at least in comparing tranches of the same seniority from CDOs with the same type of underlying collateral.

On the other hand, NAV analysis is misleading in comparing *PIK* (payable in kind) and *non-PIK* CDO tranches. The coupon payment to a non-PIK tranche comes before any OC or other cash flow diversion test in the CDO's cash flow waterfall. Thus, it would take a very severe deterioration in the collateral portfolio for a second-priority, non-PIK CDO tranche to lose its interest cash flow stream. For a second-priority PIK tranche, however, interest deferral is a certainty in reasonably stressful default scenarios. NAV analysis will not make this distinction and will undervalue a second-priority, non-PIK tranche relative to a second-priority PIK tranche.

In Exhibits 20.8 and 20.9, we show the difference in internal rate of return (IRR) profiles for two second-priority CDO tranches, one a non-PIK tranche and the other a PIK tranche. In these exhibits, we show the IRR for the two tranches over different constant annual default rate (CDRs) scenarios, a concept we will discuss more fully later on. In Exhibit 20.8, we calculate IRRs using the two tranches' NAVs as prices—70% and 52% for the PIK and non-PIK tranche, respectively. Given the

EXHIBIT 20.8 PIK and Non-PIK Mezzanine CDOs at NAVs

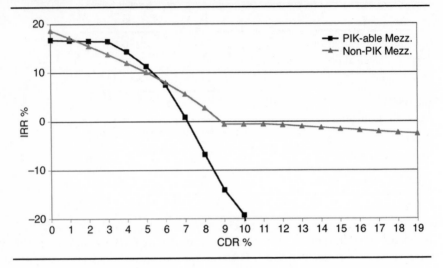

EXHIBIT 20.9 PIK and Non-PIK Mezzanine CDOs at Trading Prices

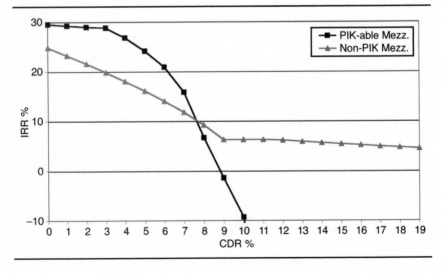

IRR profiles in Exhibit 20.8, it is a wonder that anyone would consider the PIK tranche over the non-PIK tranche. The upside in low CDRs for the PIK tranche is small compared to its downside in high CDRs.

However, the PIK tranche actually sold in the secondary market at 40% while the non-PIK tranche sold for 41%. Importantly, the PIK tranche sold at a much greater discount to its NAV (70% NAV versus 40% price) than the non-PIK tranche did to its NAV (52% NAV versus 40% price). At their trading prices, the virtues of the two tranches are more of a toss-up, as shown in Exhibit 20.9. The PIK tranche's IRR is much higher in low CDRs while the non-PIK tranche's IRR is much higher in high CDRs. Obviously, the secondary market appropriately values the non-PIK tranche higher relative to its NAV than the PIK tranche to its NAV. It is not unusual, in fact, for a non-PIK tranche with a negative NAV to trade at a substantial price based upon the certainty of its interest cash flow stream.

The major practical problem with the NAV approach is getting the market values of SF collateral. The market for structured finance tranches, especially for mezzanine tranches of esoteric asset types and any tranche of a distressed asset type, is illiquid. But because we are trying only to get an approximate *aggregate* value for the CDO's collateral portfolio, we do not have to obtain an executable level for every single asset. One can make do with a *range* for the value of esoteric and illiquid assets—for example, from 100% to 90%, from 90% to 80%, and so on. This suits structured finance traders, who will be more willing to place these kinds of values on illiquid assets. In calculating the NAV for a CDO tranche, one counts on the imprecision of individual estimates canceling each other out in aggregate.

Exhibit 20.7 shows NAV analysis for B and C. (As is usually the case for SF CDOs, we were not able to get reliable prices for A's portfolio.) We consider the two NAV percentages to be practically the same and note that they are both near the CDO's offered price.

How Good is the Manager?

Primary CDO buyers are used to interviewing CDO managers, visiting their offices, and even asking them to fill out questionnaires. Although it is not often done, secondary buyers should contact the managers of CDOs they are thinking about buying and asking them about those CDOs. Most managers are quite willing to talk to a potential secondary CDO buyer and in fact see this as opportunity to develop a new customer. Some managers produce periodic written commentaries on the performance of their CDOs and are willing to share these with prospective secondary buyers.

A convenient way to look at a manager's performance across a number of its CDOs is Moody's *Deal Score Report*, where one can find all the CDOs that a manager has done with certain underlying collateral.[5] Specifically, the Moody's report lists all SF CDOs rated by that agency, alphabetically by manager. One can then see for all SF CDOs from a specific manager:

- Compliance with the WARF test.
- Compliance with the OC test.
- A combined WARF/OC measure.
- Whether Moody's has downgraded the CDO.

These statistics can then be compared to the average for all SF CDOs and to the average for all SF CDOs issued in a particular year. We recommend that investors judge a manager's asset-specific performance. Good performance with a loan portfolio does not mean the manager would be good with a structured finance portfolio. Moreover, good performance with a CMBS portfolio does not mean the manager would be good with a diversified ABS portfolio.

One thing we notice from looking at the Moody's report is how the performance measures are pretty consistent across all of a particular manager's CDOs. That is, almost all of a manager's CDOs are doing well or almost all of them are doing poorly.

When reviewing trustee reports, we looked for evidence of detrimental trading behavior, namely, par-building trades or par-loss avoidance inactivity. It is worthwhile to look for signs of this behavior in the manager's *other* CDOs, particularly *older* CDOs. When CDOs are young, or more generally, when CDOs have not suffered collateral portfolio deterioration, the interests of equity holders, debt holders, and the manager are more aligned. As the collateral portfolio deteriorates, the manager is faced with the choice of favoring one investor over another and his own interests over those of investors. For a sign of what a manager will do under pressure, look closely at his trading of CDOs that are not doing well. We note, however, that the importance of this question becomes muted as the CDO approaches and enters its amortization stage and the CDO manager can no longer purchase new assets.

How Will the CDO's Cash Flow Structure Respond to Different Levels of Defaults, Recoveries, Interest Rates, and Collateral Prepayments?

We address this question for (1) general and structured finance-CDO specific considerations and (2) corporate-CDO specific considerations.

---

[5] We also like S&P's ROC report and Fitch's and S&P's manager reports.

General and Structured Finance-CDO Specific Considerations

Cash flow modeling is often done by the dealer to the purchaser's specifications. However, INTEX, Wall Street Analytics, and some other vendors provide CDO-specific cash flow models, updated with collateral information from the latest trustee report; investors themselves can use these models. Cash flow modeling provides the most specific, accurate estimate of a CDO tranche's future cash flows, *given the CDO collateral's future cash flows*. Unfortunately, the caveat at the end of that sentence is a pretty big one. Cash flow modeling properly takes into account OC triggers and other CDO structural features that divert cash flow from one tranche to another. But those cash flows depend upon the default frequency and loss severity of the collateral portfolio. Also implicit in cash flow modeling are assumptions about "manager behavior," that is, collateral trading and reinvestment. When cash flows are diverted from one tranche to another in a cash flow model, there is the implicit assumption that the manager will not manipulate the CDO's cash diversion tests to prevent this from happening in real life.

Other assumptions must be made regarding future interest rates and collateral prepayment speeds. We use the forward curve as our base case for future LIBOR rates. We typically recommend using historic average prepayment rates for nonmortgage-related ABS and historical experience on RMBS and Resi B&C, adjusted for current interest rate levels. Such collateral prepayment speeds are available for most SF CDO collateral from INTEX. We then map out the future cash flows of each piece of collateral assuming no defaults. For simplicity, we typically aggregate these individual-asset cash flows and model the CDO collateral portfolio as one aggregate amortizing bond with one average coupon. Annual defaults are then treated as percentage reductions off this single-aggregate bond.

A good reason to forgo the aggregate approach to the CDO's collateral cash flows exists when the CDO's collateral portfolio neatly falls into two distinct credit qualities—say an investment-grade pool and a CCC to C pool—and those pools have very different cash flow characteristics. For example, a troubled manufactured housing or home equity deal will extend to a multiple of its originally assumed average life. In this case, we would not want to treat the CDO's collateral portfolio as one average aggregate bond. Instead, we would want to inflict greater defaults on the CCC to C cash flows of the CDO's portfolio and lower defaults on the investment-grade cash flows of the CDO's portfolio in order to predict the collateral portfolio's aggregate cash flows more accurately.

We also might test the sensitivity of the cash flow model output to prepayment, reinvestment, and LIBOR assumptions. These assumptions become particularly important if the CDO is underhedged or overhedged. In different interest rate environments, cash flows will vary depending on the proportion of swaps and caps in the CDO's structure.

But the most critical cash flow modeling assumption is the amount and timing of defaults and recoveries. We now will recommend a methodology to arrive at constant annual default rates (CDRs) to apply to SF CDO collateral portfolios. The goal of this methodology is to derive CDRs that are equally likely, given the ratings and market values of the collateral portfolio. For example, a 0.5% CDR might be as likely for an investment-grade collateral portfolio as a 3% CDR is for a speculative-grade collateral portfolio. Or a 0.5% CDR might be as likely for an investment-grade collateral portfolio trading at par as a 1.0% CDR is for an investment-grade portfolio trading at 75%. (Another way to put it is that we want CDR scenarios that are *equally stressful* given the credit quality of the collateral.) Once equally likely collateral default scenarios are constructed, the *results* of the cash flow models, the cash flows to a particular CDO tranche, are also equally likely.

In this way, we can compare, for example, a senior tranche from a CDO with speculative-grade collateral with a mezzanine tranche from a CDO with investment-grade collateral. The following sections explain the methodology. In summary, we calculate the collateral portfolio's CDR from its WARF, and we calculate and recalculate the portfolio's WARF to get ever more stressful CDRs in the following ways:

1. We use the lowest rating of each rating agency, under the assumption that the lowest rating is the most up-to-date rating.
2. We haircut the rating for assets with low dollar prices, under the assumption that the market correctly identifies low-price assets as being credit risky.
3. To generate a higher, more stressful CDR, we haircut each collateral asset by one rating notch.
4. We repeat 3. to produce ever more stressful CDRs.

Lowest Rating Agency Rating   We calculate the WARF of the portfolio, using Moody's rating factors, but using the *lowest* rating of each piece of collateral from *each* rating agency. We take the lowest rating to address the concern that agency ratings on the collateral portfolio may have become stale since the collateral initially was issued and rated. Our assumption is that the lowest rating is the collateral's most up-to-date rating.

We then turn the collateral portfolio's WARF into a CDR. Recall that a collateral portfolio's WARF divided by 10,000 is related to its 10-year cumulative default probability. We want to calculate a CDR such that the collateral portfolio, sustaining the CDR over 10 years, will experience 10-year cumulative defaults at a level implied by its WARF. To do so, we apply the following formula:

$$CDR = 1 - (1 - WARF/10,000)^{1/10}$$

Thus, a WARF of 360 represents a 10-year cumulative default probability of 360/10,000 or 3.6%. The CDR that achieves 3.6% default rate over 10 years is:

$$CDR = 1 - (1 - 360/10,000)^{1/10} = 0.366\%$$

Exhibit 20.10 shows the relationship between a portfolio's average rating, its WARF, and its CDR.[6]

Price-Adjusted Haircuts   Our next concern is that perhaps *none* of the rating agencies has the right rating on the collateral. To check this, we apply *price factor haircuts* to any piece of collateral rated above Caa3/CCC−. As shown in Exhibit 20.11, collateral priced between 50% and 75% is re-rated *the lower of* its lowest agency rating and BB. Collateral priced between 20% and 50% is rerated *the lower of* its lowest agency rating

EXHIBIT 20.10   Average Ratings, WARF & CDRs

Average Collateral Portfolio Rating	Weighted Average Rating Factor	Constant Annual Default Rate
BBB+	260	0.26%
BBB	360	0.37%
BBB−	610	0.63%
BB+	940	0.98%
BB	1,350	1.44%
BB−	1,766	1.92%
B+	2,220	2.48%
B	2,720	3.12%
B−	3,490	4.20%
CCC+	4,770	6.28%
CCC	6,500	9.97%
CCC−	8,070	15.17%
Ca/C/D	10,000	100.00%

---

[6] Note that the CDR that achieves a 3.6% default rate is slightly greater than 3.6%/10 or 0.36%. This is because the CDR is applied to a decreasing balance. It is the opposite effect of interest compounding where a constant percent is applied to an increasing balance.

EXHIBIT 20.11   Price Factor Haircuts

Price	Rating Is Lower of Lowest Rating Agency Rating or
75%–50%	BB
50%–20%	B
<20%	CCC

and B. And collateral priced below 20% is rerated *the lower of* its lowest agency rating and CCC. We then recalculate the collateral portfolio's WARF and derive a new, higher, CDR.

Further Collateral Stresses   To produce *additional stresses* on the SF CDO collateral portfolio, we decrease the rating of each piece of collateral rated above Caa3/CCC– by one rating notch, recalculate the collateral portfolio's WARF, and derive a new CDR. We repeat this process until the results of the cash flow model under the CDR assumption returns a 0% or lower IRR for the CDO tranche we are considering.

Real Case CDR Stresses   In Exhibit 20.12, we show the results of this methodology. We use CDO A as an example to work through the calculations. For each piece of collateral in A's portfolio, we found the lowest rating from the three rating agencies. Then we calculated the portfolio's WARF using these worst-of-ratings and Moody's WARF scale. For CDO A, this turned out to be 856, as shown in panel A. of Exhibit 20.12 under Lowest Rating Agency Rating. For reference, the rating equivalent of this 856 WARF, Baa3.5, is shown in panel B. of Exhibit 20.12, again under Lowest Rating Agency Rating. To give a little more detail to the Moody's symbols, we added on 0.5 to show that the WARF is about mid-way between the Baa3 and Ba1 ratings. Finally, in panel C. of the exhibit, we show the CDR derived from the 856 WARF, 0.89% CDR, again under Lowest Rating Agency Rating.

In panel C. under Lowest Rating Agency Rating, the CDRs of 0.89%, 0.99%, and 1.08% for CDOs A, B, and C, respectively, are meant to be equally likely to occur, or equally stressful, given the credit quality of each of the CDOs' collateral portfolios. All these CDRs were calculated using the lowest agency ratings on the CDOs' collateral portfolios. When we use these CDRs in these CDOs' cash flows models, we expect the *output* of the cash flow models—i.e., the collateral cash flows—the tranche cash flows, and the tranche IRRs, also to be equally likely to occur. Because the cash flow model results are the result of equally likely default scenarios, they are comparable.

EXHIBIT 20.12 CDR Stresses

Lowest Rating Agency Rating	+ Price Haircut	+1 Rating Notch	+2 Rating Notches	+3 Rating Notches	+4 Rating Notches	+5 Rating Notches	+6 Rating Notches	+7 Rating Notches	+8 Rating Notches	+9 Rating Notches	+10 Rating Notches
Panel A. WARF											
A	856	910	1166	1566	1966	2423	2906	3493	4323	5498	6711	8017
B	950	1177	1538	1988	2428	2845	3328	3892	4761	6003	7262	8637
C	1031	1095	1406	1804	2214	2709	3279	3930	4669	5595	6414	7184
Panel B. WARF Rating Equivalent											
A	Baa3.5	Ba1	Ba1.5	Ba2.5	Ba3.5	B1.5	B2	B3	B3.5	Caa1.5	Caa2	Caa3
B	Ba1	Ba1.5	Ba2.5	Ba3.5	B1.5	B2	B3	B3.5	Caa1	Caa1.5	Caa2.5	Caa3.5
C	Ba1	Ba1.5	Ba2	Ba3	B1	B2	B2.5	B3.5	Caa1	Caa1.5	Caa2	Caa2.5
Panel C. Constant Default Rate Stresses											
A	0.89%	0.95%	1.23%	1.69%	2.17%	2.74%	3.38%	4.21%	5.50%	7.67%	10.52%	14.94%
B	0.99%	1.24%	1.66%	2.19%	2.74%	3.29%	3.97%	4.81%	6.26%	8.76%	12.15%	18.07%
C	1.08%	1.15%	1.50%	1.97%	2.47%	3.11%	3.90%	4.87%	6.10%	7.87%	9.75%	11.90%

The next stress we put the collateral portfolios through is to look for low-priced assets rated above Caa3. Using the price-factor haircuts in Exhibit 20.11, we lower collateral ratings to those in the exhibit, unless their ratings are already lower than those in the exhibit. In Exhibit 20.12, panel A., under + Price Haircut we show a new WARF of 910 for CDO A. This is equivalent to about a Ba1 average rating and a 0.95% CDR. The CDRs for CDOs B and C after applying price haircuts are 1.24% and 1.15%, respectively.

Again, these new CDRs are meant to be equally likely and equally stressful, given the credit quality of the CDO's collateral portfolios. The output of the cash flow models using these CDRs is also equally likely and comparable. The remaining stress CDRs in Exhibit 20.12 are created by successively lowering every collateral rating above Caa3 one rating notch, recomputing that portfolio's WARF, and computing a new CDR. Once again, the stresses are meant to be equally likely, as are the cash flow model outputs using these stresses.

Model Results

In Exhibit 20.13, we show the results of our cash flow modeling. We have calculated the IRRs of the offered CDO tranches, using the CDRs shown in Exhibit 20.12 and the offering prices of the CDO tranches shown in Exhibit 20.2.

EXHIBIT 20.13   CDO Tranche Yield versus Default Stress

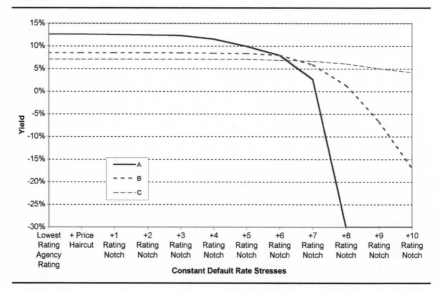

Note that no single CDO tranche dominates over the entire range of stresses. The higher the IRR in low-CDR environments, the steeper the decline in IRR in high-CDR environments. These CDOs are priced so that increasing risk correlates to increasing average return. Note that we can say this only because we have built a scale of risk, on the horizontal axis of Exhibit 20.13, based on equally likely CDR scenarios.

Which CDO should be purchased? Our first choice to purchase is the CDO A Class B-1. It has suffered very little deterioration in its average WARF. Its "Caa1"-and-below bucket is not too bad either at 3.0%. The manager has not engaged in par-building trades and has a good record on its other CDOs as reported in Moody's *Deal Score Report*. Unfortunately, we were not able to do a NAV analysis. Its high fixed coupon and low offered price gives it a 400 basis point yield advantage over its nearest competitor in the low CDR scenarios. It has a higher yield than its nearest competitor until the +6 rating notch CDR scenario. Remember, this is a very harsh scenario where we lower the collateral's rating six notches after we have taken the lowest rating of the three agencies and after we have applied price haircuts. So, in the more probable CDR scenarios, CDO A performs best.

After CDO A, we are indifferent between CDO B Class B and CDO C Class A. CDO B has suffered average WARF deterioration from 432 to 834 and its Caa1-and-below bucket is 6.5%. But is has delevered by reducing cash flow to tranches below the Class B notes. Subordination below the Class B notes has increased a bit from 12.1% to 12.8%. Because this is a static portfolio CDO, there is no question of manager behavior. Its NAV is high. Compared to the CDO A Class B-1, it has a lower yield, but that yield is more stable over more severe CDR stresses. So it is safer than CDO A Class B-1 but it also pays less. Our preference for A over B, at least at the prices that produce these IRRs, is based on our belief that the 6% and greater CDRs that cause B to outperform A are pretty unrealistic.

CDO C's average WARF deterioration has been the greatest, from 426 to 852. A whopping 7.1% of the portfolio is Caa1 and below. The manager can be depended upon to find, and buy, the bond that is just about to be downgraded—not hard when you sell B rated bonds and buy BBB rated bonds trading at the same price. But a great many sins are covered up by two facts: These are first-priority notes and the CDO soon will enter its amortization phase. First priority gives these bonds the highest NAV result of our example bonds. The imminent shut down of trading limits the amount of further damage the collateral manager can do to the portfolio. And it gives us confidence in the bond's cash flow modeling results. Without aggressive trading, the CDO really *will* begin to fail OC triggers, cut off cash flows to lower tranches, and amortize these first priority notes. We are indifferent between CDOs B and C because the 108 to 145 basis point advantage B has over C in low-CDR scenarios seems balanced out by the flatter profile C has over B in high-CDR scenarios.

Corporate-CDO Specific Considerations

In Exhibit 20.14, we describe two high-yield, bond-backed CDOs, identified as CDO #1 and CDO #2, that sold in the secondary market at the end of 2003. In Exhibit 20.15, we show IRR/CDR profiles of the two CDOs at their offered prices. CDO #2 clearly dominates in CDR scenarios less than 6%, while CDO #1 clearly dominates in CDR scenarios greater than 6%. But CDO #1 has a WARF of 4,400 while the WARF of CDO #2 is 2,850. If ratings factors indicate default risk, there is greater default potential in CDO #1 than in CDO #2. How then, should these corporate debt-backed CDOs be compared?

EXHIBIT 20.14   Two Corporate Debt-Backed CDOs

	CDO #1	CDO #2
Priority	Senior	Mezzanine
PIK?	Non-PIK	Non-PIK
WARF	4400	2850
Secondary price	95%	50%

EXHIBIT 20.15   IRR versus Absolute CDRs

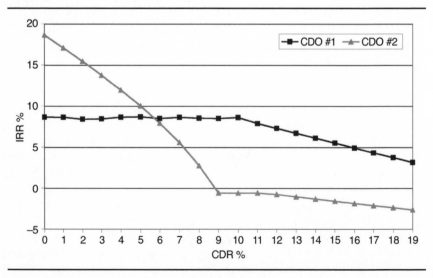

EXHIBIT 20.16   Comparison of Historic and Market Practice CDRs

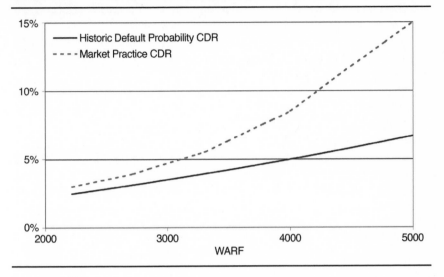

Exhibit 20.16 shows *market practice* in translating the WARF of high-yield bond CDO portfolios into CDRs and compares it to the mathematical formula we presented when discussing SF CDOs in Exhibit 20.10. By "market practice" we mean the CDRs that secondary CDO investors generally associate with different WARFs of high-yield bond portfolios. These naturally vary from investor to investor and portfolio to portfolio, but the generalization we show in Exhibit 20.16 is pretty robust. So where the solid line in Exhibit 20.16 reflects the formulaic CDRs we associated with rating factors in Exhibit 20.10, the dotted line in Exhibit 20.16 shows market practice in translating WARFs into CDRs to assess a high-yield bond-backed CDO.

Interestingly, market practice seems to favor use of default rates closer to those of the formula for low WARFs. As WARF increases, market practice CDRs increase above the formula CDRs. Our view is that at low WARFs (which exist when CDOs are on the drawing board), investors have faith that managers can meet or beat the historic market pace of defaults. Then, as CDOs season and WARFs rise, investors lose this faith and believe the manager's defaults will exceed historic averages. Another fact backing up this practice is that once bonds have been downgraded, they are more likely to be downgraded again and eventually default.

In Exhibit 20.17, we line up the two CDOs' "base-case" CDRs based on the market practice of translating WARFs into CDRs. The base-case CDR for CDO #1 with a 4400 WARF is 11%, while the base-case CDR for CDO #2 with a 2850 WARF is 4%. So we line up CDO

EXHIBIT 20.17   IRRs versus Market Practice CDRs

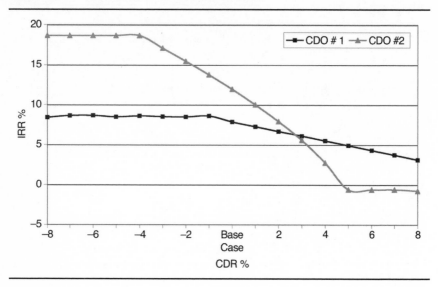

#1's IRR at 11% CDR with CDO #2's IRR at 4% CDR. Now, looking at the patterns of IRRs on this scale, it seems to us that CDO #2 is a clear choice. It has a higher IRR up to the base-case CDR plus 3% CDR (14% CDR for CDO #1 and 7% CDR for CDO #2).

One could argue that if we make an adjustment to line up the CDOs' "WARF-expected base-case CDRs," we also should make an adjustment to reconcile the potential volatility of actual results around these expectations. We might expect CDO #1, with a base-case CDR of 11%, to have wider potential swings in actual results than CDO #2, with a base-case CDR of 4%. After all, a 25% increase in CDR for CDO #1 is 2.75 CDR while a 25% increase in CDR for CDO #2 is only 1% CDR. With this in mind, we like CDO #2 even more, as it should be harder for CDO #2 to get to base-case plus 3% CDR (7%) than it is for CDO #1 to get to its base-case plus 3% CDR (14%).

PRESCRIPTION FOR MAKING PRIMARY ISSUANCES CONDUCIVE TO SECONDARY TRADING

To round out our discussion of secondary CDO assessment, we would like to suggest the things primary market investors can do to ensure that their CDOs are more salable in the secondary market. The goal is to ensure the widest dissemination of information about CDOs and to help break down the informational barrier for secondary purchasers:

1. Make sure the trustee has a reputation of producing monthly reports and collateral files on a timely basis, e-mails collateral reports in Excel format, posts old files on an accessible web site, and distributes reports to third-party vendors in electronic format.
2. Make sure the banker produces summaries of trustee reports, if for no other reason than to make sure the banker cares about, and is aware of, the quality of the trustee's service.
3. Recommend that the manager obtain and distribute collateral marks. The manager is in the best position to obtain collateral marks as he knows where he bought the collateral bonds and is in a position to demand marks from dealers.
4. Make sure that CDO will be available on a third-party modeling service. And encourage the development of more commercial "libraries" that sell CDO cash flow models and collateral updates.

CONCLUSION

In this chapter, we provided a methodology for assessing secondary CDO tranches and applied it to three live examples. We created an eight-point checklist of questions to ask about a secondary CDO in Exhibit 20.1 and followed the checklist through in evaluating three CDO tranches. In doing so, we made use of the trustee's monthly report and Excel collateral files, summaries of trustee data prepared by the CDO's banker and rating agencies, and rating agency reports on CDO managers.

We paid special attention to two techniques of analyzing CDOs in the secondary market, NAV analysis and cash flow modeling. We tried to shake the faith of those overly adherent to NAV analysis with an example involving a PIK and a non-PIK mezzanine CDO. We discussed the comparability of cash flow modeling results and argued the necessity of comparing the cash flow results of CDOs under default scenarios that take into account the credit quality of their respective portfolios. We advocate developing a range of equally likely and equally stressful CDRs for each CDO and comparing their CDR/IRR profiles in this context.

Our most unique suggestion was a methodology to produce a range of CDRs for SF CDO cash flow modeling purposes. The methodology proposed takes into account the ratings and prices of the CDO's collateral and produces CDRs that are equally stressful across different CDOs, given the credit quality of collateral portfolios, thus allowing the comparison of CDO cash flow model results across CDOs. We also formalized market practice with respect to the determination of high-yield bond-CDO default stresses.

Finally, we suggested some negotiating points for primary CDO purchasers to ensure the liquidity of their CDOs in the secondary market.

CHAPTER 21

The CDO Arbitrage

Both the pattern of CDO issuance—such as heavy or light volume, or which type of collateral dominates—as well as the *configuration* of completed deals—Are there AA or A rated tranches, or simply a larger AAA and BBB class?—are dictated to a large degree by CDO arbitrage. In this chapter, we first look at the CDO arbitrage and examine a "quick and dirty" analysis for benchmarking activity levels. We then focus on how the arbitrage dictates deal structure. Spread configurations and the exact collateral used are important in determining optimal deal structure.

BUILDING BLOCKS

In a CDO, asset purchases are financed by a combination of liabilities plus equity. The "arb" exists when those assets can be purchased and the liabilities sold with enough left over to provide a competitive return to equity holders. Mortgage market participants recognize this exercise for what it is: a kissing cousin to the collateralized mortgage obligations (CMO) arbitrage.

Like the CMO arbitrage, in any intended CDO arbitrage sample structures are always run to determine when this arb is "close." Dealers then act on those results to optimize deal structure so as to increase the likelihood that the deal can actually be executed. Let us look at some simplified examples of "arb" runs for bond and loan deals and then at how these deals can be fine-tuned to improve the arb's attractiveness.

Crude Run

The basis for the arb is the "crude run." In this run, we look for is whether return-on-equity is anywhere near the actual level needed to be attractive to potential equity buyers.

411

To calculate the arb, dealers run the assets and liabilities through a large structuring model. These models first compute the period-by-period cash flows to the equity holders and then calculate the internal rate of return of the equity cash flows. These models gives the underwriting dealer, working with the CDO manager, considerable flexibility in optimizing capital structure. For example, higher quality assets can be used. In that case, overcollateralization levels are lower, and less equity is necessary to support the deal. Or BB rated notes can be used in lieu of equity capital which, in turn, increases overall leverage. Greater asset diversity can be substituted for equity capital. Spreads, prices, and coupons of the assets and liabilities also play a role in determining the required amount of capital over which the excess return must be spread.

However, to compute whether or not any arb is close, we do not need a complex CDO structuring model. Any hand calculator, plus a dose of common sense, will do.

To illustrate our point, we use a very generic collateralized bond obligation (CBO) deal (Exhibit 21.1). The assets in this representative deal consist of high-yield bonds purchased at par and with a yield equal to the yield-to-worst on the Merrill Lynch Cash pay index, which was 12.32% as of June 200X. Our generic deal's $425 million of liabilities consist of $350 million senior notes paying LIBOR + 40, plus $75 million of BBB rated mezzanine notes at LIBOR + 200. Deal structure is supported by $75 million in equity. To be realistic, we also assumed 2% in up-front expenses, and ongoing expenses of 70 basis points per year.

The CBO Arb

Now look at the CBO arbitrage as of 6/200X (in the last column of Exhibit 21.1). After deleting 2% in up-front expenses from our $500 million amount, $490 million ($500 million × 0.98) remains to be invested. These assets earn 12.32% (yield-to-worst on the Merrill Lynch Cash pay index), or a total of $60,368,000, per year. We also assume asset defaults of 3% and recoveries of 50%; so we subtract 1.5% per year, or $7,350,000 per year, from total asset returns. Thus the initial $500 million of assets generates a return of $53,018,000 after that 1.5% loss.

We then subtract the cost of the LIBOR-indexed liabilities. That cost would be understated, and the returns to equity overstated, if the cost of the liabilities is based on prevailing LIBOR term structure at the time. This is because LIBOR at the time of the analysis was lower than forward LIBOR, as the market was expecting LIBOR to be higher over the life of the note than is reflected in current rates.

So we sidestepped that problem by using swap rates for the appropriate maturity. In our case, we used the 7.33% fixed rate on the 7.5-

EXHIBIT 21.1 CBO Arbitrage, 1st Half, 200X

($ million)	
Assets	500,000,000
Class A notes	350,000,000
Class B notes	75,000,000
Equity	75,000,000
Upfront expenses	2.0%
Investable assets	490,000,000
Losses	1.5%
Expenses	0.7%

Date	1/200X	2/200X	3/200X	4/200X	5/200X	6/200X
High-yield index	11.20%	11.31%	11.82%	12.15%	12.44%	12.32%
Class A note spread	55	50	46	45	42	40
Class B note spread	250	240	235	225	215	200
7.5-year swap yield	7.49%	7.39%	7.29%	7.42%	7.63%	7.33%
10-year swap yield	7.52%	7.43%	7.29%	7.41%	7.64%	7.32%
Class A note yield	8.04%	7.89%	7.75%	7.87%	8.05%	7.73%
Class B note yield	10.02%	9.83%	9.64%	9.66%	9.79%	9.32%

EXHIBIT 21.1 (Continued)

Arbitrage

Date	1/200X	2/200X	3/200X	4/200X	5/200X	6/200X
Gross return on assets	54,894,700	55,428,800	57,898,400	59,544,800	60,951,100	60,368,000
Losses	7,350,000	7,350,000	7,350,000	7,350,000	7,350,000	7,350,000
Net return assets	47,544,700	48,078,800	50,548,400	52,194,800	53,601,100	53,018,000
Cost of class A notes	28,147,525	27,599,775	27,113,100	27,557,425	28,187,600	27,041,525
Cost of class B notes	7,518,300	7,371,150	7,226,400	7,246,350	7,339,950	6,991,275
Expenses	3,430,000	3,430,000	3,430,000	3,430,000	3,430,000	3,430,000
Total cost and expenses	39,095,825	38,400,925	37,769,500	38,233,775	38,957,550	37,462,800
$ Return to equity	8,448,875	9,677,875	12,778,900	13,961,025	14,643,550	15,555,200
% Yield on equity	11.27%	12.90%	17.04%	18.61%	19.52%	20.74%

year swaps plus 40 basis points as the cost of the Class A notes, which is equal to 7.73%; and the 7.32% 10-year swap rate plus 200 basis points as the cost of the Class B notes, which is equal to 9.32%. Note that with the swap curve flat, tenor assumptions are immaterial to the results. Anyway, the cost of the Class A note thus becomes [($350,000,000 of Class A notes) × (0.0773 cost)] = $27,041,525. The cost of the B Notes is [($75,000,000 of Class B notes) × (0.0932 cost)] = $6,991,275.

We added to these two costs the 70 basis points of expenses ($490,000,000 × 0.007) = $3,430,000. Thus total cost of the liabilities plus expenses equals $37,462,800. That leaves $15,555,200 as a dollar return-to-equity. Dividing that return by our example's $75,000,000 of equity delivers an equity yield of 20.74%.

Caveats

This is obviously a very basic calculation for the following reasons:

1. The bonds are usually not purchased at par. Most are at a discount.
2. Losses do not kick in immediately as assumed.
3. This is a one-period calculation, a simple simulation of returns without taking into account any asset pay-down schedule.
4. No ramp-up period (versus typical ramp-ups of 2–4 months) has been assumed.
5. We overlooked the possibility of hitting some deal triggers, even at 3% defaults that would cause automatic deleveraging.
6. Once an asset manager is selected, a deal gets fine-tuned to fit that firm's style and then-current market appetites for alternative liability structures (return-to-equity may rise or drop).
7. The calculation ignores the cost to the equity holders of deleveraging.

Consequently, approximate equity returns estimated in this fashion should be regarded as a very basic estimate of actual equity returns.

Changes Over Time

We refer to the first half of fictitious calendar year 200X for our example. This is an exaggerated version of calendar year 2000. We have chosen this period because we saw a huge change to the arb from January to June of that year. Applying the crude arbitrage calculation detailed above to the month of June 200X suggests an equity return of 20.74%. That is certainly quite attractive both in absolute terms as well as relative to other equity alternatives such as public or private equity. In fact, when equity return is above 14% via this simple calculation, CBO structurers know that it pays to look more closely at whether structural changes can be made to make the CBO more attractive. If the "quick and dirty" analysis indicates a return lower than 14%, then that is generally a fruitless exercise. Of course, as detailed above, this calculation is certainly not omniscient, nor perfect. But it is certainly indicative.

Now let us move back to the market scenario in the first quarter of 200X. At the end of January 200X, the yield-to-worst on the high-yield index was 11.20%, which was 112 basis points lower than on 6/200X. The cost of liabilities was also higher in January 2000, as well. Class A notes required a yield of LIBOR + 55, while the cost on the Class B notes was LIBOR + 250. On a swapped basis, the Class A notes yielded 8.04%. That is 31 basis points higher than June 200X's 7.73% level. Meanwhile, the Class B notes yielded 10.02%, 70 basis points higher than June's level of 9.32%. Thus the lower yield on the assets and a higher cost of the liabilities only delivered a dollar return to equity of $8,448,875. Dividing that gross amount by the $75 million of equity provided an equity return of only 11.27% as seen in Exhibit 21.1. That is obviously not at all attractive. It also suggests that high-yield deals were quite noneconomic in January 200X.

Issuance Patterns and CBO Arb

As can also be seen in Exhibit 21.1, the CBO arb became increasingly more attractive during the first half of 200X. Yields on high-yield bonds increased over that period, and the cost of the liabilities declined. In February, the return-on-equity was 12.90%. It then rose to 17.04% in March, 18.61% in April, 19.52% in May, reaching 20.74% in June.

Intuitively, since equity is a levered investment, an increase in asset yield or a decrease in liability costs magnifies, gears, or levers, the impact of that specific change. Equity returns benefit the most from an increased return on the assets. Each 1 basis point-rise in asset yield increases return-on-equity in our example by 6.53 times (490/75). So, the 112 basis point-rise in asset yields from January to June of 200X increased equity yields by 732 basis points (6.53 × 112).

Correspondingly, each 1 basis point-drop in liability cost in our example increases returns on equity by 4.67 times (350/75). Therefore, the 31 basis point-drop in the cost of the liabilities added another 145 basis points to the equity return (31 × 4.67). Finally, each 1 basis point drop in the Class B notes increases the return-on-equity by an amount equal to that drop in costs (75/75). Thus, the 70 basis point drop in the cost of the Class B notes added another 70 basis points to the equity return.

Adding it all up within our simple approximation, the arb in June 200X should look 946 basis points (732 + 144 + 70) better than it did in

January 200X based on changes in the component parts (costs and returns). That is actually quite close to the market's real-life return-on-equity improvement of 947 basis points (20.74% – 11.27%).

Issuance Patterns on CLO Arb

The improvement in the collateralized loan obligation (CLO) arb in the first half of calendar year 200X was less dramatic (as shown in Exhibit 21.2). We again set up a generic bank loan deal, sized at $500 million in assets. However, the capital structure differed from our earlier bond deal. In that prior deal, we had assumed $375 million Class A notes plus $75 million Class B notes plus $50 million capital. A lower capital requirement from the rating agencies stems from the fact that bank loans are often secured, and have much higher recovery rates than do high-yield bonds.

Calendar year 200X loan spreads were consistent at about LIBOR + 315 basis points. "Loan yield" converts this to a fixed rate, which is constructed by adding in the rate payable on a 10-year swap (7.32%). June's asset yield thus becomes 10.57%. We then assume defaults are the same 3% (as on high-yield assets in our CBO deal example), but that recoveries would be higher, at 75%. Thus losses become 0.75% (= 3.0% × 0.25) per annum. We assume liability costs identical to those on the CBO at LIBOR + 40 on the AAA rated notes, with a 7.73% yield; and LIBOR + 200 on the BBB-rated notes, for a 9.32% yield. We also assume identical up-front expenses of 2% and ongoing expenses of 70 basis points. Based on these levels, Exhibit 21.2 shows that as of June 5, 2000, return to the $50 million in capital would have been 17.46%.

The CLO arbitrage improved somewhat during the first half of calendar year 200X, but not nearly as dramatically as did the CBO arbitrage. The return-to-equity on our representative CBO was 16.03% in January 200X. But by June, that return had risen to 17.46%. That improvement stems from reduction in the cost of liabilities. The Class A notes tightened 15 basis points (from LIBOR + 55 to LIBOR + 40), while the BBB rated notes tightened by 50 basis points (from LIBOR + 250 to LIBOR + 200.)

It is quite interesting to compare Exhibits 21.1 and 21.2. The disparity is the difference in asset behavior—high-yield spreads widened in the first half of 200X, while spreads to LIBOR were roughly constant for loan deals. As a result, the CBO arbitrage improved dramatically, while the CLO arbitrage improved much less.

EXHIBIT 21.2 CLO Arbitrage, 1st Half, 200X

	($ million)
Assets	500,000,000
Class A notes	375,000,000
Class B notes	75,000,000
Equity	50,000,000
Upfront expenses	2.0%
Investable assets	490,000,000
Losses	0.75%
Expenses	0.7%

Date	1/200X	2/200X	3/200X	4/200X	5/200X	6/200X
Loan spread	3.25%	3.25%	3.25%	3.25%	3.25%	3.25%
Loan yield	10.77%	10.68%	10.54%	10.66%	10.89%	10.57%
Class A note spread	55	50	46	45	42	40
Class B note spread	250	240	235	225	215	200
7.5-year swap yield	7.49%	7.39%	7.29%	7.42%	7.63%	7.33%
10-year swap yield	7.52%	7.43%	7.29%	7.41%	7.64%	7.32%
Class A note yield	8.04%	7.89%	7.75%	7.87%	8.05%	7.73%
Class B note yield	10.02%	9.83%	9.64%	9.66%	9.79%	9.32%

EXHIBIT 21.2 (Continued)

Arbitrage

Date	1/200X	2/200X	3/200X	4/200X	5/200X	6/200X
Gross return on assets	52,794,560	52,323,180	51,622,480	52,242,820	53,344,340	51,801,330
Losses	3,675,000	3,675,000	3,675,000	3,675,000	3,675,000	3,675,000
Net return assets	49,119,560	48,648,180	47,947,480	48,567,820	49,669,340	48,126,330
Cost of class A notes	30,158,063	29,571,188	29,049,750	29,525,813	30,201,000	28,973,063
Cost of class B notes	7,518,300	7,371,150	7,226,400	7,246,350	7,339,950	6,991,275
Expenses	3,430,000	3,430,000	3,430,000	3,430,000	3,430,000	3,430,000
Total cost and expenses	41,106,363	40,372,338	39,706,150	40,202,163	40,970,950	39,394,338
$ Return to equity	8,013,198	8,275,842	8,241,330	8,365,657	8,698,390	8,731,992
% Yield on equity	16.03%	16.55%	16.48%	16.73%	17.40%	17.46%

419

Activity levels should reflect the strength of the CDO arbitrage. In January and February of 200X, it was difficult to do CBO deals (since return-on-equity was too low to be appealing). This would suggest deal activity should be light, and most deals done should utilize loan collateral (CLOs). By contrast, in the second quarter of 200X, deal activity should be heavier, and most deals done should utilize bond collateral reflecting the fact that return-to-equity was higher on the high-yield bond deals than on the loan deals. And in fact this does reflect reality. The levels used for this analysis are very close to those in the first half of 2000. The total volume of deal activity in the first quarter of 2000 was $5.63 billion, mostly in CLO deals. By contrast, in the second quarter of 2000, Moody's rated over $15 billion in deals, the majority of which were backed primarily by bond collateral.

Improving the Arb

Now we know what is driving the arbitrage. And once a deal is "close," structurers can tinker and nudge it closer to the needs of equity buyers. Trade-offs can be made between leverage, the level of overcollateralization for triggering tests, asset quality, liability ratings, diversity, as well as acquisition prices and coupons. There is actually quite a basketful of structuring nuances.

Certainly, one of the ways to increase the potential equity return is to expand leverage. Greater leverage heightens yield responsiveness of the assets to default rates. To show this, we first compute yield responsiveness of our representative CBO deal (that detailed in Exhibit 21.1, a CBO with 15% equity, based on $75 million equity within a $500 million deal). We use June 200X data for the calculations. The dotted line in Exhibit 21.3 shows the yield profile for CBO equity in our representative 15% equity deal. Note that at 3% defaults, the equity return is 20.74% (That's exactly the same number as in Exhibit 21.1.) At default rates below 3%, return-to-equity is greater; at higher default rates, equity returns are lower.

To assess the effects of higher leverage, we then decrease equity capital by $10 million (to $65 million) and introduce $10 million of BB rated notes (coupon of LIBOR + 550). The resultant structure has 13% equity plus 2% BB rated notes. We also recompute return-on-equity at different default rates. Thus, as shown by the solid line in Exhibit 21.3 (at 3% defaults) return-to-equity is 21.84% in this "high leverage" deal. By contrast, it is 33.15% at 0% defaults and 3.00% at 8% defaults.

Effect of Higher Leverage

It is useful to compare results of an "average leverage" deal with what might evolve from one more highly levered. The net effect is that more highly leveraged deals have steeper return profiles. In our simple analy-

EXHIBIT 21.3 Effect of Increasing Leverage

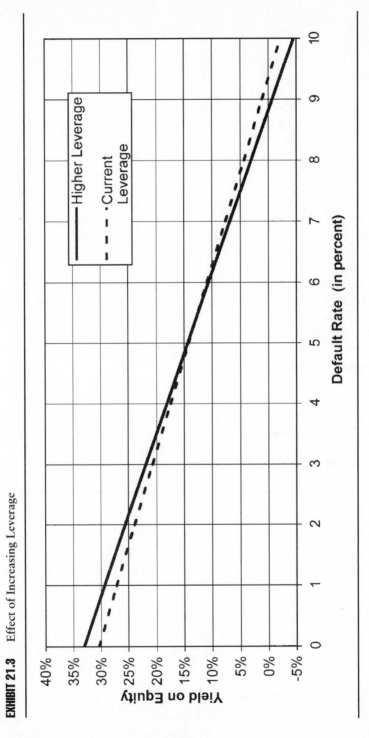

sis, at default levels below 5% to 6%, the more highly levered equity piece yields more; while at default levels above 5% to 6%, it yields less. Specifically, at 0% defaults, a deal with "average" leverage only returns 30.44%, while that with higher leverage throws off 33.15%. At 9% defaults, the average leverage deal generates 1.04%, while the deal with high leverage yields –0.77%.

In point of fact, this analysis is too kind to the more highly geared deal. The deal with greater leverage would also have tighter overcollateralization levels, which would also hit the triggers sooner and thus delever more quickly. So overall, that would create a far more negative impact on returns than shown in Exhibit 21.3. (Remember, we used a simple one-period analysis, and ignored trigger events.)

Rating agencies ultimately dictate capital structure supportable within a deal's parameters. Any increase in leverage, all other factors constant, reduces protection for the rated classes. Therefore, any such higher leverage must be accompanied by raising the quality of assets, or by tightening overcollaterization. The latter is done by decreasing the level of overcollaterization necessary to trigger a deleveraging.

Gauging Activity Levels

To create a CDO, two conditions are necessary. First, the arbitrage must be favorable. Second, CDO assets must be available.

Our basic calculation allows rated note buyers to gauge how favorable the CDO arbitrage is. Then, one needs to consider asset availability so as to figure activity levels. In June 200X return-to-equity was very attractive, as evidenced by our sample deals. If collateral was readily available, deal activity should have been heavy.

IMPACT OF CDO ARBITRAGE ON STRUCTURE

Many decisions made in the CDO structuring process are a function of the arb. If certain classes are more expensive than combinations of other classes, those classes more expensive are less apt to be created.

We make this point by looking at trade-offs inherent in deal structures. We show that greater subordination and more overcollateralization, can, at times, result in greater extension risk. It is very important for investors to examine an entire deal structure in light of their portfolio objectives.

Rules of CDO Deal Structuring

Following are two rules of CDO structuring. Rule #1 is never leave money on the table! If (all things being equal) a deal structure can support

80% AAA rated bonds, it is unlikely that any issuer will construct that deal with 78% AAA rated bonds. So if two tranches of different deals, both rated AAA by the same rating agency, are in the market simultaneously, then it is likely that both contain the maximum amount of AAA bonds supportable by their structures. If one deal carries a higher percent of AAAs, then trade-offs were made elsewhere in the structure.

Rule #2 is optimize deal structure. It is survival of the fittest out there. Issuers try various deal structures, and come up with one or two that look the "best." (Structurers' trash cans generally overflow with printouts of trials failed because they were "nonoptimal.") Optimal structure in CDOs is that for which each of the rated notes can receive a market-determined interest rate, with IRR maximized on the equity piece. If one dealer structures an equity return of 17% while another offers 18% off the same collateral at similar leverage then an investor will clearly run, not walk, to that higher return.

Interest Costs Drive Subordination

We now look at how the CDO arbitrage and current spread configuration dictates structure. Note that many investors (particularly at the AAA level) look at percent subordination as an indicator of protection. While it is certainly one such bellwether, it should not be used as the be-all and end-all. In fact, Rules #1 and #2 above are so powerful that if two tranches are created at the same time with the same rating, there is unlikely to be any strict dominance of one over the other.

Exhibit 21.4 displays three different structures, using typical combinations of structured finance collateral (ABS, MBS, CMBS, and REITs). The three structures (labeled Deals A, B, and C) are backed by exactly the same collateral. The cost of that collateral was assumed to be $97.88, which includes the CMBS IO that is often included in these deals. The diversity score is 17, also very typical of mortgage deals, and the weighted average rating factor is 345, which corresponds to the BBB level. The WAC on the collateral is 8.30%, which again, includes the effects of the CMBS IO.

In Deal A, liabilities were tranched into notes rated AAA, A–, and BB and equity, proportioned 86.67%, 9.0%, 1.67%, and 2.67%, respectively. Note that this structure maximized the amount of AAA rated notes permitted (shown in the middle section of Exhibit 21.4). The bottom part of the exhibit shows that after paying a liability holder the spreads shown separately in Exhibit 21.4, the return-to-equity (assuming no defaults) is 17.09%.

Deal B has essentially the same structure. The only difference is that the A– and BB amounts are collapsed into a BBB class. Equity yield then

EXHIBIT 21.4 Structuring Tradeoffs

	Liability Spread	Deal		
		A	B	C
Principal face		300	300	300
Total cost		97.88	97.88	97.88
Rating factor		345	345	345
WAC		8.30%	8.30%	8.30%
AAA	L + 50	86.67%	86.67%	76.67%
AA	L + 90	—	—	11.67%
A–	L + 150	9.00%	—	7.33%
BBB	L + 250	—	10.83%	—
BB	T + 700	1.67%	—	1.67%
Equity		2.67%	2.50%	2.67%
Min. AAA I/C required		122	122	144
Min. AAA O/C required		110	110	128
Equity yield		17.09%	17.24%	15.69%

expands to 17.24%, although that is not all that much different from Deal A's 17.09%.

In Deal C we recarved the AAA and A– cash flows into notes rated AAA, AA, and A–, holding constant the amounts of BB and equity. This structure would be considered suboptimal, as return-to-equity drops to 15.69%, versus Deal A's 17.09%. No matter how gifted a salesperson is, they would *not* be able to sell equity at this level when other deals are in the market with equity returns 150 bp higher.

Anyway, the reason the arb is much less attractive in Deal C is due to the spread configuration. The deals shifted 10% of the AAA rated bonds (paying LIBOR + 50) and 1.67% of the A– bonds (paying LIBOR + 150) into the AA bucket, which pays LIBOR + 90. That raised our interest costs 25.7 basis points on 11.67% of the deal. By the way, note that there is a relative value implication here: The AA rated bonds are quite attractively priced.

Debt Holders Do Not Look Exclusively at Subordination

Suppose an investor is considering buying AAA rated paper. The investor is trying to decide between the bond in Deal A or that in Deal C. Which should the investor want in his portfolio? At first glance, the one in Deal C looks "better" because of its 23.23% subordination, rather than the 13.67% subordination in Deal A. Furthermore, the minimum I/C and O/C levels are much higher for Deal C's AAA rated bond.

But do not forget that according to Rule #1, you should "never leave money on the table." Each of the deals has already maximized the amount of AAA bonds that can be created in that structure. Thus, rating agencies consider the bonds roughly equivalent.

Many believe that the AAA rated bond in Deal C could never be worse than Deal A. That is wrong. The application-of-cash waterfall typically pours collateral interest and principal cash flow into AA interest payments prior to paying any AAA principal. More precisely, rating agencies will not allow a AA rated class to defer interest payments. However, if defaults are very high, cash flows in the deal will be lower. Thus, Deal C's AAA rated notes are more likely to extend than are Deal A's. Intuitively, an additional 40 basis points of interest on 10% of the deal plus the entire interest payment on 1.67% of the deal are "earmarked" to pay the AA rated noteholders their interest; the interest on this tranche must be paid before the AAA rated notes get principal back.

CONCLUSION

In this chapter we have seen that the CDO arbitrage is the key to CDO transactions. And the arbitrage calculations also shown in this chapter allow investors to gauge activity levels. Those activity levels are especially crucial to equity buyers and to CBO managers.

Equity buyers should check the equity returns pitched by an investment bank. If that return is materially different from what you figure on your hand calculator—investors should find out what assumptions are being made about the structure, and be very sure that they are comfortable with those.

Additionally, these arbitrage calculations allow potential CBO managers to determine when they really want to press to get a deal done. Marginal arbitrage may portend that it is better to sit tight and wait for better timing. Deal performance is certainly important to any deal manager. It impacts future deals, and a manager's own pocket is directly impacted in that he or she typically retains a large chunk of the equity.

The CDO arbitrage is also a major determinant of deal structure. We have seen how different spread configurations and different collateral can make for very different deal structures. That is, deals are generally optimized to maximize returns to equity holders, while making sure to pay rated note holders their appropriate market levels. Yet with very dissimilar deal structures, investors are unable to figure relative value simply by looking exclusively at subordination in a deal, or exclusively at the amount of overcollateralization. That is because the benefits of higher subordination can be offset, depending on the waterfall rules. The benefits of higher overcollaterization can be offset by lower interest coverage ratios.

The bottom line is that since deal structures have been optimized, there are always trade-offs. Investors need to be fully aware of those choices they implicitly make.

CHAPTER 22

How to Evaluate a CDO and Manage a CDO Portfolio

In this chapter, we look at evaluating CDOs individually and as part of a portfolio. We make two points about buying CDO deals individually. First, we make the case that one of the most important points to look for in a CDO purchase is the structural protections inherent in a CDO. There is a natural tension between the interest of debtholders and equity holders that the CDO structure tries to address. Buyers of CDO debt will want to look at both the incentive structures in a CDO, as well as how the manager has done on outstanding CDOs. Second, in picking managers, track record cannot be taken at face value. Common sense goes a long way.

We then move on to managing a CDO portfolio. Some portfolio managers have quite an extensive collection of CDOs, owning 100 to 200 different CDOs. Yet they often tend to look at buying each additional CDO as if they were buying their first. They do not place the CDOs within a general portfolio framework. In the second half of the chapter, we make the case that investors should buy CDOs backed by different types of collateral. Asset class is a far more important determinant of returns than is choice of specific managers. Finally, we look at diversity on a portfolio basis. A low diversity CDO may add more diversity to a portfolio because it is backed by a different type of collateral than a high diversity CDO.

INCENTIVE CLASHES IN CDO STRUCTURES

When a deal is going well, the interests of all parties are aligned. When a deal begins to go poorly, there is a natural tension between the interests of equity holders and debt holders. And the collateral manager is

427

generally an equity holder, holding between 25 and 49.5% of a deal. (If the collateral manager held any more equity, the deal would have to be consolidated on their balance sheet.)

The source of the tension is that any violation of the interest coverage or overcollaterization tests will cut off the cash flows to the equity tranche, cutting seriously into returns. The cash flows are used to delever the deal, and repay the more senior tranches. Thus, when the manager is also an equity holder, he has every incentive to avoid tripping the overcollateralization (OC) and interest coverage (IC) triggers.

In the 2000–2002 period, there were some abuses by CDO managers, particularly in high-yield bond deals. Managers engaged in par-building trades, and avoided par-losing trades. With par-building trades, managers were able to stall violations of coverage tests by judicious portfolio trading. If the OC ratio was about to be tripped, the manager could sell $100 face of bonds trading at par, and buy $200 face of bonds trading at $100 (market value = 50% of face), boosting the OC ratios. In addition, there was an incentive not to take a loss on a bond that had lost a significant amount of value, even if the manager thought it could deteriorate further. If a bond had declined in value from par to $75, and the CDO manager thought it could go to $40, it might still be in the equity holders' interest to hold the bond. That is, selling the bond at $75 would show a $25 loss of OC, and might violate the OC test. Holding the bond would not risk tripping an OC trigger.

EVALUATE STRUCTURAL ENHANCEMENTS

In the 2002–2003 period, there were a number of structural enhancements made to alleviate these issues. The rating agencies began to require that collateral assets on watch for downgrade be treated as if they had already been downgraded one ratings notch in the WARF calculation and in all other ratings sensitive collateral tests. Principal proceeds on called or sold securities cannot be used to pay interest on the deal. Trading gains must be reinvested in new collateral assets unless OC ratios have remained at their original levels and all other asset quality tests are being met. In addition, CDOs generally contain some additional structural enhancements to protect their bondholders. These enhancements take a number of forms: increasing the effectiveness of OC test or introducing supplement OC tests, limiting the release of cash flows to equity holders and collateral gatekeeping measures, designed to keep bad assets out of a CDO portfolio.

Increasing the effectiveness of the OC test or introducing a supplemental OC test takes a number of forms. Many CDOs now place a haircut in the numerator of the OC test for assets that have been downgraded or which were purchased at a deep discount. Thus, these assets are given less than 100% credit in the OC test, lowering the OC ratio. There are often supplemental OC tests that haircut Caa assets (or speculative-grade assets for investment grade-backed CDOs). These tests go a long way toward solving two issues: par building and the reluctance of many CDO managers to sell assets at a loss.

A small number of deals have taken a more dramatic tact—limiting cash flows to equity holders. This has taken the form of equity caps as well as other limitations on payments to the equity tranche early in the life of the CDO.

Collateral gatekeeping measures are designed to align the incentive structures of equity and debt holders and keep bad assets out of a portfolio. The most common of these tests are yield tests. If the yield is too wide, the asset is either (1) barred from the portfolio, or (2) the asset can be purchased, but the amount of the coupon above the threshold cannot be used to pay interest, it must be used to purchase more collateral assets. This gatekeeping measure cuts down dramatically on par (and yield) building exercises.

In any given deal, some but not all of these protections are likely to be present. Buyers of CDO debt are well advised to look at the structural protections in a new issue or secondary CDO.

In addition to looking at the protections in the deal under consideration, investors are well advised to look at the manager's behavior on outstanding deals. It is very difficult for an equity holder to manage a deal and totally ignore its own incentives. However, some managers can be egregiously self-serving. This can usually be spotted by looking for a huge deterioration in WARF scores, or a big growth in deteriorated assets.

Realize that poor performance on previous deals is not necessarily indicative of abusive management. Often, market conditions have deteriorated, and most CDOs of that asset type have been impacted. Thus, if an outstanding deal is performing poorly, it is very important to look at the reasons why.

EVALUATING THE MANAGER'S TRACK RECORD

When marketing a CDO deal, the first words spoken to the investor are often: "The most important aspect of picking a CDO is selecting a manager; so look at the track record of this manager." But it is very difficult for investors to assess a manager on track records alone, as they do not necessarily allow easy comparison. The best one can hope to establish is that a manager has been managing that particular asset class for a long period of time, their investment approach can be articulated clearly, and risk management parameters are strictly adhered to.

There is good reason to be very skeptical about track records. They contain three biases—"creation bias," "survivorship bias," and "size bias." We briefly discuss these biases.

"Creation bias" refers to the fact that an investment can take funds that were run in another form—say a bank trust fund, a limited partnership, or an insurance company "separate" account—and convert them into a mutual fund. The mutual fund can now claim the track record of the old entity. Obviously, only "good performers" are morphed into mutual fund form, creating an upward bias to returns. Here is another example. Mutual fund management complexes often start incubator funds. Ten new funds may be created with different in-house managers, each with a small amount of seed money. Then, the mutual fund parent waits to see which are successful. Suppose after a few years, only three produced notable total returns. Then only these are marketed, with their attendant track records. There is nothing dishonest about it. It allows a mutual fund to take a chance on a number of young portfolio managers, and discover one who displays real talent. Plus, since the seed money comes from the mutual fund complex's pockets, investors have not lost money due to poor performance. But it clearly creates an upward bias to reported returns, and makes it all that much more difficult for investors to pick managers.

The bad track record for a fund can be wiped out by merging it into a sibling fund, selling it, or returning money to investors. These techniques all wipe out a fund's bad track record and create "survivorship bias" which can take another form: If a manager with a good tack record leaves one firm, both the fund and the manager can take credit for the favorable track record. (The manager does have to show that they had full control over investment decisions at the former fund.) Nevertheless, it is really difficult to apportion credit or blame for a fund's performance between a particular manager and the parent fund company. Success in one environment does not necessarily translate into success in another. For example, an outstanding manager who had an army of talented analysts may do far less well in an environment with no support, where he is his own analyst. Moreover, good track records are "adopted" by both the departing manager and the fund left behind, bad track records are used by neither, as the fund gets quietly merged into another one under a different manager.

The last bias is "size bias." As funds do better they tend to accumulate more money to invest. However, they may not be able to replicate that performance with more assets, and returns are not dollar weighted, and are hence overstated. For example, assume a fund initially sized at $10 million earned 50% one year. The fund then attracts a considerable amount of new money, say $85 million, which when added to the $5 million "profit" and the $10 million invested at inception, gives it $100 million at the end of the first year. Assume it then proceeds to lose 20% the following year. The fund will report a 9.54% annualized return, as a dollar invested at inception is worth $1.20 over 2 years [$(1.5 \times 0.8 = 1.20)$, corresponding to an annual return of 9.54%]. However, the average investor lost money. The fund made $5 million for a small number of investors the first year, then lost $20 million for a much large number of investors the second year. Again, we see that it is hard to evaluate track records.

While this discussion is very quick, there is a great deal of academic literature on these biases as they pertain to the mutual fund area.[1] The same biases apply to fixed income funds.

Common Sense

The key to evaluating manager performance is to use common sense. Do not be duped by performance numbers. Here is what to look for:

■ Make sure the firm has a track record with every asset class it is including in the CDO, and that the money manager is not stretching into asset classes in which they have not historically been active.

■ Make sure the firm has a disciplined, consistent approach to investing, which is followed in good times and bad.

■ Look at the stability of both the firm and the manager. A management team that has been at a firm for a long period of time, with significant equity, is less likely to leave. (Ideally, CDO investors would like to handcuff managers to the firm for the life of their deal. One obviously cannot do that, but bigger manager stakes mean there is less likelihood of leaving.) Moreover, the longer a group of people has been working together, the less chance of a sudden shift in strategy.

There is an assumption on the part of investors that Wall Street dealers who underwrite CDOs act as gatekeepers, allowing only the top-notch performing managers to pass through their pearly gates. That

---

[1] A fuller discussion of these issues can be found in Burton G. Malkiel, *A Random Walk Down Wall Street* (New York: Norton, 1999).

blind trust, however, is to some extent misplaced. More money management firms wish to manage CDOs than there is dealer pipeline capacity. Thus, a dealer wants to underwrite CDOs (from managers) they believe will sell quickly.

However there are often other considerations, including overall quality of the relationship between the dealer and a money manager, as well as help the asset manager can provide in marketing the deal and taking some of the equity. Consider two money managers; one has a very good track record, the other only an average one. The manager with the average track record will take all the equity in the CDOs, plus some of the subordinate securities. The manager with the better track record wants the dealer to market all the equity. Who will the underwriters pick? It's a no brainer—the manager with the average track record who is willing to provide more help in underwriting the deal.

Realize that the Wall Street dealer community does require at least a minimum performance threshold. The manager's investment philosophy and track record do have to be good enough to market the deal. Moreover, since dealers are looking at the overall quality of the relationship between the dealer and asset manager, as well as an asset manager's willingness to take down some of the equity, it is natural that larger, better established money management firms are likely to have an edge. This is a good thing for investors, per our common sense tests above.

Managing a CDO Portfolio

So far, we have examined what to focus on when looking at an individual deal—making the case that rather than focusing on the manager's track record, focus on the performance of outstanding CDO deals, and how the manager has balanced his interests with those of the noteholders. We now shift gears, and examine the argument that not only should CDO buyers look at individual deals, but they should look at their CDO holding in a portfolio framework.

The key to managing a CDO portfolio is diversification. One of the few indisputable facts is that the types of securities purchased (the style) is key—far more important than skills of a particular manager. Roger Ibbotson, one of the key researchers in the performance area, writes:

> . . . relying on past performance is not as simple as it appears. The investment styles of mutual funds typically explain more than 90 percent of the variation in returns. Just knowing that a fund is a large or small capitalization fund, a growth or value fund, an international stock fund, or a combination of these categories largely explains its

performance. The skill of the manager is demonstrated relative to the fund's investment style . . .[2]

While it is indisputable that style matters, there is a question as to whether good or poor performance in one period is indicative of the performance going forward. That is, are some managers just far superior to others? While there have been studies of mutual funds that have examined this issue, in short, the debate seems to be whether style (asset class) accounts for 90% or 99% of return variation. There is no disputing the fact that it is the key factor. Bottom line—diversify across asset classes.

Do Not Ignore CDO's with Low-Diversity Scores

Many investors buying a large number of positions still tend to look at each purchase individually. Yes, it is important to look at each deal. Some parameters, however, may be unacceptable if a particular deal was the only one purchased, and less important when the security will become part of a portfolio. Diversity is one such parameter.

In fact, it is important to look at holdings on a consolidated basis. Adding deals with low diversification may, in some circumstances, help a CDO portfolio. For example, a REIT-only deal may have a low-diversity score, but if it was part of a larger CDO portfolio, and REIT holdings elsewhere are limited, then purchasing it may actually increase diversification. By contrast, if one purchased three high-yield deals within a short period of time, each with very high-diversity scores, the additional diversification provided by buying all three deals may actually be limited, as they may own substantially the same securities.

In point of fact, one can argue that debt holders are actually better off holding a portfolio of deals with low diversity scores rather than a portfolio of deals with higher diversity scores and overlapping holdings. This is because the rating agencies tend to require more subordination on a deal with a lower diversity score. However, when an investor purchases a large number of CDOs, they are creating their own diversification.

There is a secondary effect. In trying to raise diversity scores, managers often venture into asset classes or industries they are less familiar with. We saw in Chapter 8 that a disproportionate amount of ABS CDO downgrades were from ABS CDOs with high-diversity scores. These deals added off the run asset classes such as mutual fund fee securitizations and franchise loan securitizations to boost diversity scores and yield.

The practical advice for managing a CDO portfolio is:

---

[2] Roger Ibbotson, "Style Conscious," *Bloomberg Personal* (March/April 2001).

1. An investor should not shun low diversity score deals since the investor also creates his own diversification.
2. An investor should look at holdings in his CDO portfolio on a consolidated basis.

CONCLUSION

With the rapid growth of the CDO market over the past few years, a fair number of portfolio managers have amassed large CDO portfolios. However, unlike other portfolios, CDO positions tend to be accumulated one-by-one rather than within a portfolio framework.

In this chapter, we argue the importance of evaluating each CDO deal and each CDO manager. However, it is less important to focus on a manager's overall track record and more important to focus on common sense items—length of time the management team has been together, whether they have followed a consistent investment philosophy, importance of interest risk management, and so on. It is also critical to focus on the manager's reaction to potential conflicts of interest in previous CDO deals they have managed.

Again, one should realize that the key determinant of CDO performance is likely to be the type of assets held, not the contribution of any individual manager or deal. Thus a portfolio of CDOs should consist of different types of collateral, each purchased when it is cheap. In addition, portfolio diversification should be judged in a total portfolio framework, not on a CDO-by-CDO basis. Thus it is very important to aggregate across CDOs in a portfolio to see the collateral composition and diversification.

CHAPTER 23

Quantifying Single-Name Risk Across CDOs

Single-name risk in collateralized debt obligations (CDOs) arises from the presence of the same credit in the portfolios of different CDOs. If the same credit appears in several, or all, of the CDO portfolios an investor owns, there may be an unexpectantly large exposure to that particular credit. In the extreme, if every CDO had the same exact set of underlying credits, there would be no diversification benefit from owning different CDOs. In this chapter, we quantify the extent of collateral overlap among a sample of U.S. collateralized loan obligations (CLOs) and structured finance (SF) CDOs (i.e., CDOs backed by asset-backed securities, commercial mortgage-backed securities, and residential mortgage-backed securities). We then propose a simple and consistent measure of single-name risk applicable across CDO tranches of various seniorities. Finally, we review a more complex, high tech approach to CDO single-name risk.

CLO portfolios, even from CLOs issued in different years, tend to have a lot of underlying borrower names in common, and this is especially the case for CLOs managed by the same manager. In this chapter, we name the most common underlying borrowers among a sample of CLOs.

For SF CDOs, the single name of interest is the *originator* of the ABS, CMBS, and RMBS assets in the portfolio. Many defaults in structured finance have been originator-driven, related to too-lenient underwriting standards or even to fraud by the originator. However, the high credit quality of the collateral within SF CDOs ameliorates some of the single-name originator risk. So we look closely at SF CDO risk to originators of downgraded collateral.

Our measure of single-name risk compares the concentration of a single credit across CDO portfolios to the credit protection afforded the particular tranches an investor owns. On this basis, our analysis shows little reason to be concerned about single-name risk for the CLOs and SF CDOs we studied, except perhaps at the level of subordinate debt and equity.

COLLATERAL OVERLAP IN U.S. CLOs

We examined the U.S. CLO portfolio of a major CDO investor. This investor owned the first six CLOs we list (in an opaque manner[1]) in Exhibit 23.1. Note that this investor bought two CLOs from Manager A, a 1999 vintage and a 2001 vintage. To test some conclusions about how managers buy and allocate loans across the CLOs they manage, we added a 2003 CLO from Manager A to our study. So all together we looked at seven CLOs, six purchased by a particular investor and one additional CLO. Among these seven CLOs, three have the same manager. These CLOs have collateral portfolios ranging between $350 million and $1 billion. All of these CLOs are healthy, none of their debt tranches have been downgraded, and all their tranches are passing their par and interest coverage tests by good margins.

To quantify single-name risk, we first looked at the percent of a CLO portfolio, by par amount, made up of obligations of the same credit. For a particular credit, collateral overlap is defined as the *average* percent of that single name in two CLOs. Thus, since 1.0% of 1999 A's portfolio is comprised of Invensys and 2.3% of 2000 B's portfolio is comprised of that same credit, the collateral overlap from Invensys

EXHIBIT 23.1 CLO Vintages and Managers in Study

1999 Manager A
2000 Manager B
2001 Manager A
2001 Manager C
2002 Manager D
2002 Manager E
2003 Manager A

---

[1] Why the secrecy? To protect the investor's privacy, because we are relying on underlying collateral data we cannot verify, because we wish to make general points about the CLO market rather than specific points about individual managers, and because we do not want to increase our hate mail from disgruntled CDO managers.

between the two CLOs is calculated as 1.7%. The total collateral over-lap between 1999 A and 2000 B is the sum of these individual name collateral overlaps.

Note that our measure of single-name risk focuses on exposure to a particular name *across CDOs*. It does not, however, address single-name risk *within a particular CDO*. For example, if a CDO portfolio consisted of only one credit, the CDO's debt and equity holders would bear huge single-name risk. But if that credit was not also in another CDO, our measure of single-name risk across CDOs would show 0% collateral overlap between the two CDOs. In practice, single-name risk within a particular CDO is handled by that CDO's concentration limits. In this chapter we are is concerned about single-name risk arising from the presence of a particular name across multiple CDOs.

To determine whether two CLOs contain the same credit, we first looked to the "Issuer" data field in INTEX's asset detail. Unfortunately, INTEX does not have a single unique issuer identifier across all CDOs. Nor does it group affiliated legal entities, such as holding companies and their subsidiaries. Therefore, we grouped single-name risks "by eye." Also, the portfolio for one of the CLOs was not available on INTEX, so we obtained it from Moody's EMS database.

Exhibit 23.2 shows that, by far, the greatest collateral overlap occurs among the three CLOs managed by the same manager. Pairwise overlap between Manager A's three CLOs is 71%, 68%, and 58%, respectively. The next highest collateral overlap between any two CLOs is 45%, from two CLOs issued in 2001. Apparently, having the same manager produces higher collateral overlap between CLOs than does being in the same vintage year.

The far right column in Exhibit 23.2 shows the average collateral overlap between a particular CLO and the other six. This varies from 30% to 46%. But across all possible pairs of CLOs, the collateral overlap varies from 25% to 71% and averages 38%. Ignoring the collateral overlap between the three CLOs managed by the same manager, collateral overlap varies from 25% to 45% and averages 34%.

FAVORITE CLO CREDITS

There are 531 unique borrowers represented in the seven CLO portfolios we examined; across them all, the average par exposure to any particular credit is 0.2%. But Exhibit 23.3 shows the highest single-name exposures across the seven CLOs. The biggest common holding across all of our test case CLOs is Charter Communications. On average, it

EXHIBIT 23.2 Percent of Collateral Overlap—Borrowers Common to Any Two CLOs

	1999 Manager A	2000 Manager B	2001 Manager A	2001 Manager C	2002 Manager D	2002 Manager E	2003 Manager A	Average
1999 Manager A	100	29	71	41	25	33	58	43
2000 Manager B	29	100	28	39	26	38	26	31
2001 Manager A	71	28	100	45	28	36	68	46
2001 Manager C	41	39	45	100	36	41	38	40
2002 Manager D	25	26	28	36	100	37	27	30
2002 Manager E	33	38	36	41	37	100	34	37
2003 Manager A	58	26	68	38	27	34	100	42

EXHIBIT 23.3 Most Common Borrowers in Sampled CLOs

Rank	Credit	Average CLO Exposure %	# of CLOs with Exposure
1	Charter	1.8	7
2	Huntsman	1.4	7
3	Invensys	1.3	6
4	Allied Waste	1.2	7
5	Nextel	1.2	6
6	Calpine	1.2	4
7	Owens	1.1	7
8	Dex Media	1.1	6

comprises 1.8% of each CLOs' portfolio and it is present in all seven CLOs. Huntsman, Invensys, Allied Waste, Nextel, Calpine, Owens, and Dex Media make up the balance of the eight most common credits in the CLOs. These credits' share of the portfolios averages between 1.1% and 1.4% of each CLO portfolio. Note that Calpine is only present in four CLOs. It makes the list by virtue of it making up 3.0% of one CLO portfolio and 2.6% of another. After these eight credits, single-name concentrations shrink rapidly. PanAmSat averages 1.0% across the CLOs, Graphic Packaging and Centerpoint Energy average 0.9%, and five other credits average 0.8%.

COLLATERAL OVERLAP IN U.S. STRUCTURED FINANCE CDOs

For structured finance-backed CDOs, we focus on *originator* concentrations. Many defaults in structured finance have been originator-driven, related to too-lenient underwriting standards or even to fraud by the originator. For example, 17% of all ABS defaults are traceable to problems at Conseco/Greentree. Even more dramatically, 62% of all RMBS defaults are traceable to Quality Mortgage.

Our ability to find common originators across SF CDOs was limited to those SF CDO portfolios on INTEX that include Bloomberg originator codes. In Exhibit 23.4, we show originator concentrations for seven SF CDOs for which we were able to find such data. None of these SF CDOs have had any of their debt tranches downgraded. Three different managers (Managers A, B, and C) are represented in the SF CDOs we studied.

EXHIBIT 23.4 Percent of Originator Overlap—Collateral Originators Common to Any Two SF CDOs

	2001 Manager A	2002 Manager A	2002 Manager B	2002 Manager C	2003 Manager B	2004 Manager B	2004 Manager C	Average
2001 Manager A	100	33	8	41	11	9	0	17
2002 Manager A	33	100	22	25	16	16	11	20
2002 Manager B	8	22	100	13	60	59	47	35
2002 Manager C	41	25	13	100	26	13	13	22
2003 Manager B	11	16	60	26	100	77	53	40
2004 Manager B	9	16	59	13	77	100	56	38
2004 Manager C	0	11	47	13	53	56	100	30

Originator concentrations in Exhibit 23.4 range from 0% to 77% and average 29%. The far right column in the Exhibit 23.4 shows that the average originator overlap between a particular SF CDO and the other six varies from 17% to 40%. But unlike collateral overlap in CLOs, originator concentrations show no discernable pattern associated with the SF CDO's manager. The collateral focus of SF CDOs, for example, upon CMBS or residential mortgage ABS, makes more of a difference to originator concentrations than does having a common manager.

But an assessment of single-name risk should also take credit quality into account. Or put another way, good credit quality goes a long way towards ameliorating concern about single-name risk. A SF CDO investor should be more concerned with portfolio concentration in an originator of *speculative-grade collateral* than about concentration in an originator of *investment-grade collateral*. In Exhibit 23.5, we show originator concentrations of speculative-grade collateral, whether the collateral was originally rated or downgraded to speculative-grade.

Note that the diagonal elements in the exhibit no longer equal 100%. Before, these cells represented the amount of borrowers or originators a CDO had in common with itself. By definition, this is 100%. But in Exhibit 23.5 the diagonals show the percent of speculative grade collateral the SF CDO has in its portfolio. SF CDO 2001 A is the worst off in this respect, with speculative grade collateral comprising 40% of its portfolio. Yet, its greatest overlap with any other SF CDO is only 6%. When focusing on high-risk originators, there is not very much overlap among the SF CDOs we examined. This is at least partially due to the fact that the SF CDOs we picked to examine were pretty healthy.

When we looked at the largest originators of speculative grade collateral in the seven SF CDOs, we were surprised that there was very little overlap of such originators. Again, this is probably because we picked healthy SF CDOs to examine. No originators of speculative grade collateral appear in more than two SF CDOs.

SINGLE-NAME RISK AND TRANCHE PROTECTIONS

But once the same specific credit is identified within several different CDO portfolios, then what? How can one measure and compare single-name risk to CDO tranches at different points in the CDO capital structure? For example, an investor's CLOs might own $15 million of Charter and $30 million of Huntsman. Does the CLO investor bear twice the risk to Huntsman as to Charter? Not necessarily. Suppose the investor owns senior tranches of CLOs that hold Huntsman, but subordinate

EXHIBIT 23.5   Percent of Originator Overlap for Speculative Grade Collateral Originators Common to Any Two SF CDOs

	2001 Manager A	2002 Manager A	2002 Manager B	2002 Manager C	2003 Manager B	2004 Manager C	Average
2001 Manager A	40	6	0	3	0	0	2
2002 Manager A	6	19	0	0	0	0	1
2002 Manager B	0	0	14	2	0	0	0
2002 Manager C	3	0	2	38	0	3	1
2003 Manager B	0	0	0	0	0	0	0
2004 Manager C	0	0	0	3	0	21	1

tranches of CLOs that hold Charter. A Huntsman default might have less of an impact to senior CLO tranches than the default of Charter would upon subordinate tranches.

This discrepancy in the dollar amount and significance of exposure might arise even if an investor consistently purchased CLO tranches of the same seniority. This would be the case if Charter-owning CLOs happen to suffer more collateral losses than CLOs owning Huntsman, thus making the former more sensitive to future collateral losses. The collateral overlap problem can be summarized as follows: How does a CDO investor weight the amount of exposure a CDO has to a single-name against the credit protection a tranche has against that single name? And, even more difficult, how does a CDO investor aggregate the balance of exposure and protection to a single name across a portfolio of CDOs?

EXCESS OVERCOLLATERALIZATION AND EXCESS OVERCOLLATERALIZATION DELTA

A tranche's *excess* overcollateralization (excess OC) is the excess of collateral par over the outstanding par amount of that tranche plus all the tranches *above* it in seniority. For a CLO with $100 of collateral, $70 of Tranche A, $10 of Tranche B, and $10 of Tranche C, excess OC for Tranches A and C are

$$\text{Tranche A excess OC} = \text{Collateral} - \text{Tranche A}$$
$$= \$100 - \$70 = \$30$$

$$\text{Tranche C excess OC} = \text{Collateral} - \text{Tranches A, B, and C}$$
$$= \$100 - \$90 = \$10$$

An intuitive interpretation of excess overcollateralization is that it is the amount of par the CLO could lose before the tranche is collateralized exactly 100%. Note that excess OC *increases* with the par amount of collateral and decreases with the outstanding par amount of the tranche and more senior tranches.

Now suppose that this CLO has a $2 investment in Nextel Communications. Each tranche's *excess OC delta* with respect to Nextel is the amount its excess OC would decrease if Nextel suddenly defaulted without any recovery. To calculate each tranche's excess OC delta with respect to Nextel, we compare the par amount of Nextel to that tranche's excess OC:

Tranche A excess OC Nextel Delta = $2 / $30 = 6.7%
Tranche C excess OC Nextel Delta = $2 / $10 = 20.0%

The excess OC deltas show that Tranche A would lose 6.7% of its excess OC if Nextel defaulted without recovery while Tranche C would lose 20% of its excess OC. In other words, because of the difference in tranche subordination, Tranche C is 3 times as exposed to Nextel as Tranche A (20.0% vs. 6.7%). Note that excess OC delta increases with the dollar amount of the single-name risk and decreases with the amount of the tranche's excess OC. In this manner, excess OC delta takes into account both single-name concentration and the amount of protection the tranche has from overcollateralization.

Senior and Subordinate Excess OC Deltas

Exhibit 23.6 shows senior tranche excess OC deltas for each of the most common names in the CLOs we examined. The first row of the exhibit, for Charter Communications, shows how much senior tranche excess OC would decline if Charter defaulted without any recovery. The decline in excess OC varies from 3.9% to 12.8% and averages 7.1%. Other single-names contribute much less. The bottom row of Exhibit 23.6 shows the decline in excess OC if all eight credits defaulted without any recovery. The amounts for the different CLOs range from 24.5% to 81.8% and average 40.8%.

It is obviously a remote possibility that all eight credits would default and almost an impossibility that all eight credits would default with zero recovery. Yet, in even this scenario, senior tranche *excess* OC

EXHIBIT 23.6 Senior Tranche Excess Overcollateralization Deltas (in percent)

	1999 A	2000 B	2001 A	2001 C	2002 D	2002 E	2003 A	Average
Charter	7.0	7.0	7.1	12.8	5.6	6.3	3.9	7.1
Huntsman	3.2	2.8	3.6	17.4	5.7	1.6	2.5	5.2
Invensys	4.5	9.2	4.7	11.5	2.2	na	2.6	5.0
Allied Waste	5.1	6.4	1.1	9.9	3.3	3.8	4.5	4.9
Nextel	5.9	3.7	3.5	8.1	na	6.3	6.6	4.9
Calpine	na	11.9	na	13.3	4.4	3.9	na	4.8
Owens	6.5	12.1	2.3	4.3	3.3	1.6	0.7	4.4
Dex Media	5.9	6.4	4.8	4.5	na	4.0	6.4	4.6
Sum	38.1	59.5	27.2	81.8	24.5	27.4	27.2	40.8

would not be completely eaten through for any of the CLOs. Each senior tranche would still have greater than 100% OC coverage. We therefore find it very difficult to get excited about single-name risk at the senior tranche level for healthy CLOs.

Exhibit 23.7, in contrast, shows much more severe excess OC deltas for the subordinate tranches of these same CLOs. The excess OCs for Charter across all the CLOs vary from 15.0% to 58.2% and average 35.4%. Subordinate tranche excess OC would be significantly reduced by the default of Charter.

The loss of all eight credits at 100% severity would cause every subordinate tranche in the seven CLOs to lose all its excess OC. Overcollateralization of each subordinate tranche would therefore fall below 100%. In fact, default severity could be far less than 100% and the eight defaults would still eat through subordinate tranche excess OC. For CLO 1999 A, default severity could be 49% and excess OC would be eaten through, reducing tranche OC below 100%. For 2000 B and 2001 C, severity could be as low as 29% or 27% and the eight defaults would eat through excess OC and reduce tranche OC below 100%.

Senior tranche and subordinate tranche excess OC deltas are comparable. Thus, if an investor holds tranches of different seniorities, excess OC deltas allow him to summarize his exposure to a particular name across different CLO tranches. The concentration of a particular credit across different CLO tranches can be gauged by *averaging* the credit's excess OC deltas or by looking at the range of the credit's excess OC deltas.

EXHIBIT 23.7 Subordinate Tranche Excess Overcollateralization Deltas (in percent)

	1999 A	2000 B	2001 A	2001 C	2002 D	2002 E	2003 A	Average
Charter	38.1	40.7	41.9	58.2	27.1	26.5	15.0	35.4
Huntsman	17.1	16.3	21.0	79.4	27.7	6.6	9.6	25.4
Invensys	24.5	53.8	27.8	52.5	10.7	0.0	10.0	25.6
Allied Waste	27.8	37.1	6.8	44.9	16.2	16.2	17.1	23.7
Nextel	31.8	21.6	20.8	36.9	0.0	26.5	25.0	23.2
Calpine	0.0	69.2	0.0	60.6	21.5	16.5	0.0	24.0
Owens	35.4	70.8	13.6	19.6	16.3	6.6	2.7	23.6
Dex Media	32.0	37.5	28.5	20.6	0.0	16.7	24.5	22.8
Sum	206.7	347.0	160.3	372.7	119.5	115.7	104.0	203.7

Equity Tranches and Distressed Tranches

Exhibit 23.7 also has applicability to the equity tranches of these CLOs. Excess OC for the subordinate debt tranche is also the *residual amount of par* available for the equity tranche after all the debt tranches are satisfied. Thus, each excess OC delta in Exhibit 23.7 shows the reduction in residual par available to the equity tranche if the credit defaults without any recovery. Whereas excess OC delta for the subordinate debt tranche quantifies the potential deterioration of coverage above 100%, for the equity tranche, the same statistic quantifies the potential deterioration of par otherwise applicable to equity. This same analysis is valid for any distressed CLO tranche that does not have 100% par coverage and therefore no excess par coverage.

MONTE CARLO SIMULATION OF SINGLE CREDIT RISK

The high-tech method of analyzing single-name risk in CDOs relies on Monte Carlo simulation. Rather than ratios and averages, this approach is based on default probability, default recovery, default correlation, and presents results in the form of probability distributions. This high-tech ideal may at first seem to be something of a straw man, proposed only to be criticized, because it seems unrealistic. However, a small army of CDO software engineers and vendors are currently vying to make this approach practical and, indeed, obligatory. So this chapter not only looks at two different ways to assess single-name risk, it also compares two radically different approaches to CDO analysis.

To implement this second approach, we need a default model of credits in the CDO portfolios, cash flow models of the CDO tranches, and aggregation of the results. In Exhibit 23.8 we walk through the process.

In the first row of Exhibit 23.8, the far right cell shows that the output of the default model in equally likely default scenarios. Each default scenario details whether credits did or did not default. If the credit defaulted in a particular scenario, the timing of its default and its default recovery are specified. The default model creates thousands of equally-likely default scenarios. We would need a default model that covers all of the credits in all of the CDOs in which there is an investment.

The inputs into the default model that creates these default scenarios are default probability, default recovery, and the default correlation between each pair of credits throughout all the CDO portfolios, as also shown in the first row, second column of Exhibit 23.8. The default model uses random draws based on these inputs to create the default scenarios.

EXHIBIT 23.8 Inputs and Outputs in a Monte Carlo Simulation

	Inputs	Process	Output
Default model	Default probabilities and default recovery distributions for every credit in the CDO portfolios. Default correlation among each pair of credits in all the CDOs.	Random draws taking into account default probabilities and default correlations determine whether and when credits default. Random draws also determine how much credits recover in default.	Thousands of equally likely default scenarios. Each default scenario details whether each credit in the CDO portfolios defaulted, when it defaulted, and how much it recovered.
CDO cash flow models	Thousands of default scenarios from the default model.	CDO cash flow models generate collateral cash flows and CDO tranche cash flows according to the rules of each CDO's cash flow waterfall.	In each of the thousands of default scenarios, net present value, e.g., of each CDO tranche.
Aggregation	The net present value of each CDO tranche in each of the thousands of default scenarios.	Aggregate the portfolio's net present value across all tranches in each default scenario. Calculate the distribution of portfolio's net present value across all the default scenarios.	Measures such as the mean and standard deviation of the portfolio's net present value distribution.

EXHIBIT 23.9   Illustrative Distribution of CDO Portfolio NPV: With and Without Nextel

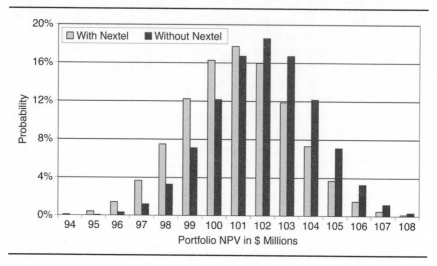

In the second row of the exhibit, each default scenario simulated by the default model is input into cash flow models of the investor's CDO tranches. These CDO cash flow models translate defaults and recoveries of the names in its portfolio into collateral cash flow and, ultimately, into tranche cash flow according to the CDO's cash flow waterfall. The sum of tranche cash flow can be quantified in a convenient measure, such as that tranche's net present value. Each default scenario implies a net present value for each of the CDO tranches the investor owns.

In the third row of Exhibit 23.8, the net present values of each tranche in each default scenario are aggregated into the portfolio's net present value. Each default scenario, then, ultimately leads to a related portfolio net present value, which is an equally likely occurrence. The average and the distribution of aggregate portfolio net present value over many simulations can be measured. To assess the sensitivity of a portfolio of tranches from different CDOs to the risk of, for example, Nextel defaulting, one would simulate aggregate portfolio net present values, assuming Nextel is default risky and default proof. The result of such a simulation is shown in Exhibit 23.9.

In Exhibit 23.9, the grey bars ("With Nextel") show the distribution of aggregate portfolio NPV given the default model of collateral and the cash flow models of tranche net present values. The black bars ("Without Nextel") also show the distribution of aggregate portfolio NPV, but this time under the assumption that Nextel never defaults. Assuming that Nextel never defaults naturally shifts the distribution of portfolio NPV a little to the right. The difference between the "with" and "without" distributions is based on all the Nextel-specific factors addressed in the modeling: the amount of Nextel in the different CDO portfolios, Nextel's default probability and default recovery, and the default correlations between Nextel and every other name in all the CDOs. The difference in the two distributions is also the result of non-Nextel factors: the subordination and credit protections of each of the tranches the investor owns, the size of the investor's investment in each particular tranche, and the maturity of the tranches.

One can summarize the distinction between the two distributions of Exhibit 23.9, with and without Nextel, by taking the difference of their two means and the difference of their two standard deviations. This directly measures the impact Nextel has on the investor's CDO portfolio. In Exhibit 23.9, Nextel reduces the investor's mean return by $1.1 million. Nextel's contribution to risk can then be compared to the contribution of other single names calculated the same way. As with excess OC delta, before buying a new CDO, one would look to see how it affects the contributions of single-name concentrations already owned. An investor would perhaps sell CDO tranches to reduce the single-name contribution of the largest risks.

We would expect, however, that an investor would want to know *why* a single name had its effect upon portfolio NPV. Accordingly, one would:

- Look at the model inputs associated with the single name, its default probability, default severity, and default correlation.
- Test the sensitivity of results to these assumptions by varying these inputs.
- Look at the tranches in which he owns the particular single name, again to figure out why that name contributes to his portfolio's risk.
- Look at the tranche's maturity, its remaining subordination, and perhaps even its excess OC delta with respect to the name.

COMPARING THE TWO APPROACHES

Our low-tech, overcollateralization-based approach has the immediate advantage of being able to be performed now and without great expense. But such older methods and measures of CDO analysis have the disadvantage of focusing on descriptive details rather than financial conclusions. For example, a CDO portfolio's WARF and diversity score do not suggest the return a CDO investor will receive. And regretfully, neither does excess overcollateralization delta.

Newer Monte Carlo methods have the advantage of making assumptions about credit risk at the lowest level of detail: default probability, default correlation, default recovery; and then putting these assumptions into an objective process to obtain not only a mean result (a tranche's expected internal rate of return (IRR), for example), but also a probabilistic distribution of that result (such as the likelihood a tranche's IRR will be between X% and Y%). If the estimation of underlying model parameters are haphazard at this point in the evolution of finance, the sensitivity of results to different assumptions can be tested (e.g., what happens to expected tranche yield and the distribution of tranche yield if default probability is higher than assumed).

Which method will win out? The newer Monte Carlo method will, because some investors will understand how to exploit the additional information it provides and because many other investors will just think it is sexy. But in interpreting and explaining the results of the new methodology, people will still fall back upon the old-fashioned, more transparent, intuitive concepts: overcollateralization, weighted-average rating factor, diversity score, and, perhaps, excess overcollateralization delta.

CONCLUSION

CLO portfolios, even from CLOs issued in different years, tend to have a lot of underlying borrower names in common, especially among CLOs managed by the same manager. The degree of collateral overlap among the CLOs we studied ranges from 25% to 71% of par.

For SF CDOs, the single name of interest is the originator of the ABS, CMBS, and RMBS assets in the portfolio. Many defaults in structured finance have been originator driven, related to overly lenient underwriting standards or even to fraud by the originator. We showed that the degree of originator overlap among these portfolios is as high as 77%. However, when investment grade assets are excluded, the highest example of originator overlap is only 6% and no single originator of speculative-grade collateral appeared in more than two of the SF CDOs we sampled.

We compared two approaches to assessing single name risk throughout a portfolio of CDO tranches. Our offering is *excess OC delta*. Software merchants are currently building or marketing simulation solutions to this and other CDO analysis problems.

The advantage of excess OC is that it is easy to calculate and relates to observable factors: the amount of excess OC a tranche has and a single name's share of that excess OC. The problem with excess OC delta is that it is an incomplete measure and does not incorporate, for example, the credit quality of the single name or the size and maturity of the tranches with exposure to the single name. While some fixes are possible for these deficiencies, excess OC delta still will not come to a conclusion in dollar-and-cent terms.

The advantage of Monte Carlo simulation is the completeness of its answer in dollar-and-cent terms. The problem with Monte Carlo simulation is that the model's answer depends on inputs whose values are guesswork: default probability, default recovery, and default correlation. While extremely specific in terms of dollars, averages, and standard deviations, it is opaque in terms of the factors leading to the result.

Of the two approaches, we think Monte Carlo methods will win out. First, because some investors will learn how to exploit the information the model can provide. Second, because the high-tech method will be perceived to be a better and more scientific way to risk manage a CDO portfolio. But we think investors will continue to fall back upon the observable, intuitive measures to check simulation results. Measures such as weighted average rating factor, diversity score, overcollateralization, and perhaps, excess OC delta.

CHAPTER 24

CDO Rating Experience

In this final chapter, we look at how CDOs have performed by rating level and types of collateral. In particular, we look at Moody's CDO rating actions on 1,049 CDOs and 3,014 CDO tranches across 22 types of CDOs and eight years of issuance. Our unique contribution to rating transition studies is a vintage-by-vintage comparison of the frequency and severity of cumulative CDO rating downgrades across different types of CDOs. This includes an analysis of the most severe downgrades, also by both vintage and CDO type.

We are conscious that there have been criticisms of the timeliness and subjectivity of ratings actions. Even so, no other CDO performance statistic has the potential to encompass all the quantitative and qualitative factors that comprise a CDO's credit quality.

We will see that most of the CDOs that experienced high downgrade frequency and severity suffered from one of two problems. For many arbitrage CDOs, poor performance was the result of an imbalance between collateral spreads on the one hand and CDO debt spreads and targeted equity returns on the other. The difficulty of satisfying all CDO constituents tempted CDO managers into low-quality, high-yielding, and misrated assets. For many balance sheet CDOs, poor performance was the result of using the CDO structure to offload credit risk upon unsuspecting CDO investors. But both of these specific manifestations arose out of a more fundamental CDO problem: poor management of the conflict of interest between CDO classes. This issue was addressed in Chapter 21.

Most of the CDOs that experienced low downgrade frequency and severity had one of two advantages. For loan and low diversity structured finance-backed CDOs, good performance resulted from timely and conservative collateral ratings. When collateral credit quality is underestimated, CDO debt investors benefit from relative overprotectiveness in the

CDO structure. For market value CDOs, good debt rating performance naturally arises from the forced liquidation of collateral assets in the event of a violation of market value coverage tests. But an exception exists when collateral liquidation is not automatic. It is our understanding that in all the cases of market value CDO downgrades, senior debt holders exercised their veto over collateral liquidation.

CDO RATING DOWNGRADE DATA

Exhibit 24.1 shows the distribution of the 1,049 CDOs and 3,014 CDO tranches we culled from Moody's ratings databases across different CDO types and years of issuance or "vintage."

Given Moody's descriptions of the CDOs they rate, we categorized CDOs in Exhibit 24.1 by the domicile of their assets (U.S., Europe, or emerging markets), their purpose (arbitrage or balance sheet), their structure (cash flow, synthetic, or market value), and their underlying assets (high-yield bonds, investment-grade bonds, high-yield loans, or structured finance assets). Structured finance-backed CDOs are further divided into those comprised of ABS, CMBS, RMBS, and REIT debt and having diversity scores less than or greater than 18, or CDOs backed by other CDOs.

In Exhibit 24.1, and in our other exhibits presenting CDO rating downgrades, we eliminated insured and principal-protected CDO tranches. This was done to focus on actual CDO performance rather than the credit quality of financial insurers and Treasury securities. We also eliminated combo tranches and tranches from the same CDO having the same rating histories, including tranches that are *pari passu* in seniority. We did this so that tranche downgrade rates are not influenced by CDOs that issued large numbers of tranches.

Note that the CDO population in Exhibit 24.1 is skewed toward U.S. arbitrage cash flow and European synthetic CDOs. This is due to the pattern of Moody's public CDO ratings. With the exception of bank and insurance company preferred stock-backed CDOs and fund-of funds-backed CDOs, we feel our capture of Moody's public CDO ratings is fairly complete. However, we note with chagrin the 130 CDO tranches, including many commercial loan master trust CDOs, whose ratings became private. Furthermore, the disappearance of a public rating seems to be associated with previous rating downgrades those CDOs experienced. In any event, we were unable to include these secretive CDOs in our study. It seems to us that if a CDO enjoys the public announcement of its ratings, then that CDO's bankers and managers should allow the public monitoring of its ratings, whatever their course.

EXHIBIT 24.1 Number of CDOs/Tranches in Study, by Type of CDO and Vintage

	1996	1997	1998	1999	2000	2001	2002	2003	All Vintages
U.S. ACF HYB	9/23	18/44	24/70	49/151	31/99	34/108	5/13	2/4	172/512
U.S. ACF HYL	3/6	6/14	17/48	26/71	31/102	26/97	37/147	30/129	176/614
U.S. ACF IGB			3/6	4/10	11/29	13/33	5/17		36/95
U.S. ACF Low-D SF				2/10	5/18	9/28	19/54	16/48	51/158
U.S. ACF High-D SF				1/2	13/36	19/60	20/64	19/64	72/226
U.S. ACF CDO^2				1/3	2/5	5/17	4/15		12/40
U.S. BS		1/2		5/18	4/9	2/2	4/13		17/48
U.S. Market Value			4/13	11/35	8/23	6/24	1/4		30/99
U.S. Syn Arb Managed					1/2	6/20	20/67		27/89
U.S. Syn Arb Static					1/3	4/15	15/45	4/7	24/70
U.S. Syn BS		1/2	1/3		6/25	4/14			12/44
Europe ACF HYB				1/4	6/15	5/11		1/2	13/32
Europe ACF HYL						4/12	6/15	10/42	20/69
Europe ACF IGB						1/3	2/4		3/7
Europe ACF SF				1/5		1/1	4/12	5/17	11/35
Europe BS			2/6	6/18	8/21	9/29	2/4	3/6	30/84
Europe BS SME Loans				1/2	2/5	1/2	6/14	7/24	17/47
Europe Syn Arb Managed						5/15	16/45	21/53	42/113
Europe Syn Arb Static				1/3	1/3	21/35	34/74	67/87	124/202
Europe Syn BS			1/3	3/11	16/58	13/51	12/58	12/40	57/221
Europe Syn SF			1/3		2/3	5/12	17/34	50/99	75/151
Emerging Market	3/4	7/13	5/7	5/12	2/5	3/8	3/9	2/5	28/58
Yearly Issuance	15/33	33/75	59/163	117/355	150/461	196/597	232/708	247/622	1049/3014

Abbreviations: ACF= arbitrage cash flow; BS = balance sheet; CDO^2 = CDOs of CDOs; HYB = high-yield bonds; HYL = high-yield loans; IGB = investment-grade bonds; SF = structured finance (ABS, CMBS, RMBS); Syn = synthetic.

Source: UBS calculations from Moody's rating data.

CDO AND TRANCHE RATING DOWNGRADE FREQUENCY

Focusing on cumulative downgrades provides a picture of ratings performance over the life of the CDO. Calculating downgrades by vintage eliminates the dampening effect that new issuance has on overall downgrade rates. For example, if all CDOs issued in previous years were downgraded, but an equal number of new CDOs are issued, then the downgrade rate for all CDOs is 50%. But a downgrade figure of 100% is more descriptive of the performance of seasoned vintages. For that reason, in Exhibit 24.1 and throughout the chapter, we exclude 2004 and later CDO issuance altogether.

Exhibit 24.2 shows the percent of CDOs with at least one downgraded tranche. This exhibit shows the cumulative frequency of CDO downgrades, irrespective of downgrade severity or the number of ratings that tranches have been downgraded. For example, the top row of Exhibit 24.2 contains cumulative downgrade rates for arbitrage cash flow CDOs backed by U.S. high-yield bonds issued from 1996 through 2003. We see that 100% of such CDOs issued in 1996 have had at least one tranche downgraded. The equivalent figure is 100% for 1997, 96% for 1998, and so on. The All Vintages column in the exhibit shows the percentage of downgraded CDOs across all vintages from 1996 through 2003. This is 75% for arbitrage cash flow CDOs backed by U.S. high-yield bonds. The Yearly Issuance row provides the percentage of downgraded CDOs across all types of CDOs in any particular vintage. This is 87% for CDOs issued in 1996.

In calculating cumulative downgrade frequency in Exhibit 24.2, and later in this chapter when we calculate downgrade severity, we focus on the lowest rating to which a CDO tranche has been downgraded. For example, if a Aa2 tranche is downgraded to A2 and then subsequently upgraded to Aaa, we treat this as a downgraded tranche with a rating migration from Aa2 to A2 rather than an upgraded tranche from Aa2 to Aaa. We note the upgrading of previously downgraded CDO tranches as a phenomenon unique to CDOs. The rating rational is that once a troubled CDO goes into early amortization, the senior tranche is often repaid quickly and its overcollateralization rises above that tranche's original overcollateralization at issuance. We rationalize our pessimistic methodology of not giving credit to upgrades that follow downgrades by likening downgrades to the finality of death, or at least that of getting fired. If an asset manager loses a job over the poor performance of the CDO portfolio, the manager is unlikely to be rehired if/when amortizing tranches are subsequently upgraded. Only if a CDO is upgraded without previously being downgraded do we give the CDO credit for the upgrade in our study. In our database, 40 of 93 CDO upgrades follow downgrades, and are thus ignored in our study.

EXHIBIT 24.2 Percent of CDOs with One or More Tranches Downgraded, by Type of CDO and Vintage

	1995	1996	1997	1998	1999	2000	2001	2002	2003	All Vintages
U.S. ACF HYB		100	100	96	88	74	38	0	0	75
U.S. ACF HYL		67	83	82	4	13	4	3	0	16
U.S. ACF IGB				33	50	73	54	0	0	50
U.S. ACF Low-D SF					0	40	22	21		16
U.S. ACF High-D SF					100	92	74	30	0	46
U.S. ACF CDO^2					100	100	20	0		33
U.S. BS			0		40	0	0	0		12
U.S. Market Value				25	18	13	0			13
U.S. Syn Arb Managed						100	67	20		33
U.S. Syn Arb Static						100	100	13	0	29
U.S. Syn BS			100	100		83	100			92
Europe ACF HYB					0	67	20		0	38
Europe ACF HYL	0%						0		0	0
Europe ACF IGB							100			33
Europe ACF SF					100		0		20	18
Europe BS				0	17	38	22	0	0	20
Europe BS SME Loans					0	0	100	0	0	6
Europe Syn Arb Managed							80	31	0	21
Europe Syn Arb Static					100	100	95	53	22	44
Europe Syn BS				100	67	38	23	0	0	21
Europe Syn SF				100		50	40	0	0	5
Emerging Market	0%	67	71	40	0	0	0	0	0	32
Yearly Issuance	0%	87	88	75	49	49	43	17	6	34

Source: UBS calculations from Moody's rating data.

457

Exhibit 24.3 shows the cumulative percent of CDO tranches downgraded by CDO type and vintage. Again, this is the frequency of tranche downgrades. For example, in the top row of the exhibit, we see downgrade rates for arbitrage cash flow CDO tranches backed by U.S. high-yield bonds issued from 1996 through 2003. The exhibit shows that 83% of these CDO tranches issued in 1996 have been downgraded. The equivalent figures are 95% for 1997, 87% for 1998, and so on. Again, the All Vintages column in Exhibit 24.3 provides the percentages of downgraded tranches across all vintages and the Yearly Issuance row provides the percentage of downgraded tranches across all types of CDOs in any particular vintage.

CDO DOWNGRADE PATTERNS

Whether by CDO or CDO tranche, clear patterns emerge in Exhibits 24.2 and 24.3. High rates of downgrade plague:

■ U.S. arbitrage cash flow CDOs backed by high-yield and investment-grade bonds.
■ U.S. synthetic balance sheet CDOs.
■ European static synthetic arbitrage CDOs.

On the other hand, downgrades are rare among:

■ U.S. and European balance sheet CDOs.
■ Low-diversity U.S. and European structured finance CDOs.
■ U.S. and European high-yield loan-backed CDOs.
■ U.S. market value CDOs.

Put in perspective, these downgrade rates are such that those of the first group are much higher than the corporate downgrade rate while those of the second group are much lower than the corporate downgrade rate. We estimate that the multiyear corporate downgrade rate, comparable to the All Vintage columns above, is around 30%. Thus on average, CDOs and CDO tranches experience about the same percentage of downgrades as corporate credits. But for the CDOs cited as having high rates of downgrade plague, tranche downgrade rates vary between 42% and 80%. For the CDOs group where downgrades are rare, tranche downgrade rates vary between 0% and 12%.

EXHIBIT 24.3 Percent of CDO Tranches Downgraded, by Type of CDO and Vintage

	1995	1996	1997	1998	1999	2000	2001	2002	2003	All Vintages
U.S. ACF HYB		83	95	87	87	65	29	0	0	68
U.S. ACF HYL		67	57	50	3	9	3	1	0	8
U.S. ACF IGB				17	50	62	48	0	0	42
U.S. ACF Low-D SF					0	28	18	17		12
U.S. ACF High-D SF					100	81	58	19		35
U.S. ACF CDO^2					100	100	24	0		30
U.S. BS			0	0	11	0	0	0		4
U.S. Market Value				8	14	4	0			7
U.S. Syn Arb Managed						50	45	10		19
U.S. Syn Arb Static						100	93	18	0	36
U.S. Syn BS			100	100		68	93			80
Europe ACF HYB					0	47	18		0	28
Europe ACF HYL	0%						0		0	0
Europe ACF IGB							67	0	6	29
Europe ACF SF					60		0	0	0	11
Europe BS				0	6	24	10	0	0	11
Europe BS SME Loans					0	0	50	0	0	2
Europe Syn Arb Managed							53	22	0	16
Europe Syn Arb Static					100	100	91	45	20	44
Europe Syn BS				100	27	29	14	0	0	14
Europe Syn SF				67		33	33	0	0	5
Emerging Market	0%	50	69	29	0	0	0	0	0	22
Yearly Issuance	0%	76	81	60	45	40	32	11	3	27

Source: UBS calculations from Moody's rating data.

WHY DOWNGRADE PATTERNS?

We chalk up poor-performing CDOs to the following causes. U.S. bond spreads were extremely tight during much of the time period studied. Tighter yields caused high-yield and investment-grade CBO managers to reach for higher-yield (and poorer-quality) assets to achieve targeted equity returns. Once high-yield and investment-grade CBO assets shrank because of defaults and forced liability pay downs, the CBOs became overhedged in losing interest rate swap positions. European high-yield CBOs also suffered from being overinvested in telecom and the fact that the fledging European high-yield bond market was in some cases the funding source of last resort for poor-quality issuers.

U.S. synthetic balance sheet CDOs worked the way they were intended, if by that it is meant as a vehicle for banks to transfer the risk of their weakest loans to the capital market. European static synthetic arbitrage CDOs did poorly because many had a balance sheet flavor to them, in that they included credit risks that some market participants wanted to get rid of, not necessarily credit risks to which market participants consciously chose to become exposed. It is significant that managed synthetic arbitrage CDOs, where risk positions are truly selected and managed, have done relatively well.[1]

A fundamental problem underlies both the imprudent pursuit of collateral yield in bond-backed CDOs and the opportunistic transfer of credit risk in balance sheet CDOs. This problem is the mismanagement (or lack of management) of conflicts of interest between CDO classes. In the past, the advantage in a CDO structure has been with managers and equity holders in arbitrage CDOs and asset sellers in balance sheet CDOs. CDO debt holders often bore a disproportionate amount of the CDO's risk. This was due to the failure of adequate structural safeguards, either because of their absence or because they could be circumvented by CDO managers. The challenge for the CDO market has been to create better protection for debt holders and a better balance among the interests of parties in a CDO.

The reason for the disparity in performance between synthetic and cash flow U.S. balance sheet CDOs is difficult to understand. A plausi-

---

[1] We point out that there is nothing inherently wrong with synthetic CDOs, either static or managed, that lack the bells and whistles of cash diversion mechanisms (i.e., synthetic CDO versions of cash flow interest and par coverage tests). In fact, we view the lack of cash flow diversion features, and the concomitant increase in subordination, as a superior structure. Subordination is a surer source of credit protection than cash flow diversion mechanisms that can be (and have been) manipulated and defeated by motivated managers. Synthetic balance sheet CDO performance problems were not caused by structure, but by reference asset selection.

ble explanation for the much better performance of cash flow balance sheet CDOs is that these CDOs are more often done for funding reasons or regulatory capital reasons, while synthetic balance sheet CDOs are usually effected to achieve credit risk transfer.

One reason that high-yield CLOs have done well is because their underlying credits are vetted by commercial banks. We also feel that public loan ratings are more timely than bond ratings and private loan ratings are more conservative than bond ratings. For whatever reason, loans historically default about half as frequently as equally rated bonds, a fact not taken into account in CLO rating methodologies.

Low-diversity structured-finance CDOs, focused on CMBS, REIT debt, RMBS, and residential mortgage-related ABS, had the advantage of underlying assets with exemplary credit histories. And as in the case of high-yield loans, this exemplary credit history goes unrewarded in the CDO-rating process. This causes structured-finance CDO debt investors to be relatively overprotected as the credit protection of the CDO's structure over compensates for the risk of the CDO's assets.

Market value CDOs really should never be downgraded. Rather, if the aggregate market price of their assets decline, assets should be sold and liabilities redeemed until the CDO regains its previous market value coverage of assets to liabilities. If this happens, CDO credit quality is maintained. The market value CDOs that have been downgraded contained a structuring flaw where the sale of assets was not automatic, but instead required the approval of senior debt holders who were in a much safer position than subordinate debt holders and decided to waive collateral liquidation.

Exhibits 24.2 and 24.3 also show two CDO sectors that have apparently reformed themselves. While every tranche of the three CDOs of CDOs issued before 2001 has been downgraded, only one of the nine CDOs of CDOs issued since has suffered a downgrade among its tranches. Nor have there been any tranche downgrades of the 13 emerging market CDOs issued after 1998.

The turnaround in the experience of arbitrage emerging market CDOs and of CDOs of CDOs shows the importance of timing to the fortunes of a CDO. This affords an example directly opposite to that of CDO collateral managers reaching for the yield on low-quality speculative and investment-grade bonds to make the arbitrage work for CBO equity. In the case of emerging market CDOs, the bursting of emerging market prices in fall 1998 meant that emerging market CDO managers could fulfill targeted equity returns and still be very selective about credit. For CDOs of CDOs, low-secondary CDO prices over much of this period also allowed managers to acquire good assets cheaply.

It is too early to say whether 2002 vintage high-yield CBOs, which also had the advantage of high-collateral yields, will turn around the experience of previous high-yield CBO vintages. But, like many 2002 vintage CDO types, they have not yet had any downgrades.

DOWNGRADE SEVERITY

Exhibit 24.4 looks at CDO downgrade activity another way, by factoring in the severity of downgrades along with their frequency. The exhibit shows cumulative average rating migration by type of CDO and year of issuance. Positive numbers mean that, on average, CDO tranches experienced a downgrade; negative numbers mean that, on average, tranches were upgraded. We compute rating migration as the change in rating in terms of number of rating notches. A "rating notch" in Moody's symbol system is the difference, for example, between a Aa2 and a Aa3 rating or between a A3 and a Baa1 rating. Exhibit 24.4 shows that U.S. high-yield bond-backed CDO tranches issued in 1996 have suffered cumulative average downgrades of 7.3 ratings notches since issuance. That would be a downgrade from A2 to Ba3, for example. The equivalent figure is 9.7 for 1997, 7.9 for 1998, and so on. The Average Drift/Year column shows average annual rating migration experience across vintages, weighting each vintage equally.

The CDOs doing well or poorly with respect to downgrade frequency in Exhibits 24.2 and 24.3 generally fare the same with respect to downgrade severity in Exhibit 24.4. An exception exists for U.S. high-diversity structured finance and CDOs of CDOs. For these, average annual severity of downgrade is much greater than what one would expect from the average cumulative frequency of tranche downgrades. In other words, it seems that when these types of CDOs are downgraded, their ratings are lowered a great deal. Otherwise, the ranking of CDOs by frequency of downgrade closely matches the ranking of CDOs by the severity of downgrade.

To put the findings reported in Exhibit 24.4 into perspective, we estimate that over the same period, corporate credits have been downgraded an average of 0.5 of a rating notches a year, or a little less than CDOs taken as a whole. However, the annual downgrade severity for U.S. and European high-yield CBOs and U.S. investment-grade CBOs has been about 1.5 times that of corporate bonds, as shown in the Average Drift/Year column in the exhibit. Annual downgrade severity of U.S. synthetic balance sheet CDOs and European static synthetic arbitrage CDOs has been about two times that of corporate bonds. But the same

EXHIBIT 24.4 Cumulative Rating Notch Change in Rating, by Type of CDO and Vintage

	1996	1997	1998	1999	2000	2001	2002	2003	Avg. Drift/ Year
U.S. ACF HYB	7.3	9.7	7.9	9.1	4.3	0.8	0.0	0.0	0.8
U.S. ACF HYL	3.3	6.0	2.9	0.1	0.3	-0.1	0.0	0.0	0.2
U.S. ACF IGB			1.3	5.0	4.4	4.8	0.0		0.7
U.S. ACF Low-D SF				0.0	3.1	1.1	0.7	0.0	0.3
U.S. ACF High-D SF				12.0	10.3	5.4	0.7	0.0	1.3
U.S. ACF CDO^2				12.0	8.0	1.9	0.0		1.1
U.S. BS		0.0	0.0	0.3	-1.0	-4.5	0.0		-0.2
U.S. Market Value			0.2	0.6	0.0	0.0	0.0		0.0
U.S. Syn Arb Managed					2.0	1.9	0.3		0.4
U.S. Syn Arb Static					7.0	6.0	0.7	0.0	0.9
U.S. Syn BS			8.0		3.8	8.0			1.5
Europe ACF HYB				0.0	6.6	1.8	0.0	0.0	0.7
Europe ACF HYL						0.0	0.0		0.0
Europe ACF IGB						2.0	0.0		0.3
Europe ACF SF				1.5		0.0	0.0	-0.4	0.0
Europe BS			-4.0	-2.0	0.6	0.7	0.0	0.0	-0.1
Europe BS SME Loans				0.0	0.0		0.0	0.0	0.0
Europe Syn Arb Managed						3.6	0.4	0.0	0.4
Europe Syn Arb Static				9.0	10.0	8.3	1.1	0.0	1.3
Europe Syn BS			4.0	1.0	2.3	0.6	-0.2	0.0	0.2
Europe Syn SF					0.0	1.2	-0.3	0.0	0.1
Emerging Market	5.0	2.9	3.7	0.0	0.0	0.0	0.0		0.2
Yearly Issuance	6.2	7.2	4.4	3.9	3.2	2.2	0.3	0.0	0.6

Source: UBS calculations from Moody's rating data.

column in Exhibit 24.4 shows that 12 out of 20 CDO categories whose annual downgrade severity is 0.3 rating notches or less and therefore much less than that of corporate bonds and the average CDO.

DOWNGRADES OF Aaa CDO TRANCHES

In Exhibit 24.5 we look at the number of original issue Aaa tranches that have been downgraded. In Exhibit 24.6 we look at the percent of such tranches. All these statistics are by type of CDO and issuance year or "vintage." Exhibit 24.5 shows that across all different types of CDOs and CDO vintages, 121 Aaa CDO tranches have been downgraded. Exhibit 24.6 shows that in percentage terms, across all types of CDOs and vintage years, 16% of Aaa CDOs have been downgraded. This statistic encompasses CDOs issued from 1996 to 2003, and it based on CDOs outstanding at least one year, and as many as 9 years. The 16% "lifetime" downgrade rate of Aaa CDOs works out to a rate of 4% per year. Meanwhile, between 1970 and 2003, Moody's has downgraded Aaa corporate bonds at a rate of 10% per year.

However, downgrade statistics vary greatly by type of CDO. Exhibit 24.6 shows that Aaa downgrades were most common amount U.S. synthetic balance sheet CDOs (64% lifetime downgrades across all vintage years), European static synthetic arbitrage CDOs (42%), U.S. high-yield bond CBOs (39%), U.S. CDOs of CDOs (25%), and U.S. static synthetic CDOs (24%). Eight types of Aaa CDO experienced 2% or fewer lifetime downgrades.

EXTREME RATING DOWNGRADES

Exhibit 24.7 provides an overall picture of CDO downgrades in a rating transition matrix. Initial tranche ratings are shown on the left of the exhibit; current tranche ratings (or, according to our methodology, the lowest rating the tranche ever had or the tranche's rating before its rating was withdrawn) are shown across the top of the exhibit. The percentages in the body of the exhibit show rating migration from the tranche's initial rating to its current rating. For example, 84% of tranches initially rated Aaa have remained Aaa, 3% have been downgraded to Aa1, 2% to Aa2, and so forth. The rightmost column in Exhibit 24.7 shows how many tranches had a particular initial rating. For example, 772 CDO tranches were initially rated Aaa after eliminating insured, principal-protected, combo, and *pari passu* tranches.

EXHIBIT 24.5 Number of Original-Issue Aaa Tranches Ever Downgraded

	1996	1997	1998	1999	2000	2001	2002	2003	Total
U.S. ACF HYB	0	0	6	28	9	2	0	0	45
U.S. ACF HYL		0	1	0	0	0	0	0	1
U.S. ACF IGB			0	0	2	2	0	0	4
U.S. ACF Low-D SF				0	1	0	0	0	1
U.S. ACF High-D SF				1	7	6	1		15
U.S. ACF CDO^2				1	2	0	0		3
U.S. BS			0	0	0	0	0		0
U.S. Market Value				1	0	0			1
U.S. Syn Arb Managed					0	1	1		2
U.S. Syn Arb Static						3	1	0	4
U.S. Syn BS		1	1		2	3			7
Europe ACF HYB				0	2	0	0	0	2
Europe ACF HYL						0	0	0	0
Europe ACF IGB						0	0	1	0
Europe ACF SF				1		0	0	0	2
Europe BS			0	0	2	0	0	0	2
Europe BS SME Loans				0	0	0	0	0	0
Europe Syn Arb Managed						1	2	0	3
Europe Syn Arb Static				1		8	10	3	22
Europe Syn BS			1	0	3	2	0	0	6
Europe Syn SF			0		0	1	0	0	1
Emerging Market	0	0	0	0			0	0	0
Yearly Issuance	0	1	9	33	30	29	15	4	121

Source: UBS calculations from Moody's rating data.

EXHIBIT 24.6   Percent of Original-Issue Aaa Tranches Ever Downgraded

	1996	1997	1998	1999	2000	2001	2002	2003	Total
U.S. ACF HYB	0	0	50	67	36	7	0	0	39
U.S. ACF HYL		0	8	0	0	0	0	0	1
U.S. ACF IGB			0	0	22	25	0	0	14
U.S. ACF Low-D SF				0	20	0	0	0	2
U.S. ACF High-D SF				100	54	33	5		21
U.S. ACF CDO^2				100	100	0	0	0	25
U.S. BS			0	0	0		0		0
U.S. Market Value				20	0	0	0		8
U.S. Syn Arb Managed					0	20	6		9
U.S. Syn Arb Static						75	9	0	24
U.S. Syn BS		100	100		40	75			64
Europe ACF HYB				0	33	0	0	0	20
Europe ACF HYL						0	0	0	0
Europe ACF IGB						0	0		0
Europe ACF SF				100			0	17	18
Europe BS			0	0	22	0	0	0	7
Europe BS SME Loans				0	0	0	0	0	0
Europe Syn Arb Managed						20	17	0	9
Europe Syn Arb Static				100		89	43	15	42
Europe Syn BS			100	0	20	17	0	0	12
Europe Syn SF			0		0	33	0	0	2
Emerging Market	0	0	0	0			0		0
Yearly Issuance	0	20	24	36	24	19	8	2	16

Source: UBS calculations from Moody's rating data.

EXHIBIT 24.7 Rating Migration of CDO Tranches

Initial Rating											Current Rating (%)											Number of Tranches
	Aaa	Aa1	Aa2	Aa3	A1	A2	A3	Baa1	Baa2	Baa3	Ba1	Ba2	Ba3	B1	B2	B3	Caa1	Caa2	Caa3	Ca	C	
Aaa	84.3	3.2	2.2	2.2	1.9	1.0	1.7	0.9	0.4	0.6	0.5	0.3		0.3	0.3		0.1					772
Aa1	2	78	3		4	3	2	3	2	3	1	1		1	1			1	1	1	1	100
Aa2	2	1	67	8	4	2	2	2	1	4	2	2		1	2	2		3	2	1		388
Aa3	1	2	8	61	5	5	3	5	2	3	3	1		2	1	2		3	1	1	1	121
A1	1	1	2	2	83	2		1	2	2	3	2		2	2							92
A2	1	0	1	0	0	83	0	2	2	4	2	1		0	1		0	3	1	0	10	223
A3	1		1		0	0	72	2	2	4	4	1		2	2	2	1	3	2	1	2	196
Baa1				1			3	85	3	1		1		1	1	3		3	1			68
Baa2		0	1			1	3		65	4	3	2	2	2	2	2		3		7		460
Baa3		0	1				1	1		41	1	2	8	6	2	2	2		6	11	3	170
Ba1							2			0	82	0		1	2	2	2		6	2	12	51
Ba2									1	0	0	66	2	2	2	2	2	2	1	7	2	203
Ba3										1		1	55	3	1	3	3	3	4	10	18	114
B1														4	1	3	3		7	11	79	28
B2															81				5	5	10	21
B3																31		8	15	8	38	13

Source: UBS calculations from Moody's rating data.

467

EXHIBIT 24.8   Worst Current CDO Tranche Ratings By CDO Type and Original Tranche Rating

	Original Rating					
	Aaa	**Aa**	**A**	**Baa**	**Ba**	**B**
U.S. ACF HYB	B2	C	C	C	C	C
U.S. ACF HYL	Aa2	Baa1	Baa3	Ca	C	Ca
U.S. ACF IGB	A3	B3	Caa3	Ca	Ca	Caa3
U.S. ACF Low-D SF	A3	A3	Caa2	C	Caa1	B2
U.S. ACF High-D SF	B2	Ca	C	C	C	
U.S. ACF CDO^2	Baa2	Baa1	Ca	C	C	
U.S. BS	Aaa	Aa2	A3	Ba3	Ba3	
U.S. Market Value	A2	Aa2	A3	Caa2	Ca	C
U.S. Syn Arb Managed	Aa1	A2	B1	Ba1	B2	
U.S. Syn Arb Static	Aa3	Baa1	Ba2	Caa2	C	
U.S. Syn BS	Ba2	B1	Caa3	Ca	C	C
Europe ACF HYB	Baa1	Aa2	Caa1	C	C	
Europe ACF HYL	Aaa	Aa3	A3	Baa3	Ba3	
Europe ACF IGB	Aaa		Baa1	Ba2		
Europe ACF SF	Caa1	Aa3	A3	Caa3	Ca	
Europe BS	Ba1	A1	Ba1	Ba3	Caa2	
Europe BS SME Loans	Aaa	A2	A2	Baa3	Ba3	
Europe Syn Arb Managed	A1	Ba3	Ba1	Ca	Ba3	B3
Europe Syn Arb Static	Baa2	Ba3	Caa3	C	C	
Europe Syn BS	A3	Ba3	Caa2	Ca	Caa3	B3
Europe SF	Aa3	Ba1	Ba1	B1	Ba1	Ca
Emerging Market	Aaa	A2	Baa2	Ca	Ba3	B2

Source: UBS calculations from Moody's rating data.

Exhibit 24.7 gives a good picture of the distribution and extremes of ratings downgrades. For example, 92.0% of tranches initially rated Aaa have remained Aa3 or better. Only 1.4% of Aaa tranches have been downgraded below investment grade while only one Aaa tranche (1/772 rounds to 0%) has been downgraded below B2. The paucity of Aaa CDO tranches falling below investment grade and below B2 in the exhibit should be of assurance to the majority of CDO investors who participate in this level of the CDO's capital structure. The Aaa rating category really seems to be a safe-harbor rating, even for volatile CDOs.

Exhibit 24.8 shows the lowest rating to which each type of CDO has been downgraded. For example, in the exhibit's top row we see the lowest rating to which any arbitrage cash flow CDO tranche backed by U.S. high-yield bonds has been downgraded. The row shows these ratings according to the original rating of the tranche. Thus, the lowest rating a Aaa tranche has been downgraded to is B2. For Aa tranches the lowest rating is C, for A tranches the lowest rating is C, and so on.

In looking at the exhibit, remember that each cell in the CDO type and initial rating matrix displays the *worst* current rating. For example, European balance sheet CDOs have generally done well, but one Aaa tranche happens to have been downgraded to Ba1. On the other hand, it seems amazing to us, given how poorly they have fared in general, that the lowest a Aaa U.S. investment-grade arbitrage cash flow CBO has been downgraded to is A3.

So what have been the very worst CDOs? It is a tie between two U.S. high-yield bond CDO tranches that have both fallen 18 rating notches since issuance. From 1998 and 1999, respectively, these tranches both fell from Aa2 to C (Moody's lowest rating). Three more U.S. high-yield bond CDOs have fallen from Aa2 to Ca.

But perhaps a better look at the performance of different ratings within different types of CDOs is shown in Exhibits 24.9, 24.10, and 24.11. Exhibit 24.9 shows the percentage of tranches initially rated Aaa that have been downgraded below Baa3. Exhibit 24.10 shows the percentage of tranches initially rated Aa that have been downgraded below Baa3. The percentage of tranches initially rated A and Baa that have been downgraded below B3 is shown in Exhibit 24.11. We picked these combinations of initial ratings and downgrade thresholds to focus on severe downgrades. Once again, we see the safety of Aaa tranches in Exhibit 24.9. Aa tranches have also suffered few downgrades below Baa3. But the relative abundance, in certain types of CDOs, of A and Baa tranches falling below B3 in Exhibit 24.11 is a concern.

CDO DEFAULTS AND NEAR DEFAULTS

To our knowledge, no study of CDO defaults has been reported. One reason is the private nature of the securities. Another reason is that even with perfect information, it would be hard to determine whether a tranche is defaulted or certain to default in the future. For example, it is often unclear whether a PIK-ing tranche is going to catch up on missed coupons and pay in full. It can also be unclear whether a non-PIK-ing performing tranche from a distressed CDO will pay back principal.

We take, as our proxy for default, downgrades to ratings below B3: Caa1, Caa2, Caa3, Ca, and C. The Ca and C ratings are traditionally reserved by Moody's for defaulted credits. By including the Caa rating

EXHIBIT 24.9 Percent of Aaa CDO Tranches Downgraded Below Baa3, by Type of CDO and Vintage

	Cumulative Downgrade Below Baa3 Rates								
	1996	1997	1998	1999	2000	2001	2002	2003	All Vintages
U.S. ACF HYB	0	0	8	10	4	0	0	0	5
U.S. ACF HYL	0	0					0	0	0
U.S. ACF IGB			0			0	0	0	0
U.S. ACF Low-D SF				0	0	0	0	0	0
U.S. ACF High-D SF				0	15	0	0	0	3
U.S. ACF CDO^2				0			0		0
U.S. BS			0	0	0		0		0
U.S. Market Value				0	0	0	0		0
U.S. Syn Arb Managed					0	0	0	0	0
U.S. Syn Arb Static						0	0	0	0
U.S. Syn BS		0	0		0	25	0	0	9
Europe ACF HYB				0	0	0	0	0	0
Europe ACF HYL						0	0	0	0
Europe ACF IGB						0	0	0	0
Europe ACF SF				100		0	0	0	9
Europe BS			0	0	11	0	0	0	3
Europe BS SME Loans				0	0	0	0	0	0
Europe Syn Arb Managed						0	0	0	0
Europe Syn Arb Static						0	0	0	0
Europe Syn BS			0	0	0	0	0	0	0
Europe Syn SF			0	0	0	0	0	0	0
Emerging Market	0	0	0	0	3	0	0	0	0
Yearly Issuance	0	0	3	5	3	1	0	0	1

Source: UBS calculations from Moody's rating data.

EXHIBIT 24.10 Percent of Aa CDO Tranches Downgraded Below Baa3, by Type of CDO and Vintage

	Cumulative Downgrade Below Baa3 Rates								
	1996	1997	1998	1999	2000	2001	2002	2003	All Vintages
U.S. ACF HYB	25	47	46	50	14	0	0		35
U.S. ACF HYL	0	0	0					0	0
U.S. ACF IGB					25	22	0	0	15
U.S. ACF Low-D SF				0	0				0
U.S. ACF High-D SF					50	11		0	10
U.S. ACF CDO^2						0	0		0
U.S. BS		0					0		0
U.S. Market Value			0	0	0	0	0		0
U.S. Syn Arb Managed						0	0		0
U.S. Syn Arb Static					0	0	0	0	0
U.S. Syn BS					50	33			43
Europe ACF HYB				0		0	0	0	0
Europe ACF HYL						0		0	0
Europe ACF IGB									0
Europe ACF SF				0	0		0	0	0
Europe BS				0	0	0		0	0
Europe BS SME Loans						0	0	0	0
Europe Syn Arb Managed						20	0	0	3
Europe Syn Arb Static						40	5	0	5
Europe Syn BS			100	0	18	11	0	0	7
Europe Syn SF					0	0	0	0	2
Emerging Market	0	0	0			0	0	0	0
Yearly Issuance	14	29	27	22	15	9	1	0	8

Source: UBS calculations from Moody's rating data.

EXHIBIT 24.11 Percent of A and Baa CDO Tranches Downgraded Below B3, by Type of CDO and Vintage

	Cumulative Downgrade Below Baa3 Rates								
	1996	1997	1998	1999	2000	2001	2002	2003	All Vintages
U.S. ACF HYB	56	94	63	71	23	0	0	0	43
U.S. ACF HYL	33	50	11	0	0	0	0	0	2
U.S. ACF IGB			0	33	25	31	0	0	21
U.S. ACF Low-D SF				0	25	10	0	0	5
U.S. ACF High-D SF				100	87	42	0		26
U.S. ACF CDO^2				100	67	13	0		26
U.S. BS		0	0	0	0	0	0		0
U.S. Market Value			0	7	0	0	0		3
U.S. Syn Arb Managed					0	0	0		0
U.S. Syn Arb Static					50	29	0	0	9
U.S. Syn BS			0		22	60	0		33
Europe ACF HYB				0	60	20	0	0	36
Europe ACF HYL						0	0	0	0
Europe ACF IGB						0	0	0	0
Europe ACF SF				50		0	0	0	8
Europe BS			0	0	0	0	0	0	0
Europe BS SME Loans				0	0		0	0	0
Europe Syn Arb Managed						20	0	0	2
Europe Syn Arb Static				0	67	47	0	0	14
Europe Syn BS			0	0	10	5	0	0	3
Europe Syn SF				0	0	0	0	0	0
Emerging Market	0	14	33	0	0	0	0	0	7
All CDOs	46	66	31	31	21	13	0	0	13

Source: UBS calculations from Moody's rating data.

categories in our definition of default, we add the wounded to the count of the dead.

Of the 3,014 tranches in our study, 306 tranches have "achieved" these ratings:

- 21 Caa1
- 40 Caa2
- 44 Caa3
- 89 Ca
- 112 C

Exhibit 24.12 shows the cumulative percent of "defaulted" CDO tranches by CDO type and rating. For example, in the second column of the exhibit we see that across all types of CDOs, 0.1% of Aaa tranches have been downgraded below B3. In other rating categories, the figures are 2.0% of Aa tranches, 4.5% of A tranches, 19.5% of Baa tranches, 25.5% of Ba tranches, and 65% of B tranches. This is the "lifetime" default rate of CDOs that have been outstanding between one to nine years, for a weighted average of 3.5 years.

Exhibit 24.12 confirms the results of our earlier exhibits that looked at CDO downgrades by frequency and severity. U.S. arbitrage cash flow CDOs backed by high-yield and investment-grade bonds, U.S. synthetic balance sheet CDOs, and European static synthetic arbitrage all have high default rates. In addition, so do U.S. arbitrage cash flow high diversity structured-finance CDOs, U.S. CDOs of CDOs, and European arbitrage cash flow CDOs backed by high-yield bonds. In contrast, balance sheet cash flow CDOs, low diversity U.S. structured-finance CDOs; high-yield loan-backed CDOs, and U.S. market value CDOs all have low-default rates.

CONCLUSION

Overall, the frequency and severity of CDO downgrades has been equivalent to those of corporate bonds. However, the performance of specific types of CDOs has been extremely variable.

The outstanding performers have been U.S. and European cash flow balance sheet CDOs, low-diversity U.S. and European structured-finance CDOs, U.S. and European high-yield loan-backed CLOs, and U.S. market value CDOs. The good performance of structured-finance and loan-backed CDOs is a result of more timely and more conservative collateral ratings not being given credit in the CDO rating process. The good performance

EXHIBIT 24.12 Percent of CDO Tranche Defaults (Downgrades Below B3)

	All	U.S. ACF HYB	U.S. ACF HYL	U.S. ACF IGB	U.S. ACF Low-D SF	U.S. ACF High-D SF	U.S. ACF CDO^2	U.S. BS	U.S. Market Value	U.S. Syn Arb Managed	U.S. Syn Arb Static	U.S. Syn BS
Aaa	0.1	0.0	0.0	0.0	0.0	0.0	0.0	0.0	0.0	0.0	0.0	0.0
Aa	2.0	13.4	0.0	0.0	0.0	1.7	0.0	0.0	0.0	0.0	0.0	0.0
A	4.5	19.0	0.0	7.7	3.1	20.0	11.1	0.0	0.0	0.0	0.0	22.2
Baa	19.5	49.7	3.9	27.6	6.1	28.1	40.0	0.0	4.5	0.0	20.0	50.0
Ba	25.5	61.4	7.6	100.0	6.3	35.7	33.3	0.0	7.1	0.0	100.0	70.0
B	64.5	94.3	40.0	100.0	na	na	na	na	18.2	na	na	100.0

	Europe ACF HYB	Europe ACF HYL	Europe ACF IGB	Europe ACF SF	Europe BS	Europe BS SME Loans	Europe Syn Arb Managed	Europe Syn Arb Static	Europe Syn BS	Europe Syn SF	Emerging Market
Aaa	0.0	0.0	0.0	9.1	0.0	0.0	0.0	0.0	0.0	0.0	0.0
Aa	0.0	0.0	na	0.0	0.0	0.0	0.0	0.0	0.0	0.0	0.0
A	25.0	0.0	0.0	0.0	0.0	0.0	0.0	9.8	2.3	0.0	0.0
Baa	42.9	0.0	0.0	16.7	0.0	0.0	4.8	20.0	4.5	0.0	11.8
Ba	33.3	0.0	na	50.0	10.0	0.0	0.0	33.3	10.5	0.0	0.0
B	na	na	na	na	na	na	0.0	na	0.0	100.0	0.0

Source: UBS calculations from Moody's rating data.

of market value CDOs is a result of their being naturally resistant to downgrade. In addition, there has been very good performance in cash flow balance sheet CDOs.

The poor CDO performers have been U.S. arbitrage cash flow CDOs backed by high-yield and investment-grade bonds, U.S. synthetic balance sheet CDOs, and European static synthetic arbitrage CDOs. For bond-backed CDOs, the problem was that low collateral spreads tempted CDO managers into lower-quality assets to achieve targeted CDO equity returns. For synthetic CDOs, the problem was the use of the CDO structure to offload poor credit risks.

The difference in good and poor performing CDOs often reflects the fundamental conflict of interest in the CDO structure that must be managed. This conflict becomes apparent in arbitrage CDOs when collateral spreads are low and managers stretch into riskier assets to meet CDO equity return targets. CDO debt investors find they are financing riskier assets without any increase in CDO protections. This was the case with many types of poor-performing CDO types. In contrast, when collateral spreads are wide, this conflict of interest remains concealed. Arbitrage CDO managers can be pickier about credit and still meet CDO equity return targets.

The importance of collateral yield is well illustrated in the histories of CDOs of assets that have experienced high default rates and significant spread widening. The performance of emerging market CDOs and CDOs of CDOs radically changed from poor to good over their histories as CDO managers took advantage of wide collateral spreads to select good credit assets.